Power and Policy in China

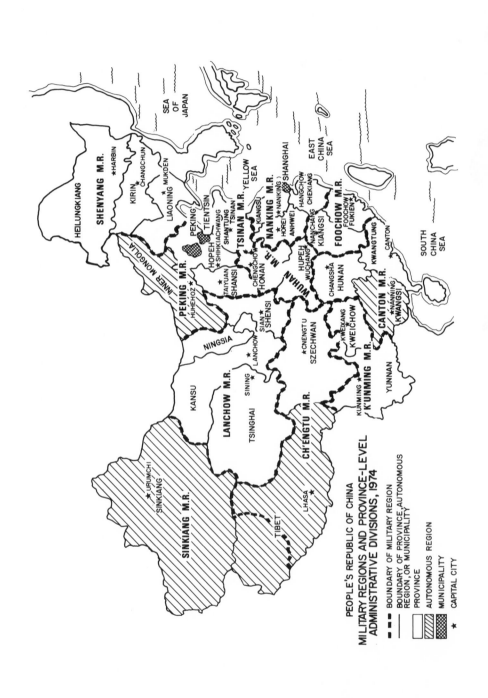

PEOPLE'S REPUBLIC OF CHINA
MILITARY REGIONS AND PROVINCE-LEVEL
ADMINISTRATIVE DIVISIONS, 1974

■ ■ ■ BOUNDARY OF MILITARY REGION
—— BOUNDARY OF PROVINCE, AUTONOMOUS
      REGION, OR MUNICIPALITY
☐ PROVINCE
▨ AUTONOMOUS REGION
▩ MUNICIPALITY
★ CAPITAL CITY

HEILUNGKIANG

SHENYANG M.R.
★HARBIN

KIRIN ★CHANGCHUN

LIAONING ★MUKDEN

INNER MONGOLIA

PEKING M.R.
HUHEHOZ★

★PEKING TIENTSIN

HOPEH
SHIHKIACHWANG★

TAIYUAN★ SHANTUNG
SHANSI

TSINAN M.R. YELLOW
          SEA

CHENGCHOW★ TSINAN★
HONAN

NANKING M.R.

HOPEI★ ★NANKING

ANHWEI KIANGSU

HANGCHOW
★SHANGHAI
CHEKIANG

NANCHANG★
KIANGSI

FOOCHOW M.R.

★FOOCHOW
FUKIEN

EAST
CHINA
SEA

WUHAN M.R.

HUPEH
★WUCHANG

CHANGSHA★
HUNAN

SIAN★
SHENSI

★CNENGTU
SZECHWAN

KWEIYANG
★KWEICHOW

KWANGTUNG

★CANTON

CANTON M.R.

NANNING
★KWANGSI

NINGSIA

LANCHOW M.R.

KANSU

LANCHOW★

SINING★

TSINGHAI

CH'ENGTU M.R.

SINKIANG M.R.

★URUMCHI
SINKIANG

TIBET

LHASA★

KUNMING★
K'UNMING M.R.

YUNNAN

SOUTH
CHINA
SEA

SEA
OF
JAPAN

Power and Policy in China

Parris H. Chang

The Pennsylvania State University Press
University Park and London

Library of Congress Cataloging in Publication Data

Chang, Parris H   1936–
    Power and policy in China.

    Bibliography: p. 256
    Includes index.
    1. China—Politics and government—1949–
I. Title.
DS777.55.C375   320.9'51'05   74–34190
ISBN 0–271–01189–0

Filmset in Hong Kong by Asco Trade Typesetting Ltd
Printed in the United States of America

APR 4   1978

To my Mother
and
To the memory of my Father

Contents

Acknowledgments

The research and publication of this book would have been impossible without help from many quarters. My debts are far too numerous to acknowledge completely, but there are a number of people and institutions whose support and assistance cannot go unmentioned.

I owe a special personal and intellectual debt to Professor Doak Barnett, who has for many years lent his encouragement and support to my studies of Chinese politics. He was my academic adviser at Columbia University, gave me a basic education on contemporary China, and stimulated and supervised the writing of my doctoral dissertation from which several chapters of this book derive. At Columbia University, I also had the good fortune to study with Professors Zbigniew Brzezinski, O. Edmund Clubb, Roger Hilsman, and James Morley, who have greatly contributed to my intellectual development.

I am grateful to several colleagues in the field who took time to read the manuscript at its various stages and offered valuable comments. In our numerous conversations in Hongkong and at the Center for Chinese Studies at the University of Michigan, Allen Whiting provided me with many illuminating insights into the dynamics of the Chinese leadership. His encouragement, understanding, and willingness to assist a beginner are greatly appreciated. I also thank Gordon Bennett, Thomas Bernstein, Seweryn Bialer, Alexander Eckstein, C.T. Hu, John Fincher, Michael Pillsbury, Robert Scalapino, Richard Solomon, Frederick Teiwes, James Townsend, and the late John M.H. Lindbeck, who read all or parts of the manuscript and whose suggestions resulted in many improvements in this book. I wish especially to thank John Fincher, who read the entire manuscript several times and gave me invaluable advice on the scope of the study, and Robert Scalapino, whose penetrating criticism led me to reshape and refine interpretations and analysis I have obstinately maintained.

I owe special thanks to Ting Wang of the Contemporary China Research Institute of Hongkong, who generously shared with me his immense knowledge of China and his lifetime collection of research materials, and to many cadres on the mainland (whom I shall not name) I talked to during my tour of China in 1972, who provided me with first-hand information on some personnel and policy issues and significantly enhanced my understanding of Chinese politics.

I wish to express deep appreciation to Vernon Aspaturian, Robert S. Friedman, and Thomas Magner, colleagues at The Pennsylvania State University, for unfailing encouragement and support.

Several institutions have generously supported and assisted the preparation of this book, and it is a pleasure to express my gratitude. Research grants provided by the Contemporary China Studies Committee of the East Asian Institute at Columbia University from 1967 to 1969 enabled me to do field research in Hongkong in 1967–1968 and complete the first draft of the study. In the final stages of research I received timely research grants from the Liberal Arts Office for Research and Graduate Studies of The Pennsylvania State University.

Various libraries and research institutions and their staffs generously provided research facilities and rendered other helpful services. I wish to thank particularly Richard Sorich of the China Documentation Center at Columbia University, Weiying Wan of the Asia Library at the University of Michigan, Yee-fei Lau of the Universities Service Center of Hongkong, and staff members at the Institute of International Relations in Taipei and the Union Research Institute of Hongkong for valuable assistance. I am grateful also to the editor of the *China Quarterly* for permission to incorporate here portions of my article published in the journal earlier.

The skills and talents of a number of people have greatly expedited the completion of this book. I wish to thank Carole Schwager, who carefully edited the manuscript and coordinated the book production; Susan Mandarino, Karen Sweeney, and June Cutler, who devoted countless hours to typing several drafts of the manuscript; and Kathleen Shelton and Marsha Church, who helped compile the index.

Finally, I am most grateful to my wife, Shirley, and to our daughters, Yvette and Elaine, who have shared and endured the travails of my academic life, and whose patience and understanding are a source of constant encouragement which sustained me in my long and arduous years of authorship.

As always, I take sole responsibility for any errors and imperfections in the subsequent pages.

Parris H. Chang

University Park
April 1975

Abbreviations

APC	Agricultural Producers' Cooperative
CC	Central Committee
CCP	Chinese Communist Party
CPGC	Central People's Government Council
CPPCC	Chinese People's Political Consultation Conference
CPSU	Communist Party of the Soviet Union
CRG	Cultural Revolution Group
GAC	Government Administrative Council
GPCR	Great Proletarian Cultural Revolution
KMT	Kuomintang (The Nationalist Party)
NCNA	New China News Agency
NPC	National People's Congress
PLA	People's Liberation Army
PRC	People's Republic of China

Introduction

Until the advent of China's Great Proletarian Cultural Revolution (GPCR) in 1966, leaders of the Chinese Communist Party (CCP) had carefully concealed their differences from the public and had largely succeeded in nurturing an image that Communist China was a monolithic society governed by a unified, cohesive leadership—an image which was accepted by quite a few outside observers. The violent leadership conflicts and the attendant political upheavals in China during the GPCR shattered that myth of monolithic solidarity. Since 1967, the Chinese Communists themselves have rewritten their own history and propagated a theory that in the CCP there was a "struggle between the two lines" extending back over many decades—between the proletarian revolutionary line represented by Mao Tse-tung and the bourgeois revisionist line represented by Liu Shao-ch'i and other "capitalist power-holders." According to the theory, these "capitalist power-holders" had attempted to restore capitalism in China and had overtly or covertly sabotaged, obstructed, and opposed Mao's revolutionary line.

Is the reinterpretation more credible than the old myth? By examining China's policy-making process and policy disputes at the decision-making level before the GPCR I hope to ascertain where the truth lies. Five major policy issues are analyzed in this book: the Twelve-Year Agricultural Program, administrative decentralization, the commune movement, the Socialist Education Campaign, and the ideological rectification campaign. In analyzing the formulation and implementation of these policy issues, this study is designed to shed light upon the following questions: In the period covered by this study, were China's policy-making processes tightly controlled by a few top leaders who, in essential agreement, made all major decisions, which were then carried out by a highly centralized bureaucracy? Or were there much more complicated political processes at work in China in those years, in a system that was in reality less cohesive and monolithic than it appeared? Were there significant differences among the CCP leaders on various policy issues? What role did Mao Tse-tung play in the policy-making process, before and after the Great Leap Forward? What were the roles of

Liu Shao-ch'i, Chou En-lai, and other leaders at the center? Were the leaders at the center divided into factions? Did leaders at the regional and provincial level play a role in the policy-making processes? To what extent were local cadres a factor influencing policy-making—at least in the implementation stage? Were policy shifts simply a matter of a few leaders who largely agreed on their objectives and shifted policies in response to changing conditions? Or were policy shifts related more to conflict among leaders and to a changing balance of power in party councils? In structural terms, where were the loci of decisions? Did the loci of decision-making change over time?

Although the answers to these and other questions will be set forth in the subsequent chapters, the major conclusion of the book can be summarized at the outset:

1. Policy-making in China involved a complicated conflict and consensus-building process with many actors and many problems which—although distinctive in many respects—had some similarities to political processes elsewhere.

2. Although Mao played an extremely important role in the system—different from the less important role he played after the early 1960s—he was frequently blocked and frustrated by other leaders, and he was not always "in command," as some scholars have maintained.

3. When Mao maneuvered on various occasions to push his policies, he sought "outside" support to overcome his opponents at the center; consequently, the arena of political conflict was expanded, and more actors were drawn into participation in the resolution of conflict.

4. Despite Mao's enormous power, policy was significantly influenced by debates and conflict among the leaders; the major shifts in policy followed an oscillating pattern between the conservative and radical orientation, as a result of shifting coalitions and balance of power in the decision-making councils.

5. Leaders and cadres at the provincial and lower levels did have an effect on policy during the implementation phase in a variety of ways, although they may not have directly participated in its formulation.

Placed in the context of political science literature, my study of the policy-making process in China falls into the tradition of so-called descriptive or behavioral decision theory, which is concerned only with how policy-makers *actually* behave, whether the outcome is admirable or not,[1] and I have adopted an elite approach, viewing policy-making in China as an elite occupation. Political scientists have questioned the validity of this approach partly because an elite is not easily identified in a political system or subsystem, and partly because those who assert the existence of elite power structures cannot empirically prove that the elite exert power over a variety of policy issues.[2] In the case of Communist China, there is no question that a ruling elite does exist; this ruling group, until the Cultural Revolution, consisted of most of the 193 full and alternate members of the Central Committee (CC) of the CCP,[3] and its total number was approximately 800.[4] These 800 persons satisfactorily meet the theoretical requirement for an elite model as suggested by Dahl: "a controlling group less than majority in size, that is not a pure artifact of democratic rules . . . a minority of individuals whose preferences regularly prevail in cases of differences in preference on key political issues."[5]

Inasmuch as an elite did exist in China, it makes sense to focus on how this elite allocated value in society. In such an analysis of the behavior of policy-makers, we are concerned with policy-makers' expectations, the values they sought to maximize, their role demands, motivational and strategic factors, the socioeconomic constraints upon them, and their interaction with one another, on the one hand, and with the bureaucracy and the society as a whole, on the other. Thus while concentrating primarily on policy-makers, this study is intended to avoid some of the pitfalls of the "totalitarian model" which concentrates on "the dictator, his whims, the political intrigues among those around him."[6]

For purpose of analysis, the policy-making process in Communist China is divided into five stages: problem-identification, initiation, consensus-building, authorization, and implementation.[7] *Problem-identification* refers to gathering of information and definition of problems. *Initiation* or recommendation embodies the generation and proposal of solutions to cope with the identified problems. *Consensus-building* involves efforts to obtain support for the proposed solutions as well as efforts to neutralize or overcome opposition. *Authorization* or prescription refers to the formal enactment of solutions by those who have the effective and legitimate authority. *Implementation* or application involves the execution of the authorized measures in specific situations.

Terms such as "power," "influence," "policy," and "decision," which appear very frequently in this book, are defined briefly here. Many definitions have been given to the concept "power" in the social science literature. "Power" is defined in terms of the capacity to affect or modify the behavior of another group or individual, or it is defined as the production of certain intended effects, or as the process of affecting the behavior, attitudes, or outcomes of others, or "power" is sometimes synonymous with the causation of a change in another's behavior or attitude.[8] In this book "power" or "influence" refers to affecting, controlling, modifying, altering, or causing some activity, behavior, attitude, or outcome in an individual or a group. The analysis of power or influence in policy-making is, in a sense, a search for an explanation of why decisions turn out the way they do.[9] When we say that Mao Tse-tung has power over a given decision, we are explaining the decision in terms of Mao. Thus "power" and "influence" are used interchangeably here, although other writers may differentiate. According to

Lasswell and Kaplan, for instance, power is a special case of the exercise of influence, and power is different from influence in general because of its implied threat of sanction.[10]

Although "policy-making" and "decision-making" are used interchangeably here, "policy" and "decision," intimately related concepts, are used differently. "Policy" refers to goals, the means chosen to carry out these goals, and the actual distribution of values which is designated by the term "decision." In other words, policy includes decisions as one form of stipulation or determination of value distribution.[11]

In addition, Chinese Communists hold a peculiar concept of "decision," which renders analysis more difficult. According to the party's general secretary prior to the Cultural Revolution, Teng Hsiao-p'ing:

> Many important directives of the Central Committee were first sent out in *draft form* to local organizations, which were asked to suggest revisions after they had discussed them and *put them tentatively into operation; they were issued in official form only after being revised in the light of the opinions received*—a process which takes several months, sometimes even more than a year, to complete. The Central Committee also permits local organizations to modify its directives according to local conditions if they really find it impossible to carry out the directives as they are.[12] (Emphasis added)

It appears that Chinese Communists did not regard a "decision" as hard and irrevocable but as an idea that would evolve continually in the course of application (implementation). In this regard, it is more productive to treat policy-making as an ongoing process, using the authoritative decision itself as a focal point of analysis, as Richard Snyder suggests.[13]

Five major policy issues constitute a good sample for examining China's policy-making process. The case study approach is used because it is not sufficient to analyze the structure of policy-making by examining only China's state and party constitutions, legal statutes, and other authoritative policy statements. This alone cannot insure an understanding of how China's political system has actually functioned. A good many of the rules and procedures of government which are followed in practice may have been the result of precedents. Such rules and procedures may be understood and observed even though they are not formalized; they may function alongside of, or in place of, formal rules. Therefore as a guide for understanding the policy-making process in China, case studies of how policies are made may prove more reliable than simple analysis of formal rules and official statements made by Peking.

Several considerations influenced the selection of the five cases. Each received substantial press coverage, and the available information about them makes it possible to undertake detailed analysis. Each was an issue of conten-

tion among the leadership and underwent a great many changes; they therefore are a good basis for the analysis of underlying influences on the Chinese
policy-making process. Although the book does not deal with the GPCR in
great detail, except its initial stage (1955–66), its focus on the issues of contention and political conflict in the CCP leadership and on some of the dynamics in the system should clarify the GPCR and Chinese politics since the
second half of the 1960s.

The main sources used in this book are materials published in the People's
Republic of China, particularly the speeches of the party leaders, official
statements, documents and regulations issued by the CCP and the government, and newspapers, periodicals, and books. These are supplemented by
secret Chinese Communist documents and unpublished speeches by Mao that
have become available outside of China, Red Guard posters and newspapers,
refugee interviews, and studies made by scholars on China. The use of Chinese
sources, particularly secret documents and Red Guard publications, raises
some methodological problems.

Questions arise as to the validity of relying on the public Chinese Communist communications as the major sources for studying a topic such as
policy-making processes in Communist China. It is argued, and with much
truth, that Chinese official statements and mass media are full of propaganda
material and often do not report "facts"; moreover, they are frequently
couched in generalities, and they obscure reality by using Marxist jargon
and cliches. Furthermore, important aspects of the policy-making process are
often deliberately cloaked in secrecy by Chinese leaders; meetings that are
held secretly and decisions made may be announced later or not at all. This
practice conceals much that an observer needs to know to follow a line of
action through from start to finish. All these facts point to the handicaps and
limitations one has to reckon with in using Chinese Communist materials.

On the other hand, however, it would be wrong to regard all information
in the Chinese mass media as mere propaganda. No ruling group can rule by
coercion alone; to govern a big country like China and to try to persuade the
vast Chinese population to support its policies, the CCP has constant need to
communicate its directives to the masses, and this is done mainly through the
mass media. More than 28 million party members (last official figure, reported
in 1973) and hundreds of thousands of party activists upon whom the CCP
relies in carrying out its policies cannot be guided effectively on the basis of
secret channels of communication alone. For these reasons, not only official
statements but the mass media as well provide important sources of information for studying various Chinese policies and the goals of the regime.[14] Even
materials used in propaganda often reveal the motivation of the leadership
and the problems encountered.

Besides materials published for public consumption, there are a number of
secret Chinese official documents that have now become available in the

West. These documents reveal much valuable information which either clarifies issues or confirms speculations made by outside observers. Surprisingly enough, the language used in the secret channels of communication does not appear to be different from the language used in open channels, and the issues raised in these secret documents are also discussed in the press (either simultaneously or subsequently), though in somewhat vaguer terms.

The most important secret documents available are twenty-nine issues of the secret military journal *Kung-tso T'ung-hsun (Bulletin of Activities)*, covering the period of 1 January to 26 August 1961.[15] The bulletin was published by the PLA General Political Department and distributed to the Communist military officers at the regimental level or higher; the top-secret issues of the bulletin were distributed only to divisional officers. These bulletins contain extremely frank speeches by top military leaders, resolutions and reports of the Military Affairs Commission of the party's CC as well as from other sections of the army, and much valuable information on China's economic and social conditions. These copies of the journal are said to have been smuggled out of China after Khanbas overran a Chinese regimental post in Tibet in the late summer of 1961; they were subsequently acquired by the U.S. State Department which, in turn, made them available to academic libraries.

Less widely known but equally important are the so-called Lienchiang Documents. In March 1964, Nationalist Chinese commandos raided Lienchiang Hsien in Fukien province and captured documents totaling more than 200,000 words. Among these documents were resolutions of the Tenth CC Plenum of the CCP, directives of the CCP Fukien Provincial Committee and of the CCP Lienchiang Hsien Committee, reports of rural communes and brigades, as well as statistical charts and circulars on the Socialist Education Campaign and on various problems in the communes. The Nationalist Chinese authorities reprinted the Lienchiang Documents for restricted distribution. An English translation of these documents, entitled *Rural People's Communes in Lienchiang*, was published by Hoover Institution in 1969.

In addition, several other secret Chinese Communist documents secured and made available by the Chinese Nationalists have been used in this study. The authenticity of these documents is supported by the fact that at the time they were drawn up, public Chinese Communist sources were making statements that reflected the contents of these documents;[16] furthermore, Chinese Communist actions strongly indicated conformity to the programs outlined in these documents.

Red Guard publications, which mushroomed in China during 1966–67 because of the Cultural Revolution, have become an important new source for students of Chinese Communist affairs. These publications carry, among other things, many articles attacking and denouncing opponents, real and imagined, of Mao Tse-tung and the Cultural Revolution, and they reveal information relevant to the period of this study. Therefore I have selectively used some of these Red Guard sources, particularly in parts of Chapters 4 and 5. The authoritativeness and accuracy of the Red Guard materials do pose problems for the users, because many articles printed in the Red Guard publications are politically motivated and frequently are obviously biased and distorted.

In using the Red Guard materials, I have always tried to doublecheck other Chinese Communist or Western sources of the 1950s and the 1960s to determine whether a particular item is corroborated or reliable. After reading most of the available Red Guard publications, I have tentatively come to the following conclusions: their value judgments on the individual purge victims (e.g., assertions on their motivations for doing or saying certain things) are generally distorted and must be viewed with skepticism; information pertaining to facts ("who did what and when?") appears to be fairly reliable. For instance, information about several unpublicized party conferences in the early 1960s and the contents of some of Liu Shao-ch'i's unpublished speeches or interviews revealed by the Red Guard publications subsequently were confirmed by the official *People's Daily*.[17]

One major methodological problem of using the Red Guard materials is to ascertain the authoritativeness of the Red Guard sources. Where did the Red Guards get the information for their articles? Were they in a position to know what happened in the CCP leadership in the 1950s and early 1960s? Available evidence indicates that some Red Guard groups were closely associated with, if not directly controlled by, the CC Cultural Revolution Group (CRG) headed by Ch'en Po-ta and Chiang Ch'ing (Madame Mao).[18] It is quite possible that articles attacking major party figures which appeared in the publications of these organizations (many of which were reprinted in other Red Guard newspapers in other cities) were based on information supplied by the CRG. Without direct access to the sources at the highest level and the classified party archives, it would have been impossible for the Red Guards to quote directly from the private correspondence and unpublished speeches of people like Liu Shao-ch'i and to report a number of top-level party meetings and decisions made there.

Undoubtedly, articles in Red Guard publications and, since 1967, in the *People's Daily* as well have reinterpreted many past facts to suit current political need, yet they have also revealed facts hitherto unpublicized and shed new light on issues of contention in the CCP leadership and on modes of operation of the political system. With care and caution, and reading between lines, it is still possible to make significant use of the Red Guard materials.

Chapters 1 to 6 of this study are devoted to events and issues centered around the five selected policy issues. Chapter 1 discusses the background and the initial intraparty disputes on the Twelve-Year Agricultural Program during

1955–57. Chapter 2 focuses on problems of administrative decentralization. Chapter 3 deals with the implementation of the Twelve-Year Agricultural Program after the fall of 1957 and the chain of events leading to the establishment of the communes in the summer and fall of 1958. Chapter 4 analyzes the adverse effects of excessive decentralization and the communization program and inner-party disputes over the Great Leap Forward. Chapter 5 deals with the fate of the Twelve-Year Agricultural Program, the reversal of administrative decentralization, the reorganization of the commune system, and the retreat from the Great Leap Forward. Chapter 6 analyzes the Socialist Education Campaign and the rectification of cultural circles as well as a series of events that set the stage of the GPCR. Finally, Chapter 7 summarizes the findings of these case studies and offers some generalizations regarding the policy-making process in China. The names and positions of approximately one hundred Chinese officials mentioned in the book are listed in Appendix A.

1

The Dispute Over the Twelve-Year Agricultural Program

Two Different Strategies of Socialist Construction

In China's economy, the role and the importance of agriculture cannot be overstated; the agricultural sector has provided not only food for the entire population but also 90 percent of the raw materials for consumer goods industries and 75 percent of the exports with which China paid for its industrial imports. Poor agricultural harvests not only affect food supply but also have an almost immediate and direct impact on industrial products and export capabilities.

Thus the lag in agricultural output has been a serious problem for China's leaders. Farm production through the years has grown only slowly, possibly just enough to keep pace with population growth. Harvests have fluctuated, depending on weather conditions. Increased rate of industrial growth clearly demands increased agricultural output.

Two distinct approaches or strategies of economic development have been contending against each other since the early 1950s. One strategy for increasing agricultural output, which will be labeled "radical" for want of a better term, stresses structural changes in the economy and assigns a greater role to political mobilization and subjective human factors such as attitudinal change and class consciousness. It advocated, for example, collectivization of agriculture to replace the system of private farming. Early agricultural collectivization, in this view, would not only facilitate a more rational and efficient organization of labor and use of land but would also make it easier for the state to collect agricultural surpluses and speed up capital accumulation. Moreover, this approach favors greater utilization of organization and political mobilization in agriculture (and in the economy as a whole) and was planned to rely on institutions of economic control as prime instruments for resource mobilization and allocation essential to economic growth.

A different strategy, which will be labeled "conservative" or "pragmatic," places a greater emphasis on providing material incentives to the peasants and supplying chemical fertilizers and modern agricultural machinery to the countryside. Citing the example of Soviet collectivization, proponents of the conservative approach opposed a premature change in the system of agricultural production and argued for the postponement of collectivization until China's industry was ready to support the creation of large-scale, mechanized collective farms. Their argument was that a lack of qualified cadres makes it unwise for the government to exert too much control over production lest it have an adverse effect on peasant zeal to produce. Rather, material incentives such as providing more consumer goods, higher farm prices, distribution of more income to the peasants, and more free markets would be the best ways to induce the peasants to produce more. Finally, though such measures would inevitably use more of the scarce resources available for the industrial (particularly heavy) sector, it was suggested that a more balanced—even though somewhat slower—economic growth would remain the wisest course.

The Zigzag Course of Collectivization

On 31 July 1955 Mao Tse-tung, chairman of the CCP, delivered a speech to a meeting of the secretaries of provincial, municipal, and autonomous-region party committees calling for an acceleration of agricultural collectivization.[1] This was Mao's first important policy statement since his major article "On People's Democratic Dictatorship" presented in July 1949, three months before the establishment of the People's Republic of China in Peking.

The speed of agricultural socialization had been a matter of dispute within the party since 1953. Attempts were made in the spring of 1953, the fall of 1954, and the spring of 1955 to increase the tempo of collectivization. As a result of serious opposition within the party, both at the center and in the provinces, and resistance from the peasants, these efforts had to be modified or slowed down.[2]

Many Chinese leaders were well aware of the lessons of the Soviet collectivization in the 1920s.[3] Vice-Premier Teng Tzu-hui, concurrently director of both the State Council (Cabinet) Seventh Staff Office and the Rural Work Department of the CC in the CCP, articulated in July 1954 the views of those who advocated a cautious approach: "As the USSR possessed the various necessary conditions [for collectivization] at the time, it was right for her to act thus. We, however, have not the necessary conditions . . . moreover, the Chinese peasants' conception of private ownership is relatively deep, while our rural task is heavy and we have not enough cadres."[4]

In March 1955 the State Council issued a "Directive on Spring Farming and Production," which ordered the cadres to slow down agricultural collectivization and reorganize and consolidate the existing Agricultural Producers' Cooperatives (APC's).[5] In line with this "go-slow" approach, Vice-Premier Li Fu-ch'un's "Report on the First Five-Year Plan" to the National People's Congress on 5 July 1955 specified that by 1957 only one-third of the peasant households would join the elementary APC's.[6] Thus, up to the summer of

1955, the principle of "gradualism" had prevailed. Then suddenly at the end of July Mao intervened and attempted to reverse the moderate policy that was being implemented.

To understand Mao's justifications for speeding up collectivization, it is useful to keep in mind China's overall economic situation in the mid-1950s. First, farm production from 1949 to 1955 had increased only slowly, possibly just enough to keep pace with population growth. Agriculture, however, occupied a decisive position in the nation's economy; the agricultural sector had provided not only food for the entire population but also 90 percent of the raw materials for consumer goods industries and 75 percent of the exports which China exchanged for capital and industrial goods abroad.[7] The poor agricultural harvest in 1954 had not only affected food supply but also had an immediate adverse impact on industrial production and export capabilities and hence on the accumulation of capital in 1955.

Moreover, the level of living in China was low and the voluntary rate of saving was correspondingly low, yet capital accumulation would have to come almost exclusively from domestic savings. Therefore some form of compulsion would be required to achieve the desirable rate of saving. Since China's population was overwhelmingly agricultural, the bulk of savings would have to be sought in the agricultural sector so that some form of agricultural organization would have to be introduced to control the volume of consumption and generate maximum agricultural surplus.

It was within this economic context that Mao argued for the acceleration of agricultural collectivization. His basic arguments, as advanced in his speech of July 1955, are summarized in the following points:

1. China's rapid industrialization would have to rely on a sustained big push in agricultural production; this could be accomplished only through collectivization.

2. Collectivization would bridge the gap between the ever-increasing demand for marketable grain and industrial raw materials, on the one hand, and the generally low yield of stable crops, on the other.

3. Collectivization would facilitate a more rational and efficient organization of labor and use of land.

4. Collectivization would enable the state to exercise a greater degree of control over the Chinese population, would allow the government to effectuate a desired high rate of capital accumulation, and would ensure the state's supply of any available surplus.

Also very much in Mao's mind was the alleged "class struggle" in the countryside (Section IX).[8] The land reform had created a class of well-to-do peasants, and some enriched themselves by money-lending and speculative activities; on the other hand, the majority of poor peasants, lacking technical know-how and sufficient means of production, were still subjected to poverty.

If tendencies toward polarization of the peasantry were not checked, Mao warned, they would negate any positive results of the land reform, and the countryside would have to undergo another violent struggle such as the one in the land reform campaign.

Finally, Mao argued that the peasant masses were strongly for the collectivization. He maintained that the poor and the lower middle peasants (who represented 60 to 70 percent of the rural population), because of economic difficulties, were "disposed to choose the socialist road and energetically respond to our Party's call for cooperation" (Section II). It was Mao's firm belief that the peasants' zeal for the new system would induce them to work harder and that collectivization would generate a "high tide of agricultural production."

Some of Mao's colleagues, while agreeing with the need for increased agricultural production and the goal of eventual agricultural socialization, differed with Mao on the methods and timing of achieving these objectives. They were very skeptical about the ability of the cadres at this stage to institute and manage the APC's and especially about Mao's claim concerning the peasants' eagerness to join the APC's. They argued that the present pace of development of the APC's had gone beyond "the level of the cadre's experience" and "practical possibilities" or "understanding of the masses" (Section VI). They also cited the experience of the Soviet Union to criticize "impatience and rashness" in carrying out collectivization in China at that time.

Up to the summer of 1955, some of Mao's colleagues had been able to argue successfully for a more gradual policy and avoidance of a too radical approach which might deprive the peasants of their incentive and enthusiasm to produce. The evidence that other top CCP leaders had slowed down the collectivization drive was revealed in Section III of Mao's speech in July 1955:

> With the adoption of a policy of what was called "drastic compression" in Chekiang province—not by decision of the Chekiang Provincial Party Committee—out of 53,000 APC's in the province 15,000 comprising 400,000 peasant households were dissolved at one fell swoop in 1955. This caused great dissatisfaction among the masses and the cadres, and it was altogether the wrong thing to do. A "drastic compression" policy of this kind was decided on in a state of terrified confusion. It was not right, too, to take such a major step without the consent of the *Party Center*. As early as April 1955, the *Party Center* gave the warning: "Do not commit the 1953 mistake of mass dissolution of APC's again, otherwise self-criticism would again be called for." But certain comrades preferred not to listen. (Emphasis added)

Subsequently, throughout China 200,000 APC's were said to have been disbanded.

Mao's words revealed the existence of a group of officials powerful enough to obstruct the will of the "party center."[9] Who were they? Mao, in this speech, used the term "some comrades" or "certain comrades" twenty times, and "they" fifteen times to refer to those who disagreed with or obstructed rapid collectivization, but he did not identify them. They were not confined to provincial-level officials who actually implemented the policy of "drastic compression," since the decision to dissolve APC's was not made at the provincial level, as Mao clearly indicated. Some powerful top-level leaders of the CCP must have been involved because they were in a position to defy the April 1955 warning of the party center and to dissolve APC's on a large scale.

The denunciations of the purged party leaders during the Cultural Revolution have shed new light on the dispute over collectivization in the spring of 1955. Liu Shao-ch'i and Teng Hsiao-p'ing are alleged to have been the prime movers in the slowdown of collectivization:

> In 1955, following Chairman Mao's great call, there was an upsurge in agricultural cooperation throughout the country. But taking the opportunity of Chairman Mao's absence from Peking, China's Khrushchev [i.e., Liu Shao-ch'i] once again plotted criminal activities against "rashness." In May of that year, he and another top Party person in authority taking the capitalist road [i.e., probably Teng Hsiao-p'ing] concocted the reactionary policy of "holding up," "contraction," and "readjustment," and he personally ratified a plan for drastically cutting down the number of cooperatives. In a little over two months, 200,000 cooperatives were disbanded in the country.[10]

Liu had long been considered a believer of the theory of "mechanization before cooperation," and he had told a Conference on Propaganda Work in 1951, "Only with the nationalization of industry can large quantities of machinery be supplied to the peasants, and only then will it be possible to nationalize the land and collectivize agriculture."

According to Liu's own account, he did not take the initiative, although he did approve the proposal to dissolve the APC's. The initiative was said to have come from Vice-Premier Teng Tzu-hui, who was then in charge of the regime's overall rural policy: "In 1955 Comrade Teng Tzu-hui proposed the retrenchment and dissolution of 200,000 cooperatives. The Central Work Conference, over which I presided, made no refutation of this proposal, and virtually approved his plan. Later Teng Tzu-hui retrenched and dissolved 200,000 cooperatives at a Central Committee Rural Work Conference."[11]

Liu's story appears to be closer to the truth. It is plain from both accounts that the proposal to disband APC's did not originate with Liu, and probably not with Teng Hsiao-p'ing; it was initially sponsored by someone else (by Teng Tzu-hui, according to Liu). When the proposal was presented to the Central Work Conference for decision, however, neither Liu nor Teng Hsiao-p'ing opposed it. Whether Liu supported the proposal cannot be determined on the basis of available evidence. It is quite probable, however, that Liu did not fight against the dissolution of these APC's; since he was the presiding official of the conference, Liu's failure to oppose the proposal might have facilitated its approval.

Teng Tzu-hui had on the record strongly advocated a policy of gradualist collectivization and material incentives for peasants.[12] Although he was never a member of the Politburo, he was in charge of the regime's rural policy; thus if, as is alleged, he did make the proposal to cut back APC's, this view would have carried great weight in the interparty circle. Li Hsien-nien, a Vice-Premier and concurrently Minister of Finance, was among those repeatedly opposed to rapid collectivization, as his self-criticism later implied.[13] Vice-Premier Ch'en Yun, a Politburo member who was in charge of China's overall economic policy, and appeared to have consistently advocated a gradualist strategy toward economic development,[14] may have also supported Teng Tzu-hui. There is also evidence that in the provinces there was a widespread feeling against rapid collectivization.[15] In short, there seemed to be a consensus (although probably not unanimity), involving an important segment of the leadership, which opposed rapid collectivization at that time. The decision of the May 1955 Central Work Conference to cut back APC's probably reflected this consensus.

Lui Shao-ch'i's confession, quoted earlier, revealed several pieces of information on China's decision-making process. Most significant is the fact that when Mao was absent, Lui was in charge. The Central Work Conference —a forum not stipulated in the party constitutions of 1945 and 1956—was actually an enlarged meeting of the Politburo or its Standing Committee attended by both Politburo members and selected non-Politburo party officials; the Work Conference could make decisions on key issues as binding as those of the Politburo or the CC.[16] And the Rural Work Conference, such as the one convened by Teng Tzu-hui, seemed to be concerned with operational and technical matters.

Mao's Call for Help from Provincial Leaders

Confronted with opposition within the party center, Mao apparently chose to bypass the regular decision-making bodies and appeal directly to provincial-level leaders. By this maneuver, Mao appeared to enlarge the arena of policy debate to include the provincial-level secretaries so that he might try to obtain their support to overcome his opponents in the center. At the end of July 1955, just after he had returned from an extensive tour of the provinces where he must have sought support from the provincial secretaries,[17] Mao convened a conference in Peking of the secretaries of provincial-level party committees (a forum stipulated in neither the 1945 nor the 1956 party constitution).

Mao severely attacked the conservative tendencies in the party in his speech to the provincial leaders; he castigated those party officials who championed a "go-slow" policy of collectivization as "tottering along like a woman with bound feet, always complaining that others are going too fast." He called for the organization of 1.3 million lower APC's by October 1956 (a 100 percent increase in fourteen months), and for the conversion of some of these into higher (advanced) APC's.[18] Mao then envisioned that all peasant households would join lower APC's by 1960. In his speech Mao also asked provincial secretaries to "go back and look into the question [of collectivization], work out a program suited to the actual situation, and report to the CC within two months." Mao promised to "hold a discussion and make a final decision" within two months.

With this instruction, Mao staked the tremendous prestige of his position and the great strength of his leadership on the issue of collectivization. Pressure was exerted and attitude on this issue became a yardstick for measuring each official, both high and low, for his loyalty to Mao. The impact of Mao's speech was swift and impressive: cadres in the provinces immediately drew up plans to intensify collectivization and new APC's were established everywhere. For instance, in Kiangsu the number of APC's increased from 35,773 in July to 121,494 in early October, and the Provincial Party Committee revised its plan to suit the new situation.[19] In Shantung more than 78,000 new APC's had been set up by the end of September 1955, surpassing the number laid down in the plan drawn up by Shantung's Provincial Party Committee. In Kwangtung, at the Provincial Party Congress, T'ao Chu spoke on Kwantung's "First Five-Year Plan Centered on Agriculture" and promised to increase the number of APC's from 16,000 to 70,000 within six months.[20]

The Speed-Up of Collectivization

By the time the Enlarged Sixth Plenum of the Seventh CC was convened on 4 October 1955, the leap in agricultural collectivization was already a *fait accompli* in many provinces. This apparent success tended to vindicate Mao's position, implying that he had been correct and decisive. On the other hand, the success also seemed to show that Mao's colleagues in the center were guilty of "rightist" deviation—they had been too conservative to properly assess the socialist consciousness of the masses and did not sufficiently believe in the ability of the party "to lead the peasants along the road to socialism." With his own position strengthened and that of his opponents weakened by the actual development, Mao now proceeded to push through his collectivization program and convened the Plenum to formally endorse and legitimize the campaign that had already been launched—as well as to criticize rightist tendencies.

When the Plenum opened on 4 October Ch'en Po-ta delivered a speech, "Explanations of the Draft Decision on the Question of Agricultural Co-operativization."[21] In the course of his speech, Ch'en revealed for the first time that he was "doing some work in the Central Committee Rural Work Department"; later he was identified as one of the Deputy Directors of that department. Until he was purged in 1970 Ch'en Po-ta had been Mao's brain-truster for over thirty years, frequently feeding ideas to Mao and giving sub-stance to Mao's visions.[22] Very likely it was Ch'en who had advised and worked closely with Mao in 1955 on the drive to accelerate the pace of col-lectivization. Therefore Mao picked Ch'en to offer official explanations for the new line, bypassing Teng Tzu-hui (director of the Rural Work Depart-ment), who was opposed to it. On 11 October the Plenum formally adopted the decision which, among other things, called for the basic completion of lower APC's by the spring of 1958.[23] This new target represented a two-year advance over the schedule set by Mao's July speech.

The meeting, however, was by no means one-sided; in Mao's own words, which were never made public in China, the conference saw "a big debate."[24] It may have been the provincial party secretaries who carried the day for Mao. Although few of these provincial secretaries were then members of the CC, and those who were not could not vote, they did attend this enlarged CC plenary session and it seems plausible that they spoke out strongly for Mao.[25] If that was the case, when the provincial leaders (who were closer to the problem of implementing rural policies than the leaders in Peking) said Yes, it may have made it difficult for the central leaders who opposed Mao's views to say otherwise. As we shall see later, on numerous subsequent occasions Mao appeared to take actions designed to mobilize support from provinces to overrule opposition in the center.

Mao thus scored an impressive victory in the fall of 1955 and his July speech was then made public for the first time. His personal intervention to impose his views appeared to settle for the time being the debate within the party on the question of collectivization which had evolved over the preceding three years; as Vice-Premier Ch'en Yi admitted at the time, this enabled certain comrades (probably himself included) "to turn from their mistaken paths to the correct road of Marxism-Leninism."[26]

A few other high party officials who opposed the collectivization drive made self-criticisms. For instance, Li Hsien-nien recanted the error of "em-piricism"; probably speaking for other colleagues as well as himself, Li stated that "in the past we were not in doubt about the general line and the center's policy on agriculture. . . . But empiricism frequently characterized our view of the tempo of agricultural collectivization."[27] Li added: "Some of our comrades heed only the negative reactions and not the positive reactions [of peasants]. They underrate the consciousness of peasantry and underrate the leadership of the Party. In these circumstances they cannot but commit serious errors."

Vice Premier Po I-po also endorsed the new policy in a *People's Daily* (17 November 1955) article entitled "Agricultural Cooperation Should be Closely Linked Up with Technical Reform of Agriculture," although between the lines he appeared to show continuing doubts and argue more strongly for technical reform than socialist transformation. In addition to agricultural cooperation (i.e., socialist transformation of agriculture), Po considered mechanization, electrification, and chemicalization of culture, or the technical reform of agriculture, another important aspect of the socialist transformation movement. He maintained that technical reform of agriculture should correspond to the needs of socialist transformation of agriculture and give an impetus to socialist transformation of agriculture, and that only the use of modern techniques could raise the productivity of agriculture continuously. He emphatically stated, "Only after the productivity of agricultural production has been highly developed can the superiority of cooperation be further demonstrated and fully developed."

Curiously enough, Teng Tzu-hui was silent. Although he was singled out for criticism by Mao during the Plenum for having committed "empirical rightist errors," he may still have clung to his own position.[28] Shortly after the Plenum, Liao Lu-yen and Ch'en Cheng-jen were appointed deptuy directors of the State Council Seventh Staff Office. As pointed out earlier, Ch'en Po-ta, a theoretician and Mao's brain-truster, had been appointed one of the deputy directors of the CC Rural Work Department before the October CC Plenum. These two institutions were the highest state and party agencies in charge of the regime's rural policy and both were headed by Teng Tzu-hui. Although Teng was not purged then, Mao appointed those who favored his programs to dilute Teng's power and authority. Teng apparently remained at cross-purposes with Mao, and he was to suffer politically for his conviction: when the First Plenum of the Eighth CC was convened in September 1956, Teng was the only vice-premier who was not elected to the Politburo.

The Initiation of the Twelve-Year Agricultural Program

A Brief Sketch of the Draft Program

It was in the context of the inner-party disputes over the tempo of collectivization and Mao's victory leading to the speed-up of collectivization that the draft "Forty-Article 1956–1967 National Program for Agricultural Development" was launched on 25 January 1956, at a Supreme State Conference meeting.[29] The draft program called for continuation of the fairly radical line pushed by Mao since the previous summer. Capitalizing on the accelerated momentum of socialist transformation in the autumn and winter of 1955–56, Article 1 stipulated that "all provinces ... should, in the main, complete agricultural cooperativization in its elementary form and set themselves the goal of getting about 85 percent of all peasant households into APC's in 1956." This was a further upward revision of the timetable set in the October 1955 CC Plenum, accelerating the schedule by two years. According to Article 2, higher-stage APC's were to be formed by 1957 in "areas where APC's are on a better foundation," and by 1958 the "main work" of organizing them was to be completed throughout the country.

Many other ambitious goals were included. By 1967 per *mou* (1 mou = 1/15 hectare or 1/6 acre) grain and cotton yields were to be increased more than 100 percent in three major regions of the country (Article 6); grain output was to increase from the 1955 figure of over 150 catties (1 catty = 1/2 kilogram or 1.1 pounds) to 400 catties in areas north of the Yellow River, from 208 to 500 catties in the areas south of the Yellow and north of the Huai River, and from 400 to 800 catties in the areas south of the Huai,[30] while the average annual yield of ginned cotton was to be increased from the 1955 figure of 35 catties to 60, 80, or 100 catties depending on local conditions. Within three to five years, 6 million two-wheeled double-bladed plows and other farm tools would be put into service as the first step toward mechanization (Article 12). The major diseases and the four prevalent pests were to be wiped out within twelve years (Articles 26 and 27). Illiteracy was to be eliminated within five to seven years (Article 19), and local road systems and broadcasting networks were to cover the country by 1967 (Articles 30 and 31).

Of these tasks, with the exception of a few that were to be undertaken by the state or with the assistance of the state such as the production of the two-wheeled double-bladed plows, the majority would have to be carried out by the peasants themselves. Liao Lu-yen, in a report explaining the draft program, said that it "principally calls for its realization by means of reliance on the peasants themselves, using the manpower, material and financial resources of the 500 million peasants."[31] The draft program was said to have been designed to raise the peasants' "material and cultural living levels," but this goal could be achieved only after the draft program was fulfilled. The draft program promised the peasants not material rewards now but a rosy future attained through hard work.

The heart of the program was to increase agricultural production by expanding cultivated areas through reclamation and irrigation and by improving the unit area yield through irrigation, application of fertilizers, close planting, deep plowing, soil improvement, conservation, pest control, and any other means possible. Thus an approach emphasizing the mass mobilization of labor, which was to become a hallmark of the Great Leap Forward two years later, originated in 1956. As Chou En-lai told the Second Plenary Session of the Second CPPCC National Committee on 30 January 1956, the draft program was only the "minimum program" for agricultural development; he said that the massive strength of the peasantry could be relied upon not only to complete but to overfulfill the draft program ahead of schedule.[32] China had 120 million peasant households. Article 23 stipulated that a man from each household would work 250 workdays and a woman 120 workdays each year, a total of 370 workdays a year for each household, making a total of 44 billion workdays for the whole country. The amount of labor that the peasant used directly in field work was said to be roughly two-thirds of all workdays. Thus, based on Chou's calculation, the peasants would still have 14.8 billion workdays each year to be used for various measures for increasing production and other work. Total and massive labor mobilization was to be the key to realizing the goals stipulated in the draft program.

The Initiation

The process through which the draft program was formulated and the manner with which it was presented to the public deserve close attention. The original suggestion of the draft program was said to have come from Mao himself;[33] in November 1955 Mao exchanged views on the development of agriculture with the secretaries of fourteen provincial party committees and together they "agreed" on the so-called Seventeen Articles. These Seventeen Articles, apparently without approval by legitimate decision-making bodies, were transmitted to the rural areas, where they produced a "colossal mobilization force." Their contents, however, are not known to the outside world. In January 1956, after more discussions with provincial party officials, Mao expanded the Seventeen Articles into Forty Articles and produced the first version of the draft program. In mid-January 1956, members of the CC, provincial party secretaries, and other community officials in the government, all of whom were then attending a meeting convened by the party's CC, were briefed by Liao Lu-yen on the contents of the draft program.[34]

In line with the regime's united front strategy at that time, Mao made efforts to involve other groups in the political process. The CC of the CCP invited 1375 prominent non-party members in Peking, including scientists, industrialists, businessmen, educators, and representatives of the "democratic" parties and groups, to attend a series of meetings to give advice and suggestions. Some valuable ideas were said to have been offered, and revisions were made accordingly. The second draft of the draft program was then adopted by the Politburo on 23 January 1956.[35]

Two days later, on 25 January, with great éclat, the draft "1956–1967 National Program for Agricultural Development" was presented to the Supreme State Conference for discussion. According to the press release concerning it, the meeting was attended by more than 300 people, including not only important Communist officials in the government but also non-Communist officials and many prominent "democratic" personages.[36] This was the first time that Mao used this symbolically important body of the Chinese government to launch a very important policy.[37] Mao has since continued to use the Supreme State Conference as a platform from which to make important policy pronouncements. The presence of non-Communist officials and representatives of "democratic" parties gave the appearance of national support for the draft program and the party.

The program, labeled a draft, was not meant to be final for at least a few months. As stated in its introduction, the draft program was to be distributed to local party committees at all levels and to all departments concerned for comments and suggestions. Opinions would also be solicited from the public by 1 April. On the basis of these opinions, the Seventh CC Plenum, which was scheduled to meet on that date, would draw up a final plan. Meanwhile, local party and government organs at all levels, as well as all departments concerned, were instructed to review their plans of work and, on the basis of the draft program, draw up new plans for their community or agency. Thus the draft program was not simply a draft, but it was in a sense to become operative even before final approval by the CC.

Publicity and Propaganda

Persuasion as well as coercion is stressed by the Chinese leadership. A mass propaganda campaign, which usually precedes and accompanies the implementation of a policy, has been an invariable ingredient of the policy-making process in China. Following the announcement of the draft program, an intensive publicity campaign was launched to publicize it and to arouse the enthusiasm of the masses as well as that of the cadres. Premier Chou En-lai made a report (cited above) to the Second Plenary Session of the CPPCC, presenting an optimistic picture of China's countryside after the goals of the draft program were attained. National newspapers published editorials and feature articles to eulogize the draft program and urge the masses to work harder to attain the goals prescribed.[38] Response from the provinces was swift and impressive. Party officials in Kiangsi, Shansi, Hopei, and Kansu immediately called meetings to study the draft program and to revise their working plans accordingly.[39] In other provinces, the press enthusiastically propagandized the draft program, and officials vowed to achieve its objectives even sooner than the projected date.[40]

Implementation

With great fanfare, various provinces began to map out plans in accordance with the spirit of the draft program. For instance, in Shensi secretaries of the special district and *hsien* party committees attended an enlarged plenary session of the Provincial Party Committee in February 1956, in which the "Plan for the Thorough Implementation in Shensi of the Draft 1956–1967 National Program for the Agricultural Development" was adopted.[41] In Kwangtung, T'ao Chu (governor and secretary of the Provincial Party Committee) presented an ambitious draft "Seven Year Plan for Agricultural Development" to Kwangtung's CPPCC, pledging to fulfill all the targets set in the draft national program by 1962, five years ahead of schedule.[42] In addition to provinces, *hsien*, cities, and even mass organizations published their programs based on the draft national program and launched campaigns to execute them. For instance, Shenyang city (Mukden) in Liaoning province drew up a "Twelve-Year Agricultural Plan" for the city.[43] The Forestry Departments of the provincial governments of Szechuan and Shensi each formulated a "Ten-Year Forestry Plan,"[44] and the All-China Federation of Democratic Women had its version of a Twelve-Year Plan.

Meanwhile, unprecedentedly large numbers of peasants were mobilized to reclaim wastelands, to repair and build irrigation and water conservancy works, and to engage in many other construction projects. A Tientsin newspaper reported that the peasants were so occupied by these assignments they had no time for subsidiary occupations.[45] The cadres, engaging in what many critics later called "reckless advance," were under great pressure from their provincial superiors to undertake many tasks at once and to achieve the goals of the draft program ahead of schedule. The draft program also gave the local cadres an added impetus in the movement for agricultural collectivization, and the target date for the completion of the socialist transformation was frequently advanced.

For instance, the plan in Shensi province cited earlier stipulated that 90 percent of all peasant households were to join the APC's (including the higher level APC's) before the spring tilling of 1956, and that more than 90 percent of all peasant households were to join the higher APC's before the spring tilling in 1957. This was one year ahead of the schedule outlined in Articles 1 and 2 of the draft national program. Kwangtung, a latecomer to land reform, also set the same target. Thus at the end of December 1955, 75 million peasant households, or 63 percent of the nation's total, had joined APC's; three months later the number of peasant households joining APC's had increased to 88.9 percent or 206,680,000, and 54.9 percent of the nation's peasant households were already in the higher APC's.[46]

The cadres, spurred on by their superiors to attain the target, evidently acted rashly in herding the peasants into APC's. They often ignored the principles of "voluntarism and mutual benefit" as prescribed by the central authorities, forcing the peasants to join APC's and surrender their properties without due compensation. In some localities peasants were forced to invest their money in the APC's against their will, and in many cases their deposits in banks or remittances from other areas were frozen by overzealous cadres.[47]

The peasants, especially those who were better off, were dissatisfied and resentful. Although peasant resistance was rarely well organized, many instances were reported. The peasants slaughtered livestock and draft animals instead of surrendering them to the APC's; this situation was serious enough, even before the initiation of the draft program, that the State Council in December 1955 issued a directive ordering cadres to protect draft animals.[48] As soon as the draft animals became the property of the APC's, their mortality rate rose rapidly. According to a survey conducted in Kiangsu province, some 60,000 head died during the winter of 1956 and the spring of 1957; in Shantung, 30 percent of the draft animals were declared to be weak or incapacitated.[49] There were also frequent reports of peasants' absence from work, indifference to common property, disregard of orders, and even acts of sabotage.[50] The news that cadres were forcing peasants to invest their money in the APC's created a panic, with peasants in many localities withdrawing their savings from banks, concealing their money, and refraining from buying even needed articles, which resulted in "an abnormal situation in the rural market."[51]

Cadres' lack of experience in managing the APC's and the resulting mismanagement further exacerbated the difficulties of the APC's. Whereas the cadres might be very skillful in political manipulation and in conducting political activities, these functions were significantly different from those of organizing and operating economic production, especially agricultural production. To formulate plans of production for an APC of several hundred households, to allocate labor and farm tools adequately among different production teams working on different crops, to compute wage points for the peasants performing different types of labor—all their new functions must have been a very complicated and difficult job to say the least. In a speech in May 1956, Teng Tzu-hui frankly admitted that mismanagement and faulty planning had greatly contributed to the defects of the APC's.[52] The rapid growth of the APC's led to a universal shortage of competent cadres to do the job of planning, managing, and accounting adequately. Many units, even after their first year of operation, could not establish regular accounting systems. Thus it was almost impossible to distribute income correctly, and irregularities dampened the enthusiasm of the members.

Many APC's, again according to Teng Tzu-hui, had no overall production plans. Food crops and cotton were overemphasized (because they were targets in the draft program) at the expense of other economic crops; agriculture was overstressed, and subsidiary occupations were neglected. According to a survey of Liaoning province during the first quarter of 1956, sideline production registered a 40–50 percent decline compared with the corresponding period in 1955.[53] Sideline production generally represented 30–40 percent of the peasants' total income, and the falling output in economic crops and sideline occupations greatly affected the peasants' cash income and increased the difficulties in their daily life. On 2 May 1956 the editorial in *Ta-kung Pao* stated that the decline of subsidiary production was one of the main causes of the occurrence of "certain stagnant conditions" in China's rural economy. According to Teng Tzu-hui, the decline of subsidiary production adversely affected not only the economic balance of society and the supply of raw materials for certain industries but also the supply of export materials.[54]

The Shelving of the Program

The First Sign

By April 1956 it must have become apparent to the Chinese leaders that the national economy was encountering some serious problems. The Seventh CC Plenum, which was originally scheduled to meet 1 April to approve the draft program, failed to meet (although the Politburo did);[55] the draft program was therefore not approved by the CC, as had been planned.

Probably as a result of the late March to early April Politburo meeting, on 4 April the CC of the party and the State Council of the government issued an important joint directive to stop the tendencies of "reckless advance" in socialist construction.[56] It reprimanded enterprises, departments of the party, and government organs at all levels for trying to do everything at once—attempting to fulfill the draft program "with a single stroke in two or three years." On the other hand, the joint directive also blamed the APC cadres for extravagance, waste, and abuse of manpower. Many APC's were said to have constructed various projects unnecessary to production, purchased farm implements and transport facilities in excess of actual need, and even built clubhouses and offices and bought large quantities of cultural entertainment equipment and nonproductive supplies.[57]

Tendencies of "reckless advance" had resulted in excessive investment, general economic overexpansion, overemphasis on production and quantity, creating bottlenecks and causing financial difficulties. The full extent of the economic crisis caused by the "reckless advance" was revealed one year later at the NPC in June 1957, when Minister of Finance Li Hsien-nien estimated total overspending at more than 2 billion *yuan*. Chou En-lai also announced a 20 percent cutback in 1957 capital construction investment.[58] A fascinating example was the overproduction of the two-wheel double-bladed plow. In the first half of 1956 alone, 1,400,000 were produced and although 800,000 were sold, many by compulsory means, only half of these were actually used because they were either too heavy for the draft animals or not suitable for the soil in most areas. One authoritative source admitted that the overproduction of these plows caused a shortage in the supply of steel and affected priority construction projects.[59]

It was under these circumstances that the Politburo met in an enlarged session from late March to early April. Both the problems afflicting national economy and the difficulties in the countryside resulted largely from the rapid collectivization drive and poor management of the APC's, as well as from the attempts to achieve the goals of the draft program ahead of time, all of which served to vindicate the position of those party officials who advocated gradualism. The issuance of the 4 April joint directive appeared to indicate that their counsel had prevailed once again in the party's highest decision-making body.

Following the Politburo meeting, another conference of the provincial secretaries was convened. At this conference, top provincial officials may have been briefed on the shift of the regime's rural policy as well as on the question of de-Stalinization in the Soviet Union.[60]

Khrushchev's sudden denunciation of Stalin at the Twentieth Congress of the Communist Party of the Soviet Union (CPSU) appeared to have created unexpected political vibrations in China, which may have hurt Mao's political standing as well as his policies, including the draft program. In light of the de-Stalinization in the Soviet Union, the Chinese leaders apparently decided to review their leadership, particularly Mao; as a result, the political atmosphere changed, and some major domestic policies, such as the draft program, changed accordingly.

It will be recalled that Khrushchev, in a secret speech to the Twentieth Congress of the CPSU in February 1956, suddenly unveiled and attacked Stalin's crimes and megalomania. That serious dismay was created in Peking by Khrushchev's action was suggested by the fact that from February to the end of March the Chinese media were silent on the question of de-Stalinization, even though the question was already being bitterly debated throughout the Communist world and had already resulted in defections from some Communist parties. The first public Chinese reaction was the publication in the *People's Daily* (30 March) of a translation of "Why is the Cult of the Individual Alien to Marxism-Leninism?," a *Pravda* editorial of 18 March which severely criticized Stalin. On 5 April, after almost two months of soul-searching, the Chinese leadership published in the *People's Daily* an editorial entitled "On the Historical Experience of the Dictatorship of the Proletariat," which was said to have been written "on the basis of a discussion at an enlarged meeting of the Politburo."

Stalin previously had been portrayed in China as almost a demigod, and the CCP had adopted many Stalinist measures. Moreover, like Stalin, Mao was pursuing a policy of rapid collectivization. Had someone in the party begun to question Mao's style of leadership and his cult of personality as a result of Khrushchev's attack on the dead *Vozhd*? For Mao, there was an urgent need to avoid the charge that he was following Stalin's footsteps.[61] Thus the editorial, while conceding Stalin's "serious mistakes," affirmed Stalin's positive role as an "outstanding Marxist-Leninist fighter" who had defended Lenin's line of industrialization and collectivization against the enemies of Leninism. The editorial contended that Stalin's errors were committed late in his life—when he indulged in the cult of the individual, violated the party system of democratic centralism and collective leadership, and fell victim to subjectivism by divorcing himself from reality and the masses.

Perhaps in anticipation of a possible challenge to Mao's leading role, the editorial emphasized the important position of leaders in history: "It is utterly wrong to deny the role of the individual, the role of forerunners and leaders." A leader begins to make serious mistakes only when he "places himself over and above the Party and the masses." However, it was implied, there seemed to be no danger of this in China now. The editorial pointed to a 1943 Party Central Committee resolution on methods of leadership which stressed the mass line. The implication was that the CCP, under Mao, had consistently observed this "Marxist-Leninist" method of leadership.

The fact that a few months later, during the Eighth Party Congress, the new Party Constitution dropped the term "thought of Mao Tse-tung" from its preamble,[62] an action allegedly first proposed by Marshal P'eng Teh-huai and then supported by Liu Shao-ch'i,[63] seemed to suggest that Khrushchev's attack on Stalin had emboldened some CCP leaders to criticize or at least question Mao's personal leadership. Even if Mao's colleagues did not wish to embarrass him in public, Mao himself may have felt compelled to observe the system of collective leadership and change somewhat his strong personal style of leadership. In a new political atmosphere when collective leadership was emphasized, other top party officials who opposed Mao's rapid collectivization policy but were forced to go along in the fall of 1955 may have reasserted themselves and argued against rash approval of the draft program. Perhaps Mao felt that in the interest of collective leadership he would have to accede to the opposition and allow the draft program to be shelved.

It is interesting to note that "collective leadership" was now applied even to the publication of the 5 April editorial, a policy statement which was based on the "discussions of an enlarged meeting of the Politburo." The editorial carried no name of any active Chinese leader, not even Mao; by contrast, only two months earlier Mao had been conspicuously identified with formulating and proposing the draft program.

It should be pointed out here that in the spring of 1956 Mao had adopted a new posture, manifested in a secret speech, "Ten Great Relationships," which he delivered to an enlarged Politburo session on 25 April.[64] Foreshadowing his celebrated speech "On Correct Handling of Contradictions Among the People" in February 1957, the speech in April 1956 called the party's attention to the ways of correctly handling ten basic relationships or contradictions confronting the Chinese polity, including the following:

1. The relationships between industry and agriculture and between heavy and light industries.
2. Those between coastal industries and inland industries.
3. Those between economic construction and national defense.
4. Relationships among the state, the co-ops and the individual.
5. Contradictions between the central and local authorities.
6. Those between the Han people and the national minorities.
7. Those between the Party and non-Party people.
8. Those between revolution and counter-revolution.
9. Contradictions between right and wrong, inside and outside the Party.
10. Problems in international relations.

What is truly remarkable about this speech is that, in addition to showing a sober recognition of the wide range of economic and political problems in China, Mao embraced a number of solutions which made him look like a "liberal," both in politics and in economics. For example, he spoke in favor of giving material incentives to the peasants, which had long been advocated by other top leaders who were in charge of economy and which Mao had criticized earlier (and was to criticize again in 1958). Did Mao adopt the new posture due to a genuine change of heart or was he responding to political pressures resulting from China's economic difficulties and the de-Stalinization campaign? This cannot be answered with certainty. In any case, the shift seemed to be good politics from Mao's point of view. By drifting to the right, Mao, a shrewd politician, may have hoped to occupy the consensus position that had emerged in the new political context of the spring of 1956 and to preempt the issues from his critics.

The Conservatives in Ascendancy

Thus in the spring of 1956 the political momentum generated by Mao's collectivization drive of the previous summer gradually slowed down, and the official enactment of Mao's draft program as a major policy was blocked or at least delayed for the time being.[65] The political current in Peking began blowing to the right, and the 4 April Central Committee-State Council joint directive and Mao's speech were straws in this new wind. A further indication of the new trend was provided by an editorial of the *People's Daily* on 20 June

1956, "Oppose Both Conservatism and Hastiness."

Ostensibly opposing both conservatism and hastiness, the editorial in fact aimed at the tendencies of "reckless advance" which were said to have occurred "after combating conservatism [since the second half of 1955]." "That hastiness is a serious question," stated the editorial, "is due to the fact that it exists not only among the cadres of the lower levels and that in many cases the hastiness manifested at the lower levels is the result of pressure applied by the higher levels." Further, "As soon as the forty-article draft Agricultural Program was announced, all organizations vied with each other to set unrealistically high targets lest they should be accused of rightist conservatism and all departments looked forward to immediate success in their work," implying that those defects were related to Mao's draft program.

Finally, the editorial admonished cadres to adopt an attitude of "seeking truth in facts" and to apply as a criterion to combat rightist conservatism and hastiness the so-called criterion of objective practical possibility (what falls behind it is rightist conservatism and what exceeds it is hastiness). It is not inconceivable that these sentences were written with Mao in mind, since he had criticized rightist conservative thinking and had said these words: "The problem today is that many people think impossible what is in fact possible if they exert themselves.[66]

According to a recent revelation of Wu Leng-hsi, former director of the New China News Agency, the editorial was first drafted by Teng T'o, the editor-in-chief of the *People's Daily*, then revised by Lu Ting-yi and Hu Ch'iao-mu, two top officials responsible for propaganda, and finally approved by Liu Shao-ch'i.[67] Mao, unenthusiastic about the editorial when Liu went to him for his last clearance, wrote "I do not want to read it" on the draft of the editorial, although it was subsequently published. The publication of this editorial may have left Mao smarting for, according to an unpublished text of Mao's speech delivered to the Nanning Conference in Kwangsi (a meeting convened by Mao and attended by some Politburo members and regional party secretaries) in early 1958, he reopened the case of that June 1956 editorial, calling it a "mistake" and criticizing it for having undermined the spontaneous initiative of the masses and cadres and resulting in losses to the national economy.[68] Wu further asserted that Mao's criticism was really directed against Liu Shao-ch'i, who allegedly was the initiator of the movement against "reckless advances."

In the course of the Cultural Revolution, everything Liu (and other purged victims) did and said in the past was reinterpreted to discredit him; therefore any specific charge against him (or others) must be treated with caution. With regard to the movement against "reckless advance" in 1956, it may not be entirely true that Liu and the aforementioned officials, all of them disgraced in the Cultural Revolution, were prime movers;[69] the main pressure could have come from any of several directions.

One source of this pressure seemed to be Premier Chou En-lai who, since the beginning of 1956, had urged the party to relax its control over the intellectuals who possessed valuable technical and intellectual resources needed for China's socialist construction but who were politically tainted in Communist eyes because of their Western or non-Communist education. In an important speech, "On the Question of Intellectuals," addressed to a special conference of the party on 14 January 1956, he called for the party to make a better use of China's underemployed intellectuals, to give them more scope and initiative, to provide them better working conditions, and to maximize their support for the task of socialist construction.[70]

Another source of pressure was a group of top party-government officials in charge of the economic administration, especially Ch'en Yun.[71] The criticism and attempts to check excesses created in the process of socialist transformation of the economy generated what Mao later called a "miniature typhoon." Even Mao himself probably unintentionally encouraged the political shift to the right. This had something to do with his "Ten Great Relationships" speech on 25 April and another speech to the Supreme State Conference on 2 May in which he signaled his support of liberalization toward intellectuals and advanced the celebrated slogan "Let a hundred flowers blossom and a hundred schools of thought contend."[72]

Taken at their face value, these two speeches by Mao showed that he was quite capable of flexibility and pragmatism and was willing to shift his stand to abide by the consensus of leadership when he confronted political difficulties. Even if he himself was merely engaged in a political maneuver and did not really subscribe to a set of policies advocated by other top leaders, his pronouncements tended to strengthen the hands of those leaders who wanted to slow down the hectic economic policies Mao initiated since the previous summer and make legitimate the more pragmatic themes they were to sound starting in May 1956.

Thus emboldened, they began to openly criticize the rashness with which the APC's were organized and the draft program was implemented. They spoke at some length their sympathy for "the peasants' burden" and began to push for more consumer goods, relaxation of control, and other measures to alleviate tensions and deficiencies generated by the socialist transformation of agriculture, industry, and commerce in Chinese society. It is true that these themes had already appeared in Mao's speech on 25 April, but other party leaders seemed willing to go farther than Mao, and other party officials apparently capitalized on the fact that Mao had endorsed those ideas to justify their advocacy and to expand the limits of economic liberalization, perhaps much to Mao's chagrin.

In early May 1956, a speech addressed to the National Conference of Model Workers by Teng Tzu-hui, which was mentioned earlier, deplored the problems caused by the rapid forced collectivization. Speaking to the same conference, Chia T'o-fu, Director of the State Council Fourth Staff Office (which was then in charge of light industry) and Minister of Light Industry, came out strongly for developing light and particularly consumer goods industries.[73] Since in both the conception and execution of the First Five-Year Plan (1953– 57) heavy industry was to receive and had thus far actually received priority while light industry had played only a limited secondary role, Chia's new theme was not insignificant. He reiterated his arguments in June when he spoke to the NPC, and he was backed up by an editorial of the *People's Daily*.[74]

New themes also emerged from the economic reports of Li Fu-ch'un, Ch'en Yun, Li Hsien-nien, and Teng Tzu-hui delivered to the third session of the First NPC in June 1956. These included placing more emphasis on light industry, improving the living conditions of the people, and the necessity for giving more incentives to the workers, peasants, and even the bourgeois capitalists.[75] Ch'en Yun stressed the importance of securing the bourgeois capitalists' cooperation and the desirability of using their production techniques and management expertise. Teng Tzu-hui regarded the proper distribution of APC income as the most pressing problem and urged "less deduction, more distribution" as the basis for solving the relationship between the state, the APC, and the members. Teng also candidly admitted that "not a few mistakes and defects" had occurred in the course of the collectivization movement. He severely reprimanded the local cadres' waste of manpower and resources, the overburdening of the peasants, unrealistic target-setting, use of coercion, mismanagement of APC's, and so on. Nevertheless, he maintained that the chief responsibility lay with "the departments concerned at upper levels," which "were hasty and bit off more than they could chew." The most severe and thorough criticisms were made by Chou En-lai in the Eighth Party Congress, which will be discussed later.

A shift toward "soft" policies was also manifested through concrete actions. It was announced that a fixed rate of interest, 5 percent, was to be paid for seven years to the capitalists whose enterprises were placed under joint state operation.[76] The NPC's Standing Committee also passed a resolution to increase the portion of land to be retained by APC members.[77] The controls exercised over former landlord elements and the rich peasants also were relaxed, and some cadres were criticized for discriminating against the former landlord and rich peasant families.[78] The Model Regulation for an advanced Agricultural Producers' Cooperative, adopted on 30 June 1956, permitted former landlords and rich peasants to join as regular members.[79]

The Eighth National Congress of the CCP, September 1956

The Eighth Party Congress was an event of great significance for the CCP. It was the first national party convention since the party successfully seized power in mainland China in 1949; in fact, it was the first such meeting since the Seventh Party Congress was convened in the spring of 1945, several months before the defeat of the Japanese in World War II. Compared with the Second Session of the Eighth Party Congress in 1958, the 1956 meeting was characterized by realism and moderation. In its proceedings, delegates were informed not only of the achievements but also of the difficulties of the regime's programs. The conservatives, who had apparently achieved ascendancy since the spring, seemed to prevail in the Congress, and many statements articulating their views were fully aired. For instance, Ch'en Yun defended the placement of many "bourgeois" capitalists in managerial positions of the joint enterprises and justified this step by stressing the need to use their know-how and managerial expertise; that is, former owners would still be useful after the change to public ownership. Ch'en also urged that the sphere of free economy be expanded and more subsidiary occupations be managed by individual APC members, so that peasants' incentive would be increased and production would rise.[80] Teng Tzu-hui's prescriptions paralleled those of Ch'en Yun, and he advocated more distribution and less accumulation in the income of the APC's.

Two other top economic officials, Li Hsien-nien and Po I-po, supported a policy of increasing material incentives by raising the procurement prices of farm products and improving people's living conditions. Po I-po said: "Experience shows that when the relationship between accumulation and consumption was properly dealt with, a harmony was evident in the economic life of the state and a favorable effect resulted in the development of industry and other branches of the economy and in the improvement of people's living conditions." He added, "Whenever we tried to undertake more industrial construction or other construction and made too big state budgets and planned too big capital investment, haste always made waste, and man-made strain was caused to the national economy."

Premier Chou En-lai's "Report on the Proposal for the Second Five-year Plan," which was adopted by the Party Congress, affirmed a moderate line for the national economy. In this report, Chou made some very factual remarks in which he frankly admitted problems and difficulties upsetting China's national economy. He candidly stated:

> Many of the shortcomings and mistakes in our work are inseparable from subjectivism and bureaucracy among the leadership. Some leading comrades sit on high, do not approach the masses, are ignorant of the actual conditions, and are subjective in dealing with questions and making arrangements for work. ... Moreover, bureaucracy at high levels fosters commandism at lower levels.

Referring critically to the draft agricultural program, Chou said that there was a tendency in some departments and localities to do everything at once and do it everywhere, taking no account of actual conditions, and recklessly running ahead. This kind of mistake, he added, affected the state's priority construction projects and gave rise to difficulties in finance and waste of manpower and material resources. He pointedly stated, "such a tendency recurred in the beginning of 1956, following the publication of the draft *National Program for Agricultural Development*."

Although Premier Chou and others openly criticized mistakes only in the implementation of the draft program, their criticisms were actually directed against the program itself. Criticisms of the faulty implementation would eventually have discredited the program politically. Such implications were not lost on the participants in the Party Congress, particularly Mao himself. The reason other top party leaders refrained from directly criticizing the program was that such a criticism would amount to a personal attack on Mao, the initiator of the program and, by extension, the myth of the infallability of the party leadership—this they would want to avoid. Even the criticism of the administrative errors was not made lightly; it was only in the context of Mao's political eclipse that other party leaders reasserted themselves to air their views.[81]

Under these circumstances, it is not surprising that the draft National Program for Agricultural Development was not adopted. Instead, a moderate document issued jointly by the CC and the State Council on 12 September 1956, on the eve of the Party Congress,[82] may have been intended as a substitute. The draft program, a major party policy document only a few months earlier, was conspicuous by its absence at the deliberations and the proceedings of the Party Congress. Teng Tzu-hui, the major spokesman for the regime's rural policy, did not refer to it in his speech on agricultural production. Liu Shao-ch'i, in his Political Report, mentioned it only once in passing.[83] Chou En-lai in his report (cited above) referred to the draft program in a critical manner. The proposals for the Second Five-Year Plan adopted by the Party Congress failed to mention the draft program, which two years later was hailed by Liu Shao-ch'i in his Political Report to the second session of the Eighth Party Congress as having set "great goals for rural work" and having given a "correct orientation for the development of the entire work of socialist construction." Thus eight months after its emergence in January 1956, the draft program had fallen into oblivion.

Mao's political eclipse was furthered by a new arrangement in the leadership hierarchy in September 1956. In line with the new political trend placing great emphasis on collective leadership, the First CC Plenum, which met on 28 September, in addition to electing Mao Tse-tung chairman of the Party CC and Politburo also elevated four other top party leaders, Liu Shao-ch'i, Chou En-lai, Chu Teh, and Ch'en Yun to vice-chairmen of these two powerful bodies. These five men and the party's General-Secretary Teng Hsiao-p'ing formed the Standing Committee of the Politburo, the leadership nucleus of the CCP. The four vice-chairmen were already top party leaders, but their elevation to vice-chairmanship, newly created posts in 1956, served to indicate their rising political influence vis-à-vis the chairman. In the summer of 1966, when Mao had his final say, these four vice-chairmen were dropped and Lin Piao was selected by Mao as the sole vice-chairman. The CCP leadership has, over time, displayed the apparently contradictory dual characteristics of one-man rule and collective leadership. The manifestation of one characteristic over the other is an obvious function of changes in the balance of power of the top leaders.

In light of political and social and economic developments since the summer of 1955, Liu Shao-ch'i's characterization of the rightist and leftist deviations from the party's general line was fairly informative and significant. Liu had the following to say in the Political Report which he presented to the Eighth Party Congress:

> In the last few years the tendency of deviating from the Party's general line to the right has manifested itself mainly in being satisfied merely with what has been achieved in the bourgeois-democratic revolution, in wanting to call a halt to the revolution, in not admitting the need for our revolution to pass on into socialism, in being unwilling to adopt a suitable policy to restrict capitalism in both town and countryside, in not believing that the Party could lead the peasantry along the road to socialism, and in not believing that the Party could lead the people of the whole country to build socialism in China. . . .
>
> The tendency of deviating from the Party's general line to the "left" has manifested itself mainly in demanding that socialism be achieved overnight, in demanding that some method of expropriation be used in our country to eliminate the national bourgeoisie as a class, or some method be used to squeeze out and bankrupt capitalist industry, and commerce, in not admitting that we should adopt measures for advancing, step by step, to socialism, and in not believing that we could attain the goal of socialist revolution by peaceful means. Our Party resolutely repudiated as well as criticized those two deviations.

Liu's reconstruction of leftist and rightist deviations was more than an exercise in rhetoric; it rather accurately pictured the debate between two different strategies of economic development or "schools of thought" and hinted at disputes among CCP leaders over the strategy and tactics of socialist construction in China.

Whereas it is fairly easy to discern these two distinct approaches to socialist construction, the identification of individual CCP leaders with the two points of view is difficult. At the risk of oversimplification, those who had the actual responsibility for running the national economy—Premier Chou En-lai, Vice-Premiers Ch'en Yun, Teng Tzu-hui, Li Fu-Ch'un, Po I-po, and Li Hsien-nien—may be considered members of the conservative group, while Mao and those who specialized in the party administration—Liu Shao-ch'i, Teng Hsiao-p'ing, and P'eng Chen—constitute the radical group. It should be emphatically stated that with the exceptions of Mao, who has consistently pushed for revolutionary change, and Teng Tzu-hui, who persisted in his own conservative viewpoints, most other leaders had often changed their positions under different circumstances and were willing to accept the policy decided by the party at any moment. Chou En-lai has been a reputed "tide-watcher," well-known for his ability to sense and move with the political tide. Leaders like Liu Shao-ch'i, Teng Hsiao-p'ing, and P'eng Chen were thought to be "hardliners" in the 1950s because they tended to take a radical stance, but they shifted and adopted the conservative approach in the 1960s in the wake of the disastrous Great Leap. On occasions even Mao was flexible and acquiesced in measures repugnant to his known preference, although after 1958 he became closely tied to the Great Leap programs and came to personify the radical approach.

The dispute between the two approaches was not the conflict of leadership factions or cliques, and those leaders who pursued the same approach did not appear to belong to the same faction. Within the CCP leadership, factions based on personal ties or historical associations (e.g., the field army ties) have in fact existed,[84] and as the leadership unity was shattered and the top leaders were locked in bitter struggle in the 1960s, the old ties were reactivated and factional cleavages became a salient element in Chinese politics. In the 1950s, however, factional conflict had little effect on the dispute over strategy of economic development, perhaps with the exception of the P'eng Teh-huai affair in 1959 (see Chapter 4 for details). The conflict over economic policies in the 1950s was conflict between "opinion groups."[85] The opinion groups consisted of leaders who shared the same view on a given issue, but the "membership" was never constant as individuals shifted their stance. Moreover, there were different opinion groups on different issues, and those who held the same view on one issue did not necessarily stand together on other issues.

Major changes in policy in the 1950s and early 1960s can be attributed to shifting coalitions of opinion groups at the center. Furthermore, when the views of the "radical" group prevailed, there would be a "big push" that unfolded radical measures. But when the views of the "conservative" group prevailed, there followed a period of retreat and consolidation which employed a different power mix in policy implementation.

Thus the shifts in policy followed an oscillating or alternating pattern, a kind of a dialectical pattern, between conservative and radical policies. Peking's pendulum had swung to the left during the fall of 1955 and throughout the winter of 1955–56 when collectivization was stepped-up and the draft twelve-year agricultural program was launched. The momentum of this leftward swing was slowed down in the spring of 1956 as the political forces in the party regrouped; thereafter, the pendulum began to swing to the right as the views of the "conservative group" prevailed. As a result, Mao's grandiose draft program failed to secure final approval while the regime devoted its efforts to making adjustments and solving "contradictions."

The 12 September 1956 party-state joint directive on the APC's, mentioned earlier, was a sober document embodying the same comparatively sober and factual line of thought found in the speeches of Chou En-lai and other top economic officials during the Party Congress. It frankly discussed a number of problems afflicting collectivization and the rural economy, particularly the importance of individual "sideline" production, realistic target-setting and plans, avoidance of "commandist" behavior toward peasants, more distribution of income for payment and less for accumulation, the institution of a free market, and the appropriate size (not too large) for APC's. Despite these prescriptions (some of them significant concessions to the peasants), they did not seem to measure up to the difficulties in the rural economy and therefore could do no more than palliate the deficiencies of the collectivization system.

It is obvious, if only from Mao's own admission, that criticism of and opposition to the collectivization within the party continued throughout the winter of 1956–57, constituting in Mao's phrase a "miniature typhoon."[86] The harvests in 1956 were disappointing, and food shortages were reported in many areas. In Kwangsi, for instance, many peasants died of starvation; the situation was serious enough that the province's first party secretary, Ch'en Mang-yuan (a candidate member of the CC), two provincial party secretaries, and several other lesser officials were dismissed.[87] Peasant discontent was widespread; as noted earlier, they slaughtered draft animals and damaged public properties, and in some places large-scale withdrawals from APC's forced their dissolution.[88]

Mao's speech on "The Correct Handling of Contradictions Among the People" in February 1957 suggested a new approach to China's economic problems primarily through political action and ideological education. He sought solutions to "contradictions" in Chinese society through attitudinal changes of the intellectuals and their active support in socialist construction, and the education of the party cadres in a new working style. The efforts to rectify party cadres and to win over intellectuals in the spring of 1957, however, unexpectedly resulted in the intellectuals' direct challenge to the foundations of the Communist rule and bitter attacks against the abuses of Communist officialdom.[89] In early June the rectification campaign of the party was transformed into an "anti-rightist" movement; thereby the party launched a counterattack against "bourgeois rightists." Nevertheless, the image of the party leadership had already been severely tarnished.

In the meantime the events of the summer of 1957 had done nothing to improve the economic and particularly the agricultural situation. The palliative measures prescribed in the joint directive of September 1956 were insufficient and hence ineffective. It is true that the weather of 1956 and 1957 was unfavorable. Typhoon Wanda, said to be the worst in fifty years, swept through many provinces in early August 1956, doing heavy damage to crops and properties, and both flood and drought were reported in large areas of China in 1957. Many poor peasants and rural cadres, however, candidly blamed the system of collectivization, the unified grain purchase policy, and other "man-made" factors for the failure in harvests. They said that collectivization had been pushed too far and too fast, that the state's grain policy had squeezed too much out of the peasantry, that the APC's were inferior to *tan kan* (private farming), and that the peasants' living conditions were worse after they joined the APC's.[90]

The Chinese campaign showed organizational skill and control techniques far superior to those of Stalin's collectivization drive in the 1920s and the 1930s, resulting in a smoother transition and little bloodshed.[91] The peasants' resistance was largely ineffective and rarely organized. It does not follow, however, that China's collectivization was a resounding success. Despite their brilliant achievement in effecting structural change in the countryside and in bringing the peasants under tight control, the Chinese Communists did not bring about the desired increase in farm output—a very important, if not the most important, goal of collectivization. There were many reasons for this failure, some technical and others political.

The view of the "pragmatic coalition" in the party, as articulated by Teng Tzu-hui, was that the policies of collectivization and of unified grain purchase had generated many "contradictions," conflicts between APC members and the cadres, between APC's and the state, between the poor peasants and the middle peasants, and so on.[92] Teng argued that to increase agricultural production, these "contradictions" must first be "correctly" handled. His prescription was, in essence, that the party must make more concessions to the peasants and give them more material incentives to promote production.

This line of argument, which may have received the support of many of the cadres specializing in agricultural affairs, seemed to have prevailed in the party up to the eve of the Third CC Plenum. A National Rural Work Conference, held in early September 1957, reviewed the party's policy toward APC's and agricultural production.[93] Presumably, conclusions reached there were then approved by a Politburo meeting, and three directives were issued in the name of the CC on 14 September 1957, one week before the Third Plenum was convened. The directive, entitled "On the Improvement of Production Administration in APC's," instructed cadres to dissolve large APC's and restrict the size of each to one hundred households (equivalent to a natural village) and each production team to twenty households, a move apparently contrary to the wish of Mao Tse-tung, who had advocated a larger organization.[94] The directive unequivocally stated:

> As a result of practice in the past years, it has been proven that big co-operatives and big teams are generally not suited to the present conditions of production. . . . Therefore, except for a few big co-operatives which are really run with success, all the existing co-operative farms which are too big . . . should be appropriately reduced in size. . . . Once the size of the co-operative farm has been fixed, an announcement should be made that there will be no change for the next ten years.

This meant that the size of the APC's was to be further reduced, for the joint directive of September 1956 had stipulated that the size of APC's should be about 100, 200, and 300 households in mountainous, hilly, and plains regions, respectively.

The same directive, in a sense, also "decollectivized" the system of collective management to a degree by transferring the authority of production from APC's down to both production teams and subsidiary occupation groups, which in turn were to delegate authority to individual households. In other words, the collective element in the management of the APC's was to be restricted: production teams and subsidiary occupation groups were to decide their own production plans within the framework of a "unified management," the "three-guarantee" system was to be widely introduced, and an individual (household) production responsibility system was to be stressed to increase incentives.[95] Unnecessary collective labor was to be avoided to conserve manpower. Another directive stipulated that concessions were to be made to the middle and rich peasants in policies concerning the means of production and distribution of collective income, and APC members were to be permitted to raise and keep a certain number of livestock.

If these measures had been fully implemented, the cooperative system as it then existed in China's countryside would have been drastically modified; collectivist elements would have been substantially reduced and the active role of individual peasant households increased.[96] Before these profound changes could take full effect, however, the "radical" segments of the party leadership again dominated the decision-making councils and mapped out a different developmental strategy that charted a new course of action. Thus the cycle was repeated: an intensive, highly organized nation-wide campaign, followed by a period of retreat and consolidation, which in turn was replaced by another intensive campaign.

The Revival of the Program

The Regroupment of Political Forces

The "hundred flowers" episode and the subsequent "anti-rightest" campaign in the summer of 1957 had enormous political and economic repercussions. Shocked by the negative responses of the "bourgeois" intellectuals, Mao and other leaders began to reassess various policy assumptions of the past. As a result, they formulated a different developmental strategy in which the role of intellectuals (such as scientists, engineers, technicians, managerial and planning staff), who were now politically tainted, was to be deemphasized in the course of socialist construction. With regard to dissensions on economic policies, events during the summer of 1957 put the supporters of a radical line, including Mao himself, in a very strong position. On the other hand, the same events made it difficult for anyone in the party to criticize the radical policy in any way without incurring the charge of rightism; the position of the "conservatives" was correspondingly weakened.

Initially, Mao's rectification and the "hundred flowers" relaxation were supported by the liberal elements in the party, who argued for the relaxation of control, and particularly by officials responsible for economic affairs, who were then pushing for a more moderate line, but it was obviously opposed by some other political groups. For instance, some officials in the cultural propaganda apparatus of the army openly voiced their dissent.[97] Party officials in various fields, either unable to genuinely grasp Mao's dialectic and theory of "contradictions" or determined to protect their own prerogatives, criticized the rectification campaign as a rightist deviation.[98] Mao's scheme of rectification, which used an extra-party force, the intellectuals and "democratic" parties, to criticize the party cadres, was understandably unwelcome by the party's organization men. There is some indirect evidence that top "organization men" Liu Shao-ch'i and P'eng Chen were against Mao's rectification policy.[99]

The shocking events of the late spring and early summer during the "hundred flowers" period finally led to a political realignment. Mao, who apparently had initially overruled the opposition of the "organization men" to launch the rectification campaign, now apparently came to a quick change of mind and joined hands with them to pursue the "anti-rightist" campaign.[100] Apparently the balance of power among the party leaders changed and soon thereafter, in the fall of 1957, there was a shift of the regime's economic policy.

Clashes Between "Radicals" and "Conservatives" at the Third Plenum

On 10 October 1957 the *People's Daily* published a brief communique announcing that the Third CC Plenum had been held between 20 September and 9 October 1957. According to the communique, the Plenum was an enlarged meeting, in which the secretaries of the provincial and autonomous regions and special district party committees participated. Three Politburo reports were delivered, by Teng Hsiao-p'ing on the rectification campaign, by Chou En-lai on wages and welfare, and by Ch'en Yun on changes in the system of economic administration and the problem of raising agricultural output. The Plenum "basically" passed the 1956–1967 National Program for Agricultural Development (revised draft), regulations for improving the system of industrial management (draft), regulations for improving the system of commercial management (draft), regulations for improving the system of financial management and of division of authority over financial management between center and regions (draft), and regulations on the question of employee wages and welfare (draft).

Dissension on policy among the party leaders was suggested by the unusual length of the proceedings and the party's subsequent failure to make public the two important Politburo reports presented by Ch'en Yun and Chou En-lai. Generally a CC Plenum is preceded by a Politburo meeting, which is held to prepare for it, and the reports of the Politburo, such as the three that were presented to the Third CC Plenum, are first approved by the Politburo and then by the CC. If this practice was observed in the September 1957 meeting, why was Teng's report published while the other two were not?

It is probable that Mao did not attend the Politburo meeting which presumably approved the three Politburo reports.[101] *Possibly he disagreed with some of the decisions made in that Politburo meeting.* As argued earlier, the supporters of a "pragmatic" economic policy had prevailed since the second half of 1956 and their influence apparently resulted in the three CC directives which were issued on the eve of the Third CC Plenum, probably upon the conclusion of the Politburo meeting. The fact that Ch'en Yun, an outspoken advocate of the "pragmatic" line, delivered the Politburo report on the economy indicated that the same approach underlying these three directives was adopted initially and that the "pragmatic coalition" still had an upper hand in the early part of the meeting.[102]

But suddenly, at the end of the CC Plenum, the draft twelve-year National Program for Agricultural Development, symbolic of a radical mobilization approach in agriculture and the economy as a whole, was unexpectedly resurrected. It was unusual that the revised draft program was introduced by Teng Hsiao-p'ing's report, which dealt primarily with the rectification campaign.[103] Furthermore, a speech (not report) on agricultural production made by Teng Tzu-hui to the Plenum, a portion of which was later made public,[104] reiterated the main points contained in the three aforementioned CC directives and failed to endorse the revised draft program, which was surprising in view of the fact that it became one of the major items on the agenda of the Plenum.

All of the evidence suggests that the draft program was reintroduced to the Plenum late in the meeting,[105] probably as a result of Mao's initiative. Mao seems to have suddenly turned the tables, as he had in 1955 on the issue of collectivization, when he was assured of new support, and challenged the opponents among his colleagues by presenting his own policy. Another parallel with the 1955 dispute over collectivization is indicated by the fact that before the Third Plenum Mao also traveled extensively in the provinces, where he may have picked up support from the provincial secretaries, many of whom had been brought into the CC since the 1956 Eighth Party Congress.[106]

The proceedings of the Third CC Plenum were said to have been punctuated with "enthusiastic discussions." The unusual length of the meeting indicated that the CC engaged in hot and serious arguments. Exactly what procedures were subsequently used to resolve policy differences among the party leaders can only be a matter of conjecture. On the basis of available evidence, formal votes seem to be a rarity in such meetings.

It has been postulated that a last minute switch from "conservative" to "radical" policies at the Third Plenum may have been triggered by the Soviet launching of Sputnik on 4 October 1957.[107] This scientific achievement might have convinced Mao—judging from his later remark in Moscow that "the East wind is prevailing over the West wind"—that the balance of forces in the world had shifted and now favored the socialist camp. Mao, Schurmann suggests, may have invoked the changed international situation to argue against the "conservative" policies and to justify pushing the revised draft program through the Plenum.

In any case, Mao's victory in the Third Plenum was not total, inasmuch as the revised draft program was only "basically" passed, implying reservations by some of the party leaders. It was stated that further revisions, based on suggestions to be solicited from the peasants, would be made; the draft would then be submitted to the party's National Congress for approval and finally be enacted as formal legislation by the state organs.[108]

Significant revisions were later made in the original draft program, presumably to placate the "conservatives." For instance, whereas the 1956 draft called for the APC's solving their need for fertilizer by their own efforts, it was now promised that the government would invest more in manufacturing chemical fertilizer (5 to 7 million tons and 15 million tons were set as the production targets to be achieved in 1962 and 1967, respectively). Several targets and requirements set in the 1957 draft were more modest than those of the 1956 draft: cotton yield per *mou* was reduced from 60 to 40 catties for some areas, the expansion of rice acreage was cut from 310 to 250 million *mou*, plans for the two-wheeled double-share plows were dropped, and the number of annual workdays required of women was reduced from 120 to 80. Another important addition in the 1957 version was a subparagraph in Article 29 recommending that "Except in a few nationality areas, birth control and planned parenthood should be publicized and encouraged in order to avoid too heavy a burden on living expenses and in order to give the children a better education and good opportunities for employment."[109]

Despite these changes, the revised draft program was still a very ambitious and unrealistic program. Its revival represented a radical departure from the more moderate economic line which the regime had pursued since the second half of 1956.

On 13 October 1957 Mao convened the Supreme State Conference to discuss the revised draft program. The conference was attended by some sixty people, including "democratic" personages as well as party leaders (as stated earlier, the meeting in January 1956, when the draft program was first made public, was attended by more than three hundred people and enjoyed great publicity). On 14 October the revised draft was submitted to a joint session of the Standing Committee of the NPC and the Standing Committee of the CPPCC for discussion; this joint session also "basically" approved the draft program. These deliberations by the Supreme State Conference and the other two institutions had not been called for, as far as is known on the basis of the public record, in the Third Plenum communique. In all probability Mao still felt it was important to use available instruments to enlist support for his program. T'an Chen-lin, a member of the CC Secretariat, made a report on the revised draft to the joint session of the NPC and the CPPCC Standing Committees. This was T'an's "debut," so to speak, as a spokesman for "radical" agricultural policy; later he would appear with increasing frequency throughout China to propagate the "radical" line on agriculture.

Honan as a Microcosm of National Politics

The provincial politics of Honan from 1955 to 1957, like national politics in the same period, went through a full cycle: big push (usually in the form of an intense, highly organized campaign), relaxation of control (adjustments and consolidation), and then another push. The province of Honan, despite its peculiarities, presented in a sense a microcosm of the leadership disputes over the strategy of socialist construction as well as the turmoil and problems which had characterized the entire country in the collectivization drive of 1955–57. An intensive study of provincial political processes in Honan may shed light on the interactions between the national capital and provincial capitals and further our understanding of China's overall political processes.

Honan, like most other provinces, responded to Chairman Mao's call in July 1955 for accelerating collectivization, creating a "socialist" upsurge in its countryside in the winter of 1955–56. Soon after the draft twelve-year agricultural program was announced by Peking at the end of January 1956, Honan also adopted a twelve-year program which provided an added impetus to the collectivization drive. In 1956 there were 26,221 APC's in the province, each having an average membership of 358 households; among them were 808 large APC's, each of which embraced over 1000 households.[110] The cadres of Honan, spurred on by the desire to meet the targets set by the party leaders, evidently had acted rashly in organizing the new APC's, and in the process they had met strong resistance from the peasants. There was large-scale slaughter of draft animals in the countryside aimed at avoiding their surrender to the management of the APC's.[111] The summer weather of 1956 was unfavorable in Honan as in many other areas of China, and there was a severe food shortage in Honan.[112] The peasants who had been induced to join the APC's by promises of increased income were discontented when benefits did not materialize.

During the winter of 1956 and the spring of 1957, widespread dissatisfaction in the villages and desertions from the APC's were reported in many areas of Honan; a party publication characterized this as an "anti-social adverse-current"; in Lingju Hsien, for instance, there was a large-scale dissolution of the APC's and much turmoil allegedly arising from sabotage by the landlords, rich peasants, counterrevolutionaries, and bad elements.[113] The circumstances were so serious that Honan's Provincial Party Committee deemed it necessary to file several reports to the CC in Peking.[114] In Yungcheng, Hsiayi, and Minchu'an Hsien, it was also reported that the landlords and rich peasants had allied with the prosperous middle peasants to oppose collectivization. They assaulted the cadres, distributed the draft animals, foodstuffs, and farm tools among themselves, and dissolved the APC's.

Honan's Provincial Party Committee, then led by Wu Chih-p'u, governor and second secretary of the party and a CC member, regarded the situation as a sharp class struggle between the landlords and peasants. The provincial committee launched a counterattack against "class enemies" and backed the local cadres in strong actions to "turn the anti-socialist tide and safeguard socialism."

In the spring of 1957 P'an Fu-sheng, first party secretary of Honan and a CC alternate, on sick leave in Peking since the summer of 1954, returned to his job in Honan. After the winter of 1956, the CC had decided to launch a "rectification" campaign to eliminate "commandism" among the cadres and keep the party in touch with the masses. Mao's speech "On the Question of Correctly Resolving Contradictions Among the People" in February 1957 set a new tone. In line with the new policy, P'an termed all the disturbances "contradictions among the people," not between antagonistic classes, and indicated that they should be settled accordingly.

During this period, P'an and his two close confidants in the Honan Provincial Party Committee, Yang Chueh (a secretary) and Wang T'ing-tung (deputy secretary-general) emphasized that the major contradiction in the rural areas was the grain question, expressed primarily in the relation between the leaders and the led. Apparently paraphrasing Mao's 1956 speech on "Ten Sets of Relationship," they set out ten major contradictions (problems) found in Honan: the shortage of grain and fodder; natural calamities which hampered production; water disputes between communities; shortage of draft animals; contradictions between the free market and the state unified purchase system; contradictions between promotions to higher schools and getting employment for their graduates; the relation between city and countryside and between supply and demand; the minority problem (Muslim members of the APC's demanded to be allowed to withdraw); contradictions between the Party and the non-Party people, especially the "democratic" personages and the intellectuals; contradictions between centralization and decentralization, between vertical and horizontal leadership.

P'an believed that most of these contradictions manifested themselves in the relations between the leaders and the led, and he blamed the "commandist" behavior of the officials for the difficulties. He subsequently repudiated the previous views and decisions of the Provincial Party Committee on the incidents in the APC's, attacked the leadership of Wu. Chih-p'u, and even took punitive action against some forty cadres who had committed "commandist" actions in those incidents.

P'an apparently had misgivings about agricultural collectivization, believing that it contributed to Honan's shortages of grain and animal power and decline in agricultural production. On one occasion P'an was alleged to have vilified the cooperative system in these words: "The peasants were not equal to beasts of burden in the past, but are the same as beasts of burden today. Yellow oxen are tied up in the house and human beings are harnessed in the field. Girls and women pull plows and harrows, with their wombs hanging down. Collectivization is transformed into exploitation of human strength."

P'an also criticized collectivization in Honan as being the result of "reckless advance"; he said that the APC's were oversized, private plots retained by peasants were too small, the peasants' lot was too hard, and production enthusiasm was low. As the First Secretary of the province, P'an was squeezed between pressures from below to feed the population and the orders from above to fulfill various state targets. His interests and responsibilities were to maintain order and develop production in a way that would satisfy both his superiors and his constituents. In the wake of difficulties resulting from collectivization, he sent his confidants Yang Chueh and Wang T'ing-tung to several counties to conduct investigations and study the ways by which the morale of the peasants could be raised and production could be developed.

In May 1957 P'an instructed the Rural Work Department of the Honan Provincial Party Committee to formulate measures to provide incentives to peasants. A simple document drafted by the Rural Work Department was found unsatisfactory by P'an; according to P'an's critics, it was then redrafted by Wang T'ing-tung in accord with P'an's wish and was later announced as "The Propaganda Outline for the Encouragement of the Development of Agricultural Production." In many aspects the outline diverged from the guidelines set by Peking: it permitted APC's to reduce their size and the peasants to withdraw, encouraged the reclamation of land by individuals, enlarged the size of private plots and raised the amount of grain reserved for APC members, encouraged the development of family subsidiary occupations, and opened the free markets.

The outline sharply divided the Provincial Party Committee's Standing Committee; some members put forth opposite suggestions, but P'an only made changes in wording and went ahead with efforts to implement it. Although it also met opposition from some officials on local levels, P'an, as first party secretary, held a strategic position for eliciting support and overcoming opposition. From the end of June to mid-July, for instance, P'an and his supporters in the Provincial Party Committee simply ignored and bypassed the Provincial Party Committee as decision-making body and proceeded to implement the new policy. P'an convened a conference of the secretaries of the Special District, *Hsien*, and City Party Committees and called two separate meetings of the directors of the staff office of the Hsien Party Committees. At these meetings he examined and reviewed the results of the implementation of the "propaganda outline" in each locality.

These conferences appeared to be effective mechanisms through which party officials could follow up and supervise the execution of policy on the local level. For instance, Lingju Hsien's party secretary, who allowed only 47 out of 743 households that applied to leave the APC's, was reprimanded and instructed to take a more liberal attitude. The Hsinhsiang Hsien Party Committee, which was lukewarm toward the new policy and had deliberately omitted in the "propaganda outline" an article permitting the peasants' withdrawal from the APC's, was ordered to correct the omission.

P'an also challenged the theory that large cooperatives were superior to the smaller ones: "Big cooperatives are nothing better. In a big cooperative there are more contradictions among the people." He cited the example of Liuling Cooperative in which members had to walk some 10 *li* and queue up before they could talk with the director.

P'an and his supporters criticized the provincial committee for its past policy of setting up big APC's and insisted on reducing the size of APC's as far as possible. It was revealed later that the number of APC's in Honan doubled in a few months—increasing from 26,221 to 54,000 from the spring to the summer of 1957, each averaging 180 households, with the smallest containing less than 30.[115] Some hard-line local cadres voiced strong opposition to the breaking up of large APC's, so that 495 large APC's (out of 808) were retained.

P'an also took a more liberal attitude toward peasants' withdrawal from their APC's. He openly stated that peasants' withdrawal from APC's did not mean they would not follow the socialist road. Seven measures on withdrawal from APC's drafted by the Rural Work Department of the Honan Party Committee in accord with P'an's instructions were vetoed by the Standing Committee of the CCP Provincial Committee. P'an, however, did not give up his attempt; he and his supporters relied on the conferences of the directors of general offices of the *hsien* committees to push lower cadres to split up large APC's.[116]

To survive and thrive in a highly centralized political system like that in China, provincial leaders must constantly keep a watchful eye on Peking to detect any shifts in the power combinations of the top leadership or in policies,[117] and they must be flexible and adequately opportunistic to bend to the political wind. In the early summer of 1957, P'an Fu-sheng was not quick enough to detect changes in the party's line, and his insensitivity seems to have hurt him politically. The orientation of the "rectification" campaign gradually changed, and by mid-June it had become a part of the "anti-rightist" struggle. The editorial "What is This For?" (*People's Daily*, 8 June 1957) was a clear call for a halt to criticisms of the party, and during the next few days a series of *People's Daily* editorials pressed the counterattack against the "rightists," signaling a reversal of policy at the highest level.

P'an apparently did not read these signals clearly. The press in Peking was violently denouncing the rightists, but P'an was slow to act. After the "anti-rightist campaign" was finally launched in the capital of Honan, P'an reportedly still urged the party members to return the stormy assault of the rightists with criticism as gentle as "a breeze or mild rain," and he restrained the party members from using mass meetings or violent methods in struggling against the rightists.[118] When the Jungyang Hsien Party Committee initiated its own anti-rightist campaign and issued instructions to the cadres in the *hsiang* and the APC's "to mobilize the masses to uncover and combat the bourgeois rightists on 9 July 1957,[119] P'an, without consulting his colleagues in the Standing Committee of the Provincial Party Committee, sent out a directive to party committees on all levels in Honan forbidding the launching of the campaign in the organs below the *hsien* level.[120] P'an continued to call contradictions between the rightists and the party "nonantagonistic," and he claimed that the struggle between the two roads in the rural areas had been fundamentally settled. He ordered the Jungyang Hsien Party Committee to revoke its instructions and reproached it for having "created artificial tension in the countryside and fostered commandist tendencies."

The evidence does not really suggest that P'an wanted to develop capitalism in Honan and that he colluded with the "rightists" outside the party to attack the CCP, which he was later accused of doing. Rather P'an appeared to be more concerned with increasing economic production and mitigating the disruptive effects of the anti-rightist movement in Honan.

The tactics used by provincial officials to cope with demands from above indicate that through their control of the flow of information, provincial officials often enjoyed a great degree of autonomy and were in a good position to evade central supervision. For instance, when P'an Fu-sheng was summoned to Tsingtao in late July 1957 to attend a conference of provincial party secretaries, he detected obvious changes of tone in Mao's speech. Being an astute politician, P'an deleted from his previously prepared report those data critical of collectivization and added other materials showing the positive aspect of the rural economy in order to please Mao. On his return from Tsingtao in early August, P'an allegedly twisted Mao's instructions to justify his policy in Honan; he revised the outlines of his report, inserted several remarks made by Mao at Tsingtao, distributed the outlines, and, in the words of his critics, "wanted to give the fifth session of the Provincial Committee an impression that the Party center had endorsed the outlines of his report."[121]

P'an's "double-dealing" tactics might have succeeded had not his chief rival in the province, Wu Chih-p'u, who had just attended a Central Grain Conference, apparently also become aware of changes in the attitude of some top central leaders, particularly Mao, which encouraged him to challenge P'an back home. Thus in the fifth enlarged session of the Honan Provincial Party Committee, P'an's policies and leadership were fiercely attacked by an anti-P'an coalition led by Wu Chih-p'u. He was accused of denying the existence of class struggle in the rural areas, opposing collectivization and the state's grain purchase policy, pursuing capitalist policies, protecting and allying himself with the rightists, conducting factional activities, and many other anti-party words and deeds. P'an was forced to revoke the propaganda outline and stop its execution; he was also compelled to review his leadership and engage in self-criticism.[122]

It is plain that political forces in Honan, as well as in the nation, had undergone a realignment, with the radical elements now holding an upper hand. Attempting to fortify his position, which had already been undermined, P'an undertook an inspection tour of the countryside and produced a report to show that he was quite aware of class struggle and that he had been tough on "capitalist" tendencies in the rural areas.[123] When Mao visited Honan soon after, P'an was able, in the words of his critics, to "show off" his survey report and "deceive the Party center and cover up his own errors."[124]

The victory of the "radical" force in the national scene, following the clashes between the "radicals" and the "conservatives" in the Third CC Plenum, had an important bearing on the fight between P'an and Wu in Honan. When the second session of the First CCP Honan Provincial Congress was held between 12 November and 2 December 1957, T'an Chen-lin, a secretary of the CC and now the spokesman for Mao's radical line, was present to speak on the "current situation at home and abroad, the rectification campaign and the leadership over the production high tide in the countryside."[125]

P'an Fu-sheng was in hot water; this can be seen from criticism leveled against him by the Provincial Congress:

> For a short while prior to the 5th Plenum of the Provincial Committee (when P'an was in command), the Provincial Committee erred in denying the struggle between the two roads in the countryside and put restraint on cadres and the masses at a time when unlawful landlords, rich peasants and well-to-do middle peasants imbued with capitalist ideas cooperated with the bourgeois rightists in cities in their attack on the socialist system. In handling the relations between the State, APC's and the peasants, the Provincial Committee also erred in speaking for the well-to-do middle peasants and took certain economic measures that suited the capitalist spontaneity.[126]

Although it was not until the Second Session of the Eighth CCP National Congress in May 1958 that P'an Fu-sheng was openly denounced by name, and not until the Ninth Enlarged Plenum of the Honan Provincial Party Committee in June 1958 that P'an was formally replaced by Wu Chih-p'u as first secretary of Honan,[127] yet there are some indications that P'an was already out of Honan's political picture by the fall of 1957.[128] Obviously, the "conservative" forces in Honan (and in the nation as well) had lost, and the radicals in Honan led by Wu Chih-p'u had won. As a result, politics in Honan was radicalized and, before long, the repercussions of events there were widely felt on the national scene—a subject we shall return to in Chapter 3.

2

Administrative Decentralization

The Background

China's Communist rulers, like their predecessors throughout Chinese history, have been plagued by the problem of a proper division of power between central and regional or provincial authorities. On the one hand, China is so large and heterogeneous that it has been proven politically unfeasible, administratively inefficient, and economically counterproductive for the central authorities to monopolize all decision-making powers and administer the entire country directly; these are strong arguments in favor of decentralization and of delegating to local authorities discretionary power. On the other hand, the Chinese leaders have been wary of the regionalism and warlordism of China's history and of powerful regional Communist leaders' tendency toward creating "independent kingdoms"; they have therefore been equally reluctant to delegate unrestricted authority to local political organizations. Over more than twenty years of Chinese Communist rule, conflicting political, economic, and ideological pressures have worked for either centralization or decentralization; consequently, the central-local power relationship has vacillated between the two poles.

From the time of Communist takeover in 1949 until 1952, the regime instituted a highly decentralized administrative system. It divided the nation into six so-called Great Administrative Areas covering North China, Northeast China (Manchuria), Northwest China, Southwest China, East China, Central-South China. Except for Manchuria and North China where "peoples' governments" were established, a Military and Administrative Committee was set up in each of these areas as the highest local organ of state power. These regional authorities, headed by top Communist leaders, had substantial power and exercised a significant degree of autonomy; they directed and supervised the work of the provincial-level units within their jurisdiction on behalf of the national government.[1]

Gradually, as the political power of the new regime was consolidated, leaders in Peking began to tighten control over the regional authorities. In November 1952 these regional bodies were abolished and in their places six less powerful Administrative Committees were established.[2] Two years later, these six Administrative Committees as well as the six CCP Regional Bureaus which functioned in the same areas were abolished. Most of the top party or government officials in the provinces were recalled to Peking during 1952–54 to work in the central party or government apparatus. (These leaders included Kao Kang, Li Fu-ch'un, Po I-po, Nieh Jung-chen, Jao Shu-shih, Ch'en Yi, Lin Piao, Teng Tzu-hui, Hsi Chung-hsun, Teng Hsiao-p'ing, Liu Po-cheng, Yeh Chien-ying and K'ang Sheng.)

Other factors also contributed to the rapid centralization of power in Peking. In the economic sphere China's First Five-Year Plan (1953–57), which essentially emulated the Stalinist model of economic development, necessitated centralized planning and execution of major economic programs. Thus the Central People's Government Council (CPGC), in announcing the abolition of the regional administrative machinery in 1954, made the following statement:

> The planned economic construction of the country demands further strengthening of the concentrated and unified leadership of central government. In order to enable the central government to lead the provinces directly, reduce the organizational levels, improve work efficiency, overcome bureaucratism . . . and to strengthen the leadership of provinces, the administrative machinery at the levels of the Great Administrative Areas shall be abolished.[3]

Another factor was political. "Independent kingdoms" allegedly created by some regional leaders, notably Kao Kang and Jao Shu-shih, also precipitated the central leadership to do away with the regional bodies and centralize power in Peking. Kao and Jao were based in Manchuria and East China, respectively, during the early 1950s, and in 1953 they headed the State Planning Commission and the Party's Organization Department, respectively. They were said to have attempted to maintain exclusive control over these areas and departments and used them as their bases to "oppose the Central Committee and usurp its authority."[4] The nature of the Kao-Jao incident was apparently a struggle between the regionally based leaders and the centrally based leaders, particularly Mao's top associates, such as Liu Shao-ch'i and Chou En-lai.[5] Kao and Jao formed an "anti-party alliance" and recruited supporters among the provincial officials. Their factional activities were detected by Mao's top associates in 1953 or even earlier, and a national conference on financial and economic work in the summer of 1953 and a national conference on organizational work in September of the same year had already tried to deal with their challenge.[6] In February 1954 the Fourth Plenum of the Seventh Central Committee, which was presided over by Liu Shao-ch'i in Mao's absence, made the decision to purge Kao and Jao; this decision was then formally approved in a resolution in the National Conference of the Party in March 1955. The Kao-Jao incident tended to strengthen those centrally based leaders who had a vested interest in curtailing local autonomy and thus fostered the tendency toward a higher degree of centralization of control in Peking.

Since then the provinces have come under the direct control and supervision of the central leadership without an intermediate regional layer of government. After the summer of 1960, six bureaus of the party's CC were reestablished to coordinate and supervise the provincial party committees, but no parallel governmental organs at the regional level were set up. The 1954 constitution prescribes a highly centralized unitary system; it vests certain powers in the provinces but the central authorities may revoke them. The provincial government is constitutionally less a self-governing political entity than the administrative arm of the central government, or in the words of the constitution, the local administrative organ of state. The same kind of tight central control also extends to a few outlying border regions, populated by a large number of non-Han minority nationalities, even though the constitution designates these areas "autonomous areas" and their governments "organs of self-government." Under such systems individual departments under the provincial governments (People's Councils) function in many respects like branches of various central ministries.[7]

The Problems of Excessive Centralization

Late in the First Five-Year Plan (1953–57) a centralized administrative system had evolved, because concentration of administrative authority was deemed necessary for unified planning and direction of many economic programs. However, the excessive growth of central bureaucratic power had generated some unanticipated problems, and the Chinese leaders began to call for a readjustment of the administrative powers and functions such as those between the central and local authorities. Liu Shao-ch'i had the following to say on this subject in his Political Report to the Eighth Party Congress in September 1956:

> ... during the past few years, some departments under the central authority have taken too many jobs and imposed too many or too rigid restrictions on local departments and ignored special circumstances and conditions in the localities. Even when they should have consulted with the local authorities, they did not do so. Some departments issued too many formalistic documents and forms, imposing too much of a burden on the local authorities. This not only did not facilitate the work of the local authorities, but dissipated the energies of the central authority and fostered the growth of bureaucracy. ... It is absolutely necessary for

the central authorities to devolve some of their administrative powers and functions to the local authorities.[8]

What had happened was that in the course of the expansion of economy and the socialization of industry and commerce, various industrial and economic ministries in the central government had come to control a large number of factories, mines, and enterprises. The concentration of authority in Peking over enterprises scattered through the country unavoidably gave rise to bureaucratic delays in making decisions and settling daily questions; for instance, permission had to be obtained from the ministries if enterprises were to acquire fixed property worth more than 200 *yuan* (approximately U.S. $100).

Since all lines of command led to Peking, the provincial authorities, limited in the allocation of resources and in management of finance and personnel, were unable to use their own initiative to examine and act upon any assessment of the potentialities of the given area from a viewpoint which transcended interindustrial boundary lines. This particularly impeded the development of provinces that were not favored by central economic planners; thus the majority of large new industrial projects built during the First Five-Year Plan were centered in Hupei (Wuhan), Inner Mongolia (Paotou), Szechuan (Chungking), Kansu (Lanchow), Shansi (Taiyuan), and Honan (Loyang).

The high degree of centralization placed enormous power in the hands of the ministries in Peking and also gave rise to a tendency toward ministerial autarky. This was partly the result of the chronic uncertainties of supplies, which led to the reluctance of any minister to rely on other ministries, so that each set up his own "ministerial" supply base. But another part of the explanation for ministerial autarky lay in the unworkability of the coordinating procedures in the face of the growing complexity of the economy. The burdens of planning and coordination had grown with the growth of the economy itself.[9]

In the words of one Western economist, the high degree of centralization of economic power had caused the system to break down.[10] As a result, there was a gradual devolution of authority to various ministerial "independent kingdoms" and in some cases even to enterprises or local government. This was indicated by Liu Shao-ch'i, who called for proper coordination of the initiatives displayed by the central economic department with those of local economic organizations:

> Some central departments did not pay enough attention to the development and overall arrangement of local authorities ... some local authorities went blindly ahead building and expanding certain industries, regardless of whether there was enough equipment in the country to spare for them, and without reference to the resources and other economic conditions in the localities concerned.[11]

A top-level Chinese economic planning official also revealed that "some areas" decided on major items of capital construction without the approval of the state or of higher levels, diverted raw material from key construction projects of the state, and in some cases even detained materials that were in transit.[12] He added that careless plan formulation, followed by repeated revisions, had resulted in priorities being neglected, as well as in waste of both capital and raw materials and in unbalanced plan fulfillment.

The Initiatives for a Change

In April 1956 Mao spoke of "contradictions" between the center and provinces in an important speech, "Ten Great Relationships," presented to an enlarged Politburo session. Referring to the excessive control of the provinces by the center, Mao stated:

> Now there are dozens of hands interfering with local administration, making things difficult for the region. Although neither the Center nor the State Council knows anything about it, the departments issue orders to the offices of the provincial and municipal governments. All of these orders are said to have initiated from the Center, thus putting great pressure on the regions. Forms and reports are like floods. This situation must change and we must find a way to deal with it.
>
> We must promote a consultative style of work with the regions. Nothing can be initiated by the Center of the Party without having consulted the regions concerned. We hope the departments of the Center will take note of this. Everything must go through the process of consultation before an order is issued, if the matter concerns the regions.[13]

Mao then set forth a principle of "combining centralization of powers with decentralization" to guide the distribution of powers between the center and the provinces, hoping to achieve both "uniformity and individuality." He claimed that the relationship between the central and local authorities was still suffering through lack of experience and suggested that the matter be further discussed, but the speech made it unmistakably clear that he favored the expansion of local power.

What had motivated Mao to champion the expansion of local power, particularly in light of the Kao-Jao affair, is intriguing. Whereas Liu Shao-ch'i and Chou En-lai may have regarded the Kao-Jao alliance as a challenge to their power, Mao did not view it as a direct threat to his own position. There is little doubt that Mao was genuinely concerned with the problems and difficulties caused by excessive centralization. The shortcomings of China's First Five-Year Plan, which was based on the Stalinist model, and the problems arising from centralization of power in the central apparatus were candidly admitted by the CCP leaders themselves and undoubtedly served as an important impetus for change.

Mao's dialectical view of the world was another important factor. Franz Schurmann reasons that because Mao believed in a dialectical process he was convinced that centralism and democracy (decentralization), discipline and freedom, or uniformity and individuality could be combined in a "unity of opposites."[14] In this dialectical view, decentralization was intended to unleash creativity and initiative from below, and democracy could be better served by giving greater scope of freedom to the regions. Here also lies a distinct Maoist strategy of economic development which explicitly rejected the Stalinist model underlying China's First Five-Year Plan and provided an alternative model in which the provinces would be given a bigger role and more initiatives in propelling China's economy forward.

Mao's dialectical view and strategy of economic development along with the shortcomings that existed in the regime's administrative system, however, may not offer sufficient explanation for the subsequent reform and the particular means of that reform. Like many other important changes in economic and political fields in China and elsewhere, the efforts to decentralize power were partly motivated by a genuine need for reform of the economy and administrative efficiency and partly devised (and opposed) by individuals or groups of political actors who had varying interests at stake.

Seen in this perspective, Mao's inclination to sponsor decentralization appears to have been motivated by political considerations: he sought to weaken the power of several top economic officials of the party identified with the central government apparatus who were opposed to his policies and to shift control of the national economy to the provincial authorities who, as evidenced by the dispute over the speed of collectivization the previous summer and fall, were generally responsive to his command. His political tactic was to balance different political groups, to play the provincial forces off against the centrally based leaders.

Mao's identification of the relationship between the central and local authorities as an important issue legitimized open discussion of the problem and obviously boosted those who favored decentralization. Speaking to the NPC in June 1965, apparently in answer to criticism, Premier Chou En-lai promised a "more concrete definition of the division of power between central and local authorities."[15] From May to August the State Council called a series of national meetings to study the question of improving the state administrative system. According to Chou, a draft resolution for improving the state administrative system was introduced into these meetings, and the State Council extensively solicited views from different circles on that plan.[16]

The pronouncements made during the proceedings of the Eighth Party Congress indicate that the CCP leaders had by that time reached a consensus that excessive centralization, which had resulted from emulating the Soviet model, must be changed to allow local authorities a larger role. This was indicated by Chou En-lai's report:

> In the Second Five-Year Plan period, an increasing number of construction projects in the country will be undertaken by the local authorities or completed through the concerted efforts of the central and local authorities. Therefore, to afford local authorities free scope for their initiative is an essential condition for the accomplishment of our socialist construction . . . we must and can, in keeping with the principles of unified leadership, level-to-level administration, devising what is appropriate in each locality and in each case, define more clearly the respective sphere of jurisdiction of the central and local authorities, and improve the state administrative system, so that local initiative can have a free scope.[17]

Chou also introduced seven general principles to be followed in the coming reform of the state administrative system, incorporated into the "Proposals for the Second Five-Year Plan" and formally adopted by the Party Congress.

Changes in the administrative system—involving an enlargement of the power of provincial authorities—were proposed in response to the pressures exerted by provincial forces. Inasmuch as the decentralization would have increased provincial control over industry, finances, and economic planning, it no doubt had substantial political appeal to the provincial leaders; therefore they themselves may have pushed for it. The growing political weight of the provincial forces—as suggested by the election of twenty-six provincial officials to the CC in the Eighth Party Congress in September 1956—would have enabled them to exert greater political pressure than before to obtain concessions from the central leadership.

The final decisions in the process of reform were slow to come. Although the CCP leaders agreed in principle that the local authorities must be granted greater powers, they appeared to disagree over the exact way by which decentralization should be instituted. In 1956 and particularly in 1957 different views found expression in various economic journals.[18] In these discussions, each official stressed the merits of his own approach, but their disagreements also had obvious political overtones.

The crux of the debate, in fact, was not merely to find a workable balance between centralized control and decentralized authority but to determine whether the central or local authorities would exercise ultimate power over many matters. Provincial officials naturally pressed for far greater decentralization and for the authority of provincial leaders to control and operate the enterprises in their regions. Economic officials who were entrenched in the state administrative apparatus favored the retention of the ministerial control system; they wanted only a modest decentralization of authority to the provinces and continued reliance on the ministries to give coherence and direction to the economy.

Clearly articulating the views of the central economic officials was an article published in September 1957 by Hsueh Mu-ch'iao, director of the State Statistical Bureau and a vice-chairman of the State Planning Commission. Proposing changes in the economic planning system, Hsueh advocated "big planning combined with small freedoms," a principle which he attributed directly to Ch'en Yun.[19] According to this principle, the central economic coordinating agencies (such as the State Planning Commission and the State Economic Commission) would impose direct control over only a small number of vital economic activities. For the other economic activities not covered by direct central control, either the central economic agencies would only set targets, thereby granting ministries, provincial authorities, and enterprises a greater degree of operational autonomy, or it would allow enterprises a free hand to set targets and formulate production plans according to market situations, and let commercial ministries exercise regulatory control according to supply and demand.

What Hsueh called for was a system of unified leadership at the top and separate management by lower-level authorities, in which various ministries, provincial authorities, and enterprises would all be allowed greater discretionary powers, which was a significant modification of the principles put forth by Chou En-lai at the Eighth Party Congress by which the provincial-level authorities alone would benefit from the proposed decentralization. For the enterprises administered by the central government, the State Council (or the economic coordinating agencies), the ministries concerned, and enterprises should each have their special responsibilities, but the local party-state authorities on the spot would have the right to "supervise" these enterprises. For the enterprises administered by the local authorities, the central government would only provide policy guidance and set broad targets, which the local authorities would be allowed to adjust.

The changes in the economic administration proposed by Hsueh called for simultaneously giving greater decision-making powers to the ministries, provincial governments, and enterprises and substantially reducing the powers of the supreme economic coordinating bodies such as the State Planning Commission and the State Economic Commission in Peking. The ministries, which would then inherit the powers of these top economic coordinating bodies, might benefit most from the new arrangement.[20] The scope of decentralization to the provincial authorities, as proposed by Hsueh's article, was limited. This may have reflected the practical consideration that not all economic agencies in the provinces were staffed with competent cadres capable of planning and directing major economic programs. For example, Yunnan,

Kweichow, and Ninghsia—all among backward parts of China—were at first excepted from taking over certain industries from central ministries on the grounds that their administration was not yet competent to do so. On the other hand, power was apparently at stake; centrally based officials were not inclined to surrender the control of the national economy to the provincial officials.

The approach outlined in Hsueh's article may well have characterized Ch'en Yun's report on the proposed changes in the system of economic administration which was presented to the Third CC Plenum in September 1957. If this was indeed the case—which I am inclined to believe—then the fact that the promulgated regulations embodied principles significantly different from those Hsueh put forth in his article suggests that Ch'en's report was not well received by the Plenum. This body, which devoted much time to examining the reform of the system of economic administration,[21] may have been divided, but a scheme of decentralization different from that proposed by Ch'en was "basically approved" (implying reservations by some CC members). Since Ch'en Yun's report was not accepted, or, at least, his proposal was not adopted completely, his report was not made public either at that time or later.

Much of what happened in the proceedings of the Third CC Plenum remains unknown. There is, however, evidence that there were serious dissensions in the Plenum and that the approval of the revised twelve-year agricultural program and the measures of decentralization, which represented a shift toward the left, came as a result of changes in the balance of power in the CC (as noted in Clashes Between "Radicals" and "Conservatives" at the Third Plenum, ch. 1). The changes were brought about by a coalition of provincial leaders (who demanded a greater decentralization of power to the provincial authorities), Mao and the "radical" group (who were pushing for a radical economic line), and party administrators[22] (who wanted a tighter party control of the government activities and saw a greater decentralization of power to the provincial authorities, in which the party maintained a dominant role, as increasing the party control of the economy and curtailing the power of the central state organs). From the fall of 1957, the party's decision-making councils tended to be dominated by forces identified with the central government apparatus, with only an occasional voice of dissent being heard.

Decentralization Measures

On 15 November 1957 the State Council, acting on the decision of the last CC Plenum, promulgated reforms in the system of industrial, commercial, and financial administration.[23] In the field of industry, the most important change was twofold: the power of provincial authorities was increased by transferring to their control many enterprises previously managed by the ministries of the central government; and the operational authority of the enterprises was increased by reducing the number of their mandatory targets.

Control of industrial enterprises in China was divided between the industrial ministries of the central government and the corresponding organs of local authorities. Before 1957–58, the industrial ministries of the central government (Ministry of Light Industry, Ministry of Textiles, various ministries of Machine Building, and so on) exercised direct control over great number of factories and mines all over the country. Until 1959 these industrial ministries in Peking were directed and coordinated by the State Council's Third, Fourth, and Sixth Staff Offices, which dealt with, respectively, heavy industry, light industry, and transport and communications; in 1959 they came under the control of the State Council's Staff Office of Industry and Communications under Vice-Premier Po I-po.[24] In the CC of the party, a Department for Industry and Communications Work directed and supervised the work of the state agencies.

By the decree of November 1957, enterprises in consumer goods industries (most of which were then controlled by the Ministry of Light Industry), nonstrategic heavy industry, and "all other factories suitable for decentralization" were to be "transferred downward" to the local (primarily provincial) authorities. Most plants of importance were to be retained under direct control of the central ministries. These included producer goods industries, large and important mining concerns, oil refineries, electricity networks, the national defense industries, and a few other key industries (e.g., paper manufacturing).

The provincial authorities now would not only assume operational responsibilities for a broad range of industries coming under their control, and receive 20 percent of these enterprises' profits, but would also achieve greater influence over centrally controlled enterprises. For the enterprises still retained under the control of central ministries, a system of "central-local dual leadership—with the central authority as the main—is to be followed, and the leadership and supervision by local authorities is to be strengthened."[25] In other words, although the vertical links of the ministries were to be paramount for these centrally controlled enterprises, the horizontal ties to and leadership by authorities on the spot were to be greater than before.

In the provinces and the lower level administrative units, the control and influence of the party committee over the government agencies was very substantial. To transfer control of an enterprise from a ministry to a local authority was to transfer immediate control of the enterprise to the party committee of that local authority. Thus the decentralization of 1957–58 had the effect of greatly increasing the economic power of provincial and other local party committees. Donnithorne and Schurmann, as well as others, have pointed out that horizontal control—control in a particular geographical area—soon became identified with control by local Party committees, particularly in the levels below the province.[26]

In the field of commerce, as in industry, considerable authority devolved from Peking to the provinces and to the local authorities. The Decree on the Reform of the Commercial Management System, promulgated in November 1957, placed a broad range of previously centrally controlled commercial agencies and enterprises under local control. For instance, processing plants belonging to commercial ministries of the central government were, with a few exceptions, to be transferred to the control of the commercial departments of local authorities. Wholesale depots, large refrigeration plants, and granaries were placed under dual central and provincial control, although the central government was to continue to be the senior partner.

The State Council now set fewer and less complex annual targets for commercial work. Profits of enterprises, like those of industries, were, by the 1957 decree, to be divided between central and provincial authorities in the ratio of 80–20; only the profits of grain sales and foreign trade were to go to the central government. Provincial authorities were given the right to set some prices in their areas of jurisdiction.

The specialized corporations which marketed various commodities were to be merged with national ministries or local departments engaged in commercial activities. These changes resulted in a great loss of power for the Ministry of Commerce, which previously had controlled many of the national and local corporations. Now the local corporations were absorbed by local departments, over which the Ministry of Commerce could exercise small influence. In fact, the ministry headed by Ch'en Yun underwent a major reorganization in 1958.[27]

Financial reforms were in line with the general decentralization of economic administration that was introduced at this period, although no major organizational changes were called for. "The major improvement," according to the 1957 directive, was "to clearly and definitely define the scope of revenue and disbursements of local finance, to appropriately enlarge local authority in finincial management, and ... to increase the flexible power of local authorities."

Before the 1957 reform, provincial-level authorities in all provinces except Peking, Shanghai, Tientsin, and Liaoning had no significant local sources of revenue and had to obtain grants from the central government to meet their "normal annual expenditure.[28] Their power in financial management was also tightly restricted, authorization from the Ministry of Finance was needed for local expenditure, and numerous items in local budgets were controlled by the central government. The reform now drastically changed the picture; the central government would no longer control each item of local revenue and expenditure, and local authorities would be assigned definite sources of revenue that they would then be expected to use to meet all their normal expenditures.

Three sources of revenue were allocated to the local authorities: fixed local revenue, the local share of profits of state and joint state-private enterprises under the central and provincial government, and the adjustable share of certain revenues.[29] Fixed local revenues were those revenues from the state and joint state-private enterprises already under local control before the 1957 decentralization, several minor taxes, and "other local revenue." The adjustable share of certain revenues to which the local authorities were entitled included commodity circulation tax, merchandise tax, industrial and commercial tax, and agriculture tax. This arrangement was designed to give the provincial authorities greater financial power and improve their financial position vis-à-vis the central authorities as it increased the scope of their initiative. In addition, provincial authorities were authorized to reallocate revenues and expenditures as needed as long as the approved figures for overall balances were not overstepped to the central government's detriment.[30]

Provincial authorities could now levy special taxes and use their own initiative in raising funds by methods they themselves chose, such as issuing bonds, although these methods were subject to approval by the higher authorities.[31] Moreover, central ministries were no longer to transmit detailed financial plans and quotas to provincial-level departments, a provision which, if strictly observed, would curtail the powers of the ministries severely.[32]

During 1958–60, local authorities at all levels appeared to have substantially enhanced their financial independence as a result of the rise in extrabudgetary funds available to them.[33] These funds were items of revenue at the disposal of local authorities (or enterprises) which were not entered in the budgets and which might be used without approval of higher authorities. They were derived mainly from a part of the profits retained by enterprises, major repair reserve funds, supplemental wage funds, and local surtaxes.[34] It was estimated that at the beginning of 1958 extrabudgetary income in general amounted to the equivalent of some 20 to 30 percent of the budgetary revenues of local authorities of all levels; for *hsien* and municipalities, the estimate was 40 to 50 percent, rising in a few cases to as much as 70 percent.[35]

Capital investment reportedly constituted the largest single item of expenditure for extrabudgetary funds. In certain departments in Taiyuan Municipality in 1959, for example, 46 percent of total expenditure from extrabudgetary funds was used for capital investment purposes.[36] Two Chinese writers pointed out that many of the local construction projects undertaken at the time of the Great Leap were financed in this way.[37] Since these funds were invested in new projects largely without prior central approval and in competition with the state's key construction projects for materials, equipment, skills, and manpower, their unsupervised use tended to render economic planning impossible and in many ways contributed substantially to the chaos of the Great Leap Forward.

Going a step further than previous decentralization measures and reflecting the much more radical atmosphere of 1958 was the reform of the planning system which was decreed by a joint party-state directive in September 1958.[38]

The major innovations of the reform were stated in an article in the State Planning Commission's journal *Planned Economy* in September 1958 as follows:[39] (1) the establishment of a new planning system—the "double-track" system—in which local equilibrium was to play a leading role and the ministries and local authorities were to cooperate; (2) decentralized control; (3) strengthened cooperation and coordination; and (4) planning by the central authorities was to cover only the "balance transfer" of major commodities and not the total production in the country.

The previous system of planning, the "single-track" system, had operated primarily on a vertical production-branch basis, with the central ministries holding the dominant position vis-à-vis the provincial authorities in the formulation of the national economic plan. Under this system, the most important "plans of balance" with respect to major commodity branches were compiled by central ministries in charge of the individual commodity branches, and provincial plans were made an adjunct of the plans of the ministries. It was, in essence, a scheme of centralized planning primarily for the benefit of the centrally controlled enterprises, and thus it tended to neglect the interests of the locally controlled enterprises.[40]

The double-track system was designed to effect the "organic integration of balancing by production branches and balancing by local authorities" with the leading role assigned to the local authorities. Thus plans for balancing the supplies and uses of major commodities were to be regionally based, and even the plans of centrally controlled enterprises were to be integrated in the regional plans. Like other measures of decentralization, the new system of planning was based on the principle of dual leadership by both the central ministries and local authorities; however, the horizontal leadership of the territorial party committees was to have priority over the vertical leadership of production branches;[41] thus in determining plans of enterprises in their areas the local authorities would occupy a position superior to the ministries.

The double-track system required the local authorities to compile and coordinate the plans of their subadministrative units (*hsien* and special district) and of the enterprises in their locale. The plan was to be constructed from the bottom up, primarily on the basis of horizontal territorial balances. After the provincial plans had been balanced by the economic cooperation regions, they were to form part of the unified national plan. These successive horizontal balances were to comprise the primary plans; the vertical production-branch plans compiled by the ministries were to take second place. The final national plan would be based on these two types of plan.

According to the directive on planning, only nine "important" items of planning were to remain under central control: the output targets of the most important industrial and agricultural commodities (e.g., steel and grain); total national capital investment, major capital projects, and new productive capacity for important commodities; the balancing and transfer of important raw materials, equipment, and consumer goods; the total state revenues and expenditures, provincial revenue remittances and subsidies, credit equilibrium, and distribution of capital grants; total wages, total number of employees, allocation of manpower at the national level; volume of railway freight and freight turnover; and so on. Other targets, including total value of industrial output, irrigated acreage, total circulation of commodities, and local transport, would no longer be fixed by the central government. They would be decided by the local authorities and the ministries between themselves in planning conferences. Even the centrally controlled targets might be adjusted by local authorities as long as state plans were fulfilled.

Subject to the overall fulfillment of state plans, the provincial authorities were now allowed considerable freedom in rearranging and adjusting output targets, using investment funds, and adjusting both the overall scale of investment and investments in individual projects. In financial matters as well as in plans for labor, commerce, local transport, and education, a similar latitude was to be allowed to the provinces.[42] If state plans were fulfilled for the main raw materials, equipment, and consumer goods, the provincial authorities might distribute these, using their own discretion; this allocation of power to provincial authorities was later extended to cover central government enterprises within their territories.[43]

Before the 1958 reform, the planning system was on a vertical production-branch basis; as noted earlier, the central ministries held the leading position, and they tended to develop an attitude of self-sufficiency. This tendency was reversed after the 1958 reform, but a tendency toward provincial autarky was generated. Under the new system the planning unit was a geographical area—usually a provincial-level unit—and every unit aspired to become as self-sufficient as possible and thus tended to ignore the needs of other units. The resulting disruption of the regular flow of supplies between areas or provinces was extremely serious in 1958–59.[44]

The 1957–58 decentralization of powers from the central government to the provinces was paralleled by a modest decentralization from the provincial level to the special districts (and municipalities) and below them to the *hsien*. The degree of this decentralization probably varied from province to province, for an editorial in *Ts'ai Cheng* (9 June 1959), the organ of the Ministry of Finance, complained that some provincial-level authorities were giving too much financial responsibility to special districts and *hsien*. As a result of decentralization of control over enterprises, *hsien*, like the provinces, divided certain revenues with higher level authorities[45] and thus derived a high portion of their revenue from profits and taxes of industrial and commercial enterprises; for example, 70 to 80 percent of the revenue of one *hsien* in Honan was reported to come from such sources. The financial position of the *hsien* authorities was further improved by the rise in extrabudgetary funds since 1958, which offered more initiatives to the *hsien* in economic activities.

For control over many agricultural functions and other economic activities the province was, of course, too large a unit, thus the leadership of the *hsien* and municipalities was increased in activities such as those relating to demonstration farms, water conservancy campaigns, and other small-scale industrial programs. During 1958–59, the leadership of the *hsien* over local industries was encouraged and given wide publicity by the regime;[46] in fact, the development of local industries was termed one major strategy that would make possible a great leap forward in industrial development.[47] At a lower level, the communes, which were established in China's rural areas after the summer of 1958, were urged to become self-sufficient units, and they exercised considerable power at the local level.

The amount of power exercised by the subprovincial authorities probably varied considerably between provinces, and there were intraprovincial variations in size and in management and distribution systems of communes. A great latitude was given to these subordinate authorities in 1958, particularly in the field of agriculture.

The decentralization that was implemented in 1958 was quite different from, and more drastic than, what was reflected in the three regulations issued in November 1957. As originally envisaged, the decentralization transferred considerable power to the provincial authorities, but the central authorities continued to retain a very high degree of control over economy. Furthermore, the decentralization measures were to be carried out "step by step," and changes in the administrative system would be tried in 1958 and then thoroughly carried through during the Second Five-Year Plan.[48] However, as the radicals' grip on the party's policy-making machinery became tighter in the winter of 1957–58, and the position of the conservatives became weaker, gradualism and caution were discarded. Hence at the Nanning and Chengtu conferences in the first quarter of 1958, both called by Mao and attended by selected Politburo members and provincial party secretaries, new decisions resulted in decentralization proceeding more quickly and covering a larger scope of activities.[49] For instance, whereas the decree of 1957 stated that for the time being only a few textile enterprises were to be decentralized, by June 1958 all factories in the textile industry were reported to have been transferred down to the local authorities. The same decree also stipulated that most plants of importance in the producer goods industries were to be retained under direct control of the central ministries, but decentralization in heavy industry in 1958 was also reported to have covered a wider range of enterprises than indicated by the original directive. Thus some 80 percent of the enterprises and institutions controlled in 1957 by the economic industries of the central government had been handed over to the provincial-level authorities by the end of June 1958, and the share of the locally controlled enterprises rose from 54 percent of the industrial value produced in 1957 to 73 percent in 1958.

The Consequences of Decentralization

The foregoing decentralization measures greatly expanded the powers of the provincial authorities. The declared purposes of the 1957–58 reform in industrial administrative systems were to "suitably enlarge" the authority of provincial-level units over the management of industry, and to "suitably enlarge" enterprise personnel's managerial authority. The reform was different from Hsueh Mu-ch'iao's proposal, which advocated, as noted before, a limited decentralization to provinces and enterprises but retained strong ministerial powers.

If these provisions had been strictly implemented, enterprise managers would have enlarged their powers, counterbalancing the new power of provincial authorities—who then might not have accumulated the immense powers that they did.[50] However, as a result of the anti-rightist movement in 1957–58, enterprise managers, most of whom were regarded as "bourgeois rightists," were subjected to heavy political attack, and the powers that they might otherwise have exercised devolved into the hands of enterprise party committees, under the control of the provincial party apparatus, in a spirit that was called "politics takes command."

Thus provincial authorities—particularly those in control of the party apparatus—not only assumed control over the enterprises assigned to them but also extended their powers, through the system of central-local dual leadership, over the enterprises in their areas which were still under central jurisdiction. They acquired greater power over allocation of resources and target-setting as well as greater control over personnel, including those working in centrally controlled enterprises. In addition, the assignment of definite sources of revenue to provincial authorities and the new measures allowing profit-sharing significantly improved the financial position of the provincial authorities. However, it is impossible to generalize on a nation-wide basis; the extent of provincial autonomy varied greatly. Which enterprises were to fall within provincial jurisdiction and the degree of provincial authority over those still under central ministries varied; provinces varied in resources and in efficiency; and some provinces benefited from the decentralization measures more than others. The relative positions of central ministries and provincial authorities depended on the ministries and provinces concerned, on the enterprises involved, the matters at issue, and the personalities involved.[51]

The chief victims of the decentralization—in terms of loss of influence—were the various industrial and commercial ministries which lost many of their powers; clearly the central government apparatus as a whole was considerably weakened in its role in economic affairs. Early in 1958, the State Council carried out a sweeping reorganization by merging and abolishing many of its ministries and directly affiliated agencies, in an intensive drive called "structural simplification." Many cadres in the State Council were transferred down to work in the provincial and lower level organs or to take part in physical labor in 1957–58. The number of ministries and other agencies was reduced from forty-one and twenty-four in 1957 to thirty-one and fifteen in 1958–59.[52]

The 1957–58 decentralization fostered tendencies toward provincial self-sufficiency and localism: as the province became the most important unit of economic planning in the national economy, each province attempted to construct an independent industrial complex within its borders.[53] This development, coupled with the unsupervised use of extrabudgetary funds in capital construction, resulted in keen competition for materials and equipment, which, in turn, led to a virtual breakdown in the allocation system and in transport. Hence the uncertainties of supply made it more necessary than ever for each province to try to become self-sufficient, disregarding the needs of other provinces.

Given these decentralization measures, some degree of localism or departmentalism was probably inevitable; this was the cost to be paid for "bringing local initiative into full play."[54] In fact, the problems of localism or departmentalism were not unanticipated, and the Chinese Communists initially seemed confident that these problems could be overcome by "strengthening the Party's leadership"[55] and by the coordination and supervision of several interprovincial agencies known as the "economic cooperation regions." In 1957–58, after the provincial authorities were given greater control over the economy, the party purged many provincial leaders who were accused of deviations of localism, ensuring that the provinces would not use their enlarged power to challenge the center.

The control of the party, unlike that of the central government, was not decentralized. Many official statements stressed the unified leadership of the party over industry and other economic activities.[56] The central party leadership, however, failed to foresee that the provincial party secretaries, who were supposed to be agents for maintaining the party's centralized control over the provinces, would become identified with the administration of their provinces; they often displayed "departmentalist" tendencies, defended the particular policies and interests of their own areas, and found themselves impelled to advance their provinces' interests in negotiation with the central government or other provinces.[57]

Another important measure—the creation of the regional coordinating bodies designed to supervise the provinces—was not effective, either. Late in 1957 the Chinese leaders had divided the country into seven large "economic cooperation regions," each embracing several provincial-level administrative areas. Each region was intended to be an administrative mechanism between center and province.[58] Each "economic cooperation region," according to a joint party-state directive issued in September 1958, was to plan and coordinate economic activities of the provinces under its jurisdiction as well as develop an integrated complex of industry, enterprises, and institutions dealing with industry, agriculture, commerce, and education within its borders.[59] By this directive, economic coordination and increased self-sufficiency were to be achieved at the regional level, not within provinces.

However, the economic cooperation regions, during the brief period of their existence, apparently did not possess and could not develop a meaningful administrative structure to handle the task originally assigned to them.[60] The scheme of economic cooperation regions seems to have been discarded by the party in early 1959, for nothing more was heard of them after this. Thus no effective regional economic coordinating agencies appear to have functioned during 1958–59, when decentralization and the Great Leap Forward attained their fullest support. Insofar as the range of political authority was a determining factor in economic decisions, economic coordination and cooperation as well as considerable economic self-sufficiency tended to develop at the provincial level.

The far-reaching decentralization carried out after the fall of 1957 seems to have contributed in many ways to the economic crisis in China from 1959 to 1962. The decentralization drive coincided with the Great Leap Forward movement. Mao believed the Chinese economy could not be operated as a single entity from Peking, and provinces must be assigned a bigger role in propelling the economy forward. In fact, decentralization was regarded as one of the strategic developments that would make the Great Leap Forward possible.

The forceful implementation of the Maoist strategy of economic development after 1957 gave the provincial authorities a greater control over the economy; they then undertook many initiatives in economic construction, including some that were irrational and ill-conceived. Since economic planning (i.e., control) had been decentralized and no effective regional coordinating bodies existed, undesirable tendencies displayed by the provincial authorities, such as the construction of independent industrial complexes within the provinces and the unsupervised use of the extrabudgetary funds in capital construction, were not checked for a long while. The cumulative effect of these developments was an excessive economic overexpansion and "overinvestment" or waste of resources.[61] As a result, the development of China's economy was retarded and the image of the CCP leadership was severely tarnished.

3

Communization in China's Countryside

The Prelude

As noted in Chapter 1, the Third CC Plenum revised the twelve-year agricultural program. Despite some modifications, the program as a whole was very ambitious and unrealistic. It now appears that the passage of this program signaled the party's switch to a radical line in economic development strategy. The new line, however, was not immediately translated into a new and full-scale economic drive. Although a large-scale irrigation and water conservancy campaign was launched soon after the Plenum, it differed little initially from the regular routine campaign conducted annually at the end of an agricultural season. The Chinese leadership itself appeared to be somewhat uncertain as to what ought to be done. Their uncertainty could be detected in the first *People's Daily* editorial on the revised draft program, which did not appear until 27 October 1957, eighteen days after the Third CC Plenum was closed. The editorial was ambiguous; it restated various targets of the draft and dutifully endorsed the revised draft program, but it failed to call for specific action.

Some cadres which seemed to have misgivings about the revised draft program resisted the idea of another "reckless advance." This was suggested by several articles written by members of provincial cadres stressing the need to overcome "conservatism" when implementing the draft program.[1] Furthermore, cadres in the APC's, *hsiang*, and even *hsien* were found, to the dismay of the central leadership, to have become too closely identified with the interests of their local communities and the peasants.[2] Unless something drastic was done, so the Chinese leadership reasoned, the party could not expect its new policy to be effectively implemented.

Uncertainty regarding Soviet aid in China's Second Five-Year Plan also may have been a factor in the delay in implementing new policies; at that time the Chinese Communists appeared to be unsure of the nature and extent of the economic assistance they would obtain from Moscow. It is now generally believed that Mao did not secure a new Soviet credit or other economic assistance when he made his second trip to Moscow in November 1957.[3] This could have removed some elements of uncertainty Chinese leaders felt concerning the new economic strategy and reinforced Mao's own belief that new measures to achieve a breakthrough in agriculture were more necessary than ever if China was to continue to step up her exports to finance her industrial imports and to repay her debts to the Soviets.

In any case Mao, soon after his return from Moscow in the second half of November, left Peking and traveled extensively in the provinces. In the course of his tours, he attended provincial party congresses in Shantung and perhaps other provinces.[4] He also held several regional meetings with provincial officials in which he may have actively promoted his new economic line and sought support.[5]

Struggle in the Provincial Party Hierarchy

The party's policy of political liberalization in the first half of 1957 (i.e., the "hundred flowers") and its sudden reversal in the summer of the same year (the "anti-rightist" movement) had produced much confusion among party members, who were already, it seems, divided over the question of the "correct" agricultural policy. The provincial party congresses held soon thereafter, in the winter of 1957–58, provided forums in which the leadership could put forth an official interpretation of recent events, defend the consistency of the party's handling of the rectification campaign and the ensuing anti-rightist campaign, and attempt to unify party members' thinking.

A report on Shanghai's Municipal Party Congress, held in December 1957, is very revealing. At this congress "some" party members were reported even to have challenged Mao's views on "contradictions among the people":

> The session accorded adequate discussion to the current domestic situation and the principal contradictions during the period of transition; it leveled criticism at the erroneous ideas cherished by some Party members. These members, since the victory in the anti-rightist struggle, had questioned the correctness of the direction of correctly handling the contradictions among the people. They described as "rightist" some of the Party's basic policies: the policy on intellectuals, the united front policy of "long-term coexistence and mutual supervision," and the policy of "letting all flowers bloom together and diverse schools of thought contend."[6]

Whereas some criticized rightist deviations in politics, others had misgivings about the leftist tendency in economic policy. In his report to the municipal party congress K'o Ch'ing-shih, the secretary of the CCP Shanghai Bureau and the first secretary of the Shanghai Municipal Party Committee, said:

> Some of our comrades have thought that our work in Shanghai has

"advanced recklessly" in all branches. . . . They have maintained a view diametrically opposed to that of the Party. They regard the revolutionary attitude of achieving "more, faster, better and more economic results" as "recklessness" and "love for pre-eminence and ostentatious achievement. . . ."

So we must criticize such rightist conservatism, because it has already caused us some damage. Since the second half of last year, 1956, there has been little mention of the policy of "more, faster, better, and more economic results," plans based on the National Agriculture Program have not been carried out with the same vigor and enthusiasm, and the revolutionary zeal for work of many people has subsided. This is really abnormal.[7]

Paraphrasing Mao's preface to the *Socialist Upsurge in China's Countryside*, K'o said that the problem now was the interference of rightist conservatism from many directions and that many things thought impossible would become possible if only adequate efforts were exerted, and he introduced a slogan: "Join the group that promotes progress, don't join the group that promotes retrogression."

K'o may well have been one of the first regional party secretaries to join "the group that promotes progress" and give enthusiastic support to Mao's policy, for a few months later he advanced to the Politburo ahead of six other Politburo alternates. K'o's report was prominently featured in the *People's Daily*, and an editorial note stated that the issues and questions raised in the report had nation-wide significance.[8]

Indeed, the problems discussed in K'o's report were not unique to Shanghai; provincial first party secretaries in some other important provinces were preoccupied with the same problems and sang the same tune in their party congresses.[9] In these congresses, those who questioned Mao's rectification policy, and particularly those who questioned the radical new economic policy, were bitterly attacked. In the winter months of 1957–58, the more moderate elements in the party were silenced, although perhaps not convinced, and the political climate in the nation became radicalized.

The Socialist Education Movement

Even before the Third Plenum, the countryside was caught up in an intensive "socialist education movement." From the Eighth Party Congress, the press emphasized the need to rectify cadres' commandism and bureaucratism, and the "correct handling of contradiction among the people" was a main theme of propaganda in the spring and summer of 1957. One of the three directives of 14 September 1957 contained instructions for APC cadres to rectify their work styles to placate the peasants and avoid commandism. The Third CC

Plenum changed this policy. Teng Hsiao-p'ing's "Report on the Rectification Campaign" did call for the rectification of the cadres, but the emphasis shifted to education for socialism, that is, intensification of the ideological indoctrination of the rural population and cadres.[10]

Under the previous policy stressing material incentives and concessions to the peasants, the influence of the well-to-do middle peasants and rich peasants had increased in the countryside, or in the jargon of the Chinese Communists, the struggle between the two roads—socialism versus capitalism—in the countryside had become very sharp. The purpose of socialist education, according to Teng Hsiao-p'ing, was to win over the peasants to the socialist road and to criticize the bourgeois ideology of the prosperous middle peasants. Socialist education was to overcome their influence, as well as expose and counterattack the alleged sabotage carried out by the landlords, rich peasants, and "bad elements."

Before the socialist education movement could be launched, the party decided that local cadres must first undergo ideological remolding. Many local cadres were found to be tainted with rightist ideology and, worse, were too closely identified with the interests of the peasants. For instance, there had been widespread criticism by cadres in Shantung and Kwangtung of the unified grain purchase policy; they said "it resulted in the peasants' shortage of food," "it squeezed too much out of the peasants," "the amount of food rationed for the peasants is too little, not enough to eat," "the government drove the people to rebellion"; many cadres allegedly adopted an attitude of "rather resisting the government than offending the peasants."[11] These cadres also complained that collectivization was proceeding too swiftly; they said "the APC was not really superior," "the advanced APC was worse than the elementary one, the elementary APC was worse than the mutual team, and the mutual aid team was no better than independent farming."

According to a survey in Tu Hsien in Shantung, of 882 cadres surveyed, 10–15 percent were opposed to the unified grain purchase policy, 10 percent considered the amount of grain rationed to the peasants to be insufficient, and 30 percent exaggerated the damage done by natural calamities, reported more people than they really had in the APC's, or concealed the amount of grain actually produced, thus permitting the APC's to deliver less to the state and distribute more among their own members.[12]

The extent to which persuasion is emphasized as a means of enforcing the party's policies has been an outstanding characteristic of China's political system. This point was clearly illustrated by a series of so-called three-level and four-level cadres' conferences held in various provinces during October 1957.[13] In these conferences of local officials, expression of dissenting views was encouraged. It was not that the Chinese Communists supported principles of unrestricted free discussion but rather that they believed it would be better to have "negative" opinions openly expressed. Once expressed they could then be discredited and refuted by means of "positive" arguments, and the people holding wrong ideas could then be educated and rectified.

Reports of these "free debates" reveal the defects, shortcomings, and "contradictions" thought to exist by those who actually implemented the party's policies. It is questionable whether the cadres who criticized the policies of collectivization and unified grain purchase were genuinely convinced by the official lines of argument used to justify these policies. Nevertheless, the Chinese Communists were willing to take the trouble to conduct "debates" and by this means to try to remold the doubting cadres' thoughts, a policy whose origin lies in the Chinese leaders' almost mystic faith in ideological remolding and attitudinal change as well as their adherence to the "mass-line" technique of leadership.

After these cadre conferences, meetings were held in the APC's to educate peasants in socialism; the "landlord" and "capitalist" elements were attacked, and the peasants were subjected to intensive indoctrination. The following report from Honan is typical of what happened in many provinces:

> In pursuance of the directive of the Party's Central Committee regarding the rectification campaign, a general debate was conducted in the cities and countryside [of Honan] as to the two roads—socialism or capitalism, repulsing the onslaught of the bourgeois rightists, landlords, rich peasants, and counter-revolutionaries, and overcoming the spontaneous tendency towards capitalism among the well-to-do middle peasants. The people were thus enabled to distinguish right from wrong on major issues, draw a clear line between the enemy and themselves, and see more clearly the necessity of pulling down the white flag of bourgeois ideas and hoisting in its stead the red flag of proletarian ideology. ....[14]

The Hsia-fang Movement

Coupled with the socialist education movement was the *hsia-fang* movement, the "transfer down" of cadres from higher to lower levels of authority. The *hsia-fang* movement proceeded gradually, beginning after the Eighth Party Congress in September 1956; the anti-rightist campaign and the decision of the Third CC Plenum gave a special impetus to the movement. For instance, at the end of October 1957 the Liaoning Provincial Party Committee convened a conference of municipal and special district party secretaries which decided, in accordance with "the spirit of the Third CC Plenum," to transfer down 200,000 cadres by April 1958. The Kirin Provincial Party Committee also held an enlarged plenary meeting which transmitted the "spirit of the Third CC Plenum" and approved plans to simplify organizational structures and to transfer down 100,000 cadres by April 1958.[15]

The motivations of *hsia-fang* were varied and complicated: the party wanted to cut down overlapping organizations in the state machinery and reduce superfluous staff to improve administrative efficiency, it wanted to reduce administrative expenses, and it wanted to keep cadres in contact with the masses. In addition, the party intended to reform the "rightist" technicians and intellectuals through labor; in the aftermath of the anti-rightist campaign, the rightists were bitterly attacked and sent down to the front line of production. Most of all, the party wanted to strengthen its leadership of the lower levels.

Since many local cadres were thought to have identified too closely with local interests, and to be unresponsive to the commands of the party, the *hsia-fang* movement in some areas may have been aimed primarily at replacing local cadres with "outsiders," thereby checking any trends toward "localization." A series of reports on *hsia-fang*, released by various provinces, stressed the aim and the achievement of strengthening the leadership in lower and basic party and governmental organizations. For instance, in Honan province 5000 cadres sent down from the *ch'u* (district) level to take over the leadership posts of *hsiang* (administrative villages), and at least three ch'u-level cadres were assigned to each *hsiang*.[16] In addition, 61 special district-level cadres were sent down from the provincial and special district party committees to the *hsien* (county) level to strengthen the party leadership at that level. Most of them became *hsien* party secretaries, and in 52 *hsien*, or 61 percent of the total, the post of *hsien* first party secretary was assumed by cadres newly transferred down. In Kwangtung, among the 180,000 *hsia-fang* cadres, 30,000 were sent down to basic units to strengthen "the leadership over agricultural production."

The developments sketched above—the anti-rightist campaign, the socialist educational campaign, the attacks on the party's moderate elements in the provincial party congresses, and the *hsia-fang* movement—silenced critics of the party's new radical policy and increasingly radicalized the atmosphere in the country. The radical atmosphere was accentuated by a so-called two-anti (anti-waste and anti-conservatism) campaign launched in the first quarter of 1958. A party directive on this campaign equated conservatism with waste; it instructed cadres to immediately do away with "obsolete" norms and systems that would hamper production and challenged cadres to "think and act" bravely to invent new ways and new models to promote a great leap in every sphere of work.

These campaigns gradually laid the political and ideological ground for the Great Leap Forward in the winter months of 1957–58. At this stage, however, measures that would be used to bring about the Great Leap had probably not yet been formulated in detail, although the concept of some sort of a big push—especially a breakthrough in agriculture—had already become evident soon after the Third CC Plenum. In many respects it was the moves toward implementation of the twelve-year agricultural program which set in motion a series of developments that led to communization and the subsequent disastrous reversals resulting from the Great Leap Forward.

The Initial Stage of Communization

The Twelve-Year Agricultural Program as a Catalyst of the Communes

The core of the twelve-year agricultural program was, as noted earlier, to step up agricultural production. The program set output targets of 400, 500, and 800 catties of grain per *mou* for three regions in the nation, and 40, 60, 80, and 100 catties of cotton per *mou* for four regions. It also set production targets for other areas of work. To accomplish these goals, the peasants were expected to improve and construct irrigation and water conservancy facilities, gather manure and accumulate fertilizer, adopt "advanced" farming methods such as deep plowing and close planting, carry out soil improvement, and undertake ten other measures designed to increase agricultural production. The key to success was total mobilization of labor for these purposes.

The APC's provided the Chinese Communists with a handy mechanism for the control and mobilization of labor. Moreover, the cadres could use this mechanism to support various construction projects through allocation of APC resources, in the form of public accumulation funds,[17] and by organizing labor to work on these projects and to launch other campaigns.

When the draft program was introduced in 1956, most of the APC's were in the process of being established, the cadres were preoccupied with organizing and consolidating the APC's, and attempts at mass mobilization could be undertaken only on a limited scale, although even this limited mobilization resulted in charges of "reckless advances" on many fronts in the first half of 1956. When the revised draft program was adopted in 1957, collectivization was complete, 97 percent of the peasant households were in the APC's, and the party had consolidated its control in the rural areas. There was therefore considerable truth in the claims made by Chinese Communist officials that the system of collectivization was one of the best ways of implementing the National Agricultural Program.[18]

In December 1957 the Communist regime called several national conferences to discuss methods of implementing the program. The aged Chu Teh, then vice-chairman of the PRC and a member of the Politburo Standing Committee of the CCP, who had rarely involved himself in agricultural matters, came to the fore and argued vigorously for the twelve-year agricultural program in these conferences. Several main ideas emerged from these meetings: the need to emphasize overall planning (to combat "departmentalism") in work, the need for the party committees at various levels to take full command and tighten control, the need to rely on local material and financial resources, and the need to mobilize the peasants on a large scale.[19]

The first measure that embodied these lines of action was the water conservancy campaign, in the winter of 1957–58. By the end of 1957 more than 60 million peasants reportedly had been mobilized to construct irrigation and flood control works. There had been a debate among the cadres as to whether small- or large-scale projects would be emphasized, and this debate carried broad economic and political implications. There were some who argued that the large-scale projects would be more economical in terms of investment, manpower, and resources, and that water conservancy work required technical knowledge; therefore, such people argued, the enthusiasm of the masses could not supplant the necessary technology.[20]

Large-scale projects, however, could be implemented only with investments from the state, and the Chinese leadership was not willing to divert to the agricultural sector resources heretofore channeled into industry. Thus small-scale projects were to be emphasized, enabling "the state to spend little money and to rely on the masses."[21] The rationale, according to T'an Chen-lin, was that small-scale projects best fitted the principle of achieving "more, faster, better, and more economical results."[22] Since they could be built in a shorter period of time with the local resources—especially the manpower—of the APC's, they were "more and faster"; since they could be expected to produce quick economic returns, from the viewpoint of production, they were "more economical, hence better." The small-scale projects did not demand much technological knowledge, therefore "politics" could take command, and the party cadres could mobilize the peasant masses to work in a water conservancy campaign of unprecedented magnitude.

The peasants were also mobilized to work in many crash programs which, like the irrigation and water and soil conservancy campaigns, were designed to bring about a great leap in agriculture. There were energetic programs for fertilizer-accumulation, expansion of double and multicrop acreage, soil improvement, deep plowing, close planting, pest control, land reclamation, the improvement and manufacturing of farm tools and machinery, and so on.

Campaigns to build and expand local industries went hand in hand with campaigns to increase agricultural production. For instance, construction projects such as dams and flood control works needed cement, pumps, equipment, water mills, and other irrigation instruments; land reclamation and other farm work required more plows, farm implements, and agricultural machinery. The local authorities, maximizing the use of labor and mobilizing all available domestic resources in the spirit of thrift and economy, built and operated tens of thousands of small factories in areas such as iron and steel (including backyard furnaces), machine shops, power generation, coal extraction, and fertilizer production as well as in the more traditional textile and food processing industries.[23]

Small and medium-sized industries were emphasized because they would "spend little money, do many things and bring about quick economic returns."[24] The rationale was based on a strategy of economic dualism, officially termed "walking on two legs" in Chinese Communist pronouncements. The bulk of the modern sector's final product would be exported or reinvested and used for its own continued expansion and growth; very little would be diverted into the agricultural sector.[25]

On the other hand, the growth of the rural sector was to rely "on the masses," that is, on local resources. Labor-intensive small-scale industries would be developed by using simple, locally manufactured equipment, local labor, and local raw materials. A typical example was the construction of more than 600 dams in Antung Hsien of Liaoning by using straw and sand to substitute for rolled steel and cement, a "feat" that was given wide publicity. The development of local industry would absorb rural surplus labor[26] and lower the cost of transporting raw material to urban industrial centers; in addition, the products of local industries could be used to satisfy rural demands for consumer goods, tools, agricultural machinery, and other requisites of farm production. The proliferation of local industries was facilitated by the decentralization of economic decision-making in many fields after 1957. The transfer of authority over a number of industrial and commercial enterprises to the provincial and *hsien* governments (where the party was in an increasingly dominant position) placed economic planning functions under greater local party control. This enabled "politics to take command" and the initiative of the masses to be given full play, while the professionals and technicians were further restricted in their activities.

Thus China had in effect adopted a new formula for economic development. During the First Five-Year Plan, China applied the Stalinist development strategy with some modifications, so that industry, especially heavy industry, was emphasized at the expense of agriculture. But since the Chinese economy depended so heavily on agriculture, the neglect of investment in the agricultural sector slowed the growth of industry. After the dispute within the party as to whether more resources should be channeled into agriculture in order to effect a more balanced growth in the economy, a strategy evolved, after much debate and improvisation, which would permit and foster the simultaneous development of agriculture and industry.

The Amalgamation of the APC's

As various crash campaigns simultaneously unfolded, many problems emerged. Labor shortages became apparent; the APC's were too small and their administrative structure inadequate to meet the situations created by the water conservancy campaign and later by the Great Leap Forward. Local cadres began to experiment with different solutions in a spirit of the new slogan: "One must dare to think and act."

Women were mobilized to take part in physical labor in the fields, mess halls, nurseries, and other institutions for collective living which began to be organized to save time and free women from household chores; new work organizations were tried as peasants were organized into specialized "squads" or "brigades" to carry out the same tasks (such as rice-planting or ground-preparing) in one field or village after another.[27] One measure that had a most important effect was the enlargement of the size and expansion of the functions of the APC's. The amalgamation of APC's, which started in March 1958, was a major step toward the subsequent communization, although the establishment of communes per se may have not been envisaged at this early date by provincial and lower officials.

The size of the APC's had been a matter of controversy within the party for years. Mao is known to have advocated a larger organization; his favorable editorial comments in an article "On the Superiority of the Large Co-ops" often were quoted by cadres to justify the enlargement of the size of APC's. In September 1957, however, as noted earlier, a CC directive instructed cadres to break up large APC's and restricted their size to 100 households.

The APC was originally conceived as an economic organization primarily engaged in agricultural production. In the course of development, however, it steadily expanded its scope of activities and, in many cases, began to compete with the government of the *hsiang* in exercising certain functions.[28]

In the summer of 1957, cadres in Fukien made an attempt to have the APC's absorb banking and commercial functions from the Credit Co-ops and the Supply and Marketing Co-ops by merging these three kinds of co-op into one single unit [*San she ho yi*].[29] The Credit Co-ops were basic units linked to the People's Bank at the *hsiang* level, and the Supply and Marketing Co-ops were the lowest unit under the All China Federation of the Supply and Marketing Co-ops. The rationale for the merger was to effect better coordination among them; with the two other institutions under the direct control of the APC's, "departmentalism" would be eradicated and harmony would prevail in all their work.

The proponents of the merger reported that many contradictions existed among these three independent units at the basic level. The Credit Co-ops often urged peasants to deposit money when the APC's were encouraging peasants to invest their money in the APC's; the Credit Co-ops, because of their special financial responsibilities, often did not respond to applications for agricultural loans when the peasants were in need. Moreover, the Supply and Marketing Co-ops maintained too rigid a standard in their purchase of local products, the merchandise they carried often did not cater to the needs of peasants, and their location and office hours were sometimes inconvenient for the peasants.

To resolve these "contradictions," the Party Committee of Ch'ing Chiang Special District in Fukien dispatched an ad hoc work group to Nanan Hsien to test the amalgamation. The results of this experiment were reported in the *People's Daily*. An editor's note accompanying the report suggests that the central authorities were not at that time particularly enthusiastic; the note termed the amalgamation a new "working method" but pointed out several problems that would arise, including changes in the command systems of each. The paper also solicited opinions from those engaged in rural work; several articles expressing conflicting views were subsequently published in the *People's Daily*. The idea of amalgamation along these lines apparently evoked little interest in Peking at the end of summer 1957, for thereafter nothing more was said about it (although, as will be noted below, the experiment continued).

However, by the spring of 1958, as a result of the massive water conservancy campaign of the previous winter and other efforts at implementing the revised draft program, the motivation for reducing the size of APC's and checking the expansion of the functions of the APC's had significantly changed. The development of numerous crash campaigns in agriculture and local industry demanded increasing supplies of manpower and resources, which most of the APC's were unable to provide. It was argued that "localism" on the part of the APC's was not conducive to overall rational planning of the water conservancy programs, that many irrigation projects constructed separately by the APC's were small and inferior in quality, and that in many cases the frequent disputes among the APC's and among *hsiang* concerning land and water adversely affected the progress of their work.

Under these circumstances, neighboring APC's, *hsiang*, and even *hsien* learned to pool resources, take concerted actions, and institute unified planning and management to build dams, reservoirs, and other construction projects. Cadres in several localities began to ask for the expansion of the APC's; for instance, at Szekutun Hsiang of Shanchen Hsien in Honan, fourteen APC's were merged into four larger APC's in March 1958, although this move was not publicized at that time.[30] Expansion of the size of the APC's was designed to solve the problems discussed above and to strengthen the party's control in rural areas by cutting across the local ties of APC cadres who allegedly had too close an identification with the interests of their own groups or communities.

In early March 1958, an *NCNA* dispatch from Fukien reported that one year of experimentation in the amalgamation of the three kinds of co-op [*San she ho yi*] in Lientang Hsiang of Nanan Hsien produced impressive results, and the Fukien Provincial Party Committee summed up the experiences and decided to popularize them throughout the province. This *NCNA* dispatch was carried by *Ta-kung Pao* (13 March 1958) but, surprisingly, not in the

People's Daily, which suggested that the central authorities still had some reservations. During the month of March, *Ta-kung Pao* continued to publicize the news of *San she ho yi* in other provinces, but the *People's Daily* was conspicuously silent.

On 2 April the *People's Daily* ended its silence on the subject of merging various co-ops and endorsed the idea by headlining the amalgamation of the APC's, the Credit Co-ops, and the Handicraft Co-ops in Shansi Province. The turning point may have come at a meeting of regional officials in Chengtu sometime in March, when Mao made a "suggestion" to provincial officials to combine small APC's into larger units.[31] No formal decision on merging the APC's was taken in this conference, but Mao's "suggestion" probably added impetus to the trend. Some provincial officials, perceiving Mao's favorable attitude, proceeded to enlarge the APC's even before formal steps were taken in this direction.[32]

In early April 1958, for instance, cadres in Fukien merged three *hsiang* into one large *hsiang* and twenty-three APC's into one very large APC; on 12 April the *People's Daily* approved such a move for the first time, in headlines on the first page. In late April more than 3000 APC's in Lu Hsien, Szechuan, were merged into some 700 large ones, with the average membership of each increasing from 60 to 250 households. Meanwhile, Honan's Hsinyang Special District Party Committee set up, on a trial basis, a large APC of 6000 to 7000 households in both Suip'ing Hsien and P'ingyu Hsien. The enlarged Weihsiang (Sputnik) APC of Suip'ing, which soon was claimed to be China's first commune, was formed out of twenty small APC's in four *hsiang* on 20 April 1958; when this was merged with seven more APC's in late June, the commune embraced a total of 9369 households.[33] In May and June small APC's of the two *hsien* were gradually amalgamated into larger units. Similar actions were taken in Liaoning in May.

The amalgamation of the APC's laid the groundwork for later moves toward communization. The Chinese Communists, in fact, claimed that the communization movement started in the spring of 1958, although many elements of the commune system had existed before that time.[34] On the other hand, however, it is not certain whether the Chinese planned communization at this early date. It now appears more likely that many policy actions were taken on an ad hoc basis and were based on improvisation and reactions to unanticipated problems, that the full implications and consequences of these actions were not clearly foreseen or totally grasped at the time, and that communization progressed piecemeal rather than being planned in advance.

The Enactment of the Great Leap Forward

In an enthusiastic, radicalized atmosphere, the Second Session of the Eighth Party Congress met in May 1958 and approved the party's new "General Line for the Socialist Construction," thereby officially launching the Great Leap Forward. The Leap had actually started a few months earlier; in fact, the NPC session of February had called for a "Great Leap Forward," demanding a huge increase in the production targets of many main branches of industry. These targets then were scrapped and raised repeatedly.

Before the opening of the Party Congress, Mao traveled extensively in the provinces for several months to promote his radical line. He came into personal contact with, and may have won support from, various provincial secretaries, seven of whom were subsequently promoted to the CC at the May session.[35] In the Fifth CC Plenum immediately following the party congress, K'o Ch'ing-shih and Li Ching-ch'üan, first party secretaries of Shanghai and Szechuan, respectively, and T'an Chen-lin, a secretary of the CC Secretariat specializing in agricultural affairs, were elevated to the Politburo, advancing over six alternate Politburo members.[36] Lin Piao, a member of the Politburo, was elected a member of the Standing Committee of the Politburo and vice-chairman of the CC of the party.[37] Two of the top economic officials, Li Fu-ch'un and Li Hsien-nien, who were also members of the Politburo, were added to the Secretariat, presumably coopted by Mao to help implement his new economic policies.

Although proponents of the Great Leap policies were firmly in control of the party, a significant number of party officials in the center and in the provinces, vaguely identified by the press as tide-watchers [kuan-ts'ao p'ai], account-settlers [suan-ch'ang p'ai], and retreat-promoters [Ch'u-t'ui p'ai], had questioned and sometimes directly opposed the wisdom of the party's embarking on the radical course. The opposition to the party's policies was considered significant enough that Liu Shao-ch'i took a clear note of it and devoted an extraordinary amount of attention to the critics of the Great Leap policies in his keynote speech to the May session of the Party Congress.[38]

According to Liu, "some comrades" had opposed the line of rapid collectivization in 1955 and had charged that the leap forward of 1956 was a reckless advance"; they had misgivings about the principle of "more, faster, better, and more economically" as expressed in the twelve-year agricultural program; and in 1957 they had dampened the initiative of the masses, thus hampering progress, particularly on the agricultural front. The introduction of the revised draft program in the Third Plenum, Mao's militant call to overtake Britain in production, and the mass initiative evoked by the rectification and anti-rightist campaigns led to an all-round leap forward, and many of those comrades who had expressed misgivings had "learned a lesson." But, Liu added: "Some of them have not yet learned anything. They say 'We will settle accounts with you after the autumn harvest.'" Liu challenged the critics to await the autumn harvest for the results of the new policy by saying: "Well, let them wait to settle accounts, they will lose out in the end."

There was further evidence of inner-party opposition in mid-May 1958, when ten provincial first party secretaries wrote a series of articles in the *People's Daily* attacking the conservatism of "some cadres" who allegedly refused to believe in the possibility of a rapid economic progress and opposed an all-round leap forward.[39] These provincial secretaries adopted a posture of all-out support for the Great Leap and tried to persuade others to make intense efforts to bring it about. If the conservative cadres were not convinced, they were at least intimidated and silenced by purges carried out in early 1958.

In the provinces, many "rightist" officials were expelled from the party or dismissed from their leadership positions in this period. These provincial purges, most of them reviewed by the Party Congress in May, covered twelve provinces. The purge victims included four alternate CC members, one provincial first secretary, eighteen members of standing committees of provincial committees, five provincial secretaries, ten members of provincial committee secretariats, four governors, and ten vice-governors, as well as approximately twenty-five other officials holding important party or government positions at the provincial level.[40] In almost every purge differences over rural policy were involved, and in seven of the twelve provinces it was apparently the most important policy issue. In eight provinces charges of localism were also leveled against the purge victims.

In the center there was no open purge, yet the influence of those who had argued for a cautious approach seemed to be considerably undermined. Vice-Premier Teng Tzu-hui, concurrently director of the CC Rural Work Department and of the State Council Agriculture and Forestry Staff Office, and hitherto the regime's top spokesman for agricultural affairs, was pushed into the background; although he was not formally deprived of his positions, at least some of his responsibilities were taken over by T'an Chen-lin, who now outranked him in the party hierarchy.

The influence of Ch'en Yun, and possibly the influence of Chou En-lai as well, was weakened in 1958.[41] Both had been critics of the "reckless advances" of 1956—and thus indirectly were critics of Mao's collectivization drive and the draft twelve-year agricultural program. Their reports to the Third CC Plenum in the fall of 1957 were not published, and they may have advocated a material incentive approach which clashed with Mao's approach. They may even have opposed the decentralization measures pushed through in the Third Plenum, whose implementation considerably weakened the central government apparatus and transferred much of the power to direct the national economy to the party cadres at local levels. For opportunistic or other reasons, three top economic officials, Li Fu-ch'un, Li Hsien-nien, and Po I-p'o, who formerly articulated conservative viewpoints, now changed their tactics and took the lead in promoting the Great Leap policies.

Against the background of the radical trend in the policy-making councils, the second revised draft of the twelve-year agricultural program was formally approved by the Party Congress in May 1958, and it was scheduled to be officially enacted by the NPC in 1959. In the mood of the Great Leap Forward, new targets were adopted and many earlier targets were raised upward.

The 1958 version of the draft program was never published, despite the fanfare it received in the summer of 1958. The revisions made at the time are known only through T'an Chen-lin's explanatory report.[42] According to T'an, targets for the production of oil-bearing crops were added to the existing production targets; the yields on products such as ground nuts, rapeseed, and soya beans were to be doubled or tripled by 1967; the target of 40 catties of cotton per *mou* for some areas was raised to 60 catties, thus restoring the original goal set in the 1956 draft. A separate article was now devoted to close planting. This "advanced" experience, after being tested in some localities with what one report called "spectacular" results, was to be emulated throughout the nation. T'an admitted, however, that "close planting" "has often run up against resistance from conservative and backward ideas." Therefore the enactment of a separate article in this connection was to "give greater impetus to the popularization of close planting."

The principle of mass mobilization and maximization of the use of local resources was also formally written into the program. According to T'an, in the section on water conservancy, "three emphases" (emphasis on small-scale projects, on water storage, and on APC resources) were inserted to give that policy greater prominence. The article on mechanization and electrification is said to have been redrafted. There is no way of knowing how the article was rewritten, however, since the text was never made public. One source suggests that the changes came as a result of Mao's intervention.[43] At the Chengtu Conference of March 1958 a policy document entitled "Opinions on the Problem of Agricultural Mechanization" was formulated on Mao's initiative, and it was later approved by the Politburo. The document is said to have called for the mechanization of agriculture through the massive manufacture of small machinery by local industries and through reliance on local economic strength. In a smiliar vein, T'an Chen-lin stated in May 1958:

> The new version of mechanization reflects the great mass movement to improve farm implements now being used in the Country. It takes into account the possibility that semi-mechanization and mechanization of agriculture may be realized through the expansion of small-scale local industries, and it makes the point that the budding technical revolution in agriculture is a stepping stone to semi-mechanization and mechanization.[44]

An important amendment was also made to the provision regarding education. Agricultural middle schools were to be established on a large scale in the countryside by using local APC resources, and "work-study" education programs were to be actively promoted. The Chinese Communist regime had undertaken a reexamination of its educational system in late 1957 and early 1958, and one of the main conclusions reached by the authorities was that the government, central and local, could not afford the tremendous expenditures required to achieve the regime's educational goals.[45] The regime therefore decided that the only realistic course to follow in pursuing its goals was to assign the major part of the task of establishing and running schools in the countryside to the APC's. Accordingly, a rapid establishment of great numbers of *Min pan hsueh-hsiao*, or "schools run by the people, took place in late winter 1957 and early spring 1958. A dispatch of the *NCNA* on 10 June 1958 said 61,000 such schools had been set up between February and May 1958.

Honan as a Pacesetter

The newly revised draft program made no mention of the communes, the new type of rural organization which was to emerge in China's countryside shortly thereafter; it is not clear whether the Party Congress in May discussed the establishment of this new form of rural organization. However, various elements of the commune system, including new institutions for collective living (such as the public mess halls, nurseries, and sewing teams), new methods of organizing labor (such as labor armies and specialized labor brigades), and trends toward the amalgamation of APC's into larger units, had already developed in the countryside before the spring of 1958. A central party directive on merging the APC's issued in May gave a further impetus to cadres to enlarge the APC's.[46]

The province of Honan was the pacesetter in the amalgamation of APC's; later it also played a significant and leading role in bringing about China's communization. Honan's prominent role in these events can be attributed to two factors.

The geographic factor is very important. Honan is crisscrossed by several major river systems, the Yellow, the Huai, the Wei, and their tributaries; rainfall in the province reaches a maximum in July, with virtually all the precipitation occurring from May through September, and floods have been frequent.[47] In fact, both in 1956 and in 1957, Honan suffered severe floods, causing serious damage to crops and properties. Drastic steps would therefore be necessary to control the floods and reduce their damage in the future. Thus Honan was in the forefront of the water conservancy campaign in the fall and winter of 1957–58,[48] and in October and December of 1957 two national conferences concerning the campaign were held in that province.

Between fall 1957 and spring 1958, 8 billion cubic meters of earth and stone had been moved in water conservancy projects (whereas only 360 million cubic meters were moved in the previous eight years), and the area of irrigated land had been extended from 4.3 to 17 million *mou* or 86.6 percent of arable land of Honan. At the peak of the campaign, as many as 10 million peasants were organized to work on various irrigation and flood control projects in that province. Peking publicly praised Honan as "the province that has made the most rapid progress in the current mass water conservancy program."[49] Thus Honan succeeded through concerted organization and use of its large population (over 44 million in 1958) combined with its relatively high incidence of natural calamities.[50] The unusual degree of organization that was introduced into the countryside to undertake the tasks of the Great Leap also laid the groundwork for the later merger of APC's. A revealing example was provided by a 9 May directive of the Honan provincial authorities:

> Collaboration shall be worked out between *hsiang* and *hsien*, among APC's and brigades and teams, between mountainous regions and the plains, and between cities and villages. ... All APC's shall make due arrangements for living requirements of their members during May and June. ... Headquarters for directing the summer harvest and cultivation shall be established in all administrative districts, *hsien* and *hsiang* to unify the forces available and to bring about concerted action.[51]

In response to this directive it was reported on 20 May that "organizations have been set up in all parts of the province to direct the summer harvesting and sowing work. ... Creches, babycare groups, sewing groups, temporary mess halls, and centers for old people have been set up to enable more peasants to be free from domestic chores."[52] It was clear that by wheat harvest time in late May the countryside of Honan had been turned into what Hofheinz called "a veritable honeycomb of local organizations."

In addition, the factional struggle in the politics of Honan, discussed in Chapter 1, was another major factor making Honan the cradle of the communes. The conservative First Party Secretary P'an Fu-sheng, who had been on sick leave since 1954 and returned to Honan in the spring of 1957, attacked the leadership of Wu Chih-p'u, the second party secretary and governor, who had ruthlessly established collectivization in Honan. P'an and his followers later broke up many large APC's, reversed extreme measures implemented by Wu, and instituted some "capitalist" measures to give peasants incentives for agricultural production.

The provincial leadership of Honan was thus divided into two major groups, one led by P'an, who favored a moderate rural policy emphasizing material incentives for the peasants and opposing a rash approach toward collectivization, and the other led by Wu, who advocated the opposite. Besides policy differences, the conflicts between these two top provincial officials in Honan were probably exacerbated by their personal feud. Whereas P'an was the superior of Wu in Honan (P'an came to the Honan Provincial Party Committee in 1953 and replaced Wu as the senior secretary there), Wu became a full CC member after September 1956, outranking P'an, who was only an alternate CC member. The accusations that P'an violated the principle of "democratic centralism" by relying on his two confidants (who had served under P'an before their transfer to Honan in 1953), disregarding the regular party decision-making organs, at least suggested that factionalism was an element in the politics of Honan.

As pointed out at the end of Chapter 1, the ascendancy of the "radicals" in the CC after the Third CC Plenum in September 1957 enhanced the position of Wu Chih-p'u and his followers in Honan and enabled Wu to gain an upper hand in his struggle with P'an. Thereafter, Wu Chih-p'u was virtually in control of Honan's policy-making and P'an was absent from Honan for "health" reasons, although his disgrace was not publicly revealed until the Party Congress in May 1958.[53]

Changing the guard in Honan probably generated pressure on cadres in that province to enlarge APC's. The motivations for doing so were mixed and complicated. Some cadres were composed of real activists, mindful of the favorable attitude of the provincial authorities. Members of other cadres were sensitive to the new atmosphere in the provincial capital and aware of Wu's attitude, perhaps wanting to play it safe and please the new boss. Officials at all levels in Honan, who might have had misgivings about the establishment of large APC's consisting of several thousand households, might well have been afraid of being linked with the "rightist-leaning" conservatism of purged P'an Fu-sheng and might have thus felt compelled to go along with their colleagues or even subordinates who dared to "think and act."

A "suggestion" to merge the APC's made by Mao at the Chengtu Conference in March 1958 probably reinforced Wu's own inclinations and was immediately acted upon. In Wu's own account, Honan had already started a large-scale amalgamation of small APC's in April, and in the following two months it assumed the proportion of a mass movement. When small APC's (each of which generally coincided with a natural village) were merged into larger units, and when work organizations were changed in response to new tasks assumed by peasants in the spring and summer of 1958, changes in the existing APC administrative framework were unavoidable.[54] The new type of rural organization—in the form of the commune—was soon introduced by the Chinese Communists.

The Establishment of the Communes

The Crystallization of a New Concept

In the summer of 1958, the Chinese Communists had created *Jen-min Kung-she*, or People's Commune, a new economic, social, and political unit in China's countryside. The reasons they chose the name People's Commune to designate the newborn organization are not totally clear. The word commune was used by the Chinese Communists before—when they staged an uprising in the city of Canton in December 1927 they set up the Canton Commune, which lasted for three days. However, the more likely source of inspiration is the Paris Commune of 1871, which was specifically compared to the People's Commune by Chinese officials in 1958.[55] It is well known that the experience of the Paris Commune fascinated the Chinese Communists,[56] and they may therefore have adopted the term to honor their romanticized image of the Paris Commune.

If the word commune was indeed borrowed from the Paris Commune, the concept of the People's Commune bore no resemblance to the source. In fact, the concept was articulated gradually over a period of several months. When Mao spoke to the Chengtu Conference in March 1958, there were several striking passages in his speech which suggest that he may have already had various features of the new system in mind at this early date. There is, for example, Mao's call on those present to study and think boldly about such issues as "the law of value," the private ownership of property, the role and future of the family, and the future "Communist distribution relationship of to each according to his need," all of which were issues prominently featured in the discussion of the commune system in the summer and fall of 1958.[57]

In late spring and early summer the concept of commune was refined further by Ch'en Po-ta, Mao's brain-truster. The first hints of the crystallized concept of the future organization appeared in the third issue of *Hung Ch'i* on 1 July 1958. Using the example of a small APC (Hsukuan No. 1 in Hupeh), Ch'en Po-ta urged other APC's to emulate this APC's methods of building and managing small industries by "transforming a co-op into a basic-level organization of agricultural and industrial cooperation, namely forming a People's Commune which combines agriculture and industry."

A more elaborate conception of the commune appeared in another article by Ch'en in the following issue of *Hung Ch'i* (16 July 1958). Entitled "Under the Banner of Chairman Mao Tse-tung," Ch'en quoted Mao:

> Our direction is to combine, step by step and in an orderly manner, workers (industry), peasants (agriculture), businessmen (exchange), students (culture and education), and soldiers (military) into a large commune, which is to constitute our nation's basic social unit. In this kind of commune, industry, agriculture and exchange are the people's material life; culture and education are the people's spiritual life which reflect their material life. The total arming of the people is to protect this material and spiritual life.

And Ch'en added his own statement: "Mao Tse-tung's thoughts on this kind of commune are the conclusion he has derived from the experiences of real life."

For the first time, a succinct statement of a new type of sociopolitical organization was forcefully put forth. These lines, written by Ch'en Po-ta, *Hung Ch'i's* chief editor, who was also reputed to be Mao's personal secretary and ghost writer, and printed in the party's most authoritative theoretical journal, could not be taken lightly. They probably reflected the fact that Mao's ideas about the commune system had crystallized to a large extent by that time.

Mao's decision (it was apparently his decision, not that of the party) to establish communes, meanwhile, was being passed down to provincial officials in mid-July 1958 by T'an Chen-lin, who attended the regional conference in Chengchow.[58] This was confirmed later by a correspondent for *Hung Ch'i*:

> The original purpose of the cadres in Hsinyang Special District (Honan) in amalgamating the APC's was merely to create a larger unit in order to facilitate construction. When they attended the meeting in Chengchow, comrade T'an Chen-lin told them the ideas of comrade Mao Tse-tung and the CC on integrating industry, agriculture, commerce, education, and militia into a large commune. Since then, they have begun to call [enlarged APC's] "communes."[59]

It thus seems probable that *Weihsing* (Sputnik) commune was formally established in July, probably after this meeting, and not in April as is often assumed.[60]

Provincial officials also indicated that they had not thought in terms of establishing a new rural organization in the form of communes before Mao instructed them to do so. Referring to what had occurred in the spring and early summer of 1958 in the countryside—the merger of APC's, changes in the methods of organizing labor, new institutions for collective living, and the expansion of local industries—Wu Chih-p'u wrote in *Hung Ch'i* (no. 8, 1958):

> This was, in essence, already the start of the movement for People's Communes. But people were not yet aware of the real nature of this development. *Only after comrade Mao Tse-tung gave his directive in July, 1958 regarding the People's Communes did they begin to see things clearly,* realizing the meaning of this new form of organization that has appeared in the vast rural and urban areas, and *feel more confident and determined to take this path.* (Emphasis added)

Party officials of other provinces made similar statements giving credit to Mao for pointing out the new direction of agricultural development—that is, communization.[61] Before totally committing himself Mao decided to take a good look at the countryside, and in the first half of August 1958 he visited the rural areas of Hopei, Honan, and Shantung.

On 6 August 1958, Mao, during a tour of Honan, inspected the Ch'iliying

Commune and its facilities; the commune was said to have been established "according to Chairman Mao's instruction." The press carried a vivid and detailed report of Mao's activities, and recorded this interesting conversation:

> Chairman Mao smiled and said to Wu Chih-p'u: "Secretary Wu, it looks very hopeful! I wish all of Honan were as good as this." Wu Chih-p'u said: "If there is one commune like this, then there will be many other communes like this." Chairman Mao said: "Right. If there is a commune like this, then there can be many more."[62]

Mao appeared to be impressed and pleased by what he had seen. On 9 August he visited a Shantung village; in the course of a briefing, when he heard that Peiyuan Hsiang was ready to set up a large collective farm, he said: "It is better to set up the People's Commune. It has the advantage of integrating agriculture, industry, trade, education and militia, and is easier to lead."[63] This seemingly casual remark was headlined in the *People's Daily* and became a "go-ahead" signal for many cadres, who began to prepare for communization even though this new form of organization had not yet been formally authorized by the party's legitimate decision-making organs.

The Formal Authorization

On 17 August 1958 the Politburo of the CCP held an enlarged session at Peitaiho, a summer resort not far from Peking, to consider, among other things, the question of communization. On 29 August the Politburo formally passed a resolution to institute communes in the rural areas—a historic decision which subsequently plunged China's national economy into a process that resulted in serious dislocations. What motivated the Chinese Communists to embark on the communization program? Why did a collegium of rational leaders authorize a social and economic change of such vast magnitude with little advance planning or preparation?

Ideologically, the communes symbolized a spurt ahead toward the ultimate goal of a Communist society. Since the spring of 1958, the prevailing atmosphere within Chinese society had tended to encourage the idea that Communism was just around the corner, and at least some Chinese Communists apparently regarded the commune system as a quick steppingstone into their utopia. The influence of ideology on the decision to institute communes is indicated by the 1958 Peitaiho Resolution, which termed the communes "the best form of organization for the attainment of socialism and gradual transition to Communism."

There were undoubtedly more practical considerations underlying the commune decision; the commune system was seen by its proponents as a solution to various problems that existed in the APC's. One of these problems was so-called localism or departmentalism, which many APC's had displayed: the APC's were concerned only with their interests, to the exclusion of the interests of other APC's and even of the state. For instance, a state farm near Peking with an abundant water supply refused to let a neighboring APC share its water, and the APC retaliated by digging a deep well near the state farm, thus drying the water supply of the state farm.[64] An experimental team from Peking University planted some valuable fruit trees on the land of an APC, but the APC workers ploughed them up to make way for food crops. And there were many other disputes among the APC's over the land and water resources.

The unprecedented massive water conservancy campaign of 1957–58 and the Great Leap Forward drive had imposed many new tasks on the APC's; the APC's, generally small in size and meager in manpower and resources, found themselves unable to meet the requirement of new circumstances. For example, forty-eight APC's in Hsiachia Hsien of Honan, in response to the call of the water conservancy campaign, had independently constructed some eighty small projects along both banks of the Tanshui; but due to lack of manpower and inability to mobilize enough resources, these projects, poor in quality, were subsequently destroyed by floods.[65] Elsewhere some APC's had iron ore but no coal, while others had coal but no iron ore, and their work was hampered.

Each of these was a minor irritation of a local nature, but hundreds of thousands of APC's throughout China had the same problems, creating serious trouble for the central leadership, which was committed to bringing about a great leap in industrial and agricultural production. Thus the commune decision may be seen as an attempt to meet immediate needs: communes which merged small APC's into larger units aimed at solving conflicts of interest among the APC's and at providing a more efficient mechanism to organize labor and mobilize local resources on a large scale and for overall planning and management.

Furthermore, the commune system was an essential component of Mao's Great Leap strategy, the strategy of "walking on two legs." The surplus garnished from the modern section of the economy would be reinvested and used for the continued expansion of that sector, whereas the rural sector was to rely on itself and the local resources for growth. Labor-intensive small-scale industries would be developed as well as operated by the communes using simple, locally manufactured equipment, local labor, and local raw materials. Thus the commune system may be seen as an economic control lever for resource mobilization and allocation as well as an instrument for rural industrialization which would make the Great Leap Forward possible.

To a certain extent, military considerations affected the decision to set up communes because some Communist leaders, particularly Mao himself, seemed to believe that the communes would enhance China's defense capability in a "people's war." Following the enlarged session of the Military Affairs Commission of the party in June 1958, which criticized those who favored foreign military theory and discarded the party's own revolutionary traditions and experiences, there was a renewed emphasis in the PLA on people's war and the party's military traditions.[66] The revival of the militia in the summer of 1958 and, to a lesser degree, the militarization of the peasantry coincided with this development. Apparently Mao saw the communes as the ideal framework within which the militia could be organized.[67] Thus the communization became connected, even if only indirectly, with questions of military strategy and national defense.[68]

These were probably some of the considerations underlying the decision of the Chinese leadership, and particularly Mao himself, to embark on the course of communization. Mao and some of his supporters in the provinces appear to have forced the hand of the Politburo. Before the Politburo met in Peitaiho on 17 August, communization had already been in full swing in some parts of China, particularly Honan, Liaoning, and Hopei; this fact and Mao's endorsement of the new system, which was widely publicized in the press, as noted earlier, tended to present a *fait accompli* to the Politburo, which had no alternative but to give formal sanction.

Chinese official statements made it clear that the Peitaiho Politburo Resolution on Communes was based on Mao's proposal. We do not know whether Mao's Politburo colleagues, particularly those who had persistently advocated a moderate policy in the past, genuinely favored such a course of action; however, none of them spoke directly against the decision to set up communes at that time.[69] The structure and functions of communes were among the topics that came under prolonged discussion in the Peitaiho Conference, which lasted two weeks, from 17 to 30 August,[70] but it appears that very little advance planning had been made to communize the countryside on a nation-wide basis.

Beginning in 1959 P'eng Teh-huai and other Chinese Communists criticized the commune movement, saying it had been launched too hastily, and indeed the suddenness of the 1958 commune decision stood in striking contrast to the debate, experimentation, and preparation that preceded the collectivization campaign of the mid-1950s. Possibly Mao had become more assertive in 1958 following his disappointment with the overcautiousness or conservatism of his colleagues. Or after the collectivization drive of 1955–56, in which Mao achieved what generally had been considered impossible by most of his Politburo colleagues in the summer of 1955, Mao may have become "dizzy with success" and hence tended to underestimate the difficulties involved in the communization campaign. It is also possible that other CCP leaders, including those who attacked the commune system later, did not regard the commune decision as irrational or disastrous in 1958 and did not anticipate that the commune system would so severely affect agricultural production in the following years.[71]

P'eng Teh-huai provided a clue to the thinking of the CCP leadership in the summer of 1958. Many top officials, including P'eng, fell victim to the party's own propaganda as they were misled by the rosy—and grossly exaggerated—reports of bumper harvest in China at the time of the 1958 Peitaiho Conference and mistakenly believed that the grain problem had been solved.[72] This ill-founded optimism, in P'eng's opinion, was largely responsible for the premature introduction of the free supply system, symbolized by the slogan "eating rice without pay" [ch'ih-fan pu-yao-ch'ien], which developed much extravagance and waste and raised false expectations. Thus the optimism about the food supply—which was not borne out by reality later—had, to some extent, affected the thinking of the Chinese leaders when they approved the commune resolution at the 1958 Peitaiho Conference.

The Peitaiho Resolution on Communes, published in the People's Daily on 10 September, almost two weeks after its approval, was a curiously vague document. It formally designated the new rural organization the "people's commune" [jen-min kung-she], although it had been called by many different names in different localities. It also outlined some broad principles for organizing and administering the communes, but these guidelines were too general and imprecise to be useful for local cadres in an innovation of such vast magnitude. This would further suggest that the Chinese Communists, even those who had earlier had a vague concept about this new form of rural organization, had not carefully planned the commune movement in advance. In fact, several months after the Peitaiho meeting, the central authorities were still unable to provide detailed operational instructions to cadres about the form, structure, and functions of communes.[73] Consequently, local cadres were compelled to improvise and make their own decisions; disorder and confusion arose from divergent practices in different communes and different localities regarding the size, structure, and system of ownership and distribution.

One week before the Peitaiho Resolution was published, the People's Daily of 4 September published the charter of the Weishing (Sputnik) Commune in Honan Province and an accompanying editorial designed to provide some guidance to cadres on how to set up a commune. The experience of establishing the commune system in Honan had received by far the largest share of publicity in the national papers between mid-August and mid-September 1958.[74] Examples of organizing and running the communes in Honan were publicized as models to be emulated by other provinces. It appears that cadres in Honan had provided Mao and other proponents of the commune system with a rough blueprint of an operative commune.

Thus policy regarding the commune system was not formulated by the top leadership alone; rather it was the product of interactions between the top leaders and local cadres. Policy could not be formulated by single decisions, however fully considered. A vast number of lesser decisions accompanied the basic ones, and the way in which each basic policy was carried out also affected its substance. The decision to launch the communes was made at the center; however, local cadres had already, on their own initiative, taken actions moving in this direction (i.e., changes in labor organization, collective life, and the amalgamation of APC's). Provincial cadres and particularly those in Honan had consequently provided some ideas relevant to the concept and management of a "commune," which inevitably affected the decision made by the top leaders on communization.

Establishing the Communes

During the enlarged Peitaiho Politburo session which met from 17 to 30 August 1958, and particularly in the period immediately following the meeting, the press, radio, *tatzepao* [wall posters], and all other mass media were mobilized to launch a propaganda campaign on communization. The mass media served not only as an instrument of persuasion to stimulate enthusiasm and mobilize the support of the masses for the commune system, but also as an important channel of official communication through which the party could quickly disseminate orders, instructions, and other official directives to local cadres to publicize those practices and examples designed to be emulated and popularized.

While the propaganda campaign was launched in the mass media, the party's channels of internal communication—meetings, official correspondence, and so on—were also employed to communicate specific instructions regarding communization from central to provincial and then to local authorities. Provincial first secretaries were present at the enlarged Peitaiho Politburo Conference; in the proceedings there they were informed of the party's new policies and of the thinking and intentions of the top leaders. Even before the official Politburo resolution to establish the communes was made public, some of the more "activist" first secretaries had already acted.

The Hopei Provincial Party Committee issued a directive to cadres in that province to organize communes on 29 August, the same day that the Politburo resolution on the communes was approved.[75] Three days after the Politburo conference opened, the Fukien Provincial Party Committee called a telephone conference of secretaries of special district, municipal, and *hsien* party committees in the late evening of 20 August. Kuo Liang, secretary-general of the Fukien Provincial Party Committee, "transmitted" the instructions of the Central Committee and of the provincial first party secretary, Yeh Fei (who was still in Peking), to organize the communes on a large scale.[76]

In most provinces, however, instructions filtered down to lower authorities only after the Politburo Conference had been concluded. Hupeh and Shansi Provincial Party Committees held meetings on 4 September to direct the work of and make arrangements for communization in their provinces. The Kwantung Provincial Party Committee's Rural Work Department sponsored a meeting of the directors of the Rural Work Departments of Special District Party Committees from 30 August to 1 September; this was designed to study "practical problems involved in organizing the communes and to make arrangements for setting up the communes on a trial basis."[77] Meanwhile, written directives were also issued by the Szechuan and Chekiang Provincial Party Committees, and these provided more detailed and specific guidance for implementing communization than did the Peitaiho resolution.[78]

Communization in Chekiang

The processes by which communes were established in Chekiang can be reconstructed from published materials.[79] Hangchow, the provincial capital of Chekiang, was an urban center surrounded by suburban districts where a high percentage of the population were peasants engaged in agricultural production. After Honan's communes and Mao's favorable remarks on organizing communes were publicized in the *People's Daily*, the Rural Work Department of the Hangchow Party Committee began to prepare for communization in its rural areas.[79] It sent cadres to Honan and other places that had already established communes to learn their experiences; at the same time, it began to organize "*shih-tien*" [experimental] communes in six *hsiang*.

Lungch'ing, Suanglin, Tangnan, Liangt'u, Choupu, and Chien Chiao were chosen as experimental sites not because they were typical *hsiang* but rather because they were not. These *hsiang* had strong and talented leadership; their cadres were able to plan the establishment of communes in addition to managing production; the level of consciousness of the masses was reported to be high; and the size of these *hsiang* was relatively small, ranging from 2500 to 3500 households; moreover, each of these *hsiang* contained a market town.

On 29 August 1958 (the day the enlarged Politburo meeting at Peitaiho passed the resolution to set up communes in the rural areas), Communization Work Teams dispatched by the Hangchow Party Committee arrived at these *hsiang* and started to work. A propaganda campaign, its content and methods already mapped out by the Propaganda Department of the Chekiang Provincial Party Committee, was launched to "liberate human thought," to elevate the class consciousness of the masses, and to establish the superiority of the commune system, which was said to be the steppingstone to an ideal Communist society.

All available resources and means, including local newspapers, wall posters, tabloids, loudspeakers, propaganda teams, theatrical groups, movie teams, and mass meetings, were mobilized to saturate the masses with intensive propaganda. Mass meetings were held in each APC to "debate" typical questions: Can we do better in the (agricultural) production? How can we do it? Do we want to set up a commune? What are its advantages? Can we sucessfully manage it?

In these "debates," according to *Chekiang Jih-pao*, different shades of opinions were expressed and the peasants gained a good education, elevated their understanding, and voluntarily called for the establishment of communes. Subsequently, tens of thousands of "petitions" to set up communes and "applications" to join them were prepared by the peasants and presented to their *hsiang* party committees.

By 9 September each of these six *hsiang* had organized one commune, and the work of experimentation had come to an end. From 16 to 19 September the Hangchow Municipal Party Committee called a four-level cadre conference attended by more than 1100 cadres from the municipality, *Ch'u*, *hsiang*, and APC's.

The conference was devoted to studying party documents, such as the Politburo Resolution on Communes, directives of the CC and the Chekiang Provincial Party Committee, and the relevant editorials of the *People's Daily*. In the course of studying documents, APC cadres' tendencies of "departmentalism" and "individualism" (manifested in misgivings toward forming communes with less well-off APC's) were criticized, and cadres undertook criticism and self-criticism. As a result, the cadres' Communist consciousness was said to have been raised, and it was claimed that they became convinced of the necessity and superiority of the commune system.

The experiences of organizing the six initial communes then were summed up in writing by the Municipal Party Committee and distributed to the cadres for study in meetings. Through this device, the officials in the Hangchow Municipal Party Committee tried to show lower cadres how to implement the party's policy of communization and directed the attention of cadres to specific problems encountered during the "*shih-tien*" phase.

For instance, the efforts of cadres to set up a commune in Liangt'u *hsiang* met with a cool reception from the peasants as the cadres there failed to stress the economic benefits that would immediately follow the establishment of the commune. On the other hand, the experiences of Suanglin *hsiang* were singled out for praise and emulation because party cadres there allegedly relied on the mass line method and fully mobilized the masses to take part in the "debates"; these cadres appear to have kindled a certain degree of enthusiasm among the peasants through promises of great economic progress and benefits.

The conference also discussed and plotted detailed programs for communization and production for various localities, made concrete arrangements for their execution, and assigned cadres to the communes which were to be set up thereafter. As soon as the conference was concluded, cadres went back to their posts and started to organize communes on a large scale.

Despite local variations, the methods and procedures for organizing the communes appeared to be fairly uniform throughout China.[80] In the beginning, a few communes were to be set up on a trial basis; these were called *shih-tien* [spot experiments]. In these experiments, techniques of operation and organizational forms for the communes were tested, modified, refined, and "perfected." Experience gained in this process was then "summed-up" and popularized so that cadres in other places would benefit from these "advanced" experiences and apply them to organizing the communes in their own localities.[81] Much valuable experience could be gained from this leadership technique. By setting up experimental communes, the party could concentrate qualified talent on a few spots to work out, through trial and error, techniques of "social engineering" suitable for use on a vast scale. The operational methods thus devised and "perfected" could then be followed by less imaginative or competent cadres in other areas. This approach not only demonstrated operational know-how to cadres in a mass drive but also helped persuade the laggards. Liu Shao-ch'i had perceived the susceptibility of the masses to persuasion as early as 1939, when he prescribed the following:

> In our work we should break through at one point to give an example to the masses and let them see and understand things by themselves. Only by giving demonstrative examples to the masses can we encourage them, particularly the intermediate and backward elements, by affording them the opportunities and facilities to understand the problems, thereby instilling in them confidence and courage to act under our Party's slogans and to culminate in an upsurge of mass enthusiasm.[82]

It must be pointed out, however, that the "*shih-tien*" technique has very little in common with the concept of scientific experiment as generally understood in the West. "Spot experiments" were undertaken by the Chinese to disarm opposition and win acceptance for party policy, to polish, to perfect, and most of all to demonstrate certain organizational methods. There was no attempt to find out whether the measure under experimentation could really work in all localities. As pointed out earlier, when the Hangchow Municipal Committee picked six *hsiang* in the suburbs of the city in which to organize communal *shih-tien*, the "samples" it chose were not typical or ordinary *hsiang* but rather were chosen because they were atypical.

The formal government machinery seems to have played a secondary role in the course of organizing the communes, since it was rarely mentioned in the press. Rather, it was the party that took charge of the operation. As in many previous mass campaigns, the party organization, from the province down, would first set up an ad hoc "Communization Campaign Office" and assign special personnel (usually party secretaries) to take responsibility for planning and directing the campaign in a given area.[83] The communization campaign office would then dispatch work teams to engage in *shih-tien*. Usually, the *hsien*-level party organization would function as the "command post" to direct the campaign;[84] occasionally, however, provincial working groups also participated at the *hsien* or even *hsiang* level, especially in setting up a few initial model communes.[85] After the *shih-tien* stage was completed, conferences of three-level or four-level cadres (*San-chi* or *ssu-chi kan-pu hui-yi*), that is, cadres from the *hsien*, *ch'u*, and *hsiang*, sometimes with cadres from the APC party organizations, were called to make systematic preparations for large-scale implementation of the commune movement.

In these meetings, cadres were required to study, through lectures and small discussion groups, such relevant documents released by the higher authorities as the Peitaiho Politburo Resolution, directives from the CC and the Provincial Party Committee, and certain editorials of the *People's Daily* and *Hung Ch'i*. The lessons gained from *shih-tien* and the "advanced" experiences of other localities or other provinces were also introduced and discussed.[86] Many provinces actually sent cadres to Suip'ing Hsien in Honan, the cradle of the commune system, to make a field study;[87] this is a further indication of the impact of Honan's communes on the other parts of China.

Concrete plans and measures for communization in each locality later were decided upon and worked out in detail. In the planning sessions, cadres were reindoctrinated with the party's premises and goals, their misgivings about or opposition to the commune system were overcome or silenced, and efforts were made to kindle their enthusiasm. Such meetings performed other important functions. They formed a link in the party's chain of command through which the authority of the top leaders could flow down and reach cadres at the basic level. They also served as training sessions in which cadres were informed of detailed provisions of the party's policy on communization and were taught organizational techniques and operational methods.[88]

Before each commune was set up, a propaganda campaign tailored to the local situations was initiated. The *hsien*-level party organization usually was in charge of the propaganda work within its territorial jurisdiction; it mobilized and organized all available resources and mechanisms to distribute intensive propaganda among the masses.[89] The Peitaiho Politburo Resolution, several editorials in the *People's Daily*, and propaganda directives issued by provincial party authorities repeatedly enjoined cadres from using coercion to force peasants into the communes; instead, peasants were to be convinced and won over through education, persuasion, and the mass line method.[90]

In this propaganda campaign the masses were subjected to intensive indoctrination in Communist ideology to elevate their class consciousness; in addition, more instrumental themes—for example, the shortcomings of the

APC's and advantages of communes—were stressed in all the propaganda activities; in particular, many extravagant promises of rapid economic progress were made to the peasants.

The mass meeting was another mechanism used for persuasion. In many *hsiang* and APC's party cadres organized meetings to "debate" typical questions: Shall we establish a People's Commune? What are its superior qualities? Can we successfully manage a commune?[91] These meetings and "debates" were carefully planned and conducted by local party cadres; dissenting views were allowed and encouraged, or even planted, and then were roundly refuted and condemned, and the arguments in favor of the commune were forcefully put forward.

"Fair play" was not the aim of the "debates"; dissenting views could not be allowed to "confuse the masses" or to appear as attractive as the "positive views." The purpose of juxtaposing two different views was "to make the red flag redder and to make the masses recognize what is a 'white flag.'"[92] In the course of "debates," the commune system was characterized first as *ta* (i.e., large in manpower and resources) and second as *kung* (public, or more socialistic, as a system of ownership); on the other hand, the APC was characterized as *hsiao* (small in capital), *shao* (having less manpower), and *pen* (characterized by *pen-wei chu-i*, i.e., departmentalism).

Even the relatively "backward" Chinese peasant could easily infer which type of organization was "preferable," and the peasants were thus "persuaded" to join the communes. Through such manipulations the Chinese Communists secured the population's consent, although the process was clearly less than fully "voluntary." Although the peasant masses may not have been heartily convinced by this kind of manipulation, yet the Chinese Communists' emphasis on persuasion, rather than merely on compulsion, was certainly a very striking feature of the process.

Furthermore, these mass meetings served a useful purpose: they provided a forum through which the party reached the peasants, most of whom were at least partially illiterate, and the party was able to propagate its policies effectively. The debates and the clear-cut dichotomy characterizing the communes as good and the APC's as bad helped peasants understand the content of the party's policies. Finally, these meetings gave the peasants a sense of participation, which probably facilitated the party's efforts in mobilizing their support.[93]

The emphasis on propaganda, education, and persuasion in mass campaigns showed that the Chinese leadership took the mass line principle seriously. This leadership doctrine preaches that the party's policy and methods of work must be based on popular support and that "commandism" must be avoided. Mao once stated this guiding principle in the following terms:

In all practical work of our Party, correct leadership can only be developed on the principle of "from the masses, to the masses." This means summing up [i.e., coordinating and systematizing after careful study] the views of the masses [i.e., views scattered and un-systematic], then taking the resulting ideas back to the masses, explaining and popularizing them until the masses embrace the ideas as their own, stand up for them and translate them into action by way of testing their correctness. Then it is necessary once more to sum up the views of the masses, and once again take the resulting ideas back to the masses so that the masses give them their whole-hearted support.[94]

The propaganda activities, the mass meetings, and the "debates" of August–September 1958 were intended to "convince" or "persuade" peasants that communization served their interests best and thus should be accepted gladly. An image of a voluntary, spontaneous movement was propagated as the masses filed "petitions" and "applications" to join communes.[95] The party propagandists claimed loudly that the communes were the result of the "spontaneous demands" of the masses.[96] On the other hand, however, since the mass line doctrine rejected "tailism" as an incorrect leadership method, the cadres were instructed not to blindly follow "wrong" demands of the masses. If the masses could not clearly see their true interests in the commune system, it was because their class consciousness had not yet been adequately elevated or because they were victims of evil propaganda and counterrevolutionary ideologies. Therefore the party was expected to do what must be done, and the party organization at all levels had to "stand in the forefront of the movement to lead the masses."

4

Intraparty Dissension over the Great Leap Forward

The Phase of Disillusion

The establishment of the communes in rural China was certainly an epoch-making event; within a brief span of several months in the fall of 1958, the Chinese Communist leaders, with minimum resistance, imposed on the vast rural population a radically new form of organization. To be more exact, one month after the passage of the Peitaiho Resolution, more than 90 percent of China's 127 million peasant households were organized into 23,397 communes.[1] At the time, however, many of these communes existed in name only; the party instructed cadres to put up the "skeleton" of communes and wait until after the autumn harvest to reorganize APC's into communes.[2]

Communization involved a structural integration of the *hsiang* or township government (administrative village) and the collectives (mainly APC's but also other co-ops) as well as a significant territorial expansion of the basic units of local administration. In addition, changes in the system of ownership and income distribution in the rural areas accompanied the reorganization. It was only after the harvest in September that cadres in many areas began to seriously face the realities of organizing communes.

Dizzy with Success

In implementing the party's programs of communization, overzealous local cadres often stepped beyond the limits set by central authorities, which resulted in many excesses. The Chinese leadership later blamed the difficulties of the national economy largely on the mistakes committed by local cadres' implementation of central policies. There was undoubtedly some basis of truth in this charge. The excesses manifested in the cadres' implementation of communization (as in the land reform movement in the early 1950s and the collectivization drive in 1955–56) were probably inevitable; a mass movement such as this, which derives its power from mass enthusiasm and initiatives, creates its own momentum. In addition, the bias of the Chinese Communists toward leftism, as reflected in the slogan "better leftist than rightist" [*ning-tso wu-yu*], resulted in a tendency, clearly recognized by top Chinese leaders, for lower cadres to advance recklessly.[3]

But it would be wrong and unfair to place the entire responsibility for the disastrous effects of communization on cadres, groups that were merely carrying out the party's policies—many of which, in fact, were unrealistic, overambitious, ill-planned, and unsound. The top CCP leadership, more than anyone else, must take the blame.

In the fall of 1958 an atmosphere of "blind optimism" seems to have pervaded Chinese society; there was much talk in the Chinese press about the prospects for an immediate transition to communism, and some party leaders, including Mao himself, appeared to be persuaded that the pace of communization could be very fast without causing serious difficulty. The CC tried on several occasions to provide guidelines and to caution local cadres to move slowly, but instructions from the top were often ambiguous and imprecise and at times self-contradictory.

For instance, the Peitaiho Resolution of 29 August had stipulated that 2000 households would be the normal size of a commune, but it also permitted some places to set up communes of 6000 or 7000 households in accordance with local needs. One provision of the resolution instructed provincial and *hsien* cadres not to encourage the formation of communes of more than 10,000 households, but at the same time it told them not to oppose communes of such vast size. The national and provincial press, attempting to stimulate peasant enthusiasm for the commune system, had meanwhile publicized the "superiority" of bigger organization. In a millennial atmosphere, local cadres either ignored the CC guidelines or took advantage of the flexibility in the Peitaiho Resolution, and they proceeded almost uniformly to set up big communes.

In ten provinces alone, there were 1628 communes having a membership of 5000 to 10,000 households, 516 communes having a membership of 10,000 to 20,000 households, and 51 communes having more than 20,000 households.[4] Party officials at the *hsien* level tended to think that "the bigger the communes the better" and ordered the formation of large units, sometimes comprising 100,000 households, which of course proved unwieldy.[5] The Peitaiho Resolution also instructed cadres to form *hsien* federations of communes; in many localities, the whole *hsien* was organized, on paper at least, into a single commune containing as many as 500,000 people.[6] The Chinese leadership must have gotten carried away, so to speak, for they made almost no effort to discourage the formation of large communes, which could not be efficiently run because of a lack of sufficient qualified cadres.

The average number of households per commune for the whole of China at the end of September 1958 was estimated to be 4600, varying from 1400 in Kweichow to 9800 in Kwangtung; in the country districts within the municipalities of Peking and Shanghai, the number of households per commune exceeded 11,000. A general pattern was discernible in the size of the communes: the largest (on the average) communes were found in China's most modernized areas, which had the best transport facilities; conversely, the smallest (on the average) number of households per commune occurred in relatively underdeveloped and sparsely populated provinces.[7]

The Peitaiho Resolution held that one *hsiang* should equal one commune; if this privision had been strictly followed, then the total number of communes would have been about 80,000 instead of 26,400, since there were approximately 80,000 *hsiang* in China before communization. It turned out that a commune usually absorbed several or even a dozen *hsiang*. Most cadres in the absorbed *hsiang* found that their positions were eliminated, and they were either sent down to the first line of production or they were demoted to work in posts less important or powerful than those they had previously held. Although cadres in the APC's continued to serve as cadres in the new production brigades after communization, they were now subject to tighter control by the communes and found their power correspondingly diminished. Dissatisfaction among this group of basic cadres was widespread; they complained that whereas the communes had become bigger, their positions had become smaller [*she ta kuan hsiao*].[8]

Besides *ta* (bigger in size), the commune system was also characterized by the Chinese Communists as *kung* (more "socialistic" in ownership and distribution system). Before communization, the major elements of production, such as land, farm implements, and draft animals, were owned by the APC's, and the peasants could still retain a small plot of land. After communization, all the properties of the APC's were converted into the collective ownership of the communes, and peasants' private plots, house sites, and other means of production which had been retained by peasants were also handed over to the communes.[9] *Hung Ch'i* on 1 September 1958 approvingly stated that in many communes the "last vestiges of private ownership" were removed, and "in certain aspects, things had gone beyond the stage of collective ownership."

Understandably, peasants were discontented, and incidents of sabotage occurred in several provinces.[10] Overzealous local cadres also confiscated the private property of peasants—including bicycles, watches, and radios—and aroused great anxiety among the peasants. The editorial in *Hung Ch'i* on 16 September, designed to refute "rumors" spread by "class enemies" that all private property would become public, instructed the cadres in unequivocal terms that certain categories of private property, like small strips of land by the side of houses, and a small number of fruit trees as well as small livestock, and personal property such as home furnishings, clothing, bedding, and items such as bicycles, watches, and radios should not be touched.

In spite of this injunction, many local cadres proceeded to confiscate not only peasants' private plots but also their personal property.[11] Domestic sideline occupations, too, were widely suppressed on the pretext that peasants would have little time for anything other than collective work. The closure of rural markets also had an adverse impact: there were severe shortages of pigs, poultry, vegetables, and fruit as well as such items as straw sandals, coir brooms and raincoats, bamboo hats and baskets.[12] Since the APC's had to turn over all collectively owned properties to the communes as "shares," some cadres took the lead in distributing APC properties and reserve funds among their members before their APC's were merged into the communes.[13] In other cases, cadres and peasants of the wealthier APC's demanded that all APC's contribute equal "shares" to the communes. The tendency toward "departmentalism" shown by these cadres and peasants led the CC to issue repeated warnings that "education in the Communist spirit should be given to the cadres and masses." The party exhorted them to "accept the difference (in shares) with an easy conscience," not to "settle every small item of accounts or to square everything, and not to haggle over minor matters."[14]

In the fall and winter of 1958 there was a widespread practice called "one equalization and two transfers" [yi-p'ing erh-t'iao]. In many places cadres which may have taken too literally the propaganda promoting the rapid transition to Communism equalized the income of each peasant and transferred properties of wealthier production brigades (equivalent to former APC's) to other brigades, sending the labor force of one brigade to work for other brigades without compensation. Although the morale and incentive of peasants in the wealthier brigades were seriously affected, this practice was not corrected until the spring of 1959.[15]

The system of distribution in communes, which had important implications for peasants' incentives, evoked a great deal of discussion within the party during the autumn and winter of 1958. In the Peitaiho proceedings, according to Vice-Premier Li Hsien-nien, "some comrades" (presumably more radical elements) proposed a system of "eating rice without pay" (a free grain supply system).[16] Initially, the party appeared to have rejected that proposal; the editorial in the People's Daily of 4 September indicated that free supply of grain would have to be postponed to the distant future. The Peitaiho Resolution, which was made public on 10 September, cautioned cadres not to hurry the change from the original system of distribution (payment according to hours and workdays) to "avoid any unfavorable effect on production."

In spite of this injunction, the supply system was introduced during September in a number of provinces.[17] Some cadres in the provinces were anxious to exceed even that swift pace set by the party leadership in the advance to Communism. On the other hand, one suspects that the impetus may have been given by the radical elements in the party, including Mao himself. Mao, in a tour of Anhwei, was quoted on 16 September: "Since one commune can put into practice the principle of eating rice without pay, others that possess the equal conditions can do the same. Since rice can be eaten without pay, clothing can be had without pay in future."[18] This was no formal directive, but for cadres in the provinces, anything Mao said would probably have the same or even greater effect.[19]

The rationale for adopting the supply system was complicated. In practical terms, the existing system of distribution tended to favor families with a strong labor force or with better skill; most of these probably belonged to middle and upper-middle peasants. It also created inequalities between peasants. The supply system would favor peasant households with a small labor force, most of whom could probably be classified as poor or lower-middle peasants—those who were dependent on the assistance of the party and were regarded as the party's allies in the communization campaign. Ideologically, the supply system, embodying the Communist principle "to each according to his need," was an advance beyond the socialist principle of "to each according to his work," and thus appealed to enthusiasts who wanted to effect the fast transition to Communism. In addition, there was a romantic yearning for the return to Yenan experiences, when the Chinese Communist supply system provided free food and goods to their cadres and troops in base areas.[20]

All of these reasons were articulated by Chang Ch'un-ch'iao in an article in *Chieh-fang (Liberation)*, the semimonthly theoretical organ of the Shanghai Party Committee.[21] The article also advocated total restoration of the Yenan supply system and complete abolition of the current wage system, which Chang termed "unequal" and "bourgeois." Wu Leng-hsi, former director of the New China News Agency, claimed that the basic ideas of Chang's article had been expressed by Mao at the Peitaiho Politburo Conference.[22] Wu also said that Mao ordered the reproduction of Chang's article in the *People's Daily* and personally wrote an accompanying "Editor's Note" basically affirming the theses of that article.[23] (It is significant that in 1975, unhappy with wage differences in China, Mao has renewed his call for changes in the remuneration and distribution system and that Chang, in strong support of Mao, has published a signed article in the April 1975 issue of *Hung Ch'i* to attack the bourgeois rights.)

In October and November, the problem of wages and supply was roundly debated, and different shades of opinion were expressed in both the *People's Daily* and *Hung Ch'i*.[24] Although the *People's Daily* did not come out editorially in favor of any particular solution, allegedly a result of inner-party dispute,[25] there were many enthusiastic reports on the free supply of grain in the provinces, and a "half supply, half wage system" was almost universally adopted throughout China.[26] In some provinces, such as Honan, the list of free supply items even included clothing, medical care, maternity benefits, education, wedding and funeral expenses, and recreation, in addition to food.[27] In this particular province, the percentage of the total commune income allocated for distribution (both supply and wages) was also very low; whereas the central authorities reportedly stipulated that 60 percent of the commune incomes were to be distributed,[28] in many communes in Honan the distributed income constituted only 30 percent of the total commune income.[29]

In late fall 1958 problems and difficulties began to emerge, caused in part by certain irrational programs of the Great Leap Forward and communization and in part by the excesses of cadres at provincial and lower levels. Many communes were simply too big, and the cadres were incapable of coordinating the multiple enterprises within them. In Shantung, most communes existed without production plans, and the press urged each commune to map out a unified production plan.[30] The peasant masses, spurred on by the cadres, had worked excessively hard since the winter of 1957; after this year of sustained intensive mobilization, they—and even the cadres—began to suffer from physical exhaustion.[31] The excessive "Communist style" (*Kung-ch'an Feng*, a pejorative term), as manifested in the cadres' overemphasis on the accumulation and investment (in relation to distribution) of the supply portion of the distribution, and in the cadres' requisition of peasants' private property, denied many peasants material incentives to work and produce.

The Wuhan Plenum—A Tactical or Genuine Retreat

In mid-October 1958 such major economic officials of the regime as Li Hsiennien and T'an Chen-lin conferred with officials from the northern and northeast provinces at an important conference; they discussed many problems that had emerged in the communes.[32] In November many Politburo members went out to the provinces to determine what had gone wrong. Between 2 and 10 November Mao called a meeting in Chengchow which was attended by some of Mao's Politburo colleagues and a few regional party leaders.[33] Later (21–27 November) Mao called a meeting in Wuchang, whose participants included the first secretaries of the provincial party committees.[34] Formal meetings and informal consultations continued, and finally the enlarged Sixth CC Plenum was held in Wuhan from 28 November to 10 December 1958.

The Plenum was the party's first systematic attempt to come to grips with organization, management, administration, and distribution problems that had arisen as a result of the establishment of communes. In the preceding few months, the central authorities, aside from giving some broad guidelines, had failed to issue detailed, concrete instructions on these questions; the cadres in the provinces, relying on the "wisdom of the masses," had largely taken things into their own hands, and much confusion had arisen from divergent practices in different places. For example, before the Wuhan Plenum, there were two, or three, four, or even five administrative layers under different communes in different places in Liaoning Province, and these administrative layers were called by different names.[35] In Wuhan, the Chinese leadership stipulated a three-level administration for communes throughout China.

The Resolution on Communes adopted by the Wuhan CC Plenum on 10 December 1958 showed that the Chinese leadership had become more sober and realistic. An examination of the issues dealt with in the resolution also reveals the unmistakable interaction of ideological and practical considerations in the party's councils. It appears that the influence of the radical elements in the party had peaked in the fall of 1958 and began to decline with the Wuhan Plenum.

Section IV of the Resolution reaffirmed the rights of commune members to retain individual means of livelihood, small farm tools, and domestic animals and stated that commune members were again permitted to engage in small domestic sideline occupations, on condition that these would not harm collective production. To increase peasants' material incentives, the resolution cautioned that the scope of free supply should not be too wide;[36] it clearly stated that the system of wages paid according to work done must take "first place for a certain period" and "an important place over a long period" and warned that any negation of the socialist principle "to each according to his work" at this stage would "dampen the working enthusiasm of the people" (Section III). The Chinese leaders obviously were aware that Communism was not just around the corner,[37] and the Resolution addressed some "good-hearted" but "overeager" comrades, who had thought the process of building a socialist country in "fifteen, twenty or more years" was too slow, saying that "every Marxist must soberly realize that the transition to Communism is a fairly long and complicated process of development" (Section II).

In the months preceding the Resolution many cadres had apparently been harsh and "commandist" in pushing peasants into communes. On many occasions central authorities told local cadres to use persuasion; nevertheless, their exhortations for local cadres "to stand in the forefront of the communization movement," to get peasants "organized along military lines," and to enforce strict discipline in agricultural production may have encouraged cadres to place greater reliance on means more effective than persuasion—coercion. The Wuhan Resolution now admonished cadres to manifest a "comradely" style of work, with no rudeness or "commandism"; it also instructed them not to become "dizzy with success" and not to exaggerate (Sections VI and VII).

Finally, the resolution called on party committees at all levels to "make full use of the five months from December this year to next April" to check up on and consolidate the people's communes in their own areas. In the second half of November 1958, Shantung, Anhwei, Honan, and other provinces had already organized 10,000-man inspection corps to go into the rural areas to study problems in the communes; they discovered that the way income was distributed (too little was allocated for distribution and too much was distributed on the basis of free supply), the long hours of work, and cadres' "commandist" behavior had aroused widespread peasant discontent.[38] These findings presumably led the party leadership to prescribe the corrective measure contained in the Wuhan Resolution.

The most astonishing news of the Wuhan Plenum, however, was Mao Tse-tung's decision not to be a candidate for a second term as chairman of the PRC in the 1959 election, which had party approval. In the spring of 1959 the NPC elected Liu Shao-ch'i to succeed Mao.

There was speculation at that time outside of China that Mao was being pushed aside or demoted because of the failure of the commune movement. There is no solid evidence for believing this to be the case;[39] indeed, although Mao relinquished his government post, he continued to hold the chairmanship of the party—the real locus of the power in the regime. One major reason for Mao to give up the chairmanship of the government, a primarily procedural and ceremonial position, was probably Mao's desire to concentrate his attention upon "questions of the direction, policy, and line of the Party and state," as indicated in Peking's official statement.

Moreover, in stepping down Mao probably was trying to avoid the kind of successional struggle that occurred in the Soviet Union after Stalin's death in 1953. In a speech in October 1966, Mao himself alluded to this:

> For considerations for the security of the country and in view of Stalin's experience, two lines [of leadership] were arranged—I was on the second line and other comrades on the first. . . . I was on the second line, I didn't take charge of the daily routine. Many things were done by others in the hope that this might increase their prestige, so that when I go to see God the country won't receive such a shock [as it may otherwise]. . . . [T]o divide the Standing Committee [of the Politburo] into the first and second lines and to let them take charge of the Secretariat was my idea.[40]

The division of the Politburo Standing Committee into "two lines" of leadership—the first at the "operational" level and the second at the policy level—in the 1950s (probably during the Eighth Party Congress in 1956) was, according to Mao, his way of training the "revolutionary successors." The elevation of Liu Shao-ch'i to the chairmanship of the PRC can thus be seen as a step to ensure that Liu would succeed Mao when he died and would settle the succession issue when Mao was still alive.

Mao's decision to step down as head of State in favor of Liu, however, certainly cannot be considered politically innocent and entirely free of other political motivations. Being sensitive to the successional struggle in the Soviet Union after Stalin, Mao may have been attempting to avoid any denunciation of his own leadership by some Chinese leaders after his death by installing one top CCP leader who had his utmost confidence and who could be relied upon to continue the course of Chinese revolution which he had chartered. Up to 1958–59, Liu was certainly this man.[41] It is also possible that in the winter months of 1958–59 Mao anticipated opposition to his leadership as a result of his Great Leap and communization programs, therefore he stepped down as head of state in favor of Liu in the hope that he would deflate his opposition and strengthen his support from Liu.[42]

In any case, the election of Liu Shao-ch'i in the NPC session in April 1959 did surprise many people. Some observers outside China had predicted that Marshal Chu Teh, then vice-chairman of the Republic, would succeed Mao, and reports reaching Western diplomatic sources in Peking had indicated that Chu Teh was an active "candidate" for the post.[43] The elevation of Liu Shao-ch'i to chairmanship of the PRC, even though it was merely a ceremonial post, gave him tremendous prestige and signaled to the party ranks that he was second in command and Mao's designated successor.

Anna Louise Strong, a veteran American Communist residing in China at that time, visualized the communization campaign as a battle—a sudden push ahead, a retreat for consolidation, and then another advance. She described the communization campaign of the summer and fall of 1958:

> Any swift advance, in battle or social organization, produces rough edges. The foremost troops outrun the main force and take posts where the new front cannot yet be stabilized.... But the drive has natural limits and a pause comes for regrouping. The general staff must be ready to fix the new front line forward which the main forces may quickly advance and which they can firmly hold. Some of the foreposts can be fortified, the rest drawn back for safety and the rear brought up. A new front is consolidated for some later advance.[44]

The autumn upsurge had pushed 99 percent of the peasants into communes —the "foremost troop" had outrun the "main force" and taken the posts which the main force could not hold. Thus the Wuhan Plenum was an occasion for consolidation. There is considerable basis of truth in Strong's observation. Late in 1958 the Chinese leaders had uncovered some problems through preliminary investigations, inspections, and various formal and informal meetings, and they then prescribed a period of five months in which to take corrective measures. However, there were no clear indications at that time that the Chinese leaders intended to backtrack from what they had done, nor did they appear to have foreseen or anticipated at the Wuhan Plenum the kind of social and economic crises into which China would soon be plunged.

In fact, at the Wuhan meeting the party continued to urge communes "to go in for industry in a big way" and optimistically put forward excessively ambitious targets for economic development in 1959. Steel output was to be increased from an estimated 11 million tons in 1958 to 18 million tons in 1959; grain output was to be increased from an estimated 375 million tons in 1958 to about 525 million tons in 1959. As it turned out, the party's "new front" was not consolidated and the party, instead of advancing, was compelled to retreat even further in 1959 and later.

Further Retreats

In the course of their checkups, the Chinese Communists began to uncover many serious problems in the communes. For example, in his "Investigation Report of the Humeng Communes," published in the *People's Daily* on 25 February 1959, T'ao Chu (first secretary of the Kwangtung Provincial Party Committee) denounced as undesirable one widespread practice among brigades and teams, who concealed their harvested crops from higher authorities and divided the concealed grain among their own members. He attributed this manifestation of "departmentalism" to the failure of the communes to take into account the differences between brigades and between teams when income was distributed. The communes were reportedly unable to provide unified production plans for their numerous brigades, work was assigned day by day, and the militarization of work methods resulted in inefficiency and waste of labor power. According to T'ao there was much discontentment with the mess halls and the new system of distribution under which malingerers and weak peasants now got the same food and benefits as hard and strong workers.

From the end of February to early March 1959, many Politburo members and provincial secretaries met quietly at Chengchow in an enlarged Politburo session—the Second Chengchow Conference—to review the state of communes and compare notes on their checkups.[45] They realized that something more than what was prescribed in the Wuhan Plenum had to be done to effectively cope with the defects they had discovered. After the conference, the party issued secret directions which instructed communes, among other things, to enforce a system of "three-level ownership, three-level accounting," with the brigade as the basic accounting unit.[46]

In the original commune system the commune owned all the means of production in its component parts (production brigades and production teams) and operated as the sole accounting unit to distribute income for all the commune members. Before the Chengchow revision, although the production brigade formed a business accounting unit, its gains and losses were pooled into those of the commune as a whole, and the brigade was not permitted to allocate its own resources; this fact had an adverse effect on the incentives of the brigades, particularly the prosperous ones. The transfer of the right of ownership back to the brigades (most of which were formerly advanced APC's, equivalent to a natural village in scope) and the move to make the brigade the basic accounting unit set the proponents of the original commune system back a long way; the transition to ownership "by the whole people" and to Communism was to be retarded further. In spite of the unfavorable ideological implications, however, the regime was compelled to attend to accounting and administrative problems at the commune level, and, particularly, to the discontent and slackened efforts on the part of the peasants in the brigades and teams who were now receiving insufficient incentives. The party also reprimanded overeager cadres for committing "one equalization and two transfers" and ordered them to return properties requisitioned improperly from brigades and teams and compensate the peasants for their losses.

By the second half of February greater emphasis was placed on establishing a system of "production responsibility."[47] Some authorities on production management were transferred from the communes down to the brigades and from the brigades down to the production teams. The brigades and the teams were required to fulfill their contracts and meet the quotas assigned to them, but they were allowed to manage their own production work. These were sensible administrative arrangements designed to restore morale and work incentives; however, ideologically they represented backsliding, showing that the "bigness" and "socialist" nature of the original commune system did not work. Target-setting had become more modest and realistic; both the *People's Daily* and *Hung Ch'i* recommended to commune cadres that targets be fixed in contracts at 15–20 percent below the highest level attainable to give production brigades extra incentives to work for bonuses.[48]

"The Whole Country as a Chessboard"—The First Attempt at Recentralization in the Spring of 1959

The 1957–58 decentralization, giving local authorities control of industrial construction and production, and the encouragement of local industries had given rise to some serious problems. The increased autonomy of the provincial authorities over the management of the economy correspondingly weakened the ability of the central authorities to plan, coordinate, and allocate resources. There was a strong tendency for provincial authorities and even communes to become self-sufficient, and this tendency toward autarky was fostered by a breakdown in the allocation system and bottlenecks in transport. Communes, in their efforts to "go in for industry in a big way," retained many superfluous materials.[49] Provincial authorities, attempting to build up comprehensive industrial complexes within their own provinces, had set up and expanded various industries, almost regardless of cost. As a result, many key raw materials were in short supply, the state's priority projects were adversely affected, and the situation was out of control.[50]

These developments greatly alarmed the central leadership, which now denounced the "departmentalism" of the provincial authorities. The party called for a return to centralized leadership in the development of industry and stressed the need for overall planning and better coordination in a *People's Daily* editorial, "The Whole Country as a Chessboard" (24 February 1959), which emphasized the need to distribute investment funds and construction projects around the country in an orderly way and to determine production targets and allocate raw materials according to a "single national plan." Probably in reply to criticism of inconsistency directed against the new line, the editorial asserted that centralized leadership as implied in the concept of "the whole country as a chessboard" did not contravene the policy of administrative decentralization and would not hamper local initiatives and flexibility. The editorial added: "Dispersionism and departmentalism violate democratic centralism and are contradictory to the spirit of the whole country as a chessboard."

In discussing problems of capital construction in an article in *Hung Ch'i* (1 March 1959), Ch'en Yun also had much to say about "the whole country as a chessboard." Ch'en emphatically stated that only when a national industrial complex had been built would it be possible to build regional industrial complexes and that only after regional industrial complexes had been set up would it be possible to establish industrial complexes in the provinces. Ch'en criticized provincial authorities for prematurely attempting to build complete, independent industrial complexes within their borders.[51] He termed these efforts "impractical," "harmful to the overall arrangement," "diluting the collective strength," and "retarding the speed of socialist construction," and he admonished provincial authorities to show their Communist spirit and to overcome departmental tendencies.

Ch'en Yun, who previously had misgivings about excessive decentralization, probably felt his earlier skepticism vindicated by the prevailing conditions. In the *Hung Ch'i* article, he virtually argued for recentralization. For instance, he proposed that a system of priorities should be instituted and the principle of a "chessboard" strictly observed. Construction projects were to be ranked in order of importance to the country according to "the purview of the central government"; materials, major equipment, and the labor force were to be uniformly controlled and allocated by concerned central government departments and provincial authorities to insure "first, the accomplishment of national plans and then, if there is a surplus, to carry out regional or local projects."

A similar proposal was expounded by Chou En-lai in his "Report on Government Work," which was delivered to the NPC in mid-April 1959. To guarantee proper fulfillment of planned targets, Chou stated, it was necessary to draw up "10-day, monthly, or quarterly time-tables" for the most important products or projects, and it was also necessary for leading organs of the central and provincial authorities to send inspectors to check on progress and quality.[52]

Some curiously contradictory overtones could be detected in Chou's speech. On the one hand, the speech contained many frank and realistic statements; it argued in favor of unified planning and coordination at the national level, further checkups and consolidation of communes, implementation of the corrective pressures decided upon in the preceding few months, adaptation of plans (targets) to objective realities, and the need to keep manpower engaged in agricultural rather than industrial tasks (agriculture should employ no less than 80 percent of the manpower). On the other hand, Chou also talked at length about the correctness of the 1958 "general line" and continued to call for another "great leap" in 1959 to achieve the fantastic targets set the previous December (525 million tons for food grain and 18 million tons for iron and steel).

The ambivalence of Chou's speech probably reflected the political and economic context of that moment. The Seventh CC Plenum had been held in early April in Shanghai, shortly before the NPC meeting. Some CC members who had had doubts about the overambitious targets for 1959 set at the Sixth CC Plenum the previous December proposed revising them downward. The CC was divided and the proposal was not approved.[53] Red Guard sources later reported that P'eng Teh-huai and Mao clashed in the proceedings; P'eng reportedly voiced opposition to Mao's "assuming command in person" and "discarding the Standing Committee of the Politburo," and, in return, Mao was said to have criticized P'eng.[54]

Apparently many top Chinese leaders were victimized by their own dramatic propaganda, as they daily assailed the public with inflated statistics. P'eng Teh-huai's account provides some clues to the confusion and bewilderment of the Chinese leadership during the last quarter of 1958 and early 1959:

> At that time, from reports sent in from various quarters, it would seem that communism was around the corner. This caused not a few comrades to become dizzy. In the wake of the wave of high grain and cotton output and the doubling of iron and steel production, extravagance and waste developed. The job of autumn harvesting was handled crudely and without consideration of cost, and we considered ourselves rich while actually we were still poor. More serious, in a rather long period of time, it was not easy to get a true picture of the situation. Even up to the Wuchang conference and the conference of secretaries of provincial and municipal Party committees in January this year [1959], we had still not been able to find out the realities of the overall situation.[55]

Other leaders felt the same way. Thus Teng Hsiao-p'ing instructed the State Planning Commission and the State Economic Commission to identify major problems and propose solutions and bring them to the following Central Work

Conference for discussion. He also ordered the New China News Agency to collect various data and information to make the top provincial leadership aware of the objective realities.[56]

Before long, however, the Chinese leadership, including Mao, grasped the seriousness of the problems confronting them and decided to make amends and slow the pace of the Great Leap. This was suggested in Mao's secret "Letter of Instruction" sent to the party committees at all levels down to the communes and production teams on 29 April 1959 through an inner-party communication medium, *Tang-nei t'ung-hsin* [*Correspondence within the Party*].[57] In the letter Mao admonished the cadres to be more modest and realistic in setting grain production quotas, to refrain from issuing impractical orders on matters such as close planting, and to speak the truth and not give false reports. He was well aware that low-level cadres were under immense pressures to falsify information because the high-level authorities bragged, applied pressure, and indulged in empty promises, and he specifically rebuked these erroneous leadership styles. The letter was significant in at least two ways. It shows that Mao had again switched to a conservative position, placing himself at the head of a more conservative consensus within the party. Moreover, by criticizing the work methods and manner of implementation, Mao intended to shift the blame for economic difficulties from the policy and the policy-maker to the cadres who improperly executed the policy.

The provincial secretaries' reaction to the low key sung by Mao was apparently mixed; some officials were dismayed or puzzled. Li Ching-ch'üan (the first party secretary of Szechuan who was promoted to the Politburo in May 1958 because of his enthusiastic support of the Great Leap programs), for instance, reportedly characterized the letter as "blowing a cold wind" and "making people waver at a crucial moment." In a meeting called to convey Mao's instructions to his own subordinates, Li allegedly warned lower officials not to "take a one-sided view of the letter and let peasants do what they like." To soften the negative impact of the letter, Li was said to have told secretaries of Special District and Municipal Party Committees to understand the letter "from the positive aspect" and allegedly refused to lower the high grain targets and change the rules for close planting (between 300,000 and 400,000 rice stalks per *mou*) set earlier by the Szechuan Provincial Party Committee.[58]

In any case, beginning with the Wuhan Conference, the party swung slowly but inexorably to the right. During the spring and early summer of 1959, the press criticized those tendencies that were closely identified with the Great Leap: too much reliance on mass enthusiasm and not enough careful and realistic planning and experiment; overestimating the capacity of the human will and subjective spontaneity while underestimating the importance of objective factors; overemphasizing speed and quantity at the expense of rising costs and lowered quality; exhibiting bureaucratism and commandism which were harmful to the cause of the party; and so on.[59]

As in 1956, the more radical elements of the party had overplayed their hand, and, in turn, the "conservatives" had much to criticize about "reckless advances." But one major difference between the debates in the summer of 1959 and those in the second half of 1956 is the fact that the disputes within the party in 1959 were not contained; rather they cracked open the party leadership.

The Showdown at Lushan

In early July 1959 an enlarged Politburo conference was convened at Lushan, a summer resort in the province of Kiangsi.[60] Attending the conference were important officials of the party, government, and the PLA, in addition to regular members and alternates of the Politburo. The tasks facing China's top leaders at Lushan required a comprehensive review of the Great Leap programs and the formulation of measures to cope with problems that had beset the national economy.

Most, if not all the participants were by this time well aware of the shortcomings of the Great Leap and were probably convinced that some revision of existing policy was inevitable. To the surprise and anger of Mao, however, many of his Great Leap policies came under direct frontal attack by a so-called anti-party group led by P'eng Teh-huai. This was the most serious opposition within the party that Mao had encountered since establishing himself as the undisputed leader of the CCP in 1942.

Before discussing the Lushan proceedings, P'eng's attack on the Great Leap policies must be placed in proper perspective. The background of the Army-party friction in the 1950s is a good starting point.

The PLA and the Party[61]

Party control over the army has been a strong tradition and accepted leadership doctrine for the CCP leadership. Since its inception in 1928, this system of party control has remained essentially unchanged in general outline, although parts of it have at times received more or less emphasis than others. However, the modernization of the PLA, the increasing emphasis on technology and modern warfare by those party officials in charge of military affairs, the rise of a young professional officer caste after the Korean War, and the adoption of the Soviet military experiences generated some unanticipated consequences. Under the vastly changed circumstances of the mid-1950s, the relevance of the pre-1949 revolutionary model, of the old procedures and practices regulating the army's internal and external social behavior, and of the Maoist military doctrines were increasingly questioned by many PLA men. In short, within the PLA there was a sense of impatience with the system of political control.

On numerous occasions the party displayed overt dissatisfaction over various "deviations" in the PLA; for instance, on 1 July 1958 the organ of the PLA charged:

> ...purely military views, warlordism, and doctrinaireism have revived among a part of the personnel. They assert that that collective leadership of Party committees is not adapted to the requirements of modernization and regularization. One-sidedly stressing the suddenness and complexity of modern warfare, they assert that the system of Party committees will impede the better judgement and concentration of command. They even openly advocate liquidation of the system of Party committee leadership. Further, they liquidated and restricted the activities of Party committees in leadership and political work.[62]

Several weeks later, the same paper also blasted those who advocated "technology first" and questioned the competence of political officers in military affairs:

> There are those who concentrate excessively on modernization, and advocate the weakening of party leadership, and try to weaken political work.... They pay lip-service to political leadership, but they believe that modernization is not related to and is in a different class from politics....[63]

Beginning in 1956, the party leadership attempted to rectify undesirable tendencies in the PLA through a rapid succession of campaigns. Political education was intensified for both officers and men; party committees in the PLA were rebuilt and strengthened; PLA officers' privileges were curtailed, and an "officer to the ranks" movement was launched. In spite of—or perhaps because of—these endeavors to strengthen political control and restore "revolutionary" traditions, the PLA's relationship with the party apparently deteriorated.

It is necessary to note that what the PLA objected to was not party control or party leadership per se, for, after all, the top leadership of the PLA consisted of party leaders; rather, what the PLA objected to was a series of specific measures which the party tried to enforce in the PLA. However, the PLA, as a distinct political group, also had its special interests. Many of the party leaders in charge of the PLA may have found that the logic of the special function of the PLA (e.g., national defense) and the special interests of their "constituents"—let alone personal ambition and other considerations—compelled them to resist or obstruct policies which they viewed as inimical to the PLA and to lobby for policies more in line with the interests of the army.

Consider the issue of PLA participation in the regime's various socialist construction campaigns.[64] The party claimed that "the PLA is the army of the people, it must regularly maintain close relations with the masses, and nourish itself with what is acquired from the struggle waged by the masses," and the party ordered the PLA to actively participate in and support socialist construction.[65] In January 1956, when the party's draft twelve-year agricultural program was launched, the PLA's Political Department drew up a twenty-article "Program for Participation and Support by Army Units in the Agricultural Cooperative Movement and Agricultural Production" by which the PLA would support the draft program with "practical action."[66] From 1956 to 1959, PLA units reportedly contributed "freely" 4 million, 20 million, 59 million, and 44 million workdays, respectively, to agricultural tasks such as sowing, harvesting, land reclamation, and irrigation work.[67]

By 1956, "a number of people [in the PLA] [took] the view that for the army to help the people in production and take part in certain social activities in leisure hours [would] hinder training."[68] The increasingly nonmilitary demands made on the PLA during the period of the Great Leap also increased misgivings and opposition within the PLA. As Hsiao Hua revealed:

> There is a definite conflict between participation in national construction and training in their respective demands for time.... Needless to say, as the Army is an armed combat organization, it must carry out its task as a "work force" in such a way that its task as a "combat force" is not affected.... It is obviously wrong to think that, as no war is going on at present, the Army should exert itself mainly in the direction of production construction, or to set too high requirements concerning the Army's participating in construction and labor production. Anything that may weaken war preparations and training tasks is impermissible.[69]

It was this kind of divergence between military priorities and other (political, economical, and ideological) priorities that was at least partly responsible for the growth of friction between the party and the PLA leadership. During 1956 and 1959, the cumulative effect of the numerous nonmilitary demands made on the PLA either brought latent opposition into the open or created new opposition. On the eve of Army Day (31 July 1958), Marshal Chu Teh, apparently speaking on behalf of the party, severely indicted some elements in the PLA in an article entitled "People's Army, People's War," in the *People's Daily*:

> There are people who advocate an exclusively military viewpoint, who have a one-sided regard for military affairs and look down upon politics,

have a one-sided high regard for vocation and technique and look down upon ideology, have a one-sided high regard for the role of individuals and neglect the collective strength of the Party and the masses. They only deal with tactics and technique, but not strategy; they only want the army but neglect the function of masses of the people; they only pay attention to national defence, but not to the significance of economic construction to national defence.

The appointment of senior provincial party secretaries to serve in the capacity of first political commissars in the military regions or military districts to strengthen party control—a trend that became discernible particularly at the height of the Great Leap—was an indication of the party's doubts about the PLA and its leadership. Marshal Lin Piao, who had been inactive for some time, was elevated to the Politburo Standing Committee and made a vice-chairman of the party in May 1958; this was generally attributed to Lin's improved health. However, Lin's promotion also may have been an early sign of Mao's displeasure with the performance of Minister of Defense P'eng Teh-huai, who was in overall charge of the regime's military affairs, and of contemplation or preparation on Mao's part for changes in the top leadership of the PLA.

In fact, immediately after this session of the Party Congress, the MAC held an enlarged meeting, from 27 May to 22 July, to undertake a comprehensive critical review of the current PLA line of military construction with the aim to "destroy slavish ideology" and "bury dogmatism." In a speech to the group-leader forum of the conference on 28 June, Mao severely criticized the PLA efforts at emulating the Soviet experiences and rebuked General Hsiao K'o, then vice-minister of defense and director of the Military Training Department, for having warlord mentality imbued with "bourgeois ideology, dogmatism, and feudal ideology."[70] Although Mao did not single out P'eng Teh-huai for criticism, there seems to be little doubt that the meeting and Mao's speech were directed against P'eng inasmuch as he was then in charge of the regime's overall military affairs and should be responsible for the shortcomings in the PLA work.

Evidence contained in the secret PLA *Bulletin of Activities* makes it clear that army-party relations worsened partly because of the differing priorities of the PLA and the party leadership, and partly because some politico-military policies which the party emphasized were opposed by leaders of the army. For instance, P'eng and some other PLA leaders were obliquely or directly accused of advocating an "erroneous military line," opposing army participation in production, favoring "unreasonable military systems and formalities," neglecting party branches at the company level, and preferring foreign military theory to Mao's own doctrines.[71]

It is argued, however, that in themselves these reasons were insufficient for P'eng to challenge Mao at Lushan in 1959; another important factor that motivated P'eng's "anti-party" activities, for which he was ultimately dismissed, is believed to have been a "fundamental disagreement over policy towards the Soviet Union with special military implications."[72] According to Gittings, an expert on Chinese military affairs, P'eng fought for military collaboration with the Soviet Union and may even have been willing to sacrifice some measure of control over China's military affairs to secure continued military assistance, possibly including nuclear weapons or technology.[73] The Chinese leadership, however, chose a different course of action, one which subsequently led to the rupture of military arrangements between China and the Soviets, reportedly on 20 June 1959,[74] less than two weeks before the Lushan Conference.

If P'eng's attack on the Great Leap policies and the commune system were motivated primarily by his dissatisfaction over China's policy toward the Soviet Union and the military relations between the two nations, as Gittings argues, P'eng did not show it at Lushan, judging by the evidence available. Information released to date suggests that he chose to act as a member of the Politburo speaking exclusively on economic matters, rather than as a dissatisfied minister of defense pleading a case on military grounds. P'eng and other PLA leaders had legitimate reasons to be concerned with the regime's economic policies. The food of the PLA had to be supplied by the peasantry, soldiers were recruited largely from the countryside, and the livelihood of the peasants had a direct impact on the troops' morale. Besides, the PLA had to help maintain peace and order, and if the peasants should revolt, it would doubtless have the ultimate responsibility for suppressing them. There is little doubt that P'eng and his colleagues were dissatisfied with the economic policies of the Great Leap and communes; his dissatisfaction was clearly reflected in a poem he composed in the fall of 1958:

> Grain scattered on the ground, potato leaves withered;
> Strong young people have left to smelt iron, only children and old
>   women reaped the crops;
> How can they pass the coming year?
> Allow me to appeal for the people.

The Challenge of P'eng Teh-huai

Considerable information, considered credible, has now come to light concerning the party's meeting at Lushan in 1959. It indicates that when the enlarged Lushan Politburo Conference started, the participants were divided into small discussion groups according to regions, and P'eng Teh-huai was assigned to the northwest group.[75] A movement to critically review the shortcomings of the so-called Policy of the Three Red Banners had been fostered by an anti-leftist campaign preceding the conference, as noted earlier, and the ground rules calling for "big democracy" at the Lushan Conference seem to have created a somewhat uninhibited atmosphere.[76] Many party leaders may thus have been encouraged to speak out more boldly than they had before. It was probably under these circumstances that Marshal P'eng Teh-huai, who reportedly attacked the Great Leap and the communes in unequivocal terms in the discussions with the northwest group during 3–10 July, set out his criticisms of current policies in a lengthy "Letter of Opinion" which he presented to Mao and distributed to the members of the Lushan Politburo Conference on 14 July.[77]

While praising the achievements made as a result of the general line and paying lip service to Mao's brilliant leadership, P'eng's attack was a strong one even though it was couched in careful terms. P'eng blamed the party leadership for being misled by an "air of exaggeration" to overestimate grain production at the time of the Peitaiho Conference in the previous year and to conclude that food problems were settled. He criticized the party leadership and, by implication, Chairman Mao, for prematurely diverting the peasants' efforts to adjust to the needs of industrial production. The party's understanding of the development of iron and steel production was characterized, in P'eng's words, by "serious one-sidedness." P'eng also criticized the party for its alleged lack of careful and realistic planning and for its failure to specify concrete and practical measures in many areas. P'eng chided "not a few comrades" who, misled by the achievements of the Great Leap and the ostensible enthusiasm of the mass movement, had developed pronounced leftist tendencies and wanted to "jump into Communism in one step."

Leftist tendencies, in P'eng's opinion, were manifested in the premature negation of the principle of "exchange at equal values," in the premature raising of the slogan "eating rice without pay," in the blind propagation of certain techniques without proper advance testing, and in the substitution of the principle "politics in command" for certain economic laws and scientific rules. He held that "petty-bourgeois fanaticism" was responsible for these leftist deviations. P'eng is alleged to have said that "if the Chinese workers and peasants were not as good as they are, a Hungarian incident would have occurred in China and it would have been necessary to invite Soviet troops in."[78]

He was not the only top leader who criticized the "Three Red Banners." Chang Wen-t'ien, a candidate member of the Politburo and the senior vice-minister of foreign affairs, is also reported to have made several speeches attacking the Great Leap.[79] Some evidence suggests that P'eng and Chang may have acted in coordination. On 24 April 1959 P'eng led a "military good will" mission to the capitals of the Warsaw Pact powers, and on the same day Chang left for Warsaw to attend a meeting of the foreign ministers of the Warsaw Pact powers in an observer's capacity. Before and during the Lushan Conference, both P'eng and Chang reportedly had many contacts, and, according to P'eng's confession,

... both comrade Chang Wen-t'ien and I harbored the right-leaning thought and also had discussed things in advance. Furthermore, because both of us harbored prejudice and malcontent against comrade Mao Tse-tung, this urged us to attack the Party together. Although no concrete plan had been mapped out for such an attack, yet it was quite obvious that we two shared the same feelings and worked in coordination.[80]

According to P'eng's own account and other sources, Huang K'o-cheng, a member of the CC Secretariat and chief of staff of the PLA, Chou Hsiao-chou, a candidate member of the CC and first secretary of the Hunan CCP Committee, and a number of other high-ranking party officials (to be identified later) also spoke against the Great Leap and the communes. Besides criticizing the Great Leap and commune policies, Chou Hsiao-chou was alleged to have given P'eng detailed information on the defects of these policies and supplied P'eng with the "ammunition" to attack the party's "Three Banners."[81]

P'eng Teh-huai and his "anti-party clique" may not have intended to overthrow Mao's leadership in the party, as charged. What they in fact attempted was the modification of the party's Great Leap policies. Yet if their endeavors had been successful, Mao's prestige and authority, which were now so closely associated with those policies, would undoubtedly have been tarnished severely.

Having received P'eng's "Letter of Opinion" on 17 July, Mao reportedly spoke for some forty minutes at the Lushan Conference on 23 July.[82] He is said to have declared that he welcomed criticism but that he hoped his audience would "withstand" criticism and not be misled or discouraged. He refuted the charges that the party was divorced from the masses and that the institution of communization, public mess halls, and other mass movements constituted "petty-bourgeois fanaticism"; he claimed that 70 percent of the 500 million rural population actively or tacitly supported the party's programs.[83] Mao asserted that the major shortcomings of the Great Leap were manifested only in "the shortages of vegetables, hairpins and soap, and a tense market situation for a certain period." He admitted that "petty-bourgeois fanaticism" had stirred up the "wind of Communism" for a few months, and for this he held cadres at the *hsien* and commune levels responsible; but he stated that this mistake had been rectified and had in fact had a "favorable" educational effect.

At one point Mao virtually made a self-criticism. He said that he was personally responsible for what went wrong during 1958–59 because he did not understand economic planning and took too much into his own hands. At the same time, however, he implicitly blamed this on the failure of Premier Chou En-lai to assume his responsibilities, and he criticized Vice-Premier Li Fu-ch'un and the State Planning Commission, which Li headed, for not having done the necessary planning work.

Mao confessed that he had originated the idea for a mass movement to smelt iron and steel, which subsequently involved 90 million people in a battle on the "steel" front. In a rather sad and emotional way, he lamented that he had no male offspring, "one son having been killed [in the Korean War] and the other being mad." Quoting a curse uttered by Confucius,[84] Mao attributed his family tragedy to divine punishment for initiating policies that had caused much human suffering.

Some of Mao's attackers may have been silenced or restrained by Mao's speech. In P'eng Teh-huai's own account, he and Chang Wen-t'ien felt "tense" after listening to Mao's talk, and Chang remarked that "things could not be discussed further."[85] P'eng, however, was determined to press his case further, to "clear up some vague ideas."[86]

Whether P'eng had organized the dissidents in advance to launch co-ordinated attacks in the proceedings of the Englarged Politburo Conference at Lushan is debatable, but it is an intriguing question. The party subsequently condemned the activities of the "anti-party clique" headed by P'eng as "purposive, prepared, planned and organized," and P'eng did not totally deny these accusations.[87] That P'eng's views were not without sympathetic hearers in the CC was barely noted by a passage of the resolution which observed that his activities "could and did mislead a number of people." Some observers now believe that P'eng launched his attack at Lushan with the fore-knowledge and support of Russians, having been in personal contact with Khrushchev himself.[88] P'eng and his "anti-party clique" do appear to have done some lobbying behind the scenes before and/or during the Lushan Conference, and many high-ranking PLA officers were reported to have endorsed P'eng's "Letter of Opinion."[89] In addition, a number of Politburo members and lesser personalities apparently supported P'eng initially but did not hold out to the end.

Lin Po-chu, member of the Politburo and a patriarch figure of the party, may have supported P'eng from beginning to end.[90] Information made available since the initiation of the Cultural Revolution claims that Marshal Chu Teh, a member of the Politburo Standing Committee and a vice-chairman of the CC, also sided with P'eng Teh-huai and voiced criticisms of the Great Leap.[91] Mao's sarcastic references to the "Military Club" [*Chun-shih chu-lo-pu*][92] and his alleged remarks that he would organize guerrilla bands "if the PLA chooses to follow P'eng Teh-huai"[93] suggest that a large number of PLA leaders were behind P'eng.

Was Mao overwhelmed by his critics at the enlarged Politburo Conference —as Khrushchev was by his opponents in June 1957?[94] Mao may have felt that his leadership position was endangered by the opposition of some of his powerful associates. As the debates between his attackers and defenders continued indecisively to the end of July, Mao reportedly sent for other CC members who were not then present at Lushan and whose support he badly needed[95]—a maneuver which General Huang K'o-cheng is reported to have labeled "calling for reinforcements."[96]

On 2 August Mao turned the enlarged Politburo Conference into a formal CC Plenum, a forum he may not have planned at the outset. Apparently confident of the support that would come from his "reinforcements," Mao's tone changed markedly; he now accused his critics of being "right opportunists" and described their criticism of his policies as the "frantic attack of right opportunists on the Party."[97] Although P'eng Teh-huai and his "anti-party" group were subsequently defeated, the defeat came only after what a *Red Flag* editorial labeled a "test of strength."[98]

From the context of events before the Lushan meeting and developments thereafter, the position taken by various CCP leaders (other than those who have already been identified) during the Mao-P'eng confrontation seems to be of interest, but precise information on this subject is not available. Lin Piao is reported by the Red Guard sources to have vigorously defended Mao's policies, and there is no reason to believe otherwise. Despite the charges to the contrary since the GPCR, Liu Shao-ch'i did throw his support behind Mao.[99] Premier Chou En-lai apparently went along with Mao too. Ch'en Yun, a vice-chairman of the party and a member of the Politburo Standing Committee, had frequently championed a conservative economic line and was a critic of Mao's Great Leap programs, yet he failed to back P'eng at Lushan. In fact, Ch'en was not even present at the Lushan proceedings; according to one Red Guard report, he was on sick leave in Manchuria when the Lushan meeting was in session and he expressed surprise and regret when informed of P'eng's activities.[100] Other top economic officials, including Li Fu-ch'un, Li Hsien-nien, and Po I-po, who had expressed misgivings on Mao's economic measures in 1956, "have now stood firm," in Mao's own words, and did not join forces with the P'eng group;[101] as noted before, they had shifted ground in 1958 to support Mao's Great Leap programs.

In view of the fact that P'eng received support from only one of the seven members of the Politburo Standing Committee (Marshal Chu Teh) and was opposed by four other members (excluding Ch'en Yun and Teng Hsiao-p'ing, who were not present), that he received support primarily from the military officials, and that he failed to recruit to his side more civilian party officials, and particularly those in charge of the economy, his opposition to Mao seemed to lack a broad political appeal. Even though a large number of the PLA leaders backed him, P'eng's challenge to the party leadership, when short of threat or use of naked force (of which P'eng was presumably capable, since both he and his collaborator, General Huang K'o-cheng, had the authority to deploy troops), and when the arena of conflict was the CC where Mao and his supporters had greater control, could result only in defeat.

During the last part of the Lushan Plenum, after being subjected to criticisms and denunciations, P'eng made a formal self-examination.[102] In addition to confessing errors in his attack on the Great Leap and Mao, P'eng also admitted a number of mistakes he had made in the 1930s and 1940s, all of which involved disputes and conflicts with Mao. P'eng is alleged to have said he had adopted a "quarrelsome attitude" toward Mao and for a long time had had "an extremely wrong personal prejudice" against Mao. He also gave a brief account of his relations with Chang Wen-t'ien and Huang K'o-cheng.

On 9 September 1959 P'eng sent a letter to Mao in which he alluded to his past mistakes, regretted his failure to follow Mao's guidance in the past, regarded Mao's "well-intentioned and sincere criticism as a blow" to him, and asked for permission to leave Peking to visit communes so that he might steel and remold himself ideologically "in the collective life of the working people."[103]

P'eng, Chang Wen-t'ien, Huang K'o-cheng, and Chou Hsiao-chou were later officially named members of the "anti-party" clique and were dismissed from their executive posts in the government and the party, but they retained their membership in the party's Politburo and CC.[104] Meanwhile, Lin Piao, Lo Jui-ch'ing, and Chang P'ing-hua replaced P'eng, Huang, and Chou as minister of defense, PLA chief of staff, and first secretary of CCP Hunan Committee, respectively. The surprisingly lenient treatment meted out to P'eng and the other members of the so-called anti-Party clique for their severe offense—challenging the party's leadership—may well have been due to the fact that they commanded substantial support.

With regard to policies concerning the communes, the Lushan Plenum reaffirmed changes in the structure of the communes that had been previously made in the Second Chengchow Conference in March:

> At the present stage a three-level type of ownership of the means of production should be instituted.... Ownership at the production brigade level constitutes the basic one. Ownership at the commune level constitutes another part.... A small part of the ownership should also rest in the production team.[105]

Thus the production brigade would recover the land, animals, and implements that had been taken over by the communes since the fall of 1958, and they again would be the basic accounting unit, whereas the powers at the commune level were drastically curtailed. The Plenum also admitted the exaggeration in the 1958 agricultural production figures released earlier and scaled down the claimed output of grain and cotton from 375 and 3.5 million tons to 250 and 2.1 millions, respectively; it also lowered the 1959 target figures about 10 percent.

The Aftermath of Lushan

Following the Plenum, an extraordinary nationwide campaign was launched against rightist tendencies and "rightist opportunists"; it was accompanied by passionate reaffirmation of the Great Leap policies and exaggerated adulation of Mao's leadership.[106] In many provinces, meetings of provincial and lower-level cadres were held to wage struggles against "rightist thinking, rightist sentiments and rightist activities"; "rightist opportunists" and those imbued with "rightist thinking" were exposed and subjected to serious criticism.[107]

As a result, many party officials, fearing guilt by association with the "rightist opportunists," were reluctant to implement a number of the more practical policies introduced in late 1958 and early 1959. Trends toward realism and pragmatism that had clearly emerged since the spring of 1959 were suddenly halted. In some respects, the momentum of the campaign actually made the Party swing again to the left.

For instance, the system of "production responsibility"—farm output quotas based on individual households [pao ch'an tao hu]—which had been acclaimed in the spring, was now denounced by the party as "reactionary"; it was held responsible for having degraded the "big and public" features of the commune system and having converted it into a "small and private" system.[108] Whereas in April and May 1959 Mao (in his Letter of Instruction) and the propaganda organs had placed great emphasis on modest target-setting and on "leaving a margin," three months later the party condemned this sober attitude as "conservatism."[109] This radical "backlash" also resulted in a nation-wide drive to restore commune mess halls and in a frenzied but abortive attempt to set up urban communes.

It subsequently became clear that many party officials were victimized by the "anti-rightist opportunist" campaign.[110] A number of officials disgraced —dismissed or demoted from their original posts—were PLA leaders who either had close working relationships with P'eng Teh-huai or were otherwise implicated in the P'eng affair.[111] The first category included at least T'an Cheng, director of the PLA General Political Department and a secretary of the Central Secretariat, Hung Hsueh-chih, director of the PLA General Rear Services Department, and Hsiao K'o, director of the PLA Military Training Department.[112] The second category included at least Teng Tai-yuan, commander of the Army Railway Corps and minister of railways, Teng Hua, commander of the Shengyang Military Region, and a few civilian officials such as Hsi Chung-hsun, vice-premier and secretary-general of the State Council, and Chang Chung-liang, first secretary of the Kansu Provincial Party Committee.[113] Since all of these PLA leaders were also members of the CC, they may have been the members of the "military club" that Mao referred to in the 1959 Lushan Conference.

Most of the other officials adversely affected by this campaign did not appear to have close relationships with P'eng Teh-huai; they probably held "rightist" views similar to P'eng's, however; that is, they criticized Great Leap and commune policies.[114] Two vice-premiers, Ch'en Yun and Teng Tzu-hui, also slipped into relative obscurity during this period, but available evidence is insufficient to establish their connections with P'eng Teh-huai's "anti-party" activities. Teng Tzu-hui, like Ch'en Yun, had consistently advocated conservative economic policies in the mid-1950s, and he is believed to have been a critic of Mao's Great Leap and commune programs, but his eclipse seemed to precede the Lushan showdown. Sources that became available during the Cultural Revolution indicated that most of the victimized officials in the "anti-rightist campaign" of 1959 were provincial and lower-level cadres.[115]

Whereas the Communist regime ended its first decade of rule on 1 October 1959 with many splendid achievements to its credit as well as serious problems to solve, the regime's second decade was beset with enormous difficulties from the outset.

Severe drought struck many provinces in 1960. In addition, a typhoon and floods, said to be the worst in fifty years, hit twenty provinces, causing very serious damage.[116] Approximately 900 million *mou* of farmland in the country were reported hit by floods, drought, wind, insects, or waterlogging; of this total, some 300 million *mou* of land were severely hit, with some areas suffering complete crop failures.[117] The calamities in 1960 were particularly disastrous since "they came on the heels of the heavy natural calamities which swept over 600 million *mou* of farm land in 1959."[118]

Overambitious Great Leap and commune programs, coupled with cadres' excesses and aggravated by severe natural calamities, resulted in acute food shortages, serious economic disarray, widespread popular discontent, and a serious loss of moral among party and military cadres. In many places calamities precipitated peasant revolt. In Honan, the cradle of the commune system and showcase of many radical Great Leap policies in 1958, for instance, there was widespread starvation and "armed banditry"; desperate peasants who had access to arms (because they were militia members) organized themselves into strong armed bands in Hsinyang, Kaifeng, and other special districts, causing social disorder, and the Chinese authorities had to launch an all-out military and political effort to "suppress the counter-revolutionaries and pacify the countryside," inflicting numerous casualties.[119]

5

Retreat from the Great Leap Forward and the Reorganization of the Commune System

The Fate of the Twelve-Year Agricultural Program

The 1956–1967 National Program for Agricultural Development, which had rarely been mentioned since the fall of 1958, came back into the news in the spring of 1960. The party reiterated the need to "fulfill" the goals of the program, even though at the height of the exhilaration (and exaggeration) of the Great Leap, many of these same goals had been reported to have been surpassed. In April 1960 the NPC formally enacted the Twelve-Year Agricultural Program.[1]

T'an Chen-lin, appointed a vice-premier of the State Council in 1959, made a report on the program.[2] T'an claimed that in 1959 504 *hsien*, 28 percent of the total 1786 *hsien* where grain is grown (or in terms of acreage, 286,700,000 *mou*, 24 percent out of a total 1,200,000,000 *mou*), had achieved or surpassed the program's targets for per *mou* grain yields (400, 500, or 800 catties); 204 *hsien*, 20 percent of 1027 cotton-growing *hsien* (or in terms of acreage, 36,484,000 *mou*, 42 percent of a total of 85,000,000 *mou*), produced over 60, 80, or 100 catties of ginned cotton. In 1959 there were more hogs, it was claimed, than the target figure for 1962. The average annual income of each member of the rural population in 1959 was claimed to have reached about 85 *yuan*, which was close to the average income level (80 *yuan* per person) of the prosperous middle peasants before agricultural cooperation, and it was reported that income reached the target set for 1962 ahead of time.

The "four pests" (rats, sparrows, flies, and mosquitoes) had allegedly been eliminated; and some diseases like smallpox and bubonic plague had already been virtually wiped out or effectively controlled. T'an further claimed that the irrigated areas in China had increased by 550 million *mou*, and that 610 million *mou* were now able to withstand drought for 30, 40, or 70 days, as called for by the program. Soil improvement had covered 450 million *mou*, or 60 percent of the total 700 million *mou* of lowlands subject to waterlogging. The area sown to better seeds reached 1.8 billion *mou*, or 80 percent of the total sown area.

Despite these extravagant claims, the 1959 and 1960 harvests were poor;[3] food shortages were severe, and Peking was forced to import grain from

Western countries to feed its population. Floods and droughts disproved the claim of "achievements" made in the irrigation and water conservancy campaign of 1957–58. Even by T'an's own admission, the efforts to increase grain and cotton—the core of the program—had achieved only a limited success; less than one-fourth of the *hsien* had met the targets for average annual per *mou* output of grain and cotton, and most of these areas had a high-yield record before.[4]

In his speech to the NPC meeting, T'an appealed to the nation to exert greater effort to fulfill the program two or three years ahead of schedule. The party's organ endorsed the call in an enthusiastic editorial;[5] immediately thereafter, cadres in the local areas were directed to mobilize the peasants to work for another great leap in agricultural production. The renewed emphasis on the program in the spring of 1960 by the CCP leadership, particularly the party's attempt to achieve the goals of the program ahead of schedule, was ill-timed, for the prevailing conditions of China's agriculture should have induced the policy-makers to prescribe more realistic measures, as they actually did subsequently, rather than attempt another leap.

The CCP leadership failed to take timely actions to salvage the agricultural crisis in the spring of 1960 for several reasons. In the wake of the Lushan affair, the leadership was apparently impelled to defend and reaffirm the correctness and validity of Mao's policies in order to uphold and restore Mao's prestige and authority, which had been tarnished at the Lushan meeting. The renewed campaign to push the twelve-year agricultural program, in addition to the urban communes, should be viewed in this political context.

It is possible that Nikita Khrushchev's attack on Mao's policies also caused the CCP leadership to react very emotionally and a bit irrationally. Khrushchev's open derision of the peoples' communes in his conversation with United States Senator Hubert Humphrey in December 1958 and his disparaging remarks about the commune system (which could only be taken as direct criticism of the communes in China) in a public speech in Poland in July 1959—both events publicized by the American press—apparently infuriated Mao.[6] A proud and stubborn man, Mao may have become more defiant in the face of Soviet criticism and more doggedly determined to prove the correctness of his policies, regardless of the consequences.[7]

A remark attributed to Liao Lu-yen, minister of agriculture in 1961, provided a clue to the thinking of the CCP leaders and highlighted their defiant mood in 1960: "That things have now come to such a pass is largely attributable to the years before and after 1960 when fired by the passion of the moment and irritated by Khrushchev's rebuke, desperate steps were taken to tackle things in a big way, regardless of consequence."[8] In the fall of 1962, Mao made an admission: "There was a period of time in 1960 when this problem [rectification of errors in agriculture and industry] was given insufficient attention."[9] Mao attributed this to the "advent of revisionism which pressured us, and our attention was shifted to opposing Khrushchev."

If the foregoing analysis has any validity, then it can be said that the actions of the Chinese leaders in the spring of 1960 were influenced at least partly by emotions aroused by Khrushchev's criticism of Chinese policies. This kind of human element is not always easy to discern and document, but it must be present in any policy-making process, since policy-makers are of course subject to emotion and human failings. Policy decisions therefore seldom result from rational deliberation alone, often reflecting the human ingredients.

The Twelve-Year Agricultural Program that was enacted by the NPC in April 1960 was identical with the revised version of October 1957 (which is less ambitious than the 1956 and 1958 versions), except the sparrow, which had been found to be the natural enemy of insect pests harmful to fruit trees, was replaced by bedbugs in the list of "four pests," as proposed by T'an Chen-lin. Even though the APC's had been supplanted by the communes, articles on and references to that institution remained intact, and the existence of the communes was not noted in the program. This may have been a case of legislative sloppiness by the NPC, but it also highlights the role of the NPC in China's policy-making process: the NPC was a rubber stamp; it simply put a seal of approval on the bill as presented by the party leadership without even making technical amendments. Interestingly enough, T'an Chen-lin, throughout his speech to the NPC, failed to make any references to the second revised draft of the program which had been approved by the second session of the Eighth Party Congress in May 1958. The 1958 version, reflecting the radicalized atmosphere of that time, contained higher targets and a number of new goals.

The 1956–1967 National Program for Agricultural Development fell into oblivion after April 1960, and little has been said about it.[10] The top policy-makers in the party, including the original proponents of the program, may have lost interest in it, for in fact it had proven to be a failure.

The approaches toward increasing agricultural production—massive mobilization of labor, intensive application of labor, greater emphasis on structural change and ideological motivation—which had been symbolized by the program and advocated by the radicals of the party, including Mao, proved counterproductive in many respects. The stress on ideological motivations and attitudinal change underlying Mao's almost mystic faith in the malleability of human nature was a poor substitute for incentives and resulted in serious peasant discontent. The structural changes in agriculture brought about by the establishment of first the APC's and then the communes, and the utilization of these control mechanisms to effect maximum resource mobilization in the rural areas, had achieved only a limited success and in fact by 1959 had reached the point of diminishing returns.

Many Chinese Communists by now were well aware that sustained agricultural growth would require major technological reforms in agricultural production. The Twelve-Year Agricultural Program was a step in that direction, but the measures it stipulated were insufficient and inadequate because they emphasized labor-intensive techniques and underestimated the need for capital investment.

In conjunction with technical improvements in agriculture, an intensive campaign had been conducted during 1958 and 1959 to implement the "eight-point charter for agriculture," which had been introduced by Mao in 1958 after he "applied the advanced principles of agricultural sciences and summarized the rich experience of the peasant masses in the practice of production."[11] The excessive and indiscriminate application of techniques such as close planting and deep plowing, in disregard of divergent soil and climate conditions, not only wasted large amounts of labor but contributed substantially to crop failures in many localities.

In light of the relatively labor-intensive farming techniques practiced in China even before collectivization, increasing agricultural production required greater capital investment in agriculture. Throughout the 1950s, however, Peking had been unwilling to divert significant amounts of investment resources, heretofore channeled into industry, and particularly heavy industry, to agriculture, and state investment in agriculture had been relatively small.

In 1958, the radical group in the party had formulated a new approach to agricultural investment: local resources and labor were mobilized on an unprecedented large scale to work on labor-intensive investment projects such as irrigation, flood control, and land reclamation and to raise unit yields in agriculture through close planting, deep plowing, and the like, as well as to promote the expansion of small-scale local industry. The party planned to use the output of these local industries to satisfy rural demands for manufactured consumer goods, tools, agricultural machinery, and other requisites of farm production, while most of the modern sector's product would still be saved and used for its own continued growth. This was one of the main ideas behind the slogan "walking on two legs"—a strategy of dualism designed to bring about the simultaneous development of agriculture and industry.[12] Instead, however, this strategy helped to produce the profound economic chaos in China between 1960 and 1962.

The "Agriculture-First" Strategy

Confronted with acute food shortages and serious economic dislocation, and shocked by the sudden withdrawal of Soviet technicians from China, the party was compelled to scrap the Great Leap, modify the commune system, and improvise measures to cope with the serious crisis from the second part of 1960 on. The regime's past policies, which had been riding the tide of the "anti-rightist" campaign, momentarily swung to the left after the Lushan Conference. Gradually, however, the prevailing crisis situations swung the pendulum back to the right as the "anti-rightist" campaign ground to a halt and "conservative" elements steadily regained a predominant voice in the councils of the party.

In the summer of 1960 a Central Work Conference was convened at Peitaiho, to be attended by all provincial first party secretaries. The proceedings of the conference were not given publicity in the media, but subsequent events indicate that the conference must have decided to change drastically the priorities of economic policy—above all by mobilizing available resources to support agriculture. Fragmentary evidence suggests that it was at this conference that the party discussed or decided upon the reestablishment of six CC regional bureaus (which had been abolished in 1954)[13]—a decision which was announced by the party at its Ninth CC Plenum in January 1961.

After the work conference, the shift toward an "agriculture-first" policy became clearly discernible. In an article in *Hung Ch'i* in September 1960 Liao Lu-yen, minister of agriculture, stressed that agriculture must be the foundation of the national economy and that the basic policy of the party must be to take agriculture as the "foundation" and industry as the "leading factor."[14] It is true that the agriculture-first policy had been discussed by various CCP officials since the fall of 1959 and that Mao was credited with initiating the policy in 1959,[15] yet the policy had not been seriously implemented up to the summer of 1960. In the last four or five months of 1960, "all the people to agriculture and food grains" became a nation-wide slogan in China, and concrete steps finally were undertaken to implement the new line.

The policy of making the production brigades the major units of ownership, accounting, and production in the communes was reiterated and reemphasized in the public media. For instance, on 16 September 1960 an editorial in the Canton *Nan-fang Jih-pao (Southern Daily)* instructed cadres to thoroughly implement the new policies and encouraged the production brigades and commune members to undertake "multiple enterprises" and subsidiary occupations in addition to growing food grains; the proceeds of such diversified undertakings were to be kept by the brigades for their members. Apparently in answer to charges that these measures represented a backsliding from the original system of ownership at the communal level, the same editorial disclosed that "On the basis of the experiences gained in the People's Communes over the past two years, our Party has recently set the period of transition from the system of ownership by the production brigade to the system of ownership by the People's communes at five years." In other words, the retreat was to be only temporary; when the situation improved, the party would advance once more.

It appears that many of the pragmatic and rational measures introduced since the spring of 1959, including the agriculture-first policy, had not been effectively implemented, and in some cases had not been implemented at all. The campaign against the "rightist opportunists" launched after the Lushan Plenum and the efforts to reassert the validity of Mao's policies were one of the major factors, as previously indicated. In mid-May 1960 T'ao Chu stated the following:

> Recently, the bud of rashness has again appeared in some places. There is a desire to speed up the transition of the system of ownership by the brigades to the system of ownership by the communes. Communes have improperly used the material resources and labor power at the lower levels to strengthen the commune-owned economy. Some other people go to the other extreme; they think that failure to observe totally the principle of exchange at equal value and distribution according to work means equalitarianism.[16]

In many localities the party's distribution policy (to each according to his labor, and payment based mostly on wages), which was clearly stipulated after the Wuhan Plenum in December 1958, was not implemented. In Kwangtung, "idealist" and extremist cadres claimed that "the more the payment in supplies and the less the payment in wages the better." The cadres added meat, fish, and fruit to the five basic items originally stipulated for free supply.[17] In the distribution of free rations, these cadres gave the same treatment to men and women, old and young, and people capable and incapable of heavy physical labor. According to *Nan-fang Jih-pao* (2 September 1960), "more and more goods are supplied while less and less is paid in wages, and some brigades cannot afford to pay wages for a long time. . . . [This] dampens the people's enthusiasm for production to a considerable degree." In the suburbs of Peking, cadres wanted to distribute less and retain more, because "the availability of more funds on hand can help develop the economies of the communes at a faster pace."[18]

Many cadres resisted the party's policies because their own interests were involved. Since the transfer of rights of property ownership and production authority from the communes to the brigades would inevitably reduce the power of cadres at the commune level, some cadres refused to carry out the changes, justifying their action on the grounds that the changes would "affect the unified leadership of the communes and hamper the fulfillment of production plans."[19]

Huang Huo-ch'ing, first party secretary of Liaoning, blamed the "departmentalism" of cadres in Liaoning, one of China's most important industrial provinces, for the failure to implement effectively the party's "support-agriculture" policy:

Not all the comrades grasped the great significance of industrial aid to agriculture as a measure to speed up agro-technical reform. Some functionaries of certain factories and mines showed rightist conservatism and departmentalism; they maintained that fulfillment of their production tasks came into conflict with the aid to agriculture. Some regarded the communes as "poverty-stricken relatives" and held that industrial aid to agriculture was "one-way help" and "additional burden."[20]

In an editorial of 17 July 1960 the *People's Daily* emphatically instructed industrial enterprises to forgo other considerations and promote the idea that agriculture should be the foundation of all things, giving top priority to supporting agricultural production.[21] And in November 1960 the party dispatched a secret "Twelve-Article Urgent Directive on Rural Work" to cadres at all levels, instructing them to carry out the provisions of the directive thoroughly and faithfully.[22]

The directive reduced the scope of power at the commune level and enlarged the authority of the brigades to make them economically and administratively viable units (articles 1 and 3). It demanded that cadres stop trying to equalize peasants' income by transferring workers without regard for the quality of work that resulted, a policy known as "one equalization and two transfers" [*yi-p'ing erh-t'iao*].[23] It returned to peasants private plots, which had been confiscated in 1958, and permitted peasants to undertake family sideline occupations (article 5) and sell their products in the rural trade fairs (article 10). The directive also stipulated that more collective income should be allocated for distribution and less for accumulation and that more than 70 percent of payment to the peasants must be in wages.

The restoration of private plots and the opening of free markets were the only provisions that had not been announced before the directive. The fact that the party deemed it necessary to reiterate the other provisions and disseminate new instructions in the form of an "urgent directive" was a further indication that policies had not been earnestly implemented by lower cadres up to that time.

China's New Economic Policy

In January 1961 the CC, which had not met formally since August 1959, held its ninth plenary session in Peking. This was a very critical moment—the food supply crisis was at its worst, and shortly before, in the summer of 1960, the Soviet government had torn up many agreements concluded with Peking and had withdrawn from China Russian experts and technicians along with the blueprints of unfinished industrial plants and factories.

The CC reaffirmed the agriculture-first policy pursued since the summer of 1960:

> The whole nation in 1961 must concentrate on strengthening the agricultural front, thoroughly carry out the policy of taking agriculture as the foundation of the national economy and of the whole Party and the entire people going in for agriculture and grain production in a big way, step up and support agricultural production by all trades and professions.[24]

Although the communique of the plenum did not specifically mention the twelve-article urgent directive, the plenum presumably discussed and approved it. The new agricultural policy was combined with an industrial policy based on "readjustment, consolidation, filling out and raising standards." In concrete terms, the new line meant that economic activities had to be readjusted, capital investment had to be cut back, consumer goods industries and industries that could produce goods of value to agriculture were to be favored, and quality rather than quantity was to be emphasized. The communique also formally announced two other important party decisions: to establish six regional CC bureaus and to intensify the rectification campaign, which was already in progress.

Recentralization and Rectification

The regional bureaus were established, in the words of the communique, to "strengthen leadership" of the party center over party committees in the provinces. In the course of decentralization and the Great Leap, provincial authorities, and particularly provincial party committees, had acquired greater power (at the expense of central government ministries) in the management of economy. Provincial party secretaries, supposedly agents of the central party control, tended to become identified with local and particularistic interests and to become preoccupied with problems of their provincial administration, so that many displayed "dispersionist" and "departmental" tendencies.

In the spring of 1959, as noted previously, heavy emphasis had been placed on the principle of "the whole country as a chess board," and some measures were put forward to recentralize and tighten control over the provincial authorities. The establishment of the new regional party bureaus was a further step toward recentralization—it would provide the central leadership with an additional organizational instrument to supervise the provinces more closely.[25] These regional bodies, judging from their institutional setup, were expected to perform major economic functions on a regional basis, in addition to their regular political functions.[26]

In 1961 the regional bureaus were assigned the priority task of supervising the ongoing rectification campaign. In the words of the communique of the Ninth CC Plenum, the rectification campaign was to be carried out throughout the country "stage by stage" and "area by area," to help cadres "raise their ideological and political level, improve their method and style of work and purify the organizations" by cleaning out the extremely few bad elements who had "sneaked into party and government organizations."

The party publicly admitted that counterrevolutionary incidents had taken place and that the party's functionaries had committed various unlawful acts. The primary targets of the 1961 rectification campaign, however, were obviously the "leftist" elements who were described by the communique as "good-willed and well-intentioned" but without a "sufficiently high level of ideological consciousness." They were accused of lacking sufficient understanding of the distinction between socialism and Communism and between the socialist ownership by the collective and the socialist ownership by the people as a whole, of the three-level ownership in the People's Commune with the brigades as the foundation, of the principles of exchange of equal value and to each according to his work. In short, the campaign was directed against "leftist tendencies."

Some of the more radical provincial-level proponents of the Great Leap were disciplined in the course of the rectification campaign. Wu Chih-p'u, Honan's first party secretary who had played a leading role in the communization movement in 1958 and ruthlessly implemented many Great Leap programs (which had helped cause widespread famine and peasant revolt) in 1958–60, was demoted to second party secretary in 1961 and was later transferred from his post in Honan.[27] Chang Chung-liang, first party secretary of Kansu, was purged in 1961, partly as a result of serious famine and starvation that had occurred in that province in 1959–60.[28] The 1960–61 purge or demotion of province-level first secretaries in Chinghai (Kao Feng), Shantung (Su Tung), and Anhwei (Tseng Hsi-sheng) also may have been related to "leftist" mistakes they committed during the Great Leap period. These three first secretaries had played a leading role in the 1958 purges of "conservative" officials in their provinces, and when these officials won reinstatement their prosecutors' positions were undermined.

Changes in the Original Commune System

After Mao relinquished the chairmanship of the Republic in April 1959, and particularly after the Lushan confrontation in which Mao's prestige and self-esteem were badly scarred, he appeared to gradually withdraw from active participation in the policy-making councils. Either because Mao was unwilling to preside over the liquidation of his utopian programs or because of opposition pressure within the leadership or preoccupation with the widening Sino-Soviet rift—or, more probably, a combination of all these factors—the reclamation of the disasters of the Great Leap and commune programs was largely carried out by Mao's colleagues. They were known to have sought Mao's final approval of major policy decisions,[29] yet Mao no longer introduced them, as he often had in the past (this may be less true in regard to key foreign policy issues, such as Sino-Soviet relations). The importance of the function of policy initiation should not be overlooked; those who initiate are in a better position to define problems, present alternatives, and structure choices. Since Mao no longer initiated policy, he lost a large measure of control over the decision-making process.

For instance, when Mao convened a Central Work Conference at Canton in March 1961 to consider, among other things, the reorganization of communes, the chairman discovered to his chagrin that, without his prior knowledge, Teng Hsiao-p'ing, the party's general-secretary, had already made certain key decisions on the plan concerning the reorganization, which was drafted under Teng's supervision.[30] Presented with the fait accompli, an irritated Mao asked sarcastically: "Which Emperor has decided these?"[31] Even though Mao expressed displeasure and scolded Teng for making decisions in advance of the meeting, he was apparently compelled by the prevailing instability of the rural economy to sanction or at least acquiesce to the plan. The meeting subsequently approved the "Draft Regulations on the Rural People's Communes."[32] It seems that when Mao no longer initiated policies and withdrew from active participation in policy-making process, those who controlled the CC Secretariat increased their power since they were in a position to exercise control over the agenda of the party conferences and over the preparation of policy proposals for deliberation at the conferences.

The new sixty-article draft redefined the nature of the communes as well as their ownership and distribution systems, watering down the original (1958) concept considerably. It clearly stipulated the various functions and division of labor among the three layers of the commune, a move intended to check abuses by officials at the commune level; it also decentralized most powers previously vested in the commune level, passing these powers down to the brigade and team levels—which in a sense was a concession to "localism."

In addition to reducing the size of the communes and brigades and prescribing that 5 percent of the farmland in a given commune be set aside for private plots, the sixty-article "Regulations" elaborated on the measures provided for in the twelve-article "Urgent Directive" and presented them in a more detailed and formalized manner. Party committees at all levels were instructed to discuss the new document and to insure its thorough understanding and faithful implementation by cadres.

Reaction to the sixty articles was apparently mixed, with most cadres and soldiers in the PLA reportedly warmly supporting the party's new policy. However, the party felt compelled to reply to "some cadres and soldiers" who articulated misgivings such as the following: Do communes still have "ten superiorities"? Is there still any difference between the people's communes and the advanced co-operatives when big communes are being divided into small ones and earnings are made proportional to labor, and when self-retained land continues to exist?[33] Where did the "five styles" come from? Why is it that the wind of "Communist style" has been blowing all over the nation?[34] And some cadres questioned whether the promotion of private plots, family sideline occupations, and free markets "would affect collective production and develop capitalism."[35]

Party propagandists were at pains to defend the party leadership from the obvious charge of having turned backward and being inconsistent. They maintained that the "Three Red Banners" (the general line for socialist construction, the Great Leap, and the communes) were still correct, and that the measures prescribed in both the twelve articles and the sixty articles had been consistently advocated by the CC and Chairman Mao, and they blamed the difficulties of the national economy on overzealous cadres who had stirred up the "communist wind" (i.e., excessively stressed egalitarian tendencies) as well as on cadres' mistakes in the execution of party policies. However, this line of argument was hardly convincing; in fact, not a few cadres reportedly attributed responsibility for the "five styles" to the central authorities, and some even said that without the commune there would be no "five styles."[36]

The CCP leadership clearly began to display a greater sense of realism. Expertise, rational planning, efficiency, and pragmatism were again emphasized.[37] The critics of the Great Leap policies who had been sidelined in 1957–58 and again in 1959–60 during the anti-rightist-opportunists campaign were gradually rehabilitated—a tacit admission that these critics had been at least partially correct.[38]

In 1961, a number of Politburo members went out to rural areas to undertake what were called "squatting investigations" [*tun-tien tiao-ch'a*]. For instance, Liu Shao-ch'i spent forty-four days in three communes in three different *hsien* in Hunan from 2 April to 15 May 1961.[39] Also in April and May, both Teng Hsiao-p'ing and P'eng Chen spent one half month in the rural areas of Hopei carrying out intensive investigation.[40] Ch'en Yun was in the suburbs of Shanghai for three weeks from June to July.[41] Even P'eng Teh-huai and Chang Wen-t'ien reportedly went out to rural areas to undertake "investigation and study."[42]

The obvious change in the top leaders' working style probably resulted from their realization that they had not received accurate information about China's political and economic conditions, which they needed to form correct workable decisions. Hence the Central Work Conference in March 1961 instructed leading cadres at all levels to conduct personal "investigation and study" to help them understand the situation on a firsthand basis.[43] The study of "On Investigation Work," an article written by Mao in 1930, was now required reading for cadres.[44]

In conducting these "squatting investigations" top leaders stayed in a given locality long enough to closely survey the grassroot conditions. Thus they obtained information that might otherwise have been concealed by lower-level officials or might have failed to reach the top levels of the party through official channels of communication. This subject is discussed further in Chapter 7.

A Realignment of Political Forces

The political climate in China had changed considerably since the second half of 1960. The CCP leadership manifested anxiety and a sense of urgency, in contrast with an earlier attitude of resolution and defiance in the face of internal difficulties and Khrushchev's criticism. Officials who had been most closely linked with the Great Leap and commune policies at the provincial level, and probably at lower levels, were disciplined, and critics of these policies who had been demoted or dismissed reasserted themselves and succeeded in "reversing the verdict" [fan an], that is, they won reinstatement.

Moderate policy views were now well received in the party. Several of the top economic officials of the regime, including Ch'en Yun and Teng Tzu-hui, who were known for their conservative views and criticisms of the Great Leap and commune policies and who had been politically inactive during 1958–60, must have felt vindicated by the prevailing conditions. From 1961 on men like Ch'en Yun and Teng Tzu-hui reemerged on the political scene and actively participated in the policy-making processes.[45] Members of the Politburo who previously had been inclined toward the "radical" group and supported Mao's economic measures, including Liu Shao-ch'i, Teng Hsiao-p'ing, and P'eng Chen, also changed their stance. Whether the lessons they learned from the failure of the Great Leap had honestly changed their minds or whether they were merely being opportunistic cannot be determined. In any case, political forces in the party underwent a gradual, almost imperceptible realignment from the second half of 1960, with the advocates of the moderate policy in charge of the party's policy-making councils.

The conversion of Liu Shao-ch'i into an ardent advocate of moderate policies in the early 1960s was both interesting and politically significant. Before the Cultural Revolution in the second half of the 1960s, Liu had generally been regarded by Western observers as a hardliner.[46] In the two speeches Liu made in 1957 and 1958, he showed himself to be a staunch supporter of the Great Leap and closely identified himself with Mao.[47] Liu succeeded Mao as chairman of the republic in April 1959, apparently because he had Mao's confidence, for although he had differed with Mao on the questions of collectivization in 1955 and the "hundred flowers" in 1957, when the party decision was made, Liu went along with Mao.

The Great Leap and commune programs generated harmful consequences by the time the Lushan Conference was called into session in July 1959, and Liu had begun to doubt their value. The Lushan meeting was originally intended to be a working conference to deal with defects in the economy and modify some of the radical policies that were being pursued, but Peng Teh-huai's attack on Mao upset the original plan.[48] Although Liu threw his support to Mao in Mao's confrontation with P'eng Teh-huai,[49] he was apparently preoccupied with the economic dislocations caused by the Greater Leap. The accusation that Liu hoisted the "ensign of combating the Left deviation" at the Lushan proceedings and schemed to "tamper with the already prepared summary of the meeting and turn it into an anti-Left document"[50] suggests that Liu was concerned with curbing excesses of the Great Leap.

Mao's withdrawal from active participation in the leadership in 1960 put Liu squarely in the forefront. The responsibility for overcoming the economic disaster now rested on the shoulders of Liu, who now was working closely with Ch'en Yun, Teng Hsaio-p'ing, P'eng Chen, and Po I-po. During his seven-week squatting investigation in Hunan Liu probably got a clearer picture of the state of the economy; in May 1961, in fact, he warned a Central Work Conference that the true situation in the nation was worse than had hitherto been realized by the leadership.[51] From that time on, Liu apparently became more outspoken in his criticism of the defects of the Great Leap and the commune programs and supported a series of measures that were long advocated by the "conservative" group in the 1950s. Although Liu's criticisms were largely directed against the cadres and their implementation of Mao's programs, Mao probably saw these criticisms as aimed at himself. The disagreement between Mao and Liu grew steadily; although there was no open and complete break between the two until 1966, in retrospect, it is clear that Liu's "rightist deviations" of 1961–62, which were criticized by Mao in the summer of 1962, undermined Mao's trust in Liu.

P'eng Chen also had generally been regarded as a "hardliner"; in 1957 he, like Liu Shao-ch'i, was said to have taken a tough position toward the party's liberalization policy.[52] Nevertheless, there is evidence to suggest that P'eng had become critical of Mao's leadership by 1961, if not earlier. It was the *Peking Wan Pao* [*Peking Evening News*] and *Ch'ien Hsien* [*Front Line Monthly*], both controlled by P'eng Chen's Peking party apparatus, which in 1961–62 published the satirical political essays entitled "Evening Chats at Yenshan" and "Three Family Village," which subtly attacked the Great Leap.[53] It is difficult to believe that this was done without P'eng's approval—or at least knowledge.

In 1961 P'eng reportedly established an "Office of Policy Research" under the Peking Municipal Party Committee and staffed it with his own "brain-trusters."[54] This office is said to have conducted a series of intensive investigations into the commune system, industry, finance and trade, and other fields. *Peking Jih-pao* also claimed that P'eng Chen organized his aides to undertake a critical examination of orders and directives issued by Mao personally and by the central authorities during 1958–60, allegedly for the purpose of uncovering errors and mistakes committed by Mao.[55] The authenticity of these reports is difficult to judge, but the evidence does suggest differences evolved between P'eng Chen and Mao.

The realignment of party leaders as well as Mao's loss of his magic grip on some of his followers had crucial implications for policy-making. In the second half of 1961, the party further reorganized the commune system, introducing revisions more extensive than those presented earlier in the sixty articles.[56] The size of the communes, brigades, and teams was reduced, and the teams (generally twenty to thirty households in size), which had already been granted greater powers in managing production, were made the basic "ownership" as well as "accounting" units of the communes.[57] Thus the widely propagandized "big and public" features of the 1958 commune system could no longer be found in the drastically reorganized communes.

In December 1961 the party formulated another major policy document— the seventy-article "Regulations on Industry, Mines and Enterprises"—to try to cope with serious disarray and pressing problems in industry.[58] This document was drafted under the close supervision of Vice-Premier Po I-po, assisted by Sung Jen-chiung (then the first secretary of the CCP Northeast Bureau and during 1956–60 minister of the Third and Second Machine-Building Ministries), and was approved by a Politburo meeting chaired by Liu Shao-ch'i.[59] As noted earlier, since the Ninth Plenum in January 1961 the party had emphasized an agriculture-first strategy and had reshuffled its priorities of economic development; the seventy-article "Regulations" now outlined concrete and systematic measures to implement these broad policy lines.[60]

The provisions of this document clearly indicate that many policies associated with the Great Leap were reversed. Except in a few specially regulated cases, all capital construction programs were to be terminated (articles 3 and 4) and all industrial enterprises set up in haste and in defiance of economic rationality (i.e., those suffering financial loss) were to be closed down (article 9). Industrial production was to be reoriented toward serving the market— that is, satisfying consumer demands (article 2). Workers' material incentives were to be more carefully studied, the piece-wage system was to be restored, and better working conditions and other welfare benefits were to be provided (articles 25, 26, 27, 67, 68, and 69). Rationality, rather than mass movement, became the dominant theme of industrial management; factory managers (*ch'ang chang*) were once again given production authority, and the importance of engineers and technicians in production processes was reemphasized (articles

30 and 52). Quality was favored over quantity, and a system of strict quality control was established (articles 34, 35, and 36).

The Reversal of Verdicts

In January 1962 an enlarged Central Work Conference was held in Peking, attended by 7000 people, most of them provincial and lower-level officials. The immediate objective of the conference was to prepare a comprehensive review and a "summing-up" of the regime's policies of the previous three years.[61] This occasion was similar to the Lushan Conference in 1959, for again the Great Leap and commune programs received heavy criticism.

The consensus that emerged from the January 1962 enlarged Central Work Conference apparently was that the party, without abandoning the slogans of the Great Leap, would have to scrap its ambitious programs and pursue a rational and pragmatic course of economic development. Liu Shao-ch'i apparently set the tone of the conference when he said that the catastrophic failures of the Great Leap were "three parts natural calamities and seven parts human failings" [san-fen t'ien-chai, ch'i-fen jen-ho] and admonished party officials to learn the necessary lessons from these painful experiences.[62] Among the top leaders only Chou En-lai and Lin Piao came to Mao's defense.[63]

The rehabilitation of the critics of the Great Leap and the victims of the 1959 "anti-rightist-opportunist" campaign, which had expanded gradually after late 1960, apparently was an important item on the agenda of the conference. Subsequently Red Guard sources reported that the official line adopted by the party was, in Liu Shao-ch'i's words, that "those who shared P'eng Teh-huai's views, provided that they had not colluded with foreign countries, would be permitted to reopen their cases."[64] The matter, however, did not rest there; those who had done the purging or had benefited from the purging seemed to have resisted the move, and the top leaders were compelled to speak out again.[65]

The following statement by Liu Shao-ch'i, republished in 1962, deserves to be quoted at length; it unmistakably reflects a negative attitude toward the "anti-rightist-opportunists" campaign and the attendant purges:

> When opportunist ideas and differences of principles arise in the Party, we must, of course, wage struggles to overcome those ideas and errors of principle. This definitely does not mean that when there are no differences of principle and no opportunist ideas in the Party, we should deliberately magnify into differences of principle divergences of opinion among comrades on questions of a purely practical nature.
>
> Comrade Mao Tse-tung has said: "... *the Party must on the one hand wage a serious struggle against erroneous thinking, and must on the other hand give the comrades who have committed errors ample opportunity to wake up to*

their errors. This being the case, excessive struggle is obviously not appropriate."
   The "Left" opportunists were clearly wrong in their attitude toward inner-Party struggle. According to these almost hysterical people, any peace in the Party was intolerable—even peace based on complete unanimity on matters of principle and on the Party line. Even in the absence of any differences of principle in the Party, they deliberately hunted out targets, dubbed some comrades opportunists and set them up as "straw men" to shoot at in inner-Party struggle. They thought that such erroneous struggle and such shooting at "straw men" were the magic formula for developing the Party and achieving victory in the revolutionary fight of the proletariat.[66] (Emphasis added)

Although this statement (based on a statement which first appeared many years earlier) restated ideas Liu had preached since 1939, the new messages contained in the revised text (the italicized sentences) are important, especially in the new political context of 1962 when Liu was attacking the "left" opportunists. We need not accept at face value charges recently leveled against Liu that the republication in 1962 of his 1939 treatise, *How to be a Good Communist*, represented an open challenge to Mao. Nor can one assume that the charges made by Maoist propagandists that Liu was behind the "anti-party" group at the 1959 Lushan meeting and later actively sought P'eng Teh-huai's reinstatement are necessarily correct.[67] Rather it is more likely that Liu's promotion of a policy of rehabilitation was motivated by his genuine concern over the harmful effects generated by the excessive purges and struggles that had taken place in the party. Undoubtedly, at a time of serious national crisis, the party needed to unite its members and mobilize all of its talent to cope with the various problems it faced. Acting as a "unifier" in the party, Liu could and must have enhanced his image and prestige among many party members.

In 1961–62 P'eng Teh-huai was dramatized as the contemporary "Hai Jui" in a historical play, *The Dismissal of Hai Jui*, which was performed throughout China and was well received by China's attentive public. Wu Han, a vice-mayor of Peking and a well-known playwright and historian, pictured Hai Jui as a righteous Ming Dynasty minister who returned land to peasants and brought oppressive and corrupted officials to justice only to be cashiered for his efforts through court intrigue. In the play, the demand was made that the unfair dismissal be reversed so that this "righteous official" could again serve the people.[68] The contemporary meaning of the drama was apparently not lost on Mao; in fact, he said that "The crux of the 'Dismissal of Hai Jui' is the question of dismissal from office; the Emperor Chia Ch'ing dismissed Hai Jui from office. In 1959 we dismissed P'eng Teh-huai from office and P'eng Teh-huai is 'Hai Jui,' too."[69]

Undoubtedly Mao was irritated, to say the least, by the demands being made to reinstate critics of Great Leap policies; and he may have been particularly embittered by open sympathy being shown to Marshal P'eng Teh-huai by the intellectuals. During 1961–62, T'eng T'o, a party secretary of the Peking Municipal Committee, Wu Han, and Liao Mo-sha, director of the United Front Work Department of the Peking Party Committee, together or separately wrote many essays "in the guise of recounting historical anecdotes, impartial knowledge, telling stories and cracking jokes" that surreptitiously mocked Mao, criticized his policies, pointed to his errors, and subtly praised his critics.[70] In domestic policy, for example, they satirized at the "follies" of the Great Leap, characterizing it as "boasting," "indulging in fantasy," and "substituting illusion for reality." In foreign policy, they indirectly ridiculed Mao's famous slogan "The East Wind Prevails over the West Wind" as "great empty talk."

The economic crisis in 1960–62 had come to vindicate P'eng Teh-huai's earlier criticisms and had made him a martyr in the eyes of some Chinese. Mao had been proven wrong, and his prestige appears to have been tarnished, judging from the writings of Wu Han, Teng T'o, and other intellectuals in the party.[71] Perhaps emboldened by the evidence of sympathy for the cause he fought for, in June 1962 P'eng produced an 80,000-word "petition" to appeal for a "reversal of verdict" in his case.[72] Mao may have been further distressed by P'eng's action, which suggested that P'eng had not learned his lesson after the Lushan incident and had not repented.

The Role of Ch'en Yun[73]

In the party's further swing to the right in 1962, Ch'en Yun appears to have been a major moving force behind many policies of economic rationalization. Supporters of Mao now claim that Liu Shao-ch'i admits that he "trusted Ch'en Yun too much and listened to his views too one-sidedly." Under Liu's aegis, Ch'en was appointed head of a "Five-Man CC Finance and Economy Group" established in 1962 to take charge of the regime's overall economic and financial policies.

From 21 to 23 February 1962, Liu Shao-ch'i reportedly convened an enlarged session of the Politburo Standing Committee in the west chamber of Chungnanhai, Peking (often referred to by the Red Guard press as the "West Chamber Conference") to follow up various suggestions made at the January CC Work Conference. The West Chamber Conference, which was also attended by the regime's top economic officials, reportedly heard Ch'en Yun present a report on "Current Financial and Economic Conditions and Certain Measures." Excerpts reported in Red Guard publications indicated that Ch'en Yun's indictment of the Great Leap was merciless but that his diagnosis of the state of the national economy was essentially realistic; he prescribed drastic measures to salvage the situation.

Teng Tzu-hui also is said to have discussed and recommended Anhwei's "responsibility farm system," under which each peasant household was to assume responsibility for agricultural production on the farmland contracted to it. The conference, according to Liu Shao-ch'i's account, "did not oppose this proposal." A "certain comrade," as Liu Shao-ch'i recalled, even went so far as to propose the permanent distribution of farmland to each peasant household and advocated the policy of "*san ho yi shao*" [three reconciliations and one reduction], that is, making peace with the imperialists, reactionaries, and revisionists and reducing aid to the world revolutionary movements.

In 1967 Ch'en Yun was identified as the "villain" who had advocated the distribution of collective lands to peasants. He was quoted as having said in the summer of 1962, when the Nationalists were threatening to invade the mainland, that the peasants could be relied upon in the coming battle with the Nationalists if they had a stake in their own land.

The Politburo, it is said, later endorsed Ch'en Yun's report to the West Chamber Conference and asked him to speak again to "leading cadres" of the CC departments and the State Council. Ch'en Yun's speech was subsequently disseminated to officials at the provincial level for "discussion"—a practice often used by Chinese leaders to inform lower officials of the thinking at the top.

In May 1962 a report prepared by Ch'en Yun's five-man CC financial and economic group was approved by Liu Shao-ch'i, who was presiding over the Politburo in the absence of Mao. Although details of this report are not available, it probably proposed a drastic reorientation of economic priorities and further extension of rational measures to boost economic production. Faced with a *fait accompli*, Mao was reportedly furious; in Liu Shao-ch'i's words, "the Chairman was not in the least in accord with our evelution of the situation and our way of doing things."

Confronted by an acute food shortage, widespread social discontent, and serious economic disruptions, the majority of the party leaders appeared to be willing to take drastic measures to boost the peasants' incentives for production and to disregard temporarily the political and ideological implications of such measures. Thus a system called *san tzu i pao* [three freedoms and one guarantee], which subsequently was denounced repeatedly during the cultural revolution,[74] is said to have been instituted in 1962. This system allowed peasants to farm private plots as well as reclaim wasteland for their own use, to operate family sideline occupations, and to sell their produce in the free markets; in addition, each household was responsible for certain output quotas on the public land assigned to it.

In some cases, collective lands were divided among peasants on a long-term basis in the 1962 period, and some peasants were even permitted to leave communes to engage in private farming. Teng Hisao-p'ing allegedly quipped: "So long as it raised output, *tan kan* (literally, going it alone, i.e., private farming) is permissible; white or black, so long as the cats can catch mice, they are good cats."[75] These concessions, a desperate attempt to salvage the Great Leap, considerably weakened the collectivist elements of agricultural production.

Retreats in the Model Province—Honan

Honan was a pacesetter in the communization movement in 1958; under the leadership of the leftist first secretary, Wu Chih-p'u, the province received much nation-wide publicity for carrying out radical Great Leap measures. In 1960–61, severe natural calamities and human failings [*t'ien tsai jen huo*] resulted in enormous economic dislocations in this province. Many areas of the province suffered complete crop failure; hunger was widespread, and large numbers of peasants fled Honan. Armed peasant revolts occurred in several special districts, and the Chinese authorities had to use troops to suppress these "counterrevolutionary" activities, inflicting numerous casualties.[76] In 1960 or early 1961, First Secretary Wu Chih-p'u was demoted to second secretary and later shifted to a position outside of Honan. Liu Chien-hsun, the first secretary of Kwangsi Chuan Autonomous Region, was transferred to Honan to head the Honan Provincial Party Committee in 1961.

Two months after the 7000-cadre enlarged Central Work Conference met (January 1962), T'ao Chu, first secretary of the Central South Regional Bureau, came to Honan to deal with the critical situation there. At Cheng-chow, the provincial capital of Honan, T'ao Chu presided over a work conference (also called the Chung-chou Guest House Conference) which was attended by secretaries of provincial, special district, and municipal party committees of Honan, to formulate measures for agricultural recovery.[77] In response to the critical conditions prevailing in Honan's rural economy, the conference prescribed several "capitalist" measures which downgraded collective management in agricultural production and placed greater emphasis on peasants' material incentives.

Some dissenting voices were raised during the conference by apparently leftist party officials. T'ao Chu ridiculed these officials as "leftist remnants" and rebuked cadres in Honan for being "inept and reckless." In reply to a suggestion that some measures were "capitalistic," T'ao Chu retorted: "You are afraid of capitalism but not malnutrition." "You are afraid of this or that, but not of people's starvation." "Capitalism is much better than 'starvationism' and 'malnutrition-ism.'" Defending a measure to lend collective land to peasants, T'ao Chu declared: "Give the peasants a piece of land, some seeds, let peasants escape with life." The conference produced two documents, "The

CCP Honan Provincial Working Conference Summary" and "The Six-Year (1962–67) Plan for Agricultural Recovery and Development of Honan Province," which T'ao Chu subsequently presented to the CC; reportedly they were approved by Liu Shao-ch'i.

Based on these two documents, the Honan People's Provincial Council issued a "Notice on the Measures for Encouraging Agricultural Production," which stipulated strong measures to boost peasants' incentives. For instance, the production teams were instructed to allocate 7 percent of the collective land as private plots of peasants; these private plots would be farmed by individual households on a long-term basis, and the proceeds were to be kept by peasants and exempted from the state's system of unified purchase. Draft animals and livestock belonging to the collective were divided among in-dividual peasants for use and care, and the peasants were to get one, two, or three "legs" for each new-born animal as a reward.

In areas that were difficult to work, peasants might be allotted additional pieces of good land on loan from the production teams. When this measure aroused strong opposition from many cadres as well as large numbers of poor and lower-middle peasants, Liu Chien-hsun, who had replaced Wu Chih-p'u as Honan's first party secretary in 1961, had a reply: "If we may eat food imported from capitalist countries, why cannot we loan land?"[78] In Feng Ch'iu Hsien, 210,000 *mou*, or 23 percent of the collective land, were loaned to peasants for private farming, and in some grave disaster areas as much as 80 percent of the collective land was farmed by peasants individually.[79] In Honan at that time, the peasants had a new adage: The private plot is a son of one's own begetting [*ching-sheng tzu*], the loaned land is an adopted son [*yang-stu*], and the collective land is an orphan [*ku-erh*].

In July 1962 the Honan provincial authorities handed down another docu-ment, "The Summary of the Provincial Party Standing Committee Confer-ence," which provided for a system of "guaranteed production quotas by households."[80] Individual households now were to underwrite the output of a piece of collective land assigned to them; they would receive rewards if they overfulfilled the quotas but would receive fines if they failed to meet the quotas. This measure undoubtedly was designed in large part to enforce a system of production responsibility and provide production incentives for the peasants; however, the measure obviously undermined collective agri-cultural undertakings which the Chinese authorities had been stressing since agricultural collectivization in the mid-1950s.

Mao Stages a Comeback

In the face of severe economic and social crisis in 1960–62, Mao either reluctantly acquiesced or was compelled to accept a Chinese version of the New Economic Policy mapped out by his colleagues, and temporarily, at least, he lost a large measure of control over the decision-making process. He apparently felt that under Liu Shao-ch'i's stewardship things had gone too far, so as soon as the economy showed signs of recovery in the second half of 1962, Mao reasserted himself, demanding repeal or restriction of various "revisionist" measures that had been taken to repair the disasters of the three preceding years.

When a Central Work Conference was held at Peitaiho in August 1962, top leaders holding different views clashed. According to later reports on this conference in Red Guard and other sources, Mao vehemently denounced the policy allowing peasants' private farming [*tan kan*] and the system of production responsibility [*pao ch'an tao hu*], which he felt threatened to undermine China's collective agriculture. He criticized Ch'en Yun by name for initiating *tan kan* and blamed Li Hsien-nien's commercial policy for having "undermined the collective economy and facilitated private farming."[81] Furthermore, Teng Tzu-hui, Mao's long-time critic who was said to have actively promoted the system of production responsibility in 1962, was ousted from the directorship of the party's CC Rural Work Department and the State Council's Agricultural and Forestry Staff Office.

At this conference Mao complained that the State Planning Commission (headed by Li Fu-ch'un), the State Economic Commission (headed by Po I-po), and the Finance and Trade Staff Office of the State Council (headed by Li Hsien-nien) had become "independent kingdoms."[82] Finally, Mao severely criticized Liu Shao-ch'i for having followed a "rightist" policy line.[83]

Apparently, for the first time since 1960, Mao actively intervened once again in the policy-making processes; according to Liu Shao-ch'i, after the Peitaiho meeting Mao took the initiative in drafting a decision for the "further strengthening of the collective economy" and a decision on commerce.[84] Another source reported that Ch'en Po-ta, Mao's confidant, clashed with Li Hsien-nien and others over the draft of a "Decision Concerning Commercial Work" at the Tenth CC Plenum, held from 23 to 27 September 1962.[85]

During the Peitaiho Conference in the summer of 1962, and at the following Tenth CC Plenum, Mao made it clear that he was opposed to the current policy of rehabilitation; he talked at great length on the importance of class and class struggle and warned his colleagues against the danger of the development of "revisionism" in China.[86] Not a few party officials obviously regarded Mao's analysis of objective conditions as inaccurate and his ideological prescription irrelevant to the concrete problems faced by the nation.[87] They were keenly aware that many measures termed "revisionist" or "capitalist" were indispensable for stimulating peasants' production through increased incentives, and they felt that such measures had, in fact, contributed substantially to the post-1961 economic recovery. Precisely because Mao was unable to refute arguments such as these, he shifted the dispute to the ideological level, and thus he attempted to turn the issue into one of political life and death for the proponents of "revisionist" or "capitalist" economic measures. In a socialist political system like China to advocate capitalism is a cardinal sin; ostensibly, the Cultural Revolution was launched to overthrow those "power-holders in the Party taking the capitalist road."

In any event, it appears that Mao did not succeed in getting all he wanted. It is true that after the Tenth Plenum the party reemphasized class struggle and increased its ideological control by violently attacking "revisionist" trends in all fields.[88] It is also true that Mao pushed the party to launch a Socialist Education Campaign in the countryside after the Tenth Plenum, and the party prohibited the practice of dividing land among individual households, cut back excessive private cultivation, again stressed collective undertakings, and tightened control over the rural trade fairs and peasants' speculative activities.[89] Most of the existing economic measures which had contributed significantly to China's post-1961 economic recovery, however, were not seriously affected by these measures or Mao's active intervention.[90] Possibly Mao's efforts to reverse current policies were blocked by a majority in the CC who were opposed to letting Mao "rock the boat" again.

The "Decision Concerning Further Consolidation of the Collective Economy of the People's Communes and the Development of Agricultural Production," which was approved by the Tenth CC Plenum, continued to uphold the principle of "agriculture first" in economic development and set the order of the priority in the economic plan as agriculture, light industry, and heavy industry.[91] It also called for a more reasonable unified grain purchase policy and higher farm prices to "mobilize the peasants' enthusiasm for the collective undertaking," and it affirmed the right of peasants to maintain private plots and to operate family sideline occupations.

The Plenum also approved a revised sixty-article document, the "Draft Regulations on the Rural People's Communes," which formalized the revisions in the original commune system that had been made de facto since late 1961.[92] The regulations now formally stipulated that production teams constituted the basic units of accounting in the communes; that is, the teams could carry out independent accounting, assume responsibility for their own gains and losses, and manage their own income and distributon—practices that had been in effect since the second half of 1961. Furthermore, the regulations emphatically stated that the size, ownership, distribution, and management systems of the reorganized communes would not be changed for at least thirty years.[93] In fact, the relatively moderate commune policies pursued before the Tenth Plenum seemed to remain essentially unchanged from 1963 to 1966, despite the widespread unfolding of an intensive "socialist education campaign" in the Chinese countryside.[94]

Although the three-level commune administrative structure continued to exist throughout the mid-1960s, many elements of the 1958 commune system were abandoned. In fact, by 1962 the commune system had been "decommunized" to a considerable degree. The production team (twenty to thirty households in size and generally equivalent to a lower APC) has since then owned the major means of production, constituted the basic accounting unit of the commune, and exercised independent production authority—a reversion in many respects to the system of lower APC's as it existed in 1955.

Before the Tenth CC Plenum in September 1962, central authorities had steadily recentralized control in the sphere of economy. As noted earlier, the creation of the six CC bureaus in 1960–61 was an important step in that direction; each of these regional bureaus was expected to supervise closely a group of provinces in the nation's six large regions. During the proceedings of the CC Working Conference at Peitaiho in August 1962 and at the Tenth CC Plenum in Peking the following month, the issue of economic planning was among the major problems discussed by the Chinese leaders.[95] Steps were being taken to strengthen the control of planning and coordination functions by the top economic agencies of the central government, although this control had been reduced in 1958–59. In November 1962 the State Planning Commission received seven notable new vice-chairmen, in addition to its original thirteen vice-chairmen. These new vice-chairmen were Po I-po, T'an Chen-lin, Li Hsien-nien, and Teng Tzu-hui, all of whom were vice-premiers of the State Council, as well as Ch'en Po-ta, chief editor of *Hung Ch'i*, and two lower ranking economic officials, Sung Shao-wen and Yang Ying-chieh, who had been dismissed from this position in 1959 for criticizing the Great Leap. In 1962, the Third Five-Year Plan was said to have been scheduled for 1963–67; therefore these appointments were probably made to strengthen the work of the State Planning Commission. The inclusion of both "radicals" (T'an and Ch'en) and "conservatives" suggested that both groups were watching closely the future direction of the nation's economy.

There were also some signs that the central authorities had further tightened their control over the financial sector. An article in *Hung Ch'i* in 1962 advocated that the banking system perform and strengthen its supervisory functions over the economy through careful extension of credits and strict loan-repayment enforcement. "All credit activities, settling of accounts, and disbursement of cash throughout the country must be concentrated in the national bank."[96] This was supported by other writers discussing financial work: "In matters of financial control, the major power must be concentrated in the central government and the power of local authorities and of economic units must be reduced."[97] The recentralization of financial power from provinces to the central government was paralleled by a similar recentralization within the provinces, to curtail the financial autonomy of lower local authorities. "Authority in the management of national finance must be concentrated in the three levels of central government, great administrative regions [*sic*], and the provinces; the authority of financial management of special districts, *hsien* and below must be reduced."[98]

The Chinese leadership was by now aware that China is too big for central authorities to administer directly from Peking. This realization, and the painful experiences resulting from excessive provincial decentralization during the Great Leap, probably accounted for the move in 1960–61 to establish CC regional bureaus to help supervise the provinces. There is some indication that these regional bodies (in theory, they are "dispatched organs" of the party's CC and are therefore different from the "military and administrative committees" and the "administrative committees" of the early 1950s, which formed a layer of local government in the overall government hierarchy) had fulfilled some of the functions of economic coordination among provinces, functions which the regime in 1958 apparently expected would be performed by the "economic cooperation regions." For instance, the CC regional bureaus were reported to have sponsored "material exchange conferences" to promote intraregional cooperation and to smooth out allocation problems within their regions.[99] In practical terms, these measures were designed to effect a more efficient use of local resources, to transfer unused supplies and equipment from one intraregional enterprise to another, and to achieve savings in transportation by stopping unnecessary interregional cross-hauling. Politically, the promotion of this policy was probably intended to check the tendency toward provincial autarky by curtailing the autonomy of provincial authorities in economic matters.

To perform the tasks of coordinating and supervising political, economic, and other activities in the provinces, the regional bureaus would need some degree of authority and administrative machinery of their own, and it appears that each of them was delegated considerable power and developed a significant set of administrative organs.

The efforts at recentralization during the 1960s, however, did not result in a return to 1957, that is, the pre-decentralization era in the distribution of power over management of the economy and the structure of economic control.[100] Centralization and decentralization now accommodated one another, in a system similar to one that Hsueh Mu-ch'iao had recommended in 1957. On the one hand, the central government apparatus regained considerable power lost in the decentralization of the late 1950s, but the earlier "ministerial system" was not restored in any full sense. On the other hand, the enterprises in the hands of managers and technicians were granted a certain degree of autonomy over the management and operation of economic production, as evidenced by several provisions in the seventy-article "Regulations on Industry, Mines and Enterprises" of 1961.

Despite various measures to curtail provincial power in the 1960s, provincial authorities retained considerable control (de jure or de facto) over many economic activities. After the decentralization of 1957–58, which had given great powers to the provinces, it was probably difficult for the provinces to relinquish these powers. Provincial-level units that had especially large resources—Szechuan, Kwangtung, Liaoning, Shanghai, and Peking—or provinces that were headed by officials of relatively high party stature—Shanghai, Szechuan, Inner Mongolia, and Peking—probably enjoyed greater power and independence in their relations with the center than other provinces with less resources or less powerful provincial officials.

The central-provincial power relationship, in fact, had undergone subtle but significant qualitative changes since 1957–58. Unlike the period preceding the Great Leap when the central leadership alone made decisions and imposed them on the provinces, since the early 1960s the central leadership regularly involved the provincial leaders in the decision-making process at the highest level. This widened political participation took place within the institutional frame-work of the central work conference, which was convened at regular intervals from 1960 to 1966 and which was connected with decisions on important policy issues.[101]

The decentralization of power to the provincial authorities in the late 1950s greatly enhanced the importance of provinces as bases of political power. Moreover, the role of local leaders in China's overall political structure continued to grow as national leaders found it politically expedient and necessary to involve local party leaders in top-level decision-making. As the top CCP leadership became divided in the 1960s, different factions attempted to enlist the support of the provincial leaders to tip the balance in a policy debate, and their political power accordingly increased. To put it in another way, as a result of the dissension in the CCP leadership in the 1960s, the arena of political conflict has been expanded and those situated below the upper echelons of the leadership hierarchy, such as the provincial leaders, became directly involved in the resolution of conflicts among top leaders; thus the scope of participation in power conflicts widened and a new elite became established.

Ironically, the party's regional bureaus, created in 1960 to serve as the central leadership's loyal "watchdogs" over the provinces, have subsequently turned out to be the centers of regional autonomy. Initially, the six bureaus were headed by three loyal provincial leaders and three other party officials dispatched from the center. In time, however, all of them became identified with their own regions and developed their own "independent kingdoms" with substantial autonomous bases of support in the regions and came to resist the command of the central authority. Such regional autonomy manifested itself most clearly at the height of the Great Proletarian Cultural Revolution (1966–67), and the central leadership could only oust these obdurate regional leaders from their regional strongholds by pushing the PLA into the picture. Since the GPCR, the PLA-dominated provincial power bases appear to be even more intractable and difficult to manipulate.

6

Setting the Stage
for the Cultural Revolution

The tumultuous events in China since the summer of 1966 created a political drama of the highest order. In a crusade called the Great Proletarian Cultural Revolution (GPCR), Chairman Mao invoked the support of China's fanatical revolutionary youth to ferret out "those in the party who take the capitalist road." The GPCR then generated political and social turmoil on a scale not approached in China since 1949. Not only have many party and government institutions been seriously disrupted, and not only have veteran officials, from the CC down to the local levels, been decimated, but the facade of a coherent, unified leadership has been shattered, and the image of the regime has been tarnished almost beyond repair in the eyes of the Chinese population.[1]

The GPCR began when Mao decided it was necessary to oust some of his "comrades-in-arms." As pointed out earlier, Mao's control over the party was weakened substantially when his grandiose Great Leap and commune programs failed, sending him to the political background as other CCP leaders came to the fore to save China from profound economic crisis. A set of pragmatic policies sponsored by Liu Shao-ch'i and others extricated China from the crisis by the fall of 1962, but Mao was alarmed by Liu's leadership, which, in his view, was leading China to the path of revisionism and "restoration of capitalism." Despite Mao's persistent efforts to reimpose his policies and assert his leadership, he found himself unable to make the party responsive to his will, for other leaders who controlled the party organizations had used sabotage, obstruction, and passive resistance to frustrate his goals. Mao became convinced that if he were to control the direction of the Chinese Revolution and carry out his own revolutionary vision, he would have to remove from positions of authority those leaders "who are taking the capitalist road."

The Socialist Education Campaign (SEC)

While a series of liberal policies adopted by the CCP leadership from 1960 to 1962 significantly contributed to China's post-Leap economic recovery, they also generated problems and consequences that Mao regarded as undesirable.

First and foremost was the peasants' "spontaneous tendency toward capitalism." The "three freedoms and one guarantee" system so weakened the regime's economic control over the peasants that they tended to forgo the collective undertakings of the communes to "rely on the private plots to get money and on speculation to get rich." Free markets had the effect of encouraging peasants to engage in peddling and in speculative activities instead of farming—which the Chinese Communists considered a dangerous tendency of the peasants to leave "the socialist road for the capitalist road." So long as the agricultural output increased and peasants' livelihood improved, many rural cadres condoned or even cooperated with those efforts.

A general relaxation of social and political control during 1960–62 encouraged a revival of "feudal" practices such as religious festivals, arranged marriages, and witchcraft. In the ranks of the party, and particularly among the rural cadres (most of whom were not members of the party), doubt, cynicism, and demoralization were widespread after the failures of the Great Leap. Members of many rural cadres, believing their burden of leadership too rigorous and incommensurate with their rewards, wanted to quit. A further problem was the widespread corruption among rural cadres, as was the growth of "commandism" and "bureaucratism" in cadres' working style.[2] It was in this broad social, economic, and political context that the SEC was initially launched in response to Mao's admonition to the Tenth Plenum: "never forget the class struggle."[3]

By February 1963, four months after the Tenth CC Plenum, the SEC was well under way in many provinces. Although officials claimed that great progress had already been made in restricting peasants' "capitalist" tendencies and in improving the morale, work habits, and political consciousness of both cadres and masses, defects in carrying out the SEC were conceded by those cadres who supervised it. Up to that time, the SEC was relatively lifeless—it clearly lacked the kind of tension, intensity, and momentum seen in many of the mass movements of the 1950s. The low key of the SEC may be attributed to two major factors: numerous cadres, both high and low, had suffered physical and mental exhaustion and become weary of mass campaigns after the experiences of the Great Leap; moreover, since agricultural output had barely recovered from the "three lean years," many party leaders and rural cadres were apprehensive that a violent SEC would once again disrupt economic production, like many of the mass campaigns of the 1950s had, and they therefore placed greater emphasis on increasing production than on waging class struggle.

This was unsatisfactory to Mao, who held that the class struggle should be the primary focus of the SEC.[4] He asserted that in Chinese society there still existed classes, class struggle, and struggle between socialism and capitalism, and he pointed out various class struggle phenomena in society. On the basis of his perception of reality in China, Mao intended the SEC to be a revolutionary movement of cosmic scale:

This struggle is one for the re-education of men; for the reorganization of revolutionary class force to wage sharp and effective struggles against the forces of capitalism and feudalism which are launching an audacious attack upon us; it is a great movement to suppress their counter-revolutionary activities and to remold the majority of these elements into new men: it is also a campaign for the joint participation of cadres and the masses in productive labor and scientific experiments, with a view to bringing our Party a step further in becoming a more glorious, greater and more correct Party, and making our cadres well-versed in politics and in business operations, both red and expert, well integrated with and supported by the masses, instead of being divorced from the masses and considering themselves officials and overlords. After the completion of this education movement, there will emerge in the whole country a climate of brightness and prosperity.[5]

To put the SEC back on the correct course, Mao intervened. In a Central Work Conference in February 1963, Mao described the "success" Hunan and Hopei provinces attained when class struggle was given prominence in the SEC, and he urged other localities to emulate that experience. Those cadres who had failed to emphasize class struggle or had paid insufficient attention to the class struggle phenomena were criticized. Many cadres were rebuked for having adopted "an attitude of indifference" toward various class struggle phenomena, thereby "letting the phenomena continue and develop."

Not much detail of the February party meeting is known; the available information indicates that Mao imposed on the party a new approach to the SEC—an approach that was underlined by Mao's slogan: "Once class struggle is grasped, miracles are possible." After the meeting, various provinces began to experiment with the new approach in selected areas. Shortly thereafter, reports from provinces began to pour into the CC claiming that many cadres had mastered socialist education work and that the work of SEC had been carried out with good results.

This would tend to prove the "correctness" of Mao's approach to the SEC and bolster his position. Subsequently, Mao put forth the "First Ten Points," which were adopted by another Central Work Conference in May 1963. He defined the characteristics of the contemporary historical stage, the nature of contradictions, and salient political issues in Chinese society, and he provided the directions and guidelines for resolving these contradictions and implementing the SEC. This document was the first major policy directive concerning the SEC and was clearly intended by Mao to guide the campaign along the course he desired.

The party professed that the document was based on reports of rural conditions filed by provincial and lower officials. Certain operational methods that were regarded as "successful" in some provinces, including Hunan, Hopei, Honan, and Chekiang, were standardized and written into the document as "advanced" experiences to be emulated by other provinces. As in the mass movement before, the top leadership did not provide concrete operational guidelines in advance; rather it relied on the "creativity" and initiative of individual provinces to work out methods suitable to their localities. In this way, the provincial and lower authorities had a considerable degree of freedom in implementing central directives. Furthermore, some provincial authorities actually affected, if only indirectly, the nationwide implementation of the central directives, as their "advanced experiences" were singled out by the central authorities as models to be emulated by other localities. The local autonomy in policy implementation and the kind of interaction between central and local authorities were among the striking characteristics of the regime's policy-making process, as noted earlier.

The implementation of the SEC is indicative of the change in Mao's role. Unlike the period of 1960–62, when Mao withdrew, to a large extent, from party deliberation of domestic policies, from the time of the Peitaiho Conference in the summer of 1962 Mao frequently interjected himself into the policy-making process. In a sense, Mao was a different political actor after the Peitaiho Conference—he had unmistakably displayed the will and tenacity to fight for his programs. This new image of Mao apparently gave him considerable political influence.

Whereas Mao was now actively involved in the deliberation of the party councils, he did not closely supervise the day-to-day party administration. According to Mao's own account in October 1966, the Politburo Standing Committee was divided into a first line and a second line, and he himself was in the second line, presumably meaning that he was to concern himself only with the most important decisions and with defining policy goals. The power of controlling and overseeing the daily tasks of governing China fell largely into the hands of Liu Shao-ch'i, Teng Hsiao-P'ing, and other members of the party Secretariat. Consequently, these party officials were able to sabotage, obstruct, or change Mao's policy if they happened to disagree with it. This is exactly what happened to the SEC.

About four months after the First Ten Points were promulgated, another directive on the SEC, "Some Concrete Policy Formulations of the Central Committee of the Chinese Communist Party in the Rural Socialist Education Movement" (also known as the "Second Ten Points"), was put forth by the party.[6] In the course of the GPCR, official Chinese sources revealed that the author of this document was Teng Hsiao-p'ing.[7] Purporting to supplement the contents of the SEC and to solve "a number of problems concerning concrete policies" emerging from the implementation of the First Ten Points in the preceding months, the Second Ten Points substantially modified the spirit and softened the impact of the SEC as set forth in its predecessor.

For example, Article II, Section 6 stressed that the development of the SEC "should be closely coordinated and connected with the production work."

The intense concentration on the SEC prompted some cadres to ignore production work; the new directive now demanded that "at no stage of the
movement should production be affected" and that "measures taken during
the course of the movement should be helpful to production." To prevent
excessive, indiscriminate class struggle from adversely affecting production,
the drafters of the new directive set limits by spelling out detailed, concrete
guidelines on all aspects of the struggle. Thus cadres were warned to carefully
distinguish between the class enemies and the "hoodwinked" backward
masses, between the spontaneous capitalist tendency and the speculation and
profiteering, on the one hand, and proper family sideline occupations (including private plots), proper activities of marketing and trading of commune
members, on the other (Article III). A set of measures, such as private plots,
sideline occupations, and "free markets," which had been provided in the
1962 sixty-article "Regulations on the Rural People's Communes," was once
again emphasized; it was also stated that whether the sixty articles have been
well implemented should be a yardstick in judging the result of the Socialist
Education Movement (Article II, Section 5).

Furthermore, despite lip service paid the class struggle, the new directive
apparently sought to moderate the disruptive effect of the SEC on production
and to prevent alienation of the majority of the peasants who were more
resourceful and enterprising farmers. The majority of upper-middle peasants
were held to be "laborers and our friends," capable of taking the socialist road,
although even they were likely to display "capitalist" tendencies. Measures of
struggle employed against enemies were forbidden against the upper-middle
peasants who showed "capitalist" tendencies; rather, Article V recommended
patient criticism and education to win them over. In the case of children of
rich peasant-landlords, the majority were said to have never directly participated in exploitation and were explicitly included in the 95 percent of the
masses who were to be "consolidated" during the SEC (Article X). With
respect to cadres who had made mistakes, most of their problems were said
to be "nonantagonistic" in nature; even those cadres who had ties with class
enemies were regarded as being qualitatively different from the class enemies
themselves and to be dealt with by education and reform (Article VI). This
optimistic assessment of contradictions and the overall lenient treatment of
the masses and cadres prescribed by the new directive seem to negate the
premise of intensified class struggle in Chinese society, which this directive
was supposed to correct.

Not surprisingly, therefore, the Maoists criticized the Second Ten Points
for using the method of "removing the burning brands from the boiling
cauldron" to negate "the essential content of the struggle between the two
classes and between the two roads and completely discard the line, principles
and policies" of the SEC as set forth by Mao.[8] The accusation obviously is
distorted and exaggerated; yet in light of what actually took place, the dis-

tortion and exaggeration in this and other charges are not totally unfounded.

Whatever discrepancies existed between the two directives, however, did not seem to be apparent to Mao. The authors of the second directive professed only to "supplement" the first and to set out clear-cut criteria for implementing concrete policies—the first directive was not contradicted directly or explicitly. Phrases and slogans were copied from the first directive to repeat very nearly the same thing on matters such as class struggle and the need to mobilize the masses. Even when the authors redefined issues and set new limits, they used terms very similar to those used by Mao. This adroit subterfuge, coupled with Mao's withdrawal from the supervision of daily policy implementation, blinded Mao for a time to the fact that the true intent of his own policy was being ignored.

Thus only in June 1964, nine months after the Second Ten Points were formulated, did Mao again step forward to intervene. In a Central Work Conference, which was a meeting of the Politburo Standing Committee attended also by the first secretaries of the party's regional bureaus, Mao formulated the following six criteria[9] for measuring the success or failure of the SEC:

1. We must see whether the poor and lower-middle peasants have been truly aroused.
2. Has the problem of the Four Uncleans among the cadres been resolved?
3. Have the cadres participated in physical labor?
4. Has a good leadership nucleus been established?
5. When landlords, rich peasants, counter-revolutionaries and bad elements who engage in destructive activities are discovered, is this contradiction merely turned over to the higher levels, or are the masses mobilized to strictly supervise, criticize, and even appropriately struggle against these elements, and moreover retain them for reform on the spot?
6. We must see whether production is increasing or decreasing.[10]

All except the last are political criteria and thus contrast sharply with the primarily economic yardstick, the sixty-article Regulations on the Rural People's Communes, as stipulated in the Second Ten Points. The introduction of new criteria at least suggested that Mao was displeased by the way with which the SEC had been pursued and that he was repudiating, even if only indirectly, those who were responsible. Apparently it was also at this meeting that "Organizational Rules of Poor and Lower-Middle Peasant Associations" were adopted.[11]

The work of organizing a "revolutionary class army" had been urged since May 1963 in the First Ten Points. Since then, efforts had been made in various parts of the country to recruit and organize poor and lower-middle peasants. The directive of the Second Ten Points was somewhat ambivalent; although it promoted the establishment of peasants' organizations in terms very similar to its predecessor, it also elaborated methods and procedures to be followed and criticized cadres who set up such organizations overnight by administrative order. By suggesting caution and by pointing out unresolved problems with regard to organizing rural class ranks (Article IV, Sections 1 and 5), the authors of the Second Ten Points may have intended to slow down such activities. In any case, the Organizational Rules adopted in July 1964 finally gave concrete form to, and formally defined the functions of the peasant organizations and settled problems that had previously been left open.

Two of the tasks of the peasant associations were to "carry on resolute struggle with the forces of capitalism and feudalism" and "to assist and supervise the various level organizations and cadres in the rural people's communes to do a good job of managing the collective economy."[12] This may mean that local party organizations failed in carrying out these tasks, for otherwise it would be unnecessary to undergo such "organizational tinkering." If the peasant associations were designed to serve as separate "watchdog" bodies in the rural areas, why were they to be subjected to the leadership and control of local party organizations, as stipulated in the "Organizational Rules"? The ambiguity of the role of the peasant associations perhaps reflected the continual dissension in the CCP leadership over the SEC.

Mao's efforts in June 1964 and on earlier occasions showed that he was determined to carry out his vision of the SEC. But his repeated intervention and assertion of his authority indicate that he was encountering resistance, and the SEC was not following the course he had charted. Other party leaders did not oppose Mao directly and they never challenged his authority to set basic policy decisions, even when they disagreed. Although Mao could and did make basic policy decisions, his overall ability to control events was diluted because other party leaders who controlled the operation of the party and supervised policy implementation were in a strategic position to revise and modify his guidelines and thwart his true intent, as they clearly did when Mao championed the SEC. He called for the campaign at the Tenth CC Plenum, but it was led "astray" soon after it was launched; from February to May 1963 Mao tried to put it back on the "correct" path, first by issuing the First Ten Points. A few months later, this "correct" orientation was sidetracked by the introduction of the Second Ten Points, and Mao felt compelled to intervene once again in June 1964. This cycle was to be repeated when Liu Shao-ch'i later took over the management of the SEC.

In the fall of 1964, the SEC entered a new phase as Liu came to the forefront to direct the campaign. There is no way to know whether he was responding to Mao's intervention in June or whether his extensive "investigation and study" tour in Hunan in August 1964 convinced him that cadres were not carrying out the SEC adequately; other considerations, or a combination of all these factors, may have motivated him to personally take charge of the implementation of the SEC. Wang Kuang-mei, Liu's wife, was also actively and prominently involved.[13] Liu's stewardship of the SEC and Wang Kuang-mei's involvement were subject to scathing attack by Maoists during the GPCR. The "crimes" Liu is alleged to have committed can be summarized as follows: on the basis of Wang's "T'aoyuan Experience," in September 1964 Liu produced the "Revised Second Ten Points" which were "left" in form but "right" in essence and in opposition to the line set by Mao; in addition, he "wrote off" the struggle between socialism and capitalism and took excessive punitive action against basic-level cadres to "protect the handful of capitalist power-holders in the party."[14]

These and other charges leveled after Liu's disgrace were obviously intended to blacken his reputation and to meet new political exigencies; they purposely distorted and obscured what Liu actually did in the second half of 1964. Maoist reinterpretation of past events notwithstanding, the fact still remains that Liu did play a guiding role in the SEC during the second half of 1964 and that his management was found wanting and repudiated by Mao as early as January 1965.

Mao was irritated by Liu's "mispresentation" of the purpose of the SEC. Following his eighteen-day tour of Hunan in August 1964, Liu delivered a speech to the high-ranking officials of the CC departments and of the Peking Party Committee in which he stated that the SEC should be oriented toward solving "the contradiction between the Four Cleans and the Four Uncleans" in politics, ideology, organization, and economy; in Liu's view, problems in Chinese society were derived from "the overlapping of contradictions within the party and contradictions outside of the party, or the overlapping of [antagonistic] contradictions between the enemy and us and the [nonantagonistic] contradictions among the people."[15] By juxtaposing the "antagonistic" and "nonantagonistic" contradictions, Liu, according to Mao, downgraded the importance of the "antagonistic" contradictions in society and thus surreptitiously shifted the focus of the SEC away from struggle between the "two lines." For this, he was subsequently accused of pursuing an erroneous policy line which was "right" in essence but "left" in form.

The "leftist" manifestations of Liu's line were to be found in the excessive purge of basic-level cadres. On the basis of Liu's own theoretical formulation, he appeared to have placed equal, or perhaps greater emphasis on the resolution of the contradiction "among the people." He held that the contradictions among the people had found expression in an "irregular relationship" between the cadres and the masses. Therefore, for him, the complete solution of the problems of cadres, that is, their "Four Uncleans," was the "most important condition for successful consolidation of over 95 percent of the peasants."[16] The cadre problem was viewed by Liu as quite serious. In his speech of August 1964 cited above, he claimed that one-third of the rural leadership was not "in our hands" and that the party had not won but actually lost the battle in the revolutionary struggle of the past year. The Revised Second Ten Points also stated that the cadres, aside from being "unclean" economically, had failed to draw a line between allies and foes, forsaken their own principles, discriminated against poor and lower-middle peasants, fabricated their background and family history, and thus they became unclean in politics and organization. Following this new critical assessment of the cadre problem, Article VI recommended harsher treatment of cadres. In practice, throughout the late fall of 1964, a great number of basic-level cadres were publicly criticized by the "mobilized masses" and many were dismissed from office.[17] Although Liu was undoubtedly responsible for this state of affairs, it does not follow that his "striking at the many" was intended to "protect the few" at the top,[18] as the Maoists have charged.

In addition, Mao and Liu apparently disputed certain operational techniques. Liu, a typical "organization man," stressed leadership and control from above and empowered the "work teams," which largely consisted of outside personnel from higher levels, to direct the SEC. The emphasis on the role of the work teams in the SEC would tend to circumscribe the revolutionary fervor of the masses below, for although the Revised Second Ten Points spoke at length of the need to boldly mobilize the masses, it clearly meant that the mobilization was to be led and directed by the work teams from above (Article II, Sections 1 and 3). Liu did not basically object to arousing the masses; rather, as an "organization man," he was likely to see any threat to the position and prerogatives of the party organization, thus he wanted mass enthusiasm kept within bounds to guard against a situation in which mass spontaneity could get out of hand.[19]

Liu and Mao also disagreed over the effective method of information gathering. Liu wanted leading personnel of the SEC to "squat at points," that is, to remain in villages to secure information directly from the masses instead of merely calling meetings to listen to reports and reading materials prepared by others (Article II, Section 2). In his August 1964 speech, Liu disparaged the method of "investigation and research," which Mao had long advocated, by claiming that the "investigation meeting," hitherto used by cadres to collect information, "did not work in many cases" and "could not uncover problems." Mao apparently took Liu's remarks as a personal insult and later pointedly reaffirmed the effectiveness and correctness of the "investigations and research" method in a formal party document, the "Twenty-Three Points"; Liu was to apologize for his "denial of the Chairman's thought" in his self-criticism in October 1966.[20] This is just one of many policy conflicts that became personalized.

By the end of 1964, the deviations in Liu's handling of the SEC had become apparent to Mao and he began to take steps to put the SEC back on the path he desired. The first such indication was a statement in the editorial of the

People's Daily on 1 January 1965: "The principal contradiction in China today is the (antagonistic) contradiction between socialism and capitalism. . . . The Socialist Education Movement . . . is directed precisely at carrying further the solution of this contradiction."[21] The shift of the orientation of the SEC was unmistakably clear in a new directive, "Some Problems Currently Arising in the Course of the Rural Socialist Education Movement" (also known as the Twenty-Three Points), which was said to have been drafted under Mao's personal guidance in a Central Work Conference in January 1965. This directive listed three different interpretations of the "contradictions" in Chinese society, which the SEC was to solve:

1. The contradictions between the Four Cleans and the Four Uncleans.
2. The overlapping of contradictions within the party and contradictions outside of the party, or the overlapping of contradictions between the enemy and us and contradictions within the people.
3. The contradictions between socialism and capitalism.

Article II of the Twenty-Three Points termed the first two (Liu's formulations) "un-Marxist-Leninist" and affirmed the third "Marxist-Leninist" and "decidedly in accord with the scientific theories" of Mao. Although Liu's name was not explicitly mentioned, it was beyond any doubt that the clarification was undertaken to correct his earlier "mispresentation."

Similarly, although the Twenty-Three Points did not explicitly and totally repudiate Liu's Revised Second Ten Points (in fact, both contained some of the same formulas and prescriptions), there was no doubt that Mao had actually intended to provide a new guideline for the SEC. Mao's intention was clearly reflected in a passage in the Preamble of the Twenty-Three Points which stated: "If this document should contradict previous central committee documents concerning the Socialist Education Movement this document should uniformly be taken as the standard." In several places, the Maoist document directly contradicted the provisions of the Revised Second Ten Points and the T'aoyuan Experience.[22] Thus Mao once again asserted his personal authority to establish a new overall policy line for the SEC.

The party meeting in January 1965 seemed to mark an important turning point in the intraparty conflict. Several sources claim that it was during the drafting of the Twenty-Three Points that Mao became suspicious of the loyalty of men like Liu and Teng, and that he had already decided to purge the highest echelons of the party in early 1965.[23] Thus the Twenty-Three Points sounded a novel and curious note by stating that the key point of the SEC was "to rectify those people in positions of authority within the Party who take the capitalist road"—a phrase that was to become a leitmotiv of the much larger struggle that began unfolding in 1966.

If Mao had actually had a plan to purge some of the top leaders in early 1965, his timetable was temporarily interrupted by the escalated war in Vietnam in February.[24] The expansion of United States war efforts aroused fear of a direct Sino-American military confrontation and an invasion of the Chinese mainland in the minds of many Chinese officials, probably including Mao himself. At a time like this, it would not be opportune to further divide the party by undertaking purges, and Mao apparently temporized. In fact, the press and radio in the spring and summer of 1965 drastically toned down the themes of class struggle in Chinese society and focused on the consolidation of cadres and masses. However, after the danger of a Sino-American confrontation subsided and when Mao's earlier doubts on the loyalty of top party leaders were reinforced by new evidence of resistance to his command in the fall of 1965—an event that will be discussed later—the GPCR could begin.

Reform in the Cultural and Ideological Spheres

During the socioeconomic crisis of 1960–62, the party had relaxed its stringent political control over society, and there was a thaw in the cultural and ideological spheres.[25] It was in this "permissive" period that dissenting writers and intellectuals, most of whom were members of the party, expressed basic disagreement with the party policies. Writings published by men like Teng T'o and Wu Han even satirized Mao's leadership and his Great Leap programs.

Mao began to fight back at the Tenth CC Plenum. For Mao, the heresy and criticism by the writers represented an assult by the "bourgeois" forces against socialism in China. Thus he told the Plenum: "Using novels to carry out anti-Party activities is a big invention. In order to overthrow a political regime, it is always necessary to prepare public opinion and carry out work in the ideological field in advance. This is true of the revolutionary class as well as of the counter-revolutionary class."[26] Mao argued that although the bourgeoisie had been overthrown in China, they attempted to use the old ideas, old culture, old customs, and old habits of the exploiting classes to corrupt the mind of man and conquer his heart to attain their goal: restoration of their rule. He therefore called for rectification in the areas of culture and ideological work.

Mao's outburst in the Plenum had an immediate, although short-lived, effect. T'eng To and his colleagues no longer published their "Evening Chats at Yenshan" after September 1962. Chou Yang, a deputy director of the CC Propaganda Department charged with overseeing the regime's literary and art work, hurriedly convened a "Symposium on Literary and Art Work" in mid-October to transmit the "spirit" of the Tenth Plenum. Adopting what the Maoists called "two-faced tactics," Chou made a mild self-criticism as a concession to Mao's criticism, on the one hand, but he affirmed his own leadership by claiming that "the basic situation of the literary and art circles is good" and "not too many things in opposition to the Party and Marxism have been published," on the other.[27] Shortly after, in November, Chou allegedly sponsored a "Symposium on Confucius" in Shantung, the birthplace of Confucius, to glorify this ancient sage and his teachings.

Later disclosures made during the GPCR presented the first clear picture of this tug-of-war between Mao and his followers, on the one hand, and those who controlled the regime's cultural and propaganda apparatus, on the other. Beginning in September 1962 Mao repeatedly called for total reform in the fields of culture and ideology, and his followers sought to bring this about. Yet those in the "Establishment" were at best lukewarm to Mao's demand, which they apparently viewed as an attack on the particularist concerns of their profession. Outwardly, they bowed to the Maoist demands for reform and rectification; in reality, they paid lip service to Mao's criticism while continuing to ignore his demands. Each time Mao spoke out, they would convene meetings to transmit Mao's instructions and undertake rectification, but each rectification campaign would soon peter out with exaggerated claims of the very accomplishment the campaign had not actually produced.

Closely involved in Mao's efforts to rectify the cultural and ideological spheres was his wife, Chiang Ch'ing. Late in 1962 she became actively engaged in the reform of Peking Opera and energetically promoted the "revolutionary modern drama." She demanded that art serve politics and that the Peking Opera and other theatrical forms primarily portray workers, peasants, and soldiers in socialist revolution and construction, turning from "ghosts," "emperors," "generals," "ministers," "scholars and beauties"—themes that had hitherto dominated China's theater. The Peking Party Committee and the Ministry of Culture, which controlled the best known and most prestigious Peking Opera organizations, refused to cooperate, and her endeavors in Peking were obstructed and sabotaged.[28] This was not surprising. Officials in the cultural "Establishment," some of them China's best known literary figures, resented the intrusion of Chiang Ch'ing in their affairs, since they regarded her as a layman in cultural work. Her personality did not win friends either; on occasions her sharp tongue, arrogance, assertiveness, and disregard for "protocol" irritated party leaders P'eng Chen, Lu Ting-yi, Chou Yang, and others, who perhaps then became more determined to stand in her way.[29] Thus policy differences were intertwined with personal conflicts. Frustrated in Peking, Chiang Ch'ing turned to Shanghai to seek support for her theatrical reform.

The Shanghai Party Committee was then headed by K'o Ch'ing-shih, a Maoist stalwart, who was concurrently first secretary of the party's East China Bureau, mayor of Shanghai, and a Politburo member. K'o expressed total support for Mao's art and literary reform and had already in early 1963 urged workers in the art and literary fields to emphasize the successes of the past thirteen years. K'o's proposal was given a cold reception by key officials in the party's Propaganda Department; when a meeting on "Literary and Art Work" was convened by that department in April 1963, Chou Yang was quoted as having said that "All themes in writing can reflect the spirit of our time" and that writers should "not consider the portrayal of the present as our only major task."[30] In spite of the cold shoulder of officials in the central apparatus, K'o and Chang Ch'un-ch'iao, director of the Propaganda Department of the Shanghai Party Committee, mobilized the manpower and resources under their control to provide Chiang Ch'ing with a base of operation. Shanghai became the pacesetter of "revolutionary modern drama" and in late 1963 sponsored a festival of modern drama, the first of its kind in the nation, to show off the achievements of theatrical reforms in the East China area. The activities of Chiang Ch'ing and K'o Ch'ing-shih were apparently disliked by the officials in the regime's cultural establishment and therefore failed to receive any publicity in the national media at that time.[31]

The foot-dragging of key party officials in the cultural and propaganda hierarchy stymied the reform and rectification campaign that Mao had demanded. Seeing his wishes largely ignored, Mao intervened again and again and kept pressing those in charge to carry out his will. In December 1963, when commenting on a report submitted by K'o Ch'ing-shih, Mao sharply criticized the serious problems in literary and art circles:

> In all forms of art—drama, ballads, music, the fine arts, the dance, the cinema, poetry and literature, and so on—problems abound; and the people involved are numerous; in many departments very little has been achieved so far in socialist transformation. The "dead" still dominate in many departments. Isn't it absurd that many Communists are enthusiastic in promoting feudal and capitalist art, but [show] no zeal in promoting socialist art?[32]

Mao's sharp remarks drew immediate response. On 3 January 1964 Liu Shao-ch'i and Teng Hsiao-P'ing called a symposium on literature and art in the name of the Party CC to discuss criticisms Mao had raised.[33] Chou Yang, in his report to the symposium, sidestepped Mao's criticism and described the shortcomings of the leadership in literature and art as a "failure on some occasions to exercise a tight enough grip" on work and "failure to make enough effort in cultivating and affirming the new things of socialism," but basically he affirmed the achievements in literary and art circles. Liu approved Chou's speech and declared that "The question is one of comprehension for the great majority in literary and art circles. There also are some who are double-minded and anti-Party. They must be criticized but must not be opposed as though they are rightists." With regard to the reform of drama, Liu echoed the Maoist demand on the staging of plays on contemporary themes, but he also affirmed the value of historical plays and voiced opposition to "dogmatism in art." In the following months, rectification meetings were convened by organizations in literary and art circles and they basically parroted the line set by Chou and Liu in January.

In June and July 1964, under the aegis of Mao, a "Festival of Peking Opera with Contemporary Themes" was held with fanfare in Peking, and many plays with contemporary themes were staged for a vast audience including Mao and other top party leaders. Bowing to the pressure of Mao and his followers, officials in charge of the party's cultural and ideological affairs now feigned great enthusiasm in promoting the revolutionary drama and seized initiatives from Chiang Ch'ing and her followers. Thus Lu Ting-yi made the opening address, P'eng Chen presented a keynote speech, and Chou Yang made the summation remarks at the festival.[34] The speech Chiang Ch'ing gave on 23 June to a symposium of artists and theatrical workers taking part in the festival was not reported,[35] nor the two operas produced under her personal supervision given any special attention in the media at that time. Although Establishment officials now endorsed the idea of infusing the Peking Opera with contemporary themes, they continued to uphold traditional art; official accounts of the festival made it clear that "plays on contemporary themes, traditional items, and new historical plays will coexist" in the future.[36]

At the end of June 1964, the CC Propaganda Department submitted a report to Mao intended to call a halt to the rectification campaign in the All-China Federation of Literary and Art Circles (ACFLAC) and its affiliated associations —a campaign which it had reluctantly launched six months earlier in response to Mao's criticism.[37] Mao, who was obviously enraged by the perfunctory manner in which his instructions were carried out, again made an extremely harsh indictment:

> In the last 15 years, these associations and most of their publications (it is said that a few of them are good) and by and large the people in them (that is not everybody) have not carried out the policies of the Party. They have acted as high and mighty bureaucrats, have not gone to the workers, peasants and soldiers and have not reflected the socialist revolution and construction. In recent years, they have slid down to the brink of revisionism. If serious steps were not taken to remold them, at some future date they are bound to become groups like the Hungarian Petofi club.[38]

It was probably around this time that a special organ of the CC, the "Five-Man Cultural Revolution Group," was set up to direct and oversee a sweeping "cultural revolution"; P'eng Chen was the head of this group, and Lu Ting-yi, K'ang Sheng, Wu Leng-hsi, and possibly Chou Yang were its members.[39]

On 2 July, less than a week after Mao's outburst, the CC Propaganda Department again called the officials of the ACFLAC and the Ministry of Culture to a meeting to make arrangements for carrying out a rectification campaign.[40] From the second half of 1964 on, after repeated intervention by Mao, it looked as if the rectification campaign that Mao had envisaged was finally "taking off" in earnest.

Thus many literary figures and their works were subject to attack in the press and magazines. The "crimes" for which they were assailed ranged from propagating revisionist themes such as "class harmony," "bourgeois humanism," and "ghosts are harmless," to beautifying capitalists and uglifying peasants and workers and party cadres, to eulogizing capitalism and opposing socialism.[41] Various literary journals were also criticized for publishing "poisonous weeds," for failure or lack of enthusiasm in responding to Mao's earlier call for rectification, for laying more stress on the past than on contemporary subject matter, and for refusal to publish the works of young writers.[42] During the rectification campaign of 1964–65, the careers of numerous literary figures and cultural officials were adversely affected; the notable ones included T'ien Han, Shao Ch'uan-lin, Yang Han-sheng, Mao Tun (minister of culture), and Hsia Yen, Ch'i yen-ming, and Ch'en Huang-mei (three vice-ministers of culture). In the ideological field, the most notable casualty was Yang Hsien-chen, a member of the CC and principal of the Higher Party School (1955–61), who advocated a bizarre theory of "combining two into one," allegedly in opposition to Mao's theory of "dividing one into two."

Chou Yang, the regime's "cultural czar," and his superior in the CC Propaganda Department, Lu Ting-yi, who were most responsible for the conditions in the cultural and ideological fields that caused Mao's wrath, emerged unscathed from the rectification campaign; Lu was even appointed minister of culture in January 1965 when the Ministry was reorganized. They were able to weather the storm by publicly repudiating their subordinates—a tactic which the Maoists described as "sacrificing the knights to save the commander."

In the mind of Mao, the campaign had not gone far enough, however. Several outspoken critics of his, including Teng T'o and Wu Han, had been spared. Apparently Mao neither forgot nor forgave his detractors, particularly Wu Han, who wrote the play "The Dismissal of Hai Jui," which, Mao believed, had sung the praises of P'eng Teh-huai and clamored for P'eng's rehabilitation. Hence when a Central Work Conference was held in September 1965, Mao singled out the play and its author for criticism and proposed that those in charge of the "cultural revolution" take action to publicly condemn the play and its author from the perspective of class struggle.[43]

Mao's demand at the conference went unheeded. Some party leaders were genuinely concerned with the war in Vietnam, which had grown more intense in February, and feared a possible direct Sino-American military confrontation; they may have reasoned that it would be wise to rally all segments of society behind the party and not alienate and further divide the population by waging struggle against the intellectuals at a time of national crisis. In fact, Liu Shao-ch'i and Teng Hsiao-p'ing had considered the campaign too excessive since 1964 and at a meeting of the Secretariat on 3 March 1965 had decided to end it; soon after that the great majority of newspapers and magazines quietly dropped criticisms of "bourgeois" writers and "reactionary academic authorities."[44] Personal considerations may have motivated several party leaders such as Teng Hsiao-P'ing and P'eng Chen to shield Wu Han; they maintained that he did not warrant the kind of struggle that Mao called for. Wu was a vice-mayor of Peking and P'eng Chen's protege—his disgrace certainly would reflect unfavorably on the prestige and authority of his boss. Allegedly, Wu was also a close friend and a bridge partner of Teng Hsiao-p'ing.[45]

As pointed out earlier, Mao had already entertained doubts on the loyalty of those in the first line of leadership; these doubts were now strengthened by fresh evidence of resistance to his command, so he decided to act. Since the central party apparatus and the Peking party machine were in the hands of his opponents, Mao was compelled to turn to the Shanghai Party Committee for a base to prepare and launch attacks against Wu Han and, by implication, his powerful protectors. This was recounted by Mao himself in October 1966:

> Then Peking couldn't do a thing; nor could the center. It was in September or October last year when this question was raised: If there was revisionism in the Center, what would the regions do about it? I felt that my views couldn't be accepted in Peking. Why wasn't the criticism of Wu Han started in Peking but in Shanghai? This was because there were no available men in Peking.[46]

Thus on 10 November 1965 the *Wen Hui Pao* of Shanghai published an article by a young leftist literary critic, Yao Wen-yuan. The article, innocently entitled "On the New Historical Play 'The Dismissal of Hai Jui,'" proved to be the first shot of the Great Proletarian Cultural Revolution. Although the article used the name of Yao, it was actually written at the instigation of Mao, who was in Peking, and under the close supervision of Madame Mao, who took a special trip to Shanghai.[47]

The attack on Wu Han and his play immediately alarmed P'eng Chen and his aides in Peking. After careful deliberation, P'eng decided to ignore Yao's article by not reproducing it in the media of Peking; but he was not ignoring the attack—he instructed his aide to ring the *Wen Hui Pao* to find out who was the "backer" of Yao's article.[48] For two weeks, Yao's article seemed to have generated no public impact—it was reproduced by only one newspaper, Shanghai's *Chieh-fang Jih-Pao*, on 12 November. To give greater publicity to Yao's article and to reach more readers outside Shanghai, on 24 November Mao arranged for the Hsin Hua Bookstore of Shanghai to print the article in pamphlet form, and the bookstore sent urgent cables to its sister stores throughout the country soliciting orders. On the same day, four provincial newspapers, *Chekiang Jih-Pao*, *Fukien Jih-Pao*, Nanking's *Hsin-hua Jih-Pao*, and Shantung's *Ta-chung Jih-Pao*, reprinted Yao's article, and *Anhwei Jih-pao* and *Kiangsi Jih-pao* followed suit on 25 and 26 November, respectively, but all of these papers were in the East China area. It looked as if P'eng Chen had largely succeeded in circumventing the publicity and minimizing the impact of Yao's attack on Wu Han.

Meanwhile, Mao appeared to be actively working behind the scene and was gradually receiving active support from other top leaders. A politically astute Chou En-lai, who has often joined the winning side, apparently jumped on Mao's bandwagon at this critical juncture, for on 28 November he called a meeting to press P'eng to have Yao's article reproduced in Peking's newspaper. Bowing to the pressure, P'eng permitted the organ of the Peking Party Committee, *Pei-ch'ing Jih-pao*, to print the article on 29 November.

Mao's most crucial support, however, was to come from Lin Piao, a vice-chairman of the party and the minister of defense, and a few other PLA leaders. Similiar to his maneuver during the 1950s in which he enlisted the support of provincial political forces to overcome opposition at the center, Mao turned to the PLA for support, broadened its political roles, and involved the PLA in political conflict resolution in the 1960s. He succeeded in coopting Lin Piao and used the PLA as a new base of power to fight his opponents who controlled the party machinery.

The first sign of PLA open support for Mao came on 29 November 1965, when the army organ, *Chieh-fang-chun Pao (Liberation Army Daily)* reproduced Yao's article. Furthermore, the army paper added an "Editor's Note" attacking Wu Han's play for having propagated politically erroneous themes and denouncing it as a "big poisonous weed." On the following day the *People's Daily* also reproduced Yao's article but added its own "Editor's Note," said to have been written by P'eng Chen, to counter the indictment made by the army paper. The note asserted that the issues involved in Wu Han's play were "academic" and that the evaluation of Hai Jui and the play should center on "questions of how to treat historical characters and historical plays, of using what perspectives in studying history, and of employing what artistic forms to reflect historical characters and historical events," and it urged those in the fields of history, philosophy, and literary studies to take part in a free debate on these "academic" questions.[49]

Clearly, the note was drastically different from that of the *Liberation Army Daily* and it said nothing of the political offenses of Wu Han's play. It seems likely that P'eng Chen intended to divert public attention from dangerous political implications that Mao had drawn from the play and to confine the debate to less harmful issues of historical scholarship and historiography. According to Mao himself, however, the crux of Wu Han's play, "The Dismissal of Hai Jui," was not faulty scholarship but its insinuation that the dismissal of P'eng Teh-huai at the 1959 Lushan Conference had been unjust and its portrayal of Marshal P'eng as the righteous Hai Jui.[50] Mao wanted to have Wu Han punished for political "crimes" in attacking his own leadership; he suggested this to P'eng Chen on several occasions. Only in this light can the significance of P'eng Chen's maneuver, and his audacity in resisting Mao, be fully appreciated.

For several months, beginning in December 1965, the criticism of Wu Han's play in the media largely revolved around the theoretical questions of historical scholarship in accordance with the tone set by the *People's Daily*, the prestigious authoritative organ of the party's CC. Although there were many articles criticizing Wu Han on various theoretical grounds, some defended him and attacked Yao's article.[51] Wu Han himself published a "self-criticism" in the *Peking Daily* on 27 December in which he confessed errors in the theories of "moral legacy" and of "historical materialism" but dodged the political offenses he was accused of in Yao's article.[52]

This episode concerning Wu Han once again demonstrated that Mao, despite his persistent efforts, was unable to enforce his will when party leaders who disagreed with him controlled the party machine. P'eng Chen, however, did not oppose Mao openly and directly; the tactics P'eng used were those of subterfuge, obstruction, and passive resistance. When repeatedly pressed by Mao to repudiate Wu Han openly, P'eng went along outwardly, but in fact he shifted the basic orientation of the attack and used different ploys to shield Wu Han from political criticism. P'eng's efforts at evasion and diversion culminated in the "Outline Report on the Current Academic Discussion" (also known as the "February Outline Report"), which he produced in the name of the Five-Man CC Cultural Revolution Group in early February 1966.[53] With the support of both Liu Shao-ch'i and Teng Hsiao-p'ing, the report was allegedly approved *pro forma* in a Politburo Standing Committee session chaired by Liu on 5 February; it was issued to the party organization on 12 February to serve as the guideline for the cultural revolution.[54] By this manipulation, P'eng had hoped to use the sacred aura of party authority to legitimize his policy and to ward off the attack of Mao and his supporters.

Those in the Maoist camp now were preparing for a final showdown with P'eng Chen and his allies, and the PLA under Lin Piao's stewardship become more closely involved in the conflict. On 2 February 1966 Madame Mao was entrusted by Lin Piao to convene a "Forum on the Literary and Art Work in the Armed Forces" in Shanghai.[55] At the conclusion of the eighteen-day forum, a summary report was prepared under Chiang Ch'ing's guidance; it was revised three times by Mao before its release.[56] The "Forum Summary" did not confine itself to the literary matters in the armed forces, it spelled out the Maoist position, policy, and intention on the cultural revolution in the nation. It pointed out that the literary and art circles had basically failed to carry out Mao's instructions and that the cultural front was dominated by an anti-party and anti-socialist "black line"; moreover, it called for a "great socialist revolution on the cultural front" and the complete elimination of this black line and stated that the PLA "must play an important role in the socialist cultural revolution."[57] The Maoists later claimed that the summary was "in direct opposition to the counter-revolutionary 'February Outline Report,' and launched a vigorous attack on the counter-revolutionary revisionist line."[58] Clearly, Mao had secured the full backing of Lin Piao and was involving the PLA on his side to fight P'eng Chen and his allies in the central party apparatus.

Mao's opponents, undoubtedly aware of the dire consequence if all the PLA leaders were to intervene and to side with Mao, desperately tried to ward off the involvement of the PLA in the domestic power struggle. To accomplish this aim, they sought to turn the attention of the PLA toward the external enemy—the Americans—by advocating a bigger and more active Chinese role in the Vietnamese war.

To fully understand how the Vietnamese war became intertwined with China's domestic politics, we must briefly review the dispute over foreign policy at that time. As the war in Indochina escalated after February 1965, and the Chinese leaders feared an eventual American invasion of the Chinese mainland, a heated debate arose among the CCP leadership as to what China should do under these dangerous circumstances. One "hawkish" option, as articulated by Lo Jui-ch'ing, then PLA chief of staff, was that China should adopt a "forward" or "active defense" strategy in that China would "give more effective support" to the Vietnamese Communists and intervene actively in the war to defeat the Americans. To deter the Americans from using nuclear weapons against China and to bolster China's defense, Lo favored China's reconciliation and united front with the Soviet Union.[59]

On the other hand, a "dovish" option supported by Mao and Lin Piao sought to avoid a direct military confrontation with the superior armed might of the United States by following a low-risk response. They rejected Lo's hard line because it would greatly increase the risk of war with the United States and opposed the demand for reconciliation with Moscow because they regarded the Soviet "Modern Revisionists" as an even worse enemy than the American Imperialists.[60] Instead, they advocated a "defense in depth" or "people's war" strategy. As articulated in a major treatise by Lin Piao, "Long Live the Victory of People's War," published with éclat in the People's Daily (3 September 1965), the strategy called for a people's war on China's soil against the invading enemies. Unlike Lo's hawkish stance asking China to intervene in the Indochina war, the Mao-Lin group wanted to fight only after China was attacked or invaded by the Americans. To justify such a low profile, Lin's essay asserted: "Revolution or people's war in any country is the business of the masses in that country and should be carried out primarily by their own efforts"; the people must not rely upon foreign assistance.

Although the "dovish" posture gained an upper hand and Lo Jui-ch'ing was purged in December 1965,[61] the "war and peace" debate continued and was entangled with domestic political considerations. For example, P'eng Chen, who previously supported the Mao-Lin option and was vehemently opposed to a united front with Moscow,[62] shifted his position in the first quarter of 1966, when he endorsed the formation of a "broadest international united front" in opposition to American imperialism in the course of negotiations with a Japanese Communist Party delegation which sought to rally the support of the Chinese, Russian, and other Asian Communists to aid Hanoi.[63] A Chinese report that P'eng Chen proposed to head a CCP delegation to attend the Twenty-Third Congress of the CPSU in Moscow in March 1966—a proposal which was turned down by Mao—also suggested that he had adopted a more conciliatory attitude toward Moscow.[64] Apparently, realizing that his handling of the ideological rectification campaign had alienated Mao and that his political survival was in danger, P'eng Chen reversed himself and joined those who favored rapprochement with the Soviets and a tougher policy against the United States in Indochina.[65]

Standing together with P'eng Chen on this issue were Liu Shao-ch'i and Teng Hsiao-p'ing.[66] Several domestic political considerations appear to have underlain their advocacy of a united front with the Soviet Union and a more active Chinese role in the Indochina conflict. First, if China should go to war with the United States, or if the crisis intensified, the PLA and its leaders would be preoccupied with the external situation, and Mao would be denied the use of the PLA in the internal power struggle. Failing that, Mao's opponents may have seen the militant policy they advocated as a means to captivate the anti-American elements in the party and the PLA so as to win their support in the eventual showdown with Mao and his supporters.

It is well known now that the controversy over China's policy toward the Vietnamese war was decided in favor of the Mao-Lin group. China did give substantial materiel to Hanoi and even dispatched highway construction and maintenance workers, but the Chinese refrained from sending combat personnel to Vietnam to fight with the Vietnamese. The assurance by Washington that the United States had no intention of escalating the conflict beyond the borders of Vietnam and did not seek the destruction of the Hanoi regime may have been used by Mao to win the approval of his "dovish" policy in the party. Ironically, as Karnow points out, "by minimizing the American threat to China, President Lyndon Johnson unwittingly provided Mao with the respite he required to trigger the Cultural Revolution."[67]

In late March 1966 Liu Shao-ch'i left Peking to visit Pakistan, Afghanistan, and Burma; he did not return to North China or East China until 20 April. Soon after Liu was away, P'eng Chen came under attack. On 28 March Mao denounced P'eng Chen and the "February Outline Report" for undermining the Cultural Revolution and protecting bad people; he confided to K'ang Sheng his intention to disband the Five-Man Cultural Revolution Group and to reorganize the CC Propaganda Department and Peking Party Committee.[68] After being informed of Mao's criticism, P'eng on 1 April set up a "three-man group" in the Peking Party Committee to repudiate Teng T'o, thus attempting to pacify Mao.[69] From 9 to 12 April K'ang Sheng and Ch'en Po-ta specified and denounced P'eng's "crimes" in a session of the CC Secretariat which was also attended by Chou En-lai.[70] The meeting resolved to revoke the February Outline Report and set up a new organization under the Politburo Standing Committee to carry out the Cultural Revolution. On 16 April Mao convened a meeting of the Politburo Standing Committee at Hangchow and P'eng Chen was summoned to account for his wrongdoings.[71] On 18 April the organ of the PLA issued an editorial, "Hold Aloft the Great Red Banner of Mao Tse-tung's Thought, Actively Take Part in Socialist Cultural Revolution"; the editorial paraphrased the Forum Summary of the PLA and declared war on the anti-party, anti-socialist "black line" in the cultural front.[72] At the end of a four-day struggle in the Hangchow Politburo Standing Committee, on 20 April (the second day after Liu Shao-ch'i returned from Burma), P'eng was for practical purposes removed from power. Whether Liu had been deliberately kept away at a crucial moment when one of his important allies was being removed can only be a matter of conjecture.[73]

The political demise of P'eng Chen was subsequently made official by a CC circular issued on 16 May after a Politburo Standing Committee meeting which had been in session in Hangchow since the second week of May. The 16 May circular revoked the February Outline Report and announced the dissolution of P'eng Chen's Five-Man CC Cultural Revolution Group and the formation of a new Cultural Revolution Group under the Politburo Standing Committee.[74] By this time, the cultural establishment which had obstructed Mao's demands for reform had crumbled. Lu Ting-yi, who made his last public appearance on 28 February, seemed to be in political disgrace soon afterward; his political fate was sealed on 8 May during a Politburo meeting when his "crimes" were exposed.[75] Chou Yang had become ill in January 1966, and he then began to relinquish his official duties. The targets of Mao and his supporters, however, were not confined to these persons. The 16 May circular had called for repudiation and dismissal of the "bourgeois representatives" who "had wormed their way" into the party, the government, the military, and various cultural organizations.

In response to Mao's "mobilization order," "revolutionary students and teachers" in Peking's educational institutions began to rise up to attack officials of the school administration. The students were further encouraged when the old Peking Party Committee was reshuffled and Li Hsueh-feng, then first secretary of the North China Bureau, became its new chief. On 25 May Nieh Yuan-tzu, a teaching assistant at the Peking University, and her six followers put up what Mao later called "the first Marxist-Leninist big-character poster in the entire country" to denounce an educational official of the Peking Party Committee and Lu P'ing, the president of the Peking University and secretary of its Party Committee.[76] Lu immediately organized his supporters in the university to demonstrate in support of the university administration and to wage a struggle against Nieh and her followers, who were denounced as counterrevolutionary traitors, bad elements, and so forth.[77] As a result of Mao's phone call to K'ang Sheng, the text of Nieh's poster was broadcast by Radio Peking throughout the nation on 1 June and published in the *People's Daily* the following day accompanied by a positive commentary.[78] Emboldened, Maoist students in Peking and other cities soon followed the example of Nieh to attack their school administration, thus ushering in a new mass movement of the GPCR. Maoists later referred to Mao's intervention in the Nieh incident as Mao's "great strategic measure" which kindled the flame of the GPCR throughout China.

Liu Shao-ch'i and Teng Hsiao-p'ing had no alternative but to fight back in self-defense. Like P'eng Chen, they could not afford to oppose the GPCR openly; what they did was to control its direction and circumvent the mass movement which threatened to disrupt the established political order. In early June, Liu hurriedly convened a Central Work Conference in Peking to formulate a guideline for the GPCR, the "Eight Articles of the Central Committee," which prescribed restrictions on the actions of the "revolutionary masses."[79] The meeting also authorized the dispatch of "work teams" by central and local party organizations to various schools and institutions on the pretext of giving leadership to the GPCR. Liu himself gave the following account:

At a certain period before 18 July, Chairman Mao was not in Peking. I took the lead in carrying out the daily, regular business of the party Central Committee. The state of the cultural revolution in various sectors of Peking city was reported at the central conference, over which I presided, and I made mistaken decisions and gave mistaken approval there. One wrong decision I made, for example, was the decision that a work team would be dispatched at the request of the various central ministerial committees and the Chinese Young Communist League headquarters. At the time, the various central ministerial committees and the Chinese YCL headquarters quite actively requested the dispatch of work teams to various areas. Through the recommendation of the new Peking municipal committee, work teams were dispatched not only to various schools but also to various organs.[80]

On 3 June the first work team was sent to Peking University by the Peking Party Committee. Bowing to the pressure of the Maoists, the new Peking Party Committee dismissed Lu P'ing and took measures to reorganize the Peking University administration, but it authorized the work team to assume all the power of the University Party Committee, thereby retaining the control of the GPCR in the university. Just as in the various stages of the SEC, work teams were the instrument with which the "organization men" in the party attempted to control the mass movement from above. In accordance with the current central policy, and following the example of the Peking municipal authorities, various provincial authorities soon dispatched work teams to schools to provide similar leadership. Initially the work teams appear to have been welcomed by most students and to have established their "revolutionary credentials." In the name of the provincial authorities, they quickly removed the top officials in the school administration and organized students to wage a struggle against the deposed school administrators, blaming them for having suppressed and undermined the GPCR.[81]

Soon, however, leftist students discovered that the work teams, in assuming the power of university authorities, were simply a new manifestation of their former suppressors, and the repeated struggle sessions (e.g., Kangaroo courts, trials) organized by the work teams against the school administrators and alleged rightist professors and students represented a cunning attempt to confine the GPCR within schools and to shift the targets of attack away from "capitalist powerholders" in the provincial party apparatus. Therefore, at least if later Maoist reports are to be credited, opposition against the work teams gradually rose and subsequently became widespread. But the work teams hit back hard at their critics. They were able to manipulate the slogan "To oppose the work teams is to oppose the party"[82] to maximum advantage, and in most instances they won support from the majority of students.

If we are to believe later reports—most of them emanating from Maoist sources—the work teams were very harsh toward the "revolutionary masses." In many cases, the work teams struck at those who had the audacity to oppose their leadership as "counterrevolutionaries," "conspirators," and so forth, and organized their supporters to struggle and persecute the dissidents. In Peking's Tsinghua University, for example, K'uai Ta-fu, a student leader, and his followers hung a big-character poster attacking the work team, Wang Kuang-mei (Madame Liu Shao-ch'i) and other members of the Tsinghua work team allegedly instigated the "hoodwinked masses" to struggle against K'uai and branded K'uai and more than 800 "revolutionary teachers and students" as "counterrevolutionaries" and "pseudo-leftists but actual rightists," and they enforced "white terror" (i.e., police brutality, considered characteristic of the capitalist system) that caused the death of one person and impelled many persons to commit suicide.[83]

There are indications that student opposition to the work teams was directed and manipulated behind the scenes by Mao's top aides in the CRG or at least had their blessing. When the case of K'uai was brought up at a high-level party meeting in early July, K'ang Sheng defended K'uai. Allegedly, Liu Shao-ch'i denounced K'ang for "failure to understand the situation," and K'ang pointed out that "forbidding K'uai Ta-fu to bring his complaint to the Central Committee at least is not in accord with state law and is in contravention of Party regulations." Reportedly, Ch'en Po-ta supported K'ang's viewpoint and sent two CRG members, Kuan Feng and Wang Li, to Tsinghua to pay a visit to K'uai, who was in custody.

Mao quickly learned of the Liu-Teng efforts to counterbalance and "subvert" his opening moves; there followed a massive and decisive Maoist attack. By June 1966 Lin Piao had already moved reliable troop units to the Peking area and appointed General Fu Ts'ung-pi as the new commander of the Peking garrison. On 18 July 1966, after an absence of almost eight months from the nation's capital, Mao returned to Peking to personally direct the campaign against the Liu-Teng leadership. For example, he called a Central Work Conference on 21 July to review the product of work teams and pushed through the conference a decision to recall the work teams. On 26 July the *People's Daily* publicized with great fanfare the news and picture of Mao's swim in the Yangtse ten days earlier—a ploy to dissipate doubts in the minds of many Chinese officials about Mao's state of health and to signal to cadres at all levels that he was still in active control. And on 5 August, four days after the opening of the acrimonious Eleventh CC Plenary Session, which was packed by "revolutionary teachers and students," Mao himself wrote a big-character poster to "bombard" the "bourgeois headquarters"; the poster assailed the leadership of the GPCR by Liu Shao-ch'i and Teng Hsiao-p'ing in June and July 1966 and attacked Liu's policy errors in 1962 and 1964.[84]

In the course of the Plenum, Mao and his supporters, under circumstances which still remain mysterious to outsiders,[85] managed to discredit the leadership of Liu and Teng and censured them for having produced and enforced an erroneous "bourgeois reactionary line." The Plenum also reshuffled the Politburo, elected Lin Piao as the sole vice-chairman of the party and Mao's successor, and formally approved Mao's blueprint for the GPCR—the now-celebrated "Sixteen-Point Decision," which endorsed Mao's call to purge "those power-holders within the Party who take the capitalist road."[86]

The censure of Liu and Teng and the attack on their policies in the Plenum suddenly put the provincial leaders in a highly vulnerable political position. It had been demonstrated that Mao possessed the power to redefine issues and he had ruled the policies of Liu and Teng both politically and ideologically erroneous. Thus the provincial leaders, to their dismay and horror, found themselves the executors of a policy line denounced by none other than Mao himself as having "enforced a bourgeois dictatorship and struck down the surging movement of the great cultural revolution of the proletariat."[87] Few provincial leaders had any intention of opposing Mao; indeed, all of them had been at great pains to display their loyalty to Mao by carrying out the policies laid down by Liu and Teng in the name of the central leadership, policies which they very likely believed had Mao's endorsement. Yet now, in the midst of rapidly changing events, they found themselves standing on the opposite side of Mao and directly involved in a furious political conflict. Consequently, they had good reason to fear and suspect that they would become primary targets in the purge projected in the Plenum's Sixteen-Point Decision.

The Maoist leadership did nothing to allay their misgivings. On the contrary, it added to the provincial leaders' fears and suspicions by both words and deeds. Rightly or wrongly, the provincial leaders interpreted a rapid succession of developments as an unmistakable sign that a sweeping purge by Mao was under way: Lin Piao's speeches at the Peking Red Guard rallies on 18 and 31 August; the simultaneous press campaign which enthusiastically acclaimed the "rebellion" of the Red Guards and "revolutionary rebels" and encouraged them to go to provinces to storm the "bourgeois headquarters" and "drag out" the capitalist power-holders; and the subsequent activities of the Red Guards and "rebels" in response to these orders. Under the prevailing conditions, the provincial leaders felt they could not take a chance, so they used all the resources at their disposal to devise a number of strategies for self-preservation. Their efforts in turn provoked the Maoist leadership to press harder and to attempt to oust the recalcitrant provincial officials from positions of power. As a result, the conflict escalated rapidly and continuously on both sides, up to the end of 1966, when there was no turning back.[88] Then, in 1967 and 1968, the Maoist effort to remove these officials and to destroy the party-government organization in which they were firmly entrenched resulted in almost total disruption of Chinese society and brought China to the brink of civil war.

Mao's Sources of Power and His Political Strategies

After the Tenth Plenum in September 1962 Mao on several occasions forcefully intervened in the policy-making process, yet he still had to overcome considerable resistance by other party leaders before he was able to impose on the party the policy lines he desired. In fact, these policy lines were often surreptitiously modified by other leaders in the course of implementation, increasing Mao's anger and frustration. He felt compelled to launch an all-out attack on his opponents and to recapture control of the direction of Chinese revolution. During the spring and summer of 1966, although Mao and his supporters were apparently in the minority, he succeeded in disposing of powerful opponents like P'eng Chen, Teng Hsiao-p'ing, and Liu Shao-ch'i even though they controlled the party machine and commanded a large number of followers in the CC. A few observations on Mao's sources of power and his political tactics are in order.

One important source of Mao's power is organizational: he has been the chairman of the CC of the party since 1945. As the party's head, he had the authority to make basic decisions and direct the party organizations, and this authority gained wide acceptance in the polity. One informal arrangement in the leadership operation, the division of "first line" and "second line" in the Politburo Standing Committee, may have solidified Mao's authority. This arrangement had others manning the first line—the actual management of society—while Mao was in the second line concerning himself with defining basic policy goals and making important decisions.[89] Although this arrangement was not strictly followed in the 1960s and other party leaders did in fact exercise the power of definition, they rarely challenged Mao's leadership position in the open, even when they were fighting against him.

Mao's power never depended only on the office he held. It also derived from the history of the CCP movement: Mao was the principal organizer of the party and the architect of the Chinese Communist revolution after 1935. Furthermore, the force of his personality and intellect gave him immense influence; he was characterized by charisma, total political commitment, great self-confidence, and imagination and originality in applying theories to specific conditions as well as an outstanding ability to evoke strong loyalty from followers.

Mao's ability to assert his authority has been greatly enhanced by his capacity as the top ideologist of the regime: he has made numerous authoritative ideological pronouncements and constantly manipulated political symbols. He alone possessed the prerogative to assess the state of the nation and define the salient issues in society. Mao's ideological role contributed much to his political influence; his ideological pronouncements set goals, constrained choices, and set the parameters within which specific problems were tackled. This was clearly reflected in the SEC. Even when other party leaders did not genuinely share Mao's diagnosis of and prescription for China's problems, they were obliged to justify their own policies on Mao's ideological formulations and base the legitimacy of these policies on Mao's thought. Although they often resorted to a tactic that the Chinese Communists fittingly describe as "waving the red flag to oppose the Red Flag," they had to accept the Maoist premises and, in the long run, reinforce the primacy of Mao.[90]

Furthermore, the elevation of the "thought of Mao Tse-tung" to the level of a new political creed and Mao's skill in manipulating political symbols gave him tremendous leverage over his opponents. The formation of a strong personal cult of Mao gradually turned Mao into an institution, and the thought of Mao became "a new standard of legitimacy and correctness with which the actions and opinions of many top leaders were to be judged."[91] Other party leaders were thus disarmed from opposing or attacking Mao publicly, inasmuch as Mao had become the source of authority and correctness and they could not base a claim to legitimacy in opposition to Mao.

In addition to taking full advantage of his political and ideological authority, Mao also skillfully manipulated issues to get what he wanted. One of the issues he manipulated was Sino-Soviet relations. There is no question that Mao, for a variety of reasons, was bitterly hostile to the Soviets, and particularly to Khrushchev. It now appears that Mao deliberately escalated the dispute between Peking and Moscow so that he could deter his colleagues from taking the "revisionist" road and compel them to adopt the anti-revisionist programs he favored at home. For example, the celebrated July 1964 article "On Khrushchev's Phoney Communism and Its Historical Lesson for the World" launched a scathing attack on revisionist trends in the Soviet Union not merely to criticize the CPSU leadership but to hold the Soviet Union up as a "negative example" for the entire international Communist movement, and most specifically for China.[92] Khrushchev's revisionism, the article asserts, "sounds the alarm for all socialist countries, including China, and for all Communists and Workers' Parties, including the Communist Party of China." In the course of providing an ideological diagnosis of the origins, nature, and consequences of Khrushchev's revisionist policies in Russia, the article also diagnosed what had been going amiss in Chinese society:

> Classes and class struggle still remain, the activities of the overthrown reactionary classes plotting a comeback still continue, and we still have speculative activities by new and old bourgeois elements and desperate forays by embezzlers, grafters, and degenerates. There are also cases of degeneration in a few primary organizations; what is more, these degenerates do their utmost to find protectors and agents in the higher leading bodies.

From Mao's point of view, combating foreign revisionism worked to prevent revisionism at home. This strategy had enormous consequences. The bitter attack on the Soviet Union generated in Chinese society hostility toward the Soviets and had the effect of deterring those in the CCP leadership who, for whatever considerations, might push for a rapprochement with Moscow. The attack on Khrushchev's revisionism tended to discredit ideologically policies that smacked of revisionism and to deprive of legitimacy those who might justify their policies, whether in the military, economic, or other fields, on the "advanced" Soviet experiences. Most important, the attack on Khrushchev's revisionism committed the CCP politically and ideologically to what must be done about preventing revisionism in China and enabled Mao to impose on the party his anti-revisionist programs. Thus, not surprisingly, the SEC and many other measures taken by the regime from 1962 to 1966 were based on Mao's fifteen-point program (put forth in the treatise "On Khrushchev's Phoney Communism") and on his other prescriptions to prevent revisionism and to ensure successful continuation of the revolution in China.

Another issue that he manipulated was his own succession. When he called for training and bringing up China's "revolutionary successors" in July 1964, he was genuinely concerned with the future of China's revolution and wanted to cultivate worthy revolutionaries of the younger generation who would carry out his revolutionary vision. In raising the question of "revolutionary succession," Mao also appeared to be raising the issue of his own succession,[93] although he had earlier designated Liu Shao-ch'i as his heir-apparent and the issue of his succession seemed to have been settled. Before the Eleventh Plenum in the summer of 1966, Liu's status as Chairman Mao's successor had added much political weight to his already enormous power and enabled him to speak with very great authority on a wide range of issues, yet, precisely because Liu had become so powerful and because his leadership had not lived up to Mao's expectations, Mao was having second thoughts.[94] Mao's grooming of Lin Piao and the approbation of the PLA before the nation may be seen as an attempt to build up a new heir or a "counterheir." When Mao listed five requirements for the "worthy successors to the revolutionary cause of the proletariat" (in "On Khrushchev's Phoney Communism") he introduced the yardstick with which he wanted to measure the "candidate" to his mantle.

Mao's manipulation of his own succession served definite political purposes. He could pressure Liu to display unquestioned loyalty to Mao and whole-hearted support for his policies; failing that, Mao could undermine Liu politically through withdrawal of endorsement. He could also sow dissension among other top leaders by making them compete to succeed him. Furthermore, he could use his succession as "bait" to cajole and win supporters from the ambitious aspirants among the top leaders. P'eng Chen, until his downfall widely regarded by outside observers as a contender to succeed Mao, appeared to have been "courted" by Mao. In September 1964 the press accorded him the honor of being Mao's "close comrade-in-arms" for the first time; after that his responsibilities steadily increased (e.g., he was appointed head of the Five-Man CC Cultural Revolution Group and first vice-chairman of the NPC Standing Committee).

Mao's victory in the political struggle in 1966 should also be attributed to his ability to gain the allegiance of Lin Piao and to mobilize the support of the PLA at crucial moments. Beginning in 1963, Mao had gradually built up the PLA as a "counterinstitution" to the party. As a result of his call for the nation to emulate the PLA, PLA methods of organization, operation, and ideological training were presented as models to be learned by all political, economic, and social organizations, including the party itself. Mao's call was an indirect rebuke to those who administered the party, for it meant they had not done their jobs properly, and the nationwide campaign to emulate the PLA in the mid-1960s boosted the prestige of the PLA. The establishment in the party and government organizations of a network of "political work departments," clearly modeled after the PLA's political commission system, enabled the PLA to extend its influence into the operations of the party and government, since these political departments were staffed largely by political cadres transferred from the PLA and by civilian cadres who were sent to PLA schools for training.

In the course of Mao's tug-of-war with P'eng Chen over the Wu Han case, the *Liberation Army Daily*, the organ of the PLA, voiced strong support to Mao's cause and helped sway to Mao's side those party officials who were uncommitted. In the spring of 1966, the army paper openly rivaled the *People's Daily* and clearly indicated the PLA's intervention on Mao's side, which enabled him to overcome the stubborn resistance of P'eng Chen.[95]

In the summer of 1966, PLA support was crucial to Mao's defeat of Liu and Teng. There were reports that troops loyal to Lin Piao were moved into Peking in June 1966; in fact, Fu Ts'ung-pi, a long-time aide of Yang Cheng-Wu, the newly appointed acting chief of staff, took over the command of the Peking garrison at this juncture, and the *People's Daily* editorial board was reorganized on 1 June and placed under the control of the PLA. It is not known whether troops were used to intimidate Mao's opponents during the Eleventh Plenum. Nevertheless, it seems obvious that PLA leaders played a vital role in the victory of Mao and the defeat of his opponents in the Plenum; this can be seen from the fact that three marshals of the PLA, Yeh Chien-ying, Hsu Hsiang-chien, and Nieh Jung-chen, were rewarded by their promotions to the Politburo.

Finally, Mao's long experience in political in-fighting and his political acumen served him well in his struggle with his opponents in 1965–66. When situations were unfavorable, before he could be certain of victory, Mao would temporize, wait for "suitable climate and soil," and avoid hasty actions. Behind the scenes, however, Mao carefully prepared the ground for a decisive assault— he formed the coalition and recruited political allies (Chou En-lai, Lin Piao, etc.) and organized his supporters into action. His tactics of "divide and rule" and "take one at a time" kept his targets isolated politically and prevented them from taking concrete actions. Such clever maneuvers often misled his opponents and kept them in the dark as to his true intent, thus enabling him to concentrate his strength to strike at them one by one, first Lo Jui-ch'ing in December 1956, then P'eng Chen in April 1966, and finally Liu and Teng in July and August 1966.

7

Conclusion:
A "Pluralistic" Policy-Making Process

Thus far we have examined in some detail the formulation and implementation of a number of policies. The following pages summarize the major findings of this study and make additional observations on China's political system.

Politics of Conflict

Despite Mao's continual imposition of his own policies on China's political process, disputes and dissensions in the leadership were frequent and intense, even during the period when Mao exercised a fairly tight reign. Consequently, policy was significantly affected. The policy shift tended to assume an alternating pattern between conservative and radical policies, following a change in the balance of power in the decision-making councils. In other words, when the radical view prevailed in the party, the political pendulum would swing to the left, policies to effect rapid revolutionary changes would be pushed, and the leadership would stress mobilization of the masses and the ability of human will to overcome objective limitations. When the conservative view gained an upper hand, however, the political pendulum would swing to the right, the radical policies would be moderated and "consolidation" (retreat) would become the order of the day, and material incentives for the people as well as objective conditions would receive attention.

This peculiar pattern of policy oscillation was noted by Skinner and Winckler, who identified eight cycles of "radicalization" and "deradicalization" at the national level between 1949 and 1968.[1] Each cycle, according to these authors, went through six phases: normalcy, mobilization, high tide, deterioration, retrenchment, and demobilization; and each phase witnessed changes in the goals of the regime, its prescriptions for leadership style, the actual behavior of cadres, and the compliance behavior of the population. Dynamics that caused these changes, according to Skinner and Winckler, were provided by the interactions between the leadership and the population on the one hand and among the leaders themselves on the other.

That disputes and conflicts have divided the CCP leadership is now beyond doubt. Are these conflicts the manifestations of the "struggle between the two lines" (capitalism versus socialism), as the Chinese communists have asserted since the GPCR? It seems clear from this study that CCP leaders, including those disgraced during the GPCR, shared a common belief system and agreed on many basic goals. Commitment to a common ideology and goals notwithstanding, there are enormous diversities in all the sources and components of the CCP ideology and there are many levels of understanding and diverse interpretations to which each ideological tenet is susceptible. It is far from the truth for the Maoists to claim that Liu Shao-ch'i and other fallen leaders are "capitalist power-holders" who intend to restore capitalism in China. Their disputes with Mao, as shown in the case studies here, pertained to timing, speed, methods, and tactics of socialist construction.

Were these policy disputes and conflicts merely "honest disagreement" among the CCP leaders or did they involve a struggle for power? Some policy disputes arose from differences in judgment among leaders who, due to the different nature of their work, maintained divergent perspectives. Teng Tzu-hui, the regime's top agricultural official until his political eclipse in the autumn of 1957, showed genuine concern for the burden of the peasants and consistently fought against Mao's radical rural policy through the 1950s. He paid a heavy political price for his conviction: he was removed as director of the State Council Staff Office of Agriculture and Foresty (until 1959 State Council Seventh Staff Office) in October 1962, and the CC Rural Work Department (the highest agricultural organ in the party), which he had headed, was abolished in September 1962.

Teng Tzu-hui's conservative outlook was shared to different degrees by leaders such as Ch'en Yun, who specialized in economic affairs. Inasmuch as they were in a better position to know China's economic realities, they became more sensitive to objective limitations. These economic officials in the party, in contrast with party officials working in other functional areas, tended to be more cautious and placed greater emphasis on "economic" methods rather than "political" methods to foster economic development.

Teng and other economic officials, however, were not entirely oblivious to their roles and the interest of their bureaucracies. It is a truism that bureaucracies everywhere generate and guard their own special interests. In fact, one can argue that it was in Teng's interest to promote measures that would increase the peasants' zeal for production, for he depended on the peasants to fulfill the targets on the basis of which the agencies he headed were to be judged. Similarly, other top economic officials also had vested interests in increasing agricultural production because agricultural output directly and immediately affected the performance of other sectors in the economy. The PLA leaders from time to time also displayed their "departmentalist" tendencies; for example, when the PLA was asked by the party to take part and assist in various economic construction tasks during the second half of the 1950s, many military leaders demurred because they feared these tasks would interfere with the training and normal routines of the PLA. Thus policy disputes in China manifest many of the traits characteristic of bureaucratic politics generally.

P'eng Teh-huai's attack on the Great Leap and commune policies, which resulted in his dismissal as minister of defense, has been attributed by some writers to his conflict with Mao in other policy areas, notably military policy and Sino-Soviet military relations.[2] To what degree P'eng's criticism of Mao's leadership at Lushan was motivated by P'eng to settle his old scores with Mao in their personal conflict can only be a matter of conjecture.[3] Political actors are human beings; on occasions their human hopes and fears, human greatness and human failings—impossible to document—can become the overriding motivation of their political action.

Policy conflicts frequently were intimately tied to power struggle among leaders. In the case of administrative decentralization, those party officials who were entrenched in central ministries wanted only a gradual limited transfer of power to provincial authorities because it was in their interest to have ministries retain control over economic planning and administration. On the other hand, for obvious reasons, the provincial leaders generally supported a far-reaching decentralization of power to the provinces. Although arguments were presented on the merits of the various types of decentralization measures considered, the stake was power to be gained or lost.

Similarly, events on the eve of the GPCR provided ample evidence of power plays among the rival leaders. Power considerations figured prominently in the disputes over the Socialist Education Campaign, ideological rectification campaign, and China's policy toward the Indochina war. Both the Maoists and their opponents used the conflicts to enhance their own positions and to undercut their rivals.

Multiplicity of Political Participants

Another outstanding characteristic of China's policy-making process was its relative openness—"open" in the sense that the process was not monopolized by a few top leaders who largely agreed on their objectives and made major decisions alone. Rather, the process was accessible to a significant number of party officials below the top level of the leadership hierarchy (the Politburo and its Standing Committee), many of them from the provinces, and these officials affected, in various ways and in varying degree, the formulation and implementation of the regime's policy.

Although the CC, as an institution, rarely initiated policy measures, the top leadership sought and took into account opinions of CC members, many of whom occupied key positions in both the central and provincial apparatus relied upon to implement central directives. Exactly how the "anticipated reaction" of the CC members conditioned and shaped a decision of the Politburo is hard to gauge; nonetheless, the influence was certainly present, although perhaps indirect or limited. When the top leadership was deadlocked, however, policy conflicts at the top were carried to the CC for resolution; consequently, members of the CC were drawn into participation in settling disputes and making momentous decisions which, at times, changed the political fate of powerful leaders (e.g., P'eng Teh-Huai and Liu Shao-ch'i).

There seemed to be a special kind of political actor in Communist China, one who did not occupy high official position and rarely appeared in the public limelight, yet was able to shape the course of events from behind the scene. Some of these "silent power-wielders" were the personal aides or advisers to the top party leaders. For instance, Teng Li-ch'un, Liu Shao-ch'i's political secretary, was able to get things done through phone calls he made,[4] for what he said was thought by other party officials to reflect the wishes of his boss. Ch'en Po-ta, Mao's brain-truster and political confidant, had been underrated by outside observers in the past; materials available since the Cultural Revolution reveal that he often made "suggestions" to other party officials or fed ideas to Mao which led Mao to intervene, but he was apparently resented by others for having both access to and the ear of the Chairman.[5] Chiang Ch'ing, Chang Ch'un-ch'iao, and Yao Wen-yuan have become prominent political figures since the second half of the 1960s, but before the Cultural Revolution they largely operated behind the scenes. They advised Mao on various issues and he seems to have lent a willing ear to their views, which subsequently became political stimuli in the policy-making process.[6] Hsu Li-ch'un's official position was not very high—he was one of the several deputy directors of the CC Propaganda Department after 1961—but he allegedly was P'eng Chen's political advisor and frequently assisted P'eng in drafting important party documents, including the February Outline Report of 1966. We lack detailed and complete knowledge of the "silent power-wielders" in China, but it is possible that there were Chinese counterparts of Harry Hopkins, Theodore Sorenson, Richard Goodwin, Bill Moyers, H.R. Haldeman, and the like in Peking, advising and influencing the thinking of top CCP leaders and thus decisively affecting the policy of the regime.[7]

Cadres at the provincial and lower levels also had a significant impact on the policy-making processes. These cadres controlled the flow of information and through the manipulation of information they affected the leaders' perception of realities and indirectly shaped their policy choices. A good example is the highly exaggerated reports on industrial and agricultural production and on the miraculous results of deep plowing and close planting during 1958 and

1959, all of which either misled the top leaders or reinforced their established predilections. Nevertheless, they constituted an input which ultimately affected the policy output of the regime.

Moreover, the top leadership relied on the bureaucracy to project its will. Policy defined at the top by the leaders had to be translated into concrete actions by cadres at lower levels, who had to make a host of secondary decisions which frequently affected—and even altered—the substance of original policy. The character of the policy formulated by the CCP leadership seems to have contributed substantially to the leeway lower cadres had in the implementation stage. More often than not, policy directives by the top leaders only defined broad goals and left the cadres to "*hsiang pan-fa,*" that is, to use their ingenuity to get things done. Since lower cadres were compelled to find and mobilize the necessary resources, human and material, to accomplish prescribed goals, they often had to take implementation very much into their own hands Bureaucrats in China, as elsewhere, had their own motivations and particularistic interests. They would not automatically implement central directives that clashed with their interests; they had to be pushed into action. At times they evaded or tried to bend the directives to suit their needs. Frequently the action of the leadership was a response to problems created by bureaucratic evasion or inertia.

The CCP leadership seemed well aware of the difficulties in maintaining a responsible bureaucracy and had developed an elaborate set of bureaucracy-controlling techniques to enforce its ruling priorities [8] One of the techniques was the use of a "campaign approach" to policy implementation. The reliance on this technique, as Barnett points out, enables the leadership to mobilize and concentrate all efforts on achieving the defined objective at a given time, to break through the bureaucratic routines, and to combat the tendency toward bureaucratization.[9]

The use of the campaign approach in implementing policy may have solved some problems, but it created others. "Crash" campaigns inevitably resulted in undesirable side-effects and excesses. This was the case in the wake of the accelerated collectivization drive and the implementation of the twelve-year agricultural program and in many "crash" programs during the Great Leap Forward. Spurred on by higher authorities to fulfill and overfulfill various targets, and under constant political pressure and ideological exhortation to appear "progressive," local officials were often compelled to opt for targets even higher than those imposed on them and to do everything to achieve the impossible.

A mass movement which derives its power and effectiveness from the initiative and enthusiasm of lower cadres necessarily generates its own momentum, which the top leadership cannot always control. The tendency toward excesses in the course of such campaigns probably is an inescapable hazard in a totalitarian regime; the same phenomenon was also present in the

Soviet system, particularly during Stalin's collectivization campaign in the 1930s.[10]

The actions of the lower officials in the implementation stage—whether they involved evasion, distortion, poor compliance, or overcompliance—inevitably created new situations and new problems ("feedback") to which the top leaders had to react; they then had to make new decisions. In this sense, lower cadres can be said to have participated, at least indirectly or negatively, in policy initiation.

On certain occasions, however, lower cadres played a less indirect and more positive role in originating policies. The communization movement in 1958 is a good example. The available evidence indicated that the decision to establish communes was first made by Mao and then formally ratified by the Politburo in the Peitaiho Conference in August 1958. Mao, however, and perhaps his Politburo colleagues as well, were greatly influenced by local leaders and cadres in Honan, the cradle of the commune system, who provided not only ideas relevant to the concept of the new rural organization but also concrete examples of operative communes. In other words, the choices of the top leadership were, in a sense, structured by cadres in Honan. In fact, several communes in Honan were selected by the CCP leadership as models to be emulated throughout China[11] and as such they greatly affected the ways in which the commune system developed throughout China in the fall of 1958.

Thus policy in Communist China was not made by a few top leaders alone; actors possessing different political resources participated, directly or indirectly, in each stage of the policy-making process and affected, in a variety of ways, the decision-output of the regime. A political actor's resources may come from his control of a segment of the party-state apparatus, or from one or more official positions which grant decision-making authority in a formal sense; or a political actor with no important official position still may have access to the top party leaders. Political resources may also stem from the functions the political actors perform, such as cadres' implementation of leadership policies, and from the opportunities to control or manipulate the flow of information. An actor may also derive political influence from his expertise on a given issue or from the fact that he speaks for a wide public; for instance, an agricultural official will have influence on agricultural matters.

Expansion of Political Participation

According to the CCP constitution of 1956, when the CC is not in session (as was often the case) the Politburo or its Standing Committee is the highest decision-making body in the party. The principle of democratic centralism, on which the CCP is organized, is designed to keep the effective decision-making power of the party in the hands of a few people at the top of the leadership hierarchy. In fact, when the top leaders in the Politburo (those in the Politburo Standing Committee) were in essential agreement among themselves, matters rarely went beyond this inner circle, for the decision they made by themselves would carry enough political weight to gain acceptance by others.

Despite the fact that Mao wielded enormous political influence, he did not always carry the day. As shown in our case studies, many of the programs he favored were modified or blocked by other party leaders who held different views. As leadership unity broke down and top leaders were involved in policy conflict, they were compelled to go to the CC or other large political forums to settle their differences. Consequently, officials outside the inner circle increasingly took part in policy decision and conflict resolution.

To project his will, Mao often engaged in politicking to seek wider support and used various maneuvers to overcome his opposition. In July 1955, for example, Mao appealed directly to provincial leaders, over the heads of his colleagues in the Politburo, to gain support of a radical collectivization policy. This maneuver enabled Mao to secure the overwhelming support of most provincial party secretaries and to disarm opposition from his colleagues at the center. In the late 1950s, when Mao was promoting his Great Leap programs, he actively enlisted the backing of provincial leaders and used such support to overcome resistance at the center.

Such maneuvers by Mao, designed to redress the balance of power in his favor, resulted in the expansion of the arena of political conflict and mobilization of new participants into the policy-making process.[12] Furthermore, after the collapse of Mao's utopian programs in the early 1960s, and as Mao was opposed and politically eclipsed by other party leaders who controlled the party machinery, he went outside the party to seek support. As is well known now, Mao turned to the PLA, coopted it, and used PLA intervention to remove P'eng Chen, Liu Shao-ch'i, Teng Hsiao-p'ing, and others from positions of power in the regime in 1966.

From the summer of 1966 on, Mao went one step further by extending the political conflict to the "public" arena; he mobilized extra-party forces—the student Red Guards and "revolutionary rebels" drawn from workers and youth—to push his GPCR crusade. The resistance to Mao's radical goals was so widespread and prevalent in the party organization at the center and in the provinces and Mao's supporters within the party councils were in the minority, that he had no alternative but to enlarge the area of conflict and invoke the aid of the "masses" to crush his opposition within the party. The participation of the masses in the political conflict reached a climax after January 1967 when they were extolled by the Maoist leadership to launch an unprecedented all-out assault against the entire power structure and to seize power from the "capitalist power-holders." In emulation of the 1871 Paris Commune rebellion, the Red Guards and "rebels" rioted, occupied party headquarters and government buildings, ousted and in many instances handcuffed party and government officials, paralyzed the party and government authorities, and produced chaos in public social order.

Some political scientists have measured the degree of political development in a polity by the scope of political participation. The explosion of political participation in China after January 1967, which was unstructured and anomic, can hardly be seen as a sign of political development, however. Rapid increase in mobilization and participation, in the absence of effective and strong political institutions, produced not political development but what Huntington calls "political decay."[13]

The subsequent intervention by the PLA and the tight control it imposed on the Red Guards has considerably arrested the trends toward political decay. PLA intervention in politics has generated new problems, however; during and since the GPCR, PLA leaders have assumed important political functions and their political influence expanded enormously at the expense of civilian officials. Opening the floodgate to military intervention when he pushed the PLA into the political arena, Mao now finds himself plagued by the refusal of PLA leaders to "return to the barracks."[14]

The Policy-Making Structure

The final question is where, in structural terms, the real loci of power lay in China's system in the period covered by this study. During the second half of the 1950s, when Mao was an active participant in the policy-making process, the process was, in a sense, more personalized and less routine; Mao had used various institutional devices to initiate policies and mobilize support for them. One of these was the Supreme State Conference which he convened on fifteen occasions as chairman of the People's Republic from 1954 to 1959. Another device Mao used was the meeting of provincial party secretaries and the ad hoc party conference. Mao also frequently used the press, through interviews, articles he wrote, and news reports, to initiate policies and make known his approval or disapproval of certain measures. And still another device he used was to write comments on reports that were submitted to him by his colleagues and subordinates, which frequently induced these officials to undertake new actions. In contrast, when Mao was less active in the 1960s, forums such as the Supreme State Conference and meetings of provincial party secretaries and the ad hoc party conference were rarely convened. The policy-making process was, in a sense, routine and institutionalized; work conferences of the Politburo and the CC were used regularly to discuss and approve policies which appeared to have been initiated by individual Politburo members, and mass campaigns became less frequent as policies were implemented through established normal institutional channels.

The supreme political authority in China, before the Cultural Revolution, was clearly vested in the CCP. In the CCP, the Politburo or its Standing Committee was the most important locus of decision; all major policy measures of the regime had to be approved, at least formally, by the Politburo or its Standing Committee. When the Politburo was divided, as it was over the pace of collectivization in 1955 and over a number of economic issues in the fall of 1957, party officials outside of this innermost circle appeared to become involved in the decision phase. On these two occasions,[15] as at the Lushan Plenum in August 1959, the CC apparently was the ultimate organ for deciding the issues and settling the disputes among the top leaders.

On various occasions when the top leadership appeared to be divided, forums such as enlarged Politburo sessions, central work conferences, and enlarged CC plenums, which were attended by nonmembers as well as members of the Politburo or the CC, were apparently used to decide major policy decisions. When Mao actively intervened in the policy-making processes in the 1950s, he frequently used regional party conferences which were attended by both Politburo members and provincial leaders to discuss and apparently also decide major policy questions.

Thus the locus of decisions may be seen as the arena of political conflict, and the choice of a particular arena was itself "political," since it would determine the political actors to be involved and the procedures to be used in solving conflict. We may also conclude that when the top leadership was divided, the arena of political conflict expanded, and those who were below the topmost level in the leadership hierarchy became involved in decision-making and conflict resolution.

In analyzing the operation of the Politburo, it is possible, on the basis of our case studies, to distinguish, tentatively, between decisions which have not been made by the Politburo as an institution but only formally approved by it and those that have been subject to full-dress debate in the Politburo. Reportedly, certain important economic measures in 1962 were proposed by the Five-Man Central Financial and Economic Group established in 1962 and headed by Ch'en Yun and were formally approved by the Politburo presided over by Liu Shao-ch'i. Similarly, the seventy-article Regulations on Industry, Mines, and Enterprises were reportedly drafted under the auspices of Po I-po (who was in charge of the regime's overall industry and communications policy) and approved by a Politburo meeting chaired by Liu Shao-ch'i. Most individual Politburo and CC Secretariat members had areas of specialization and appeared to be in charge of different broad functional areas (e.g., the military, foreign affairs, propaganda). It is possible, on the basis of available evidence, to postulate that these Politburo and Secretariat members in their individual capacities made some important decisions within their own special areas of responsibility, and that these decisions were probably then approved by the Politburo with or without full-dress debates.

Thus it appears that issues and measures that finally reached the Politburo had already been screened to some extent, and the ultimate choices of the top leadership had to some extent been defined in advance. This situation may have been inevitable. Unless individual Politburo and Secretariat members had screened issues and defined problems, decision-making in the Politburo would have been hopelessly clogged.

Although various state institutions are empowered by the 1954 state constitution with important policy-making functions, their actual role in the policy-making process is much less significant than that of the party. The NPC, according to the constitution, is the highest legislative organ of the nation; in reality, however, its functions were merely dressing decisions of the CCP leadership with legality and serving as the "transmission belt" of the party leadership; it had little to do with actual initiation or authorization of the government programs. The NPC was convened regularly in the 1950s and was, presumably, informed of the developments in the nation, but the party even dispensed with this formality in the 1960s. The party did present the twelve-year agricultural program to the NPC for formal enactment in April 1960. By this time, however, all the basic decisions about the program had been made, and the approval of the NPC was only the culminating formal ratification of the policy-making processes which had preceded it. The establishment of the communes, which resulted in major changes in the local administrative structure of the state, was effected by a party directive alone, without the NPC's formal action.

The State Council, on the other hand, was more directly involved in the regime's policy-making processes. It was the party's "executive arm," responsible for the implementation of the regime's policy. Most important, the State Council, with its ministries and agencies, administered the nation's economy. During the period covered by this study, the premier and nine of the sixteen vice-premiers of the State Council were also members of the Politburo and obviously participated in the making of decisions within the party. Even when basic policy guidelines were set by the party, the State Council had to make many administrative decisions in the course of implementation.

Thus several institutions were involved throughout the policy-making process. For instance, those agencies connected with planning, decision, and execution of rural policies in the center would at least include the Ministry of Agriculture (headed by Liao Lu-yen), the State Council Seventh Staff Office (later renamed Agricultural and Forestry Staff Office, headed by Vice-Premier

Teng Tzu-hui), the CC Rural Work Department (also headed by Teng Tzu-hui), the Secretariat (in which T'an Chen-lin had the primary responsibility over rural policies), the Politburo, and the CC.

The twelve-year agricultural program and the commune program would require the support or at least cooperation of each of these six groups. Opposition by any of the first four groups would presumably be handled by removing the dissenting official or officials. In the fall of 1955, Teng Tzu-hui's power in the State Council Seventh Staff Office and in the CC Rural Work Department was already diluted by several newly appointed deputy-directors, and from 1957 on, his functions were largely taken over by T'an Chen-lin, although he was not formally removed from those two posts. Vigorous disagreements within the Politburo would be settled by the CC or by removing dissenting individual members. Ch'en Yun was rendered inactive in 1959–60 and after fall 1962 presumably because he was critical of many Great Leap measures.

Beyond these central party and government bodies, a host of organizations from the provinces down to the communes are also involved in national policy-making processes, primarily because they have to carry out the central directives. The purge of provincial and lower-level cadres in 1957–58 and in 1959–61 suggested that the performance of these officials was not equal to the expectations of the top leadership and they had to be removed to facilitate the goals of the leadership.

The regime's most important decision-making bodies in the period covered by this study were, of course, the Politburo (its regular session and working conference), the CC (the regular and enlarged sessions), and the ad hoc party conference. The ad hoc party conference, such as the Tsingtao Conference of July 1957, Hangchow Conference and Nanning Conference of January 1958, or Chengtu Conference of March 1958, is not a formal party organ, for there is no provision in the party constitution for its existence and functions. In practice, however, it did make important decisions, and the legitimacy of these decisions were never questioned in Communist China.

Once a policy decision was adopted at the top, it then filtered down through various communication channels for implementation by lower levels. One of these channels was the mass media, particularly the party's central organs, the *People's Daily* and *Hung Ch'i* (which replaced *Hsueh-hsi* in June 1958), and the provincial newspapers published by provincial party authorities. Another channel was official directives of all sorts issued by the party and the government, some of which were made public in the press. And still another important channel was the conferences, such as those meetings convened regularly by the party and by government functional departments (the rural work conferences, the conferences of the party secretaries in charge of industry, etc.), and "conveyance meetings" (*ch'uan-ta hui-yi*), which were convened by the leading official of a functional or geographical unit specifically for conveying to his subordinates instructions from above. The meetings of the NPC, the CPPCC, and the CC also performed important communication functions.

To a very striking degree, rarely seen in other political systems, the Chinese Communists used oral communication to transmit vital information. Although this mode of communication had certain advantages,[16] often it blocked the flow of information. Transmitting central directives by word of mouth, local officials could easily reinterpret or distort them to suit their needs, thus frustrating the goals of the central leadership.

Top leaders were aware of this problem and used various means to ensure the compliance of executing agencies. For example, party and government organizations regularly filed reports, which filtered up the bureaucratic hierarchy. Another mechanism was conferences in which officials not only received information or instructions from above but also presented reports [hui pao] informing the higher authorities of the work of their units. The higher authorities frequently sent investigation teams or the top leaders themselves undertook inspection tours to gather information. In addition, agencies such as the State Statistics Bureau and the New China News Agency and, to some extent, letters written to the party, government, and the People's Daily also provided information on the state of the nation.

Was the Chinese leadership insulated from reality by the nature of the system it presided over or by the character of its own information-gathering agencies? Available evidence makes it clear that there are pressures built into the Chinese political system which operate to block channels of communication. Every dictatorship has a tendency to breed sycophancy and conformity, and Communist China is no exception. When the views of the leadership on certain issues were known, lower officials tended to send back reports that confirmed its preconceptions. For example, when Mao suggested in 1958 that close planting could increase farm production, many provincial party secretaries went out of their way to "prove" the correctness of Mao's idea, and its indiscriminate application later resulted in severe crop failures. In 1958–59, when the Chinese leadership demanded a great leap in industrial and agricultural production, lower officials, responding to the pressures or the climate of expectations at the top, transmitted false information and inflated statistics to higher authorities. Since the Chinese Communists often equated caution with rightist deviations, cadres felt compelled to juggle data to conceal failure of performance or compelled to opt for targets that could not realistically be met.

The so-called squatting investigations undertaken by many top leaders since 1961 indicate that the CCP high command tried very hard to collect information on a first-hand basis. This type of investigation is somewhat different from what the Chinese leaders had done in the 1950s. They did conduct inspection tours frequently in the 1950s, but these tours appeared to be superficial; it is questionable whether the top leaders, whose entourages usually consisted of local senior party officials, would have the opportunity to hear or see things objectionable to the local leaders in their "guided" tours.[17]

This was precisely the point raised by Liu Shao-ch'i. In an interview with the "work group" of the Hunan Provincial Party Committee in April 1961, Liu allegedly criticized Mao's method of "investigation and study" and stated that investigators sent by higher authorities were often deceived by local officials who were skillful in concealing failures and falsifying data.[18] Liu was said to have prescribed a new method of investigation which called for investigators to undertake investigation at their own hometowns. The rationale, according to Liu, was that investigators, instead of relying merely on the official sources of information and the cooperation of the investigated, could count on their relatives and friends, who would be inclined to tell the truth about the local conditions and would thus be able to uncover problems and obtain needed information.[19] Whatever merits Liu's method of "squatting investigation" may have had, it would appear to be too wasteful for top officials to "squat" in the countryside to collect information and not to attend to other important tasks in Peking.

Mao's Roles

In studying China's political system, one can hardly fail to be impressed by the enormous power Mao wields. He is the undisputed leader in the Chinese system; on many occasions, he has displayed an impressive ability to defy all institutions and intervene in any policy matter he considered of vital importance. In China's policy-making process, Mao plays several important roles.

First he is an ideologist. On numerous occasions (his speeches on collectivization in the summer of 1955, on contradictions among the people in February 1957, and on class struggle in September 1962; his statement incorporated in the treatise "On Khrushchev's Phoney Communism" in July 1964) Mao provided an authoritative assessment of the state of the nation and pointed toward a purposeful goal for the next phase. In other words, Mao determined the nature of a given period, identified different social forces and contradictions in society, and defined problems in the political arena at each important turning point. Pronouncements such as these tended to condition the policy alternatives the regime subsequently mapped out; even Mao did not dictate policy measures, but his political diagnosis had the effect of establishing the parameters within which problems were tackled.

A second role Mao played in the policy-making process was political balancer and arbiter. Mao, as the leader of the party and the nation, had to mediate conflicting interests of society (which were represented to a certain degree by his colleagues who were in charge of different segments of the bureaucracy or different functional "systems") and fix priorities among their conflicting goals. Mao's speech "Ten Great Relationships," addressed to an enlarged Politburo session on 25 April 1956, is typical of Mao's efforts to reconcile contradictions in the major sectors of Chinese society—contradictions between agriculture and industry, between light and heavy industry, between national defense and economic construction, between the central and local authorities, between the collective and the individuals, between the Han people and minority nationalities, and many others.

Furthermore, Mao plays the role of an innovator in the policy-making process. In many instances, it was Mao's initiative that resulted in launching a new policy or reversing an ongoing policy. For example, he promoted the collectivization drive in the summer of 1955. At that time, when other party leaders had clearly favored a "go-slow" approach toward organizing peasants into the APC's, Mao argued vehemently for stepping up the tempo of collectivization in a secret speech to a meeting of provincial party secretaries at the end of July 1955; consequently, the "go-slow" approach was discarded and an intense nation-wide campaign was launched to accelerate agricultural collectivization.

In addition to his intervention in the issue of collectivization, numerous other examples of Mao's vigorous initiative can be cited. In January 1956 he initiated the ambitious twelve-year agricultural program—reportedly he not only provided basic ideas for the program but also personally supervised its formulation and drafting. In the spring of 1956 he actively promoted a liberalization policy toward intellectuals, and in the first quarter of 1957 he pushed for a party rectification campaign, apparently against the counsels of many of the "organization men" in the party. He resurrected the twelve-year agricultural program in the CC Plenum of September-October 1957, and in doing so he again reversed a more cautious rural policy pursued by the party up to that time. In a series of conferences with provincial leaders at Hangchow, Nanning, and Chengtu in late 1957 and the first quarter of 1958, Mao actively and vigorously campaigned for his ambitious Great Leap programs. In the summer of 1958 he gave a "go-ahead" signal to launch the communes throughout China. In the fall of 1962 he pushed the party to launch the Socialist Education Campaign, and in the fall of 1965 he set in motion the Great Proletarian Cultural Revolution.

Political Constraints upon Mao

Enormous as Mao's power has been, he did not always have his own way. This study provides ample evidence that other party leaders frequently were able to block his policy or modify its substance. In other words, Mao was not "in command" all the time; he encountered opposition from his Politburo colleagues, and his capacity to enforce his policy fluctuated considerably.[20]

For example, the disaster of the Great Leap politically eclipsed Mao, and other party leaders seized the opportunity to initiate new programs. The question of who exercises power to initiate policy is of great political significance, for the initiator is in the position of choosing problems or issues to be placed on the agenda of the political system and determines the subjects for debate. He who defines problems and proposes alternatives carries enormous political power. In the context of the American political system, one writer has observed:

> The definition of alternatives is the supreme instrument of power; the antagonists can rarely agree on what the issues are because power is involved in the definition. He who determines what politics is about runs the country because the definition of the alternatives is the choice of conflicts, and the choice of conflicts allocates power.[21]

To a considerable degree, this observation is equally applicable to Mao's participation in China's policy-making process. In the second half of the 1950s when Mao constantly intervened in the policy-making process to exercise "leadership," his influence was paramount. After the Lushan confrontation with P'eng Teh-huai and in the wake of the disastrous failures of the Great Leap and commune programs in the early 1960s, for a variety of reasons Mao no longer played the role of an innovator who initiated policies, especially domestic policies, and he abstained, to a considerable extent, from participation in the policy-making process. Consequently, Mao's influence in the policy-making process declined substantially.

With Mao's reduced role in the initiation of policy, there was a corresponding growth in the power to initiate by other CCP leaders, particularly Liu Shao-chi'i, Chou En-lai, Teng Hsiao-p'ing, Ch'en Yun, Lin Piao, P'eng Chen, and Po I-po. The CCP was experiencing a different kind of leadership in the early 1960s as political power appeared to become more diffuse and individual Politburo members appeared to exercise greater influence over policy on their special functional "systems." Although Mao was undoubtedly kept informed of major domestic developments and his approval was sought for important decisions, yet as he was now in the "second line" and "did not take charge of the daily routine," he increasingly found himself unable to impose his will on the party.

It seems clear from the events in 1965–66 that Mao found himself "stone-walled" by other party leaders like Liu Shao-ch'i, Teng Hsiao-p'ing, and P'eng Chen, who tightly controlled the party machinery, and felt compelled to launch the GPCR to purge these "capitalist power-holders," thus removing constraints upon himself and regaining control of the party.

Scholars frequently compare Mao with Stalin and consider Mao China's Stalin. It is doubtful whether Mao ever held the kind of absolute power that the Soviet dictator wielded after 1935. True, Mao clearly dominated China's policy-making process in the second half of the 1950s; but even then he had to resort to extensive politicking to win support outside the Politburo. In the 1960s, however, Mao appears to have lost much of his "power to persuade," thus he had to use extraordinary measures to destroy his opponents politically. Although he succeeded in creating a wreckage—personal and institutional—during the GPCR, his destructive acts reflect more of the failure of his leadership and the loss of his ability to persuade than his power to command compliance.

To fully understand the constraints Mao faced, it is necessary to analyze the roles and power of other top leaders in the CCP and some of the "operational codes" the CCP leadership observed. First, most Politburo members, and particularly those in the Politburo Standing Committee (or those in the Secretariat before the 1956 Party Congress) were leaders of great stature; they fought alongside Mao against the Japanese and the Chinese Nationalists, and each of them made significant contributions to the success of the Communist revolution in China. In other words, these leaders achieved positions of power by their own merits and did not owe their positions to Mao. Unlike the relationship between Joseph Stalin and other Politburo members of the Soviet Communist Party after the 1930s, which can be characterized as the master and lackeys, the relationship between Mao and most of his Politburo associates was one of coequals, with Mao as the first among equals.[22]

Over the years, Mao's growing cult of personality and his acquisition of the "routinized charisma"[23] of the party after the Communist victory in 1949 gave him enormous prestige and influence among the rank and file and tended to enhance Mao's position vis-à-vis his Politburo colleagues and undermine the one-time relationship of relative equality. For political expediency, Mao's colleagues often inflated Mao's cult and publicly affirmed his undisputed leadership position. Nevertheless, Mao's power was never absolute; other CCP leaders did share with Mao control of important political resources in the system, the most important one being control of the party organization and the authority vested in it, and they represented in varying degrees counterweights to Mao's power. Even in the 1950s when Mao was actively and closely involved in policy formulation and execution, he by no means monopolized all the policy-making power. On occasion, such as after Khruschchev's de-Stalinization speech in 1956, other party leaders invoked the principle of collective leadership to constrain Mao.[24]

Moreover, decision-making is not a one-man show; because of inherent limits on the time, energy, and intelligence of a single individual, Mao simply could not decide all vital issues in a wholly planned society like China. Therefore, if for no other reason than this, Mao had to, and did, in fact, divide the labor and share the power with other top leaders. Thus Liu Shao-ch'i, the party's senior vice-chairman, was in charge of party affairs in the 1950s, and after succeeding Mao as head of state in the spring of 1959, he wielded more power than before. Liu was virtually the acting chairman of the party in Mao's absence from the national capital, which was quite frequent in the 1960s. Liu presided over the Politburo meetings and exercised the important and powerful functions of balancing, coordinating, and integrating conflicting interests of various sectors of the system.

Other members of the Politburo Standing Committee, with the exception of the very elderly Chu Teh, also took charge of a major functional area.[25] For instance, Premier Chou En-lai had the overall responsibility for government administration and the conduct of foreign relations (probably with the exception of intra-Communist bloc affairs); Ch'en Yun was responsible for overall economic policies until his political eclipse in 1959; Lin Piao was in charge of military affairs after he was elected to the Politburo Standing Committee in May 1958; and Teng Hsiao-p'ing supervised the party apparatus and probably also managed intra-Communist bloc affairs. Aside from these seven top leaders in the Politburo Standing Committee, other members of the Politburo and the secretaries of the CC Secretariat who were not Politburo members also had their special areas of responsibility;[26] they tended to become closely identified with particular sectors of the political system and strove to protect the special interests of their "departments."

It can be argued that in a nation as huge and diversified as China, some measure of division of labor and collective decision-making is certainly necessary, as in all political systems. Moreover, China does not have real collective leadership when Mao stands above all others and repeatedly throws his weight decisively into the political arena. Nevertheless, other party leaders were able to severely checkmate Mao by vetoing and blocking policies Mao favored. The alleged division into "first line" and "second line" in the Politburo Standing Committee, which allowed other top party leaders to exercise operational or administrative power while Mao, in the "second line" exercised "legislative power" (making basic decisions), did not prevent those in the "first line" from making basic decisions either. For one thing, there cannot be clear-cut distinction between operational and "legislative" power in China, and those who execute policy can and frequently do remake policy. At times Mao either elected or was forced to abstain from deliberations of the party councils; consequently, other party leaders made their own decisions and the thin line between the operations and "legislative" functions became totally blurred.

As pointed out, Mao sometimes was much less involved in actual implementation of policy in the 1960s, and the control of the party apparatus devolved into the hands of Liu Shao-ch'i, Teng Hsiao-p'ing, and others. These leaders built up water-tight "independent kingdoms" to spurn the interference of Mao and his supporters. Mao himself actually complained in October 1966 that Teng Hsiao-p'ing had "stonewalled" for six years, and had not informed him of the work in the CC Secretariat. What Teng and others did, especially after January 1965, was more than bureaucratic foot-dragging; they used their positions of strength and mobilized resources available to them to fight for their political survival.

Moreover, these leaders, sensing Mao's intention to remove them after January 1965, allied with one another and took concerted actions for mutual defense. These leaders included Liu, Teng Hsiao-P'ing, P'eng Chen, Lu Ting-yi, Yang Shang-k'un, and possibly Lo Jui-ch'ing, all of them entrenched in control of the party apparatus (the last five being members of the CC Secretariat, the party's highest administrative body). In opposition to the Liuist faction was the Mao-Lin faction, which included Mao, Lin Piao, Chou En-lai, Ch'en Po-ta, and K'ang Sheng, who plotted and made preparations separately or together for the final showdown. Factional cleavages and struggle, which apparently had little part in the policy conflicts over economic issues during the 1950s and were not the salient element in Chinese politics prior to the 1960s, suddenly assumed a pivotal importance in the political scene in the 1960s as the two groups were locked in bitter conflict.

Under such circumstances, former personal and working ties gained new significance. A large number of CC members who had worked under Liu Shao-ch'i and P'eng Chen in north China during the 1930s, many of whom (including P'eng Chen) were imprisoned by the KMT authorities and allegedly signed an anti-Communist manifesto to regain freedom, rallied to the side of Liu and P'eng.[27] Their political survival would depend on the fate of Liu and P'eng, for they knew too well from past experience that purges of a top leader would also victimize his former associates. This apprehension was further reinforced by the Maoist propagandists who, through a reinterpretation of history, insinuated that those who had written self-incriminating statements were cowards and traitors and deserved to be purged. Such twists and turns of events reactivated the historical ties, exacerbated the factional conflict, and hardened the opposition to Mao, all of which would in time force Mao and his supporters to go outside normal party channels in order to launch the GPCR.

Political constraints upon Mao have come not only from his opponents but often from his allies and supporters. To secure the backing of Lin Piao and his followers in the Fourth Field Army group, for example, Mao reluctantly made concessions to Lin even in matters which he considered of crucial importance. Thus Lin became the authoritative spokesman and interpreter of Mao's policy and thought after 1965, greatly expanded his base of power, particularly during the GPCR, by placing his own followers in key positions, and was made the sole vice-chairman of the party and Mao's successor during the Eleventh CC Plenum in August 1966. All of these matters had undoubtedly received Mao's consent, something which he would in time regret; but, in retrospect, the consent appears to have been a *quid pro quo*, a political payoff, which he had to give to obtain Lin's all-out support.

The case with Premier Chou En-lai seems somewhat similar. Although Chou has been regarded by most Western observers as the symbol of moderate political forces in China, he has been a political "swinger," ready to take any stance and swing to the side that served his own interest, as the case studies in this book show. In the course of the seesaw conflict between the Liuists and the Maoists in the mid-1960s, Chou lent his support to Mao and may have advised and planned with Mao since late 1964 to depose P'eng Chen and Liu. Chou's support during this crucial period and whatever contribution he made to the ultimate defeat of Liu Shao-ch'i in the summer of 1966 were undoubtedly appreciated by Mao. Nonetheless, Mao is known to harbor serious reservations about Chou. In a letter to Lin Piao on 15 September 1966, for example, Mao criticized Chou for being eclectic and "not consistently honest" and expressed doubts on Chou's integrity (loyalty) in "his late years."[28] However, what refrained Mao from turning the spearhead of struggle against Chou at that time, according to the letter, was that Chou "had done a great deal of beneficial work for a long time, and few in the Party can match his ability"; hence Mao thought it politically expedient to have Chou join "the proletarian headquarters for the time being and let him handle a few problems."

Regardless of his real feelings toward the radical goals of the GPCR, Chou went along with the Maoists at least on record, chanting the radical line and heaping praises on Chiang Ch'ing, and permitted his State Council subordinates to be attacked by the Red Guards, or even engaged in self-criticism. By such acts, Chou managed to establish his identification with Mao's "proletarian headquarters" and enhance his revolutionary credentials. Furthermore, political turmoil and economic disruptions caused by the GPCR, particularly after the winter of 1966, made Chou highly indispensable to Mao. His eloquence, political skill, and administrative talent enabled him to mediate among rival political groups, moderate excesses of the Red Guards, and maintain a modicum of order in China's national economy and foreign relations in the face of massive upheaval. Such were the circumstances under which Chou, perhaps against the wishes of Mao, was allowed to gradually assume the overall management of the GPCR from the Cultural Revolution Group (CRG), a body which was set up in May 1966 to propel Mao's crusade.

The shift might not have been significant had Chou and the CRG leaders seen eye to eye on the goals of the GPCR and on methods of carrying out the goals, but obviously they did not. On the one hand, the CRG leaders such as

Ch'en Po-ta and Chiang Ch'ing were political radicals; they wanted to change the status quo completely, they extolled violence, incited the revolutionary rebels to launch an all-out attack on the Establishment, and sought to destroy the existing power structure in China through a revolution from below to be carried out by the masses, in the image of the Paris Commune. On the other hand, however, Chou En-lai was politically moderate or conservative during the GPCR, inasmuch as he was devoted more to restricting the scope of political conflict, curbing violence and other excesses, and, most important, preserving the very political system which the CRG radicals vowed to overturn. Of course, Chou was pragmatic enough to accept reforms when they seemed inevitable, but he would effect as little change as possible to the power structure; he was a "reformist" at most, and not a revolutionary like many of the CRG leaders. At times he professed the same radical goals, but he was not really committed to them; his cooptation of the radical line, however, did facilitate his takeover of the management of the GPCR as well as the moderation of its radical goals.

Mao and the CRG leaders were fully aware of Chou's "double-dealing" but could do very little to change the situation. For one thing, Mao highly valued Chou's ability and regarded Chou as indispensable to him. For another, Chou's management of the GPCR appears to be supported by powers in the party and the military hierarchy. Perhaps most important, Mao may have perceived the threat of Lin Piao, who had expanded his influence too much during the GPCR, and Mao considered Chou a would-be ally against Lin Piao. There is some evidence that Chou was an element of Mao's anti-Lin Piao coalition, which carried out a step-by-step struggle with the Lin Piao group after the Lushan CC Plenum in August-September 1970.

Siding with Mao in every round of intra-party struggle since the 1950s, Chou En-lai has displayed his consistent loyalty to the Chairman. Whatever reservations Mao may have, he is not in a position to deny Chou a place in the top leadership hierarchy. This fact, coupled with the absence of leaders who can match Chou's seniority and merits, after the elimination of Chou's peers Liu Shao-ch'i and Lin Piao, allowed Chou to emerge from the Tenth Party Congress in August 1973 as a leader with power second only to Mao.

The political rehabilitation of Teng Hsiao-P'ing, denounced by the Maoists as the Number Two top "capitalist power-holder" during the GPCR, is still another illustration that Mao has not ruled by fiat but has engaged in political "give and take." After Lin Piao's downfall and Mao's attempt to remove or neutralize the opposition of Lin's followers entrenched in the party and PLA leadership hierarchy, Mao had to rally the support of all political forces and make deals with them. Possibly Teng's rehabilitation, revealed in his first public appearance in April 1973, was one such deal exacted from Mao by Teng's allies and associates of the former Second Field Army. Since then, Teng has gained suprising political prominence, including elevation to the Politburo around January 1974. Given his extensive military background during the period of struggle, and his ties with PLA leaders, Teng is one of the very few top CCP leaders who has empathy toward the PLA leaders and at the same time is respected and trusted by them; hence he is believed to have been instrumental in the orderly carrying out of the major reshuffle of the PLA regional leaders in December 1973.

In addition, certain rules of the party apparently had the effect of limiting Mao's power. One such rule, for example, is to ban the use of terror against dissenting cadres in the party, particularly members of the CC. This rule, which was formalized in the early 1940s by the Chinese Communists to avoid the repetition of Stalin's methods in the CCP, has been observed with consistency. In handling the disgraced cadres, particularly those who held high positions in the leadership hierarchy, Mao either reduced their power, as the case of Ch'en Yun and Teng Tzu-hui, or relieved them of it, as the case of P'eng Teh-huai, P'eng Chen, Liu Shao-ch'i, Teng Hsiao-P'ing, and a host of "capitalist power-holders" in 1966–68, but he did not threaten them with death. Some of Mao's critics in the 1950s, such as Ch'en Yun and Teng Tzu-hui, and more recently Teng Hsiao-P'ing, came back to reassert their political influence after a period of political eclipse; similarly, a large number of lesser party officials, some in the center but mostly in the provinces, who were disgraced because of their criticism of the Greap Leap or their opposition to the GPCR in the 1960s succeeded in winning "reversals of verdict" and secured rehabilitation—not posthumously.

Whatever political merits this particular mode of management of opposition may have, over the years it may have tended to reduce Mao's ability to elicit compliance and impose his will. Inasmuch as the punishment for those who dared to criticize or oppose the top leadership was simply personal disgrace and retirement, and not a matter of life or death, they were less inhibited in asserting themselves. That P'eng Teh-huai wrote an 80,000-word letter to the CC in June 1962 in which he attacked Mao's policies and demanded reversal of the verdict on him should be viewed in this context. Conceivably, those who have been purged in the course of the Cultural Revolution may plot a comeback in the future. Their physical existence alone resembles something of a political alternative to those in power, and the availability of a "counter-elite" constitutes a continuing threat to the "ins" and makes it difficult for them to consolidate their control in the wake of the Cultural Revolution.

Appendix A

Major Positions Held by
Chinese Communist Officials

Chang Ch'un-ch'iao* Director of Literary Work Department (1956–63), director of Propaganda Department (1963–66), secretary (1965–66) of the Shanghai CCP Committee, deputy director of the CRG (1966–68); currently member of the Politburo Standing Committee, first secretary of the Shanghai CCP Committee, and director of the Shanghai Revolutionary Committee; since 1975, vice-premier and director of the PLA General Political Department.

Chang Chung-liang† First secretary of the Kansu CCP Committee until his purge in 1961.

Chang P'ing-hua† First secretary of Hunan (1959–66); purged in 1966 but was rehabilitated after 1971; currently second party secretary of Hunan.

Chang Wen-t'ien‡ Until his political disgrace in 1959, alternate member of the Politburo and the senior vice-minister of foreign affairs.

Ch'en Cheng-jen† Deputy director of the State Council Seventh Agriculture and Forestry Staff Office (1955–66), deputy director of the CC Rural Work Department of the CCP (1956–64), minister of agricultural machinery (1959–65), minister of the Eighth Ministry of Machine Building (1965–66); suspended during the GPCR; deceased in 1973.

Ch'en Huang-mei Vice-minister of culture (1963–65); purged in 1965.

Ch'en Mang-yuan† Dismissed as first secretary of the Kwangsi-Chuang CCP Committee in 1957; appointed vice-minister of state farms and land reclamation in 1963.

Ch'en yi (marshal)‡ Vice-premier (1954–72), minister of foreign affairs (1958–67), member of the Politburo (1956–69); in political eclipse during the GPCR; deceased in 1972.

*Member of the Tenth CC of the CCP elected in August 1973.
†Alternate member of the Eight CC of the CCP elected in 1956 and 1958.
‡Member of the Eight CC of the CCP elected in 1956.
§Alternate member of the Tenth CC elected in August 1973.

Ch'en Yun*‡   Currently vice-chairman of NPC; vice-premier (1949–74); member of the Politburo (1945–69), vice-chairman of the CC and Politburo (1956–66); politically inactive since 1962.

Ch'en Po-ta‡   Alternate member of the Politburo (1956–66), editor-in-chief of *Hung Ch'i* (1958–67), member of the Politburo Standing Committee (1966–70), director of the CRG (1966–69); until his purge in 1970 was Mao's brain-truster and ghost-writer.

Chiang Ch'ing (wife of Mao Tse-tung)*   First deputy director of the CRG (1966–69), member of the Politburo after 1969.

Chia T'o-fu‡ ˙ Deputy director of State Council Fourth Staff Office and minister of light industry (1954–59); purged in 1959.

Chou En-lai*‡   Premier since 1949; vice-chairman of the party (1956–66, and since 1973).

Chou Hsiao-chou†   Purged as first secretary of the Hunan CCP Committee in 1959.

Chu Teh (marshal)*‡   "Father" of the Red Army, vice-chairman of the Republic (1949–59), chairman of the Standing Committee of the NPC since 1959, vice-chairman of the party (1956–66; also since 1973).

Fu Ts'ung-pi (general)   Commander of the Peking garrison (1966–68); purged in 1968; partially rehabilitated in 1974.

Hsi Chung-hsun‡   Secretary-general of the State Council (1954–62), vice-premier (1959–62); purged in 1962.

Hsia Yen   Vice-chairman, All-China Federation of Literary and Art circles (1960–65), vice-minister of culture (1954–65); purged in 1965.

Hsiao Hua (general)‡   Director of the PLA General Political Department (1964–67); purged in 1967.

Hsiao K'o (general)‡§   Vice-minister of defense (1954–59), vice-minister of the Ministry of State Farms and Land Reclamation (1959–66); in eclipse during the GPCR, but partially rehabilitated in 1973.

Hsu Hsiang-ch'ien (marshal)*‡   Vice-chairman of the NPC since 1965, also concurrently vice-chairman of the Military Affairs Committee of the CCP.

Hsu Li-ch'un   Deputy editor-in-chief of *Hung Chi* (1958–66), deputy director of the party's Propaganda Department (1961–66), P'eng Ch'en's brain-truster; purged in 1966.

Hsueh Mu-ch'iao   Economist, vice-chairman of the State Planning Commission (1954–66), chairman of the National Commodity Price Commission (1963–66); purged in 1966.

Hu Ch'iao-mu‡   Party theoretician, alternate secretary of the CC Secretariat (1956–66); purged in 1966 but partially rehabilitated in 1974.

Huang Huo-ch'ing† Mayor of Tientsin (1955–58), first secretary of the Liaoning CCP Committee (1958–67); purged in 1967.

Huang K'o-cheng (general) PLA chief of staff (1958–59), secretary of Secretariat (1956–59); relieved of these positions in 1959; appointed vice-governor of Shansi in 1964.

Hung Hsueh-chih (general)† Korean War veteran, director of General Rear Service Department (1956–59); purged in 1959; reappeared in 1974.

Jao Shu-shih First secretary of the CCP East China Bureau (1949–54), director of the CCP Organization Department (1952–54); purged in 1954.

K'ang Sheng*‡ Member of the Politburo (1945–56), alternate member of the Politburo (1956–66), secretary of the CC Secretariat (1962–66), member of the Politburo Standing Committee since 1966, vice-chairman of the party since 1973.

Kao Kang Vice-chairman of the Central People's Government and member of the Politburo (1949–54), chairman of the Northeast People's Government (1949–54), first secretary of the CCP Northeast Bureau (1949–54), chairman of the State Planning Commission (1952–54); purged in 1954 and committed suicide.

K'o Ch'ing-shih‡ First secretary of the Shanghai CCP Committee (1955–65), member of the Politburo (1958–65), first secretary of the CCP East China Bureau (1960–65), vice-premier (1965); died in 1965.

K'uai Ta-fu Maoist Red Guard leader in TsinghuaUniversity.

Kuan Feng Writer on Chinese philosophy, member of the CRG (1966–67), deputy director of the All-PLA Cultural Revolution Group (1966–67); purged in 1967.

Kuo Liang Secretary-general (1958) and alternate secretary of the Fukien CCP Committee.

Liao Lu-yen† Deputy director of the party's Rural Work Department (1953–64), minister of agriculture (1954–66); purged during the GPCR.

Li Ching-ch'üan*‡ First secretary of the Szechuan CCP Committee (1953–65), member of the Politburo (1958–67), first secretary of the Party's Southwest China Bureau (1960–67); purged during the GPCR but partially rehabilitated in 1973, appointed vice-chairman of NPC in 1975.

Li Fu-ch'un*‡ Vice-premier (1954–74), chairman of the State Planning Commission of the State Council (1954–67), member of the Politburo (1956–69), secretary of the CCP Secretariat (1958–66), politically inactive since 1967; died in 1975.

Li Hsien-nien Vice-premier and minister of finance since 1954, member of the Politburo since 1956, secretary of the CCP Secretariat (1958–66), reappointed vice-premier in 1975.

Li Hsueh-feng‡   Member of the CCP Secretariat (1956–66), first secretary of the CCP North China Bureau (1960–66), first secretary of the Peking CCP Committee (1966–67), director of Hopeh RC (1968–70), alternate member of the Politburo (1969–70); purged in 1970.

Liao Mo-sha   Director of the United Front Work Department of the Peking CCP Commitee (1961–66); purged in 1966.

Lin Piao (marshal)‡   Vice-premier (1954–71), member of the Politburo (1955–71), vice-chairman of the party (1958–71), minister of defense (1959–71), senior vice-chairman of the Military Affairs Committee of the party (1959–71), designated Mao's successor in 1966; purged and allegedly died in an airplane crash in 1971.

Lin Po-ch'u‡   Member of the Politburo (1956–60); died in 1960.

Liu Chien-hsun*†   First secretary of the Kwangsi CCP Committee (1956–61), first secretary of the Honan CCP Committee (1961–66), secretary of the Peking CCP Committee (1966–67), director of the Honan RC since 1968, first secretary of the Honan CCP Committee since 1971.

Liu Shao-ch'i‡   Vice-chairman of the Central People's Government (1949–54), chairman of the Standing Committee of the NPC (1954–59), chairman of the Republic (1959–66), senior vice-chairman of the party (1956–66); purged in 1966; died in 1972.

Lo Jui-ch'ing (general)‡   Minister of public security (1949–59), vice-premier (1959–66), PLA chief of staff (1959–66), secretary of CCP Secretariat (1962–66); purged in 1965–66.

Lu P'ing   President of Peking University (1960–66); purged in 1966 for suppressing student movement in GPCR; partially rehabilitated in 1975.

Lu Ting-yi‡   Alternate member of the Politburo (1956–66), director of the CCP Propaganda Department (1956–66), vice-premier (1959–66), minister of culture (1965–66), secretary of the CCP Secretariat (1962–66), member of the Five-Man Cultural Revolution Group under P'eng Ch'en; purged in 1966.

Mao Tse-tung*‡   Chairman of the party since 1956, chairman of the Military Affairs Committee of the party since 1935, chairman of the Central People's Government (1949–54), chairman of the Republic (1954–59).

Mao Tun (Shen Yen-ping)   Minister of culture (1949–65), chairman of the Union of Chinese Writers (1953–65).

Nieh Jung-chen (marshal)*‡   Vice-premier since 1956, chairman of National Scientific-Technological Commission since 1958, vice-chairman of the CCP Military Affairs Committee.

Nieh Yuan-tzu Instructor at Peking University, her big-character poster on 25 May 1966 kindled the fire of GPCR at Peking University, deputy director of Peking RC (1967–70), alternate member of the CC (1969–70); purged in 1970.

P'an Fu-sheng† First secretary of the Honan CCP Committee (1953–58); purged in 1958 for rightist deviations; first secretary of the Heilunkiang CCP Committee (1966–67), director of the Heilunkiang RC (1967–70); purged in late 1970.

P'eng Chen‡ First (ranking) secretary of the Peking CCP Committee (1949–66), mayor of Peking (1951–66), member of the Politburo (1949–66), secretary of the CCP Secretariat (1956–66), head of the Five-Man Cultural Revolution Group (1964–66); purged in 1966.

P'eng Teh-huai (marshal)‡ Commander of the Chinese People's Volunteers in Korea (1950–54), member of the Politburo (1954–66), vice-premier (1954–65), minister of defense (1954–59); in political disgrace since August 1959.

Po I-po Chairman of State Construction Commission (1954–56), chairman of State Economic Commission (1956–66), vice-premier (1956–66), alternate member of the Politburo (1956–66), director of the State Council Industry and Communications Staff Office (1961–66); purged in 1966.

Shao Ch'uan-lin Writer, vice-chairman of the Union of Chinese Writers (1960–65); purged in 1965.

Sung Jen-chiung (general)‡ Minister of Third—Second Ministry of Machine Building (1956–60), first secretary of CCP Northeast China Bureau (1960–67); purged in 1968; partially rehabilitated in 1974.

Sung Shao-wen Vice-chairman of the State Planning Commission (1962–66).

T'an Cheng (general)‡ Director of the PLA General Political Department (GPD) (1956–60), secretary of the CCP Secretariat (1956–62), deputy director of the PLA GPD (1960–64), vice-minister of defense (1956–65), vice-governor of Fukien (1965–66); public appearance in 1975 was first in nine years.

T'an Chen-lin*‡ Governor of Chekiang (1951–52), governor of Kiangsu (1952–54), secretary of CCP Secretariat (1956–66), member of the Politburo (1958–67), vice-premier (1959–67), director of State Council Agriculture and Forestry Staff Office (1962–67); purged in 1967 but partially rehabilitated in 1973 and appointed vice-chairman of NPC in 1975.

T'ao Chu‡ Ranking (first) secretary of the Kwangtung CCP Committee (1955–65), first secretary of CCP Central-South China Bureau (1960–66); vice-premier (1965–66), member of Politburo Standing Committee and a secretary of CCP Secretariat (1966); purged in December 1966; died in 1974.

Teng Hsiao-p'ing*‡   Vice-premier (1952–66), member of the Politburo (1955–66), general secretary of CCP and member of Politburo Standing Committee (1956–66); purged in 1966 but rehabilitated in 1972; currently vice-premier, member of the Politburo SC, vice-chairman of the party, and PLA chief of staff.

Teng Hua (general)‡§   Commander of Chinese People's Volunteers in Korea (1954), commander of the Shenyang MR (1955–59); implicated in the 1959 P'eng Teh-huai anti-party incident and demoted to vice-governor of Szechuan (1960–66); partial rehabilitation in 1972.

Teng Li-ch'un   Deputy editor-in-chief of *Hung Chi* (1962–66), Liu Shao-ch'i's political secretary.

T'eng Tai-yuan‡   Minister of Railways (1949–65), implicated in the 1959 P'eng Teh-huai anti-party incident, was vice-chairman of Chinese People's Political Consultative Conference until his death in 1974.

Teng T'o   Editor-in-chief of *Jen-min Jih-pao* (1954–57), secretary of the Peking CCP Committee (1959–66), published articles in 1961–62 attacking Mao's policies; purged in 1966.

Teng Tzu-hui‡   Vice-premier (1954–65), director of the State Council Seventh (Agriculture and Forestry) Staff Office (1954–62), director of the CCP Rural Work Department (1954–62); opposed Mao's rural policies and politically inactive since 1962; died in 1972.

T'ien Han   Playwright, chairman of the All-China Dramatic Association (1949–65), vice-chairman of the All-China Federation of Literary and Art Circles (1960–65); in political disgrace after 1966.

Wang Li   A section chief in both the International Liaison Department and Propaganda Department of the CCP prior to 1964, deputy director of the CCP International Liaison Department (1964–66), deputy editor-in-chief of *Hung Chi* (1964–67), acting director of the CCP Propaganda Department (1967); purged and dismissed from all posts in October 1967.

Wang T'ing-tung   Deputy secretary-general of the Honan CCP Committee (1955–58), deputy director of Shansi RC since 1972.

Wu Han   Playwright and historian, vice-mayor of Peking (1949–66); purged in 1966 for having authored an anti-Maoist play "The Dismissal of Hai Jui."

Wu Leng-hsi   Director of New China News Agency (1952–66), editor-in-chief of *Jen-min Jih-pao* (1957–66); purged in 1966; reinstated editor-in-chief of *Jen-min Jih-pao* in 1973.

Wu Chih-p'u‡   Second secretary of the Honan CCP Committee (1949–58, 1961–62), first secretary (1958–61), governor of Honan (1949–62), secretary of the CCP Central-South China Bureau (1962–66); disappeared from public view in 1966.

Yang Cheng-wu (general)† Commander of the Peking MR (1954–59), deputy PLA chief of staff (1959–66), acting PLA chief of staff (1966–68); purged in 1968; partial rehabilitation in 1974.

Yang Chueh Secretary of the Honan CCP Committee (1958–65).

Yang Han-sheng Vice-chairman of the All-China Federation of Literary and Art Circles (1960–66); branded an anti-party element in 1966.

Yang Hsien-chen† Marxist theorist, president of the Higher Party School (1955–61), promoted to a full CC member in 1958; purged in 1964–1965.

Yang Shang-k'un‡ Director of the CCP CC Staff Office (1945–65), alternate secretary of the CCP Secretariat (1956–65); in political disgrace since 1965.

Yang Ying-chieh Vice-chairman of the State Planning Commission (1954–59, 1962–65).

Yao Wen-yuan* Editor-in-chief of the *Shanghai Chieh-fang Jih-pao* (1965–66), member of the CRG (1966–68), currently member of the Politburo, editor-in-chief of *Hung Ch'i*, and second secretary of the Shanghai CCP Committee.

Yeh Chien-ying (marshal) *‡ Member of the Politburo since 1966, currently vice-chairman of the party and of its Military Affairs Committee and minister of defense.

Yeh Fei†§ First secretary of the Fukien CCP Committee (1955–66), promoted to full CC member in 1958; purged in 1966; partially rehabilitated in 1972 and appointed minister of communications in January 1975.

Appendix B
Members of the CC Politburo

Seventh Central Committee (1945–56)

Elected in 1945

Mao Tse-tung*
Liu Shao-ch'i*
Chou En-lai*
Chu Teh*
Jen Pi-shih (died in 1950)*
Ch'en Yun*
Chang Wen-t'ien
K'ang Sheng
Lin Po-chü
Tung Pi-wu

Elected in 1949

Kao Kang (purged in 1954)
P'eng Chen

Elected in 1954

P'eng Teh-huai

Elected in 1955

Lin Piao
Teng Hsiao-p'ing

*Also members of the Central Committee Secretariat.

†Also members of the Politburo Standing Committee; concurrently, Mao was the chairman, Teng was the general secretary, and the rest of the Standing Committee were the vice-chairmen of the CC.

‡Concurrently members of the Politburo Standing Committee; Mao retained the chairmanship of the CC and Lin Piao was the only vice-chairman of the CC.

§Concurrently members of the Politburo Standing Committee; Chou, Wang, K'ang, Yeh, and Teng are also vice-chairmen of the CC. Teng was elected to the Politburo in January 1974 and elevated to the Politburo SC and vice-chairman at the January 1975 CC Plenum; Li Teh-sheng, elected a Politburo SC member and vice-chairman in August 1973, was demoted to an ordinary member of the Politburo in January 1975.

Eighth Central Committee (1956–69)

1956–66

Full Members (elected in 1956)

Mao Tse-tung†
Liu Shao-ch'i†
Chou En-lai†
Chu Teh†
Ch'en Yun†
Teng Hsiao-p'ing†
Lin Piao†
Lin Po-chü (died in 1960)
Tung Pi-wu
P'eng Chen
Lo Jung-huan (died in 1963)
Ch'en yi
Li Fu-ch'un
P'eng Teh-huai (purged in 1959)
Liu Po-cheng
Ho Lung
Li Hsien-nien

Full Members (elected in 1958)

K'o Ch'ing-shih
Li Ching-ch'üan
T'an Chen-lin

Alternate Members (elected in 1956)

Ulanfu
Chang Wen-t'ien (purged in 1959)
Lu Ting-Yi
Ch'en Po-ta
K'ang Sheng
Po I-po

1966–69

Full Members (elected in 1966)

Mao Tse-tung‡
Lin Piao‡

Chou En-lai‡
T'ao Chu (removed in December 1966)‡
Ch'en Po-ta‡
Teng Hsiao-p'ing (removed in December 1966)‡
K'ang Sheng‡
Liu Shao-ch'i (removed in November 1966)‡
Li Fu-ch'un‡
Ch'en Yun
Tung Pi-wu
Ch'en Yi
Liu Po-cheng
Ho Lung (removed in December 1966)
Li Hsien-nien
T'an Ch'en-lin (removed in June 1967)
Li Ching-ch'uan (removed in May 1967)
Hsu Hsiang-ch'ien
Nieh Jung-chen
Yeh Chien-ying

Alternate Members (elected in 1966)

Ulanfu (removed in December 1966)
Po I-po (removed in January 1967)
Li Hsueh-feng
Sung Jen-chiung (removed in 1968)
Liu Lan-t'ao (removed in December 1966)
Hsieh Fu-chih

Ninth Central Committee (1969–73)

Full Members

Mao Tse-tung‡
Lin Piao (purged and died in 1971)‡
Chou En-lai‡
Ch'en Po-ta (purged in 1970)‡
K'ang Sheng‡
Chu Teh
Tung Pi-wu
Chiang Ch'ing

Chang Ch'un-ch'iao
Huang Yung-sheng (purged in 1971)
Yeh Chun (purged and died in 1971)
Yeh Chien-ying
Yao Wen-yuan
Liu Po-cheng
Li Hsien-nien
Hsieh Fu-chih (died in 1972)
Wu Fa-hsien (purged in 1971)
Li Tso-p'eng (purged in 1971)
Ch'iu Hui-tso (purged in 1971)
Hsu shih-yu
Ch'en Hsi-lien

Alternate Members

Chi Teng-kuei
Li Teh-sheng
Wang Tung-hsing
Li Hsueh-feng (purged in 1970)

Tenth Central Committee (1973–19—)

Full Members

Mao Tse-tung§
Chou En-lai§
Wang Hung-wen§
K'ang Sheng§
Yeh Chien-ying§
Teng Hsiao-p'ing§
Tung Pi-wu§ (died in 1975)
Chu Teh§
Chang Ch'un-ch'iao§
Chiang Ch'ing
Yao Wen-yuan
Liu Po-cheng
Li Hsien-nien
Ch'en Hsi-lien
Hsu Shih-yu

Chi Teng-kuei
Wang Tung-hsing
Hua Kuo-feng
Wu Teh
Ch'en Yung-kuei
Wei Kuo-ch'ing
Li Teh-sheng§

Alternate Members

Su Cheng-hua
Saifudin
Ni Chih-fu
Wu Kuei-hsien

Appendix C
Known Party Meetings (1949–66) and their Possible Agendas*

5–13 March 1949. Second (Enlarged) Plenum of the Seventh CC held at Shih-chia-chuang and attended by thirty-four full and nineteen alternate members; Mao delivered a work report on behalf of the Politburo (reissued on 25 November 1968). **[*JMJP*,† 15 September 1956.]**

6–9 June 1950. Third (Enlarged) Plenum of the Seventh CC;‡ reports by Mao on financial and economic rehabilitation, by Liu Shao-chi on land reform, by Chou En-lai on united front work and diplomatic affairs, by Ch'en Yun on financial and economic work, and by Nieh Jung-chen on military affairs were discussed and approved; a decision on the rectification of the party's working style and organization was adopted. **[*JMJP*, 13 June and 1 July 1950.]**

March 1951. National Conference on Organizational Work; resolution on tidying up the party's organization at basic units and the "eight qualifications" for party membership adopted. **[*Hsin-Hua Yeh-pao*, no. 3 (1953): 23; *Hsin-hua Jih-pao* (Chungkeng), 23 October 1952; and *Thoroughly Destroy the Counter-revolutionary Revisionist Organizational Line of Big Traitors Liu Shao ch'i and An Tzu-wen* (a phamphlet distributed by a rebel group of the CC Organization Department in April 1967).]**

May 1951. National Conference on Propaganda Work; on 7 May Liu Shao-chi made a speech attacking "utopian agricultural socialism," which sought to realize agricultural collectivization before mechanization. **[*PR*, no. 49, (1967): 14; *SCMM*, no. 633, p. 8.]**

---

*I am grateful to Mr. Ting Wang, of the Contemporary China Research Institute in Hong Kong, for valuable assistance on certain technical points, and to Professor Michael Oksenberg of the University of Michigan, who generously made available to me a list of party meetings which he compiled. Chinese official and Red Guard sources as well as circumstantial evidence were also used.

†See Notes for key to abbreviations.

‡Unless specified otherwise, all meetings were held in Peking.

Early December 1951. Politburo conference; decision made to carry out a nation-wide "three-anti" campaign. **[*JMJP*, 10 January 1952.]**

15 December 1951. Politburo conference; the "Decision on Mutual Aid and Cooperation in Agricultural Production" adopted. **[*JMJP*, 26 March 1953; *JMST* 1955, p. 477.]**

15 February 1953. Politburo conference; formation of mutual-aid teams and elementary APC's discussed and the 15 December 1951 "Decision on Mutual Aid and Cooperation in Agricultural Production" revised. **[*JMJP*, 26 March 1953.]**

13 June–11 August 1953. National Conference on Financial and Economic Work; devoted to a review of the economic work of the preceding years and preparation for the First Five-Year Plan. **[*JMST* 1957, p. 31, and *Thoroughly Destroy*....]**

September–October 1953. National Conference on Organizational Work. **[*JMST* 1957, p. 33.]**

10–12 October 1953. National Conference on Planned Purchasing and Marketing of Grain; a system of "planned purchase and planned supply" of grain instituted. **[*JMST* 1957, p. 31.]**

October 1953. Politburo conference; the "General Line in the Period of Transition to Socialism" adopted. **[Communique of the Fourth Plenum of the Seventh CC in *JMST* 1955, p. 343.]**

October 1953. National Conference on Agricultural Mutual Aid and Co-operation Work; Mao asserted in the meeting "If socialism does not occupy the rural front, capitalism will inevitably do so." **[*JMST* 1956, p. 93.]**

16 December 1953. Politburo conference; a CCP "Decision on the Development of APC's" adopted. **[*JMST* 1955, p. 343.]**

24 December 1953. Politburo conference; deviations of Kao Kang and Jao Shu-shih exposed; Mao proposed "Resolution on Strengthening Party Unity" (which was approved by the subsequent CC Plenum in February 1954). **[*JMST* 1955, pp. 342–43.]**

6–10 February 1954. Fourth (Enlarged) Plenum of the Seventh CC, attended by thirty-five full and twenty-six alternate members with Mao absent (fifty-two non-CC party officials were also present); Liu Shao-chi delivered a report on behalf of the Politburo attacking Kao Kang and Jao Shu-shih. **[*JMST* 1955, pp. 342–43.]**

February 1954 (following the Plenum). Politburo conference; disciplinary actions taken against Kao and Jao and their followers. **[*JMST* 1957, p. 32.]**

October 1954. Politburo conference; a decision to speed up collectivization made (i.e., to set up half a million new APC's). [*JMST 1956*, **p. 81.**]

21–31 March 1955. National Party Conference; attended by 62 full and alternate CC members and 257 representatives elected from party organizations at all levels; resolutions on the "Kao Kang–Jao Shu-shih Anti-Party Alliance," on the draft "First Five-Year Plan" and on the Establishment of the CCP Central and Local Control Committees" adopted. [*JMST 1956*, **p. 77.**]

4 April 1955. Fifth CC Plenum; the three resolutions of the National Party Conference approved; Lin Piao and Teng Hsiao-P'ing elected to the Politburo. [*JMST 1956*, **p. 77.**]

May 1955. Central Working Conference (presided by Liu Shao-ch'i); a plan to cut back 200,000 APC's, reportedly submitted by Teng Tzu-hui, was approved. [**Liu Shao-ch'i, "Confession,"** *MS*, **28–29 January 1967.**]

May 1955. National Conference on Rural Work in which Teng Tzu-hui carried out the decision authorizing the dissolution of the APC's. [**Liu, "Confession."**]

31 July–1 August 1955. Conference of Secretaries of Provincial and Municipal Party Committees; Mao spoke on "The Question of Agricultural Co-operation," seeking the support of provincial-level leaders to speed up collectivization. [*JMST 1956*, **pp. 80, 87, 92.**]

4–11 October 1955. Sixth (Enlarged) Plenum of the Seventh CC, attended by 38 full and 25 alternate members (388 non-CC party officials were also present); "Decision on Agricultural Cooperation," proposed by Mao, adopted; measures related to the Eighth National Party Congress in 1956 discussed and approved. [*JMST 1956*, **p. 87.**]

16–24 November 1955. Conference on the Transformation of Capitalist Industry and Commerce; decision to increase the pace of socialist transformation of capitalist industry and commerce. [*JMST 1957*, **p. 31.**]

December 1955–January 1956. Politburo conference; discussions on questions of intellectuals and Twelve-Year Agricultural Program. [**Circumstantial evidence.**]

14–20 January 1956. Conference on the Question of Intellectuals, attended by 1279 party officials; Chou En-lai spoke on "The Question of Intellectuals" and Liao Lu-yen explained the Twelve-Year Agricultural Program. [*JMJP*, **30 January 1956.**]

23 January 1956. Politburo conference; Mao's draft 1956–1957 National Program for Agricultural Development approved. [*JMST 1956*, **p. 64.**]

Late March–early April 1956. (Enlarged) Politburo conference; decision to slow down the economic drive; deliberation on China's response to the "de-Stalinization" movement which resulted in the publication of "On the Historical Experience of the Dictatorship of the Proletariat" in *JMJP* (5 April). [*JMJP*, 5 April 1956, and circumstantial evidence.]

25 April 1956. (Enlarged) Politburo conference; Mao spoke on "Ten Great Relationships." [*HCS*, no. 6 (1960) : 4.]

25–28 April 1956. Conference of the Secretaries of Provincial and Municipal Party Committees; questions of the forthcoming party congress, "de-Stalinization," and major problems outlined in Mao's speech discussed. [*JMST 1957*, p. 31; *NCNA* (Peking), 14 September 1956, in *CB*, no. 411, p. 3.]

6 July 1956. Politburo conference; the opening date (15 September 1956) and major items on the agenda of the forthcoming Eighth Party Congress decided. [*NCNA* (Peking), 6 July 1956, in *CB*, no. 411, p. 2.]

Late August–6 September 1956. Seventh Plenum of the Seventh CC attended by forty-four members and twenty-three alternates; devoted to the preparation of the Eighth Party Congress—the political report and other documents to be submitted to the congress examined and approved. [*NCNA* (Peking), 14 September 1956, in *CB*, no. 411, p. 5.]

15–27 September 1956. Eighth National Party Congress, attended by 1026 delegates; New Party Constitution, the Political Report, and the Second Five-Year Plan adopted; 97 full and 73 alternate CC members elected. [*JMST 1957*.]

28 September 1956. First Plenum of the Eighth CC, attended by ninety-six full and seventy alternate members; a twenty-three-man Politburo (seventeen full members and six candidates), a ten-man Secretariat (seven secretaries and three alternate secretaries), and a six-man Standing Committee of the Politburo (Mao [chairman of the CC and Politburo], Liu, Chou, Chu Teh, and Ch'en Yun [vice-chairman of the CC and the Politburo] and Teng Hsiao-P'ing [general-secretary of the CC]) were elected. [*JMST 1957*, p. 69.]

10–15 November 1956. Second Plenum of the Eighth CC, attended by 84 full and 65 alternate members (147 non-CC party officials were also present); three Politburo reports were presented by Liu on international situations (the Suez and the Polish and Hungarian crises), by Chou on national economy in 1956 and 1957, and by Ch'en Yun on the grain problem; summing up the conference, Mao called for all party members to "struggle, through rectification of work style, against the tendencies toward subjectivism, sectarianism, and bureaucratism." [*JMST 1957*, p. 147.]

Late December 1956. Enlarged Politburo conference; crises in Poland and Hungary and the international Communist movement discussed. **[*JMJP*, 29 December 1956, and circumstantial evidence.]**

January 1957. Conference of the Secretaries of Provincial and Municipal Party Committees; questions of inflation, of balance of payments, of "reckless advance" in economic construction and international situation discussed. **[*MTTT* (1969), pp. 73–90; *Pei-ching Kung-she* [*Peking Commune*], no. 5, 28 January 1967.]**

March 1957. National Conference on Propaganda Work; Mao made a speech (on 12 March) persuading the party's propaganda workers to support his "hundred flowers" campaign. **[*NCNA* (Peking), 1 September 1968, in *SCMP*, no. 4253, p. 22.]**

25 May 1957. Politburo Standing Committee Conference(?); Mao spoke on "Things are Undergoing a Change," which marked the beginning of the reversal of the party rectification campaign. **[*SCMP*, no. 4253, pp. 22–23.]**

Late July 1957. Tsingtao Conference, attended by provincial-level party secretaries and some CC members; Mao promoted a radical line in economy; Mao spoke on "The Situation in the Summer of 1957," which reassessed the state of the nation. **[*JMJP*, 19 October 1957; *Chung-kuo Shui-li*, no. 1 (1958): 7; *SCMP*, no. 4000, p. 18.]**

(First half of September 1957). National Conference on Rural Work; discussion on the reorganization of APC system and ways to increase agricultural production which probably formed the basis of the three CC directives on the APC's on 14 September. **[*JMST 1958*, p. 520.]**

Mid-September 1957. Politburo conference(?) with Mao absent; preparation for the forthcoming CC Plenum and the approval or three Politburo reports to be submitted to the Plenum.

21 September–9 October 1957. Third (Enlarged) Plenum of the Eighth CC, attended by 91 members and 62 alternates (416 other party officials were also present); three Politburo reports by Teng Hsiao-p'ing on party rectification, by Ch'en Yun on administrative decentralization and agricultural production, and by Chou En-lai on wages and welfare were presented; revised draft Twelve-Year Agricultural Program, draft regulation on wages and welfare, and three other draft regulations for improving the system of industrial management, of commercial management, and of financial management were "basically" approved. **[*JMST 1958*, p. 182.]**

January–March 1958. The Hangchow Conference (early January), the Nanning Conference (11–12 January), and the Chengtu Conference (10–22 March), all attended by provincial-level party secretaries and some Politburo members including Mao; in these meetings Mao actively promotes the Great Leap Forward programs; "Sixty-articles on Method of Work" were formulated as a result of discussions in the Hangchow and Nanning Conferences; Mao proposed the merger of small APC's into larger units in the Chengtu Conference. **[CB, no. 509, p. 6; CB, no. 892, p. 1; JMST 1959, p. 25; JMJP, 29 August 1959; SCMP, 1929, p. 34; MTTT (1969), pp. 145–54, 159–80.]**

April and June 1958. Conferences on educational work. **[Lu Ting-yi's article in Hung ch'i, 1 July 1958.]**

2 May 1958. Fourth Plenum of the Eighth CC; preparation of the forthcoming Party Congress. **[JMST 1959, p. 32.]**

5–23 May 1958. Second Session of the Eighth Party Congress; Liu Shao-chi delivered a political report on behalf of the CC; Teng Hsiao-p'ing reported on the November 1957 Moscow Meetings of the Communist and Workers' Parties; second revised Twelve-Year Agricultural Program approved; provincial purges reviewed; additional twenty-five alternate members of the CC elected. **[JMST 1959, p. 16.]**

25 May 1958. Fifth Plenum of the Eighth CC; Lin Piao elected vice-chairman of the CC and the Politburo, and member of the Politburo Standing Committee; K'o Ching-shih, Li Ching-chuan, and T'an Chen-lin elected to Politburo, surpassing six Politburo candidates; Li Fu-chun and Li Hsien-nien elected secretaries of the Secretariat. **[JMST 1959, p. 32.]**

May 1958. The CC Secretariat convened a conference to study work of Party School (e.g., educational materials). **[SCMM, no. 639, p. 3.]**

30 May 1958. (Enlarged) Politburo meeting; educational work discussed. **[SCMM, no. 653, pp. 22, 29.]**

27 May–22 July 1958. (Enlarged) Military Affairs Commission (MAC) Conference; current PLA line of military construction (e.g., emulation of Soviet experiences) criticized. **[Mao's 28 June speech to MAC in Mao Chu-hsi tui P'eng-Huang-Chang-Chen Fan-tang Chi-tuan ti P'i-p'an.]**

June 1958. Politburo Conference on Wage Problems. **[JPRS, 1 August 1967.]**

August 1958. National telephone conference of provincial party secretaries; reform of farm tools discussed. **[SCMM, no. 633, p. 12.]**

17–30 August 1958. Enlarged Politburo conference (first secretaries of the provincial-level party committees and other party officials in the center who were not in the Politburo were also present); "Revolution of the Establishment of People's Communes in the Rural Areas" adopted. [*JMST 1959*, p. 32.]

2–10 November 1958. The Chengchow Conference; attended by some Politburo members and some provincial party secretaries. [*JMST 1959*, p. 37.]

21–27 November 1958. The Wuchang Conference, attended by first party secretaries of the provincial-level party committees and some Politburo members; problems arising from the establishment of communes were among the topics discussed in this and the Changchow Conference. [*JMST 1959*, p. 37.]

28 November–10 December 1958. Sixth Plenum of the CC at Wuchang, attended by eighty-five full and eighty-two alternate members (unspecified number of non-CC members were also present); "Resolution on Some Questions Concerning the People's Communes (Wuhan Resolution)" adopted; Mao's decision to step down as chairman of the Republic approved. [*JMST 1959*, pp. 37, 39.]

January 1959. (Enlarged) Politburo conference (also identified as the Peking Conference); the 1959 economic tasks and the candidate to succeed Mao as Chairman of the PRC discussed. [**CLG, 1, no. 4 (1968–69): 45 and information supplied by Roderick MacFarquhar.**]

Late February–Early March 1959. Second Chengchow (Enlarged) Politburo Conference; changes in the original commune system—the three-level ownership system in communes—introduced. [*JMJP*, 28 and 29 August 1959; *CLG*, 1, no. 4 (1968–69): 22–23.]

Late March–early April 1959. (Enlarged) Politburo conference at Shanghai; continual discussions on problems arising from excesses in the Great Leap and commune programs; preparation for the forthcoming CC Plenum. [*JMST 1959*, p. 45.]

2–5 April 1959. Seventh Plenum of the Eighth CC held at Shanghai; attended by eighty-one full and eighty alternate CC members; checkups of the problems in the communes reviewed; the 1959 draft National Economic Plan adopted; candidates for government posts nominated. [*JMST 1959*, p. 45.]

2 July–1 August 1959. (Enlarged) Politburo conference at Lushan; P'eng Teh-huai, in his "Letter of Opinion" (14 July) and subsequent speeches, attacked Mao's Great Leap and commune policies—a fierce intra-party struggle between P'eng and his supporters and Mao occurred. [*PR*, no. 34 (1967): 8.]

2–16 August 1959. Eighth Plenum of the Eighth CC at Lushan, attended by seventy-five full and seventy-four alternate members (fourteen non-CC members were also present); P'eng Teh-huai and his "anti-party" clique disgraced; exaggeration of 1958 production figures admitted; the three-level ownership system in communes reaffirmed. Lin Piao and Lo Jui-ch'ing became minister of defense and PLA chief of staff, respectively, after the Plenum. [*JMST 1960*, p. 159; *PR*, no. 34 (1967): 8–10.]

September 1959. (Enlarged) Military Affairs Commission Conference; P'eng Teh-huai and his followers in the PLA and their leadership in the PLA affairs repudiated. [*CLG*, 1, no. 4 (1968–69): 79; *CB*, no. 834, p. 18.]

July–August 1960. Central Working Conference at Peitaiho; decision to reestablish six CC regional bureaus made (formally announced in the CC Plenum in January 1961); problems of national economy and possibly the withdrawal of Soviet technicians discussed. [*Chih-k'an Nan-yueh* (Canton: **Proletarian Revolutionary Rebels of Literary and Articles in the Canton Area), no. 3, 1 October 1967.**]

September–October 1960. (Enlarged) Military Affairs Commission Conference; Lin Piao launched an intensive campaign of political indoctrination in the PLA; "Resolution on the Strengthening of Indoctrination Work in Troop Units" adopted. [**J. Chester Chang, ed.,** *The Politics of the Chinese Red Army* **(Stanford: Hoover Institution, 1966), p. 64.**]

November 1960. Politburo conference; a twelve-article "Urgent Directive on the Rural Work" issued. [**Cheng,** *Chinese Red Army*, **p. 137.**]

14–18 January 1961. Ninth Plenum of the Eighth CC, attended by eighty-three full and eighty-seven alternate CC members (twenty-three other party officials were also present); a basic change in economic development strategy —agriculture as the foundation and industry as the leading factor—announced; establishment of six CC regional bureaus made public. [*JMST 1961*, p. 11.]

March 1961. Central Work Conference at Canton; a sixty-article "Draft Regulations on the Rural People's Communes" adopted; a new work style— "investigation and study" by party officials—stressed. [**Cheng,** *Chinese Red Army*, **pp. 405–6, 466–67.**]

May–June 1961. Central Work Conference and possibly a Politburo conference; the state of the economy reviewed. [*PR*, **no. 34 (1967): 17–18;** *CCP* **(Peking), no. 12 (1967).**]

August–September 1961. Central Work Conference held at Lushan (the Second Lushan Conference); further reorganization of the commune system decided. [*CCP* **(Peking), no. 12 (1967);** *SCMM*, no. 640, p. 19.]

December 1961. Conference of party secretaries in charge of industrial work [*Kung-Yeh Shu-chi Hui-yi*]; the seventy-article Regulations on Industry discussed. [*CCP* (Peking), no. 12 (1967).]

January–February 1962. (Enlarged) CC Work Conference, attended by 7000 party officials; a comprehensive reappraisal of the state of the nation— more measures of economic liberalization introduced; guidelines for "reversal of verdict" established. [*PR*, no. 34 (1967): 18, 20.]

21–26 February 1962. Central Work Conference (an Enlarged Politburo Standing Committee Conference, also called Hsi-lou or West Chamber Conference); Ch'en Yun presents a report diagnosing the economic problems in the aftermath of the Great Leap and prescribing solutions. [**Liu, "Confession"**; *Pei-ching Kung-she* (Peking), no. 19 (1967); *CB*, no. 884, p. 20.]

August–September 1962. Central Work Conference held first at Peitaiho then in Peking; Mao called a halt to further retreat, disputes among the CCP leaders over future course of action on China's economic development; several top economic officials (Ch'en Yun, Li Fu-chun, Li Hsien-nien, Poi-Po, and Teng Tzu-hui) criticized by Mao; Teng Tzu-hui dismissed as director of both the party's Rural Work Department and the Staff Office of Agriculture and Forestry of the State Council. [**Liu, "Confession"**; *Pei-ching Kung-she* (Peking), no. 19 (1967); *CB*, no. 884, p. 21.]

24–27 September 1962. Tenth Plenum of the Eighth CC, attended by eighty-two full and eighty-eight alternate members (thirty-three other party officials were also present); Mao spoke on "class struggle" in China; resolutions on "Further Consolidations of the Collective Economy of the People's Communes and the Development of Agricultural Production" and on "commercial work" adopted; the revised sixty-article "Draft Regulations on the Rural People's Communes" approved; problems related to industry and economic planning also discussed; the decision to launch the socialist education campaign adopted; K'ang Sheng, Lu Ting-yi, and Lo Jui-ch'ing elected secretaries of CC Secretariat. [*JMST 1963*, p. 1; **Richard Baum and Frederick C. Teiwes**, *Ssu-Ch'ing: The Socialist Education Movement of 1962–1966* (**Berkeley: Center for Chinese Studies, University of California, 1968), app. B.**]

September 1962. Meeting of Secretariat. [*SCMP* (supplement), no. 208, p. 22.]

November 1962. Central Work Conference. [*SCMP* (supplement), no. 208.]

February 1963. Central Work Conference; the SEC of the preceding five months reviewed; Mao introduced the "successful" experience of the campaign attained in Hunan and Hopei and urged other provinces to emulate that experience. [**Baum and Teiwes**, *Ssu-Ch'ing*, p. 63; *CB*, no. 884, p. 23.]

May 1963. Central Work Conference at Hangchow, experiences of conducting the socialist education campaign formalized and codified in "Draft Resolution of the Central Committee on Some Problems in Current Rural Work" (the so-called First Ten Points), a document reportedly drafted under Mao's supervision. **[Baum and Teiwes, *Ssu-Ch'ing*, app. B.; *MTTT* (1969), pp. 440–46.]**

June 1963. Politburo conference at Hangchow; the twenty-five-point "Proposal Concerning the General Line of the International Communist Movement" formulated by Mao, P'eng Chen, Ch'en po-ta, and K'ang Sheng. **[*SCMM*, no. 651, p. 5, and circumstantial evidence.]**

September 1963. Central Work Conference; reform of the education system and rectification of art, literature, and drama discussed. **[*CB*, no. 842, p. 10.]**

3 January 1964. Symposium on Literature and Art convened by Liu in the name of the CC. **[*CB*, no. 842, p. 11.]**

May 1964. Central Work Conference at Peitaiho; the system of temporary and contract workers discussed. **[*SCMM*, no. 616, p. 24.]**

June 1964. Central Work Conference and Politburo Standing Committee Conference; among the issues discussed were the socialist education campaign—"Organizational Rules of Poor and Lower-Middle Peasants Association" adopted and Mao put forth six criteria for measuring the success of the campaign—the campaign to rectify art and literature and to reform Peking Opera, and the question of cultivating revolutionary successors. **[Baum and Teiwes, *Ssu-Ch'ing*, p. 120; *JMJP*, 18 June 1969; *CB*, no. 884, p. 24.]**

October 1964. Politburo conference; the ouster of Khrushchev discussed— Liu Shao-ch'i allegedly stated that the new CPSU leadership would be 30 degrees different from the old leadership. **[*Ching-kang shan* (Peking Ching-kang Shan Corps, Tsinghua University), no. 16 (1967): 6.]**

December 1964–January 1965. Central Work Conference; Liu Shao-ch'i's administration of the socialist education campaign criticized—"Some Problems Currently Arising in the Course of the Rural Socialist Education Campaign" (the so-called Twenty-Three-Points) formulated under Mao's leadership. **[Baum and Teiwes, *Ssu-Ch'ing*, p. 118; *CB*, no. 884, p. 24.]**

September–October 1965. Central Work Conference (Politburo Standing Committee session attended by the first secretaries of the regional party bureaus); rectification of art and literature discussed—Mao issued a call to criticize Wu Han and "bourgeois reactionary thinking" in the party. **[16 May "CC Circular" in *PR*, no. 21 (1967): 6.]**

November 1965. (Enlarged) Politburo Conference presided over by Liu Shao-ch'i; the questions of education reform discussed. **[*Ching-kang Shan*, no. 16, p. 5; *SCMM*, no. 653, p. 28.]**

December 1965. Politburo Standing Committee meeting at Shanghai; Lo Jui-ch'ing came under attack by Lin Piao, a CC "Work Group" was subsequently set up to investigate Lo's "crimes." **[CB, no. 894, p. 22.]**

5 February 1966. Politburo Standing Committee meeting presided over by Liu in Mao's absence; the "February Outline Report" drafted by P'eng Chen's five-man "Cultural Revolution Group" approved on 5 February and issued on 12 February. **[SCMM, no. 640, p. 7.]**

17–20 March 1966. Politburo Standing Committee (at Hangchow) chaired by Mao; Mao spoke on the question of the GPCR, expressed misgivings on China's intellectuals, and criticized the CC Propaganda Department. **[JPRS, no. 42,349, p. 9.]**

30 March 1966. MAC meeting; a summary of the "Forum on the Literary and Art Work in the Armed Forces" (which Lin Piao entrusted Chiang Ch'ing to convene in February 1966)—a document that spelled out the Maoist position, policy, and intentions on the GPCR—approved. **[JPRS, no. 42,349, p. 9; JMJP, 29 May 1967.**

9–12 April 1966. CC Secretariat meeting, also attended by Chou En-lai; K'ang Sheng and Ch'en Po-ta repudiated a series of mistakes committed by P'eng Chen on the GPCR and other issues, and K'ang conveyed Mao's criticism of P'eng. The meeting resolved to revoke the "February Outline Report" and to set up a new Cultural Revolution Group. **[SCMM, no. 640, p. 12.]**

16–20 April 1966. Politburo Standing Committee Meeting convened at Hangchow to wage struggle against P'eng Chen; on 20 April, Mao endorsed seven documents repudiating P'eng's "crimes." **[SCMM, no. 640, pp. 13–14.]**

4–18 May 1966. Enlarged Politburo Standing Committee Conference in Hangchow; on 16 May the meeting approved the "May 16 Circular," which countermanded the "February Outline Report," dissolved the "Five-Man Cultural Revolutionary Group," and set up a new "Cultural Revolutionary Group" under the Politburo Standing Committee; the fate of P'eng Chen was sealed; on the same date, the meeting also endorsed an investigation report submitted by the CC "Work Group" on Lo Jui-ch'ing's mistakes and problems and decided to dismiss Lo from all posts he held; Lin Piao delivered a speech on 18 May warning against a counterrevolutionary coup. **[JPRS, no. 42, 349, p. 10; CB, no. 884, p. 27; CLG, 2, no. 4 (1969–70): 43–62.]**

Early June 1966. Central Work Conference presided over by Liu; decisions were made to dispatch "work teams" to educational institutions to direct the Cultural Revolution, and an eight-point directive was adopted. **[Liu, "Confession"; CB, no. 834, pp. 26–27.]**

9 June 1966. Politburo Standing Committee at Hangchow; Mao cautioned against wanton dispatch of "work teams." [*JPRS*, **no. 42,349, p. 16.**]

20–31 July 1966. Central Work Conference chaired by Mao; the leadership of Liu and Teng Hsiao-p'ing in the Cultural Revolution attacked by Mao, and "work teams" recalled. [*CB*, **no. 891, pp. 58–60.**]

1–12 August 1966. Eleventh Plenum of the Eighth CC; the sixteen-article "Decisions Concerning the Great Proletarian Cultural Revolution" adopted on 8 August; the Politburo reshuffled—Lin Piao elevated, T'ao Chu, Ch'en Po-ta, and Kang Sheng promoted while Liu, Teng, and others were demoted. [*CB*, **no. 884, pp. 28–29**; *SCMP*, **nos. 3761, 3762.**]

23 August 1966. Central Work Conference; approaches to implementing the Cultural Revolution discussed; on 23 August Mao made a speech in which he rejected a suggestion to reorganize the leadership of the Communist Youth League. [*CB*, **no. 891, p. 68.**]

8–25 October 1966. Central Work Conference; policies of, and problems arising from the Cultural Revolution in the two preceding months reviewed; Liu made a self-criticism on 23 October. [*CB*, **no. 891, pp. 70–75**; *SCMM*, **no. 651, pp. 2, 4–6.**]

Notes

Abbreviations

BFPC	*Birth of the First People's Communes in Shanghai* (Shanghai: Jen-min Ch'u-p'an-she, 1958)
CB	*Current Background* (Hongkong: U.S. Consulate-General)
CCP	*Chin-Chun Pao*
CCYC	*Ching-chi Yen-chiu (Economic Research)*
CFCP	*Chieh-fang-chun Pao (Liberation Army Daily)*
CFJP	*Chieh-fang Jih-pao (Liberation Daily)*
CHCC	*Chi-hua Ching-chi (Planned Economy)*
Chairman Mao's Repudiations	*Mao Chu-hsi Tui P'eng-Huang-Chang-Chou Fang-tang Chi-tuan Ti P'i-p'am (Chairman Mao's Repudiations of the P'eng-Huang-Chang-Chou Anti-Party Group)* (Photoduplicated; presumably published in Mainland China and released in 1968 by the U.S. Department of State, Office of External Research, Center for Chinese Research Materials, Association of Research Libraries [group 11, reel 2, part 9]; English translation in *CLG*, 1, no. 4 (1968–69).
CJP	*Chekiang Jih-pao*
CKCN	*Chung-kuo Ch'ing-nien (China Youth)*
CKCNP	*Chung-kuo Ch'ien-nien Pao (China Youth Daily)*
CLG	*Chinese Law and Government: A Journal of Translations* (White Plains, N.Y.: International Arts and Sciences Press)
Compendium	*Compendium of Laws and Ordinances of the Central Government* (Peking: Jen-min Ch'u-pan-she)
Compendium (PRC)	*Compendium of the Laws and Regulations of the People's Republic of China* (Peking: Fa-lu ch'u-pan-she, 1958)
CQ	*China Quarterly*

Down with P'eng	*Down with Big Conspirator, Big Ambitionist, Big Warlord P'eng Teh-huai* (Peking: Tsinghua University Chingkang-shan Corps Under the Capital Red Guard Congress, November 1967; *CB*, no. 851)
ECMM	*Extracts from China Mainland Magazines* (Hongkong: U.S. Consulate-General)
8NCCPC	*Eighth National Congress of the Communist Party of China* (Peking: FLP, 1956, 2 vols.)
FLP	Foreign Language Press
HC	*Hung Ch'i (Red Flag)*
HCS	*Hsien Chien-she (New Constructions)*
HH	*Hsueh Hsi (Study)*
HHPYK	*Hsin-hua P'an-yueh-k'an (New China Semi-monthly)*
JMJP	*Jen-min Jih-pao (People's Daily)*
JMST	*Jen-min Shou-ts'e (People's Handbook)*
JPRS	Joint Publication Research Service (Washington, D.C.: U.S. Department of Commerce)
KJP	*Kiangsi Jih-pao*
KMJP	*Kwang-ming Jih-pao (Illumination Daily)*
LJP	*Liaoning Jih-pao*
Lienchiang Documents	*Fan-kung Yu-chi Tui T'u-chi Fukien Lienchiang Lu-huo Fei-Fang Wen-chien Hui-pien (Collected Documents Captured During an Anti-Communist Commando Raid on Lienchiang County, Fukien)* (Taipei: Ministry of National Defense, 1964; English translation: C.S. Chen, ed., *Rural People's Communes in Lien-Chiang* [Stanford, Cal.: Hoover Institution, 1967])
MS	*Mainichi Shimbun* (Tokyo)
MTTT	*Mao Tse'tung Ssu-hsiang Wan-sui (Long Live Mao Tse-tung's Thought)* (Peking, 1969)
NCAS	*New China Advances to Socialism* (Peking: FLP, 1956)
NCNA	*New China News Agency* (Peking)
NFJP	*Nan-fang Jih-pao (Southern Daily)*
PJP	*Peking Jih-pao*
PKS	*Peiching Kung-she (Peking Commune)* (Peking: Central Finance and Monetary Institute, Peking Commune August 8 Fighting Detachment)

PLA Bull.   *PLA Bulletin of Activities*, in J. Chester Cheng, ed., *The Politics of the Chinese Red Army* (Stanford, Cal.: Hoover Institution, 1966)

PR   *Peking Review*

"Resolution concerning Peng"   "Resolution of the 8th Plenary Session of the 8th Central Committee of the CCP Concerning the Anti-Party Clique Headed by P'eng Teh-huai" (16 August 1959) (First published in *PR*, no. 34 [1967])

SCMM   *Selections from China Mainland Magazines* (Hongkong: U.S. Consulate-General)

SCMP   *Survey of China Mainland Press* (Hongkong: U.S. Consulate-General)

SUCC   *Socialist Upsurge in China's Countryside* (Peking: FLP, 1956)

TC   *Ts'ai Cheng (Finance)*

TFHP   *Tung-fang-hung pao* (Peking: Editorial Department of the Peking Institute of Geology)

TKP   *Ta-kung Pao (Impartial Daily)*

TMHC   *Ts'ai-mao Hung Ch'i* (Peking: The Finance and Trade System Rebels Liaison Committee)

URS   Union Research Service (Hongkong: Union General Research Institute)

WHP   *Wen-hui Pao*

Introduction

1. This tradition includes works such as Harold Lasswell and Daniel Lerner, eds., *The Policy Science* (Stanford: Stanford University Press, 1951), Robert Dahl and Charles E. Lindblom, *Politics, Economy and Welfare* (New York: Harper & Row, 1953), and D. Braybrooke and C.E. Lindblom, *A Strategy of Decision* (New York: Free Press, 1963). These works, however, also are in the tradition of so-called normative decision theory, which is concerned with how people *should* act to achieve better (or best) results, inasmuch as they intend to provide a basis for improving rational, efficient methods of policy formulation to maximize the outputs of public policy in accordance with the values of democratic society. See Enid B. Schoettle, "The State of the Art in Policy Studies," in *The Study of Policy Formulation* eds. Raymond A. Bauer and Kenneth J. Gergen (New York: Free Press, 1968), for a discussion of the evolution of methodology on policy formulation in the public arena.

2. These are the major deficiencies of both local community studies such as Floyd Hunter's

Community Power Structure: A Study of Decision Makers (Chapel Hill: University of North Carolina Press, 1953) and national community studies such as C. Wright Mills' *The Power Elite* (New York: Oxford University Press, 1956), which identified elites solely by associational role or socioeconomic status. In *Who Governs?* (New Haven: Yale University Press, 1961), Robert A. Dahl offers a different model of the elite in which there is no singular interlocking elite but several elites, each exerting power over a specific issue area.

3. For an analysis of the CC members, see Donald W. Klein, "The 'Next Generation' of Chinese Communist Leaders," *CQ*, no. 12 (1962).

4. This figure was revealed by "a man very high in the Party" in an interview with Edgar Snow (*The Other Side of the River* [New York: Random House, 1962], p. 331).

5. Robert A. Dahl, "Critique of the Ruling Elite Model," *American Political Science Review* 52, no. 2 (1958): 464.

6. Michael Oksenberg, "Occupational Groups in Chinese Society and the Cultural Revolution," in *The Cultural Revolution: 1967 in Review* (Ann Arbor: Center for Chinese Studies, University of Michigan, 1968), p. 1.

7. Harold D. Lasswell, *The Decision Process: Seven Categories of Functional Analysis* (College Park: Bureau of Government Research, University of Maryland, 1956), as discussed in James A. Robinson, *Congress and Foreign Policy-making* (Homewood, Ill.: Dorsey, 1962), p. 6.

8. See Dorwin Cartwright, ed., *Studies in Social Power* (Ann Arbor: Institute for Social Research, University of Michigan, 1959), p. 186, and Robinson, p. 4.

9. Robinson, p. 4.

10. H. D. Lasswell and A. Kaplan, *Power and Society: A Framework of Political Inquiry* (New Haven: Yale University Press, 1950), pp. 76–77.

11. These are borrowed from Robinson, pp. 2–3.

12. Teng Hsiao-p'ing, "Report on the Revision of the Constitution of the Communist Party of China," *8NCCPC*, 2: 188–89.

13. Richard Snyder, "A Decision-making Approach to the Study of Political Phenomena," in *Approaches to the Study of Politics*, ed. Roland Young (Evanston, Ill.: Northwestern University Press, 1958), p. 17.

14. It is no secret that "all the news that is fit to print" is decided by the party, and many "news reports" are supplied by the party committees at various levels. Those in charge of newspapers are constantly informed of the party's policies and the leadership's intentions, and their work is primarily to promote the party's goals. Mao once instructed two provincial secretaries as follows: "It is necessary for the first secretary to take command and to personally revise major editorials." See Liu Chien-hsun, "Seriously Carry out Chairman Mao's Instruction on the Newspaper Work," *HHPYK*, no. 24 (1958).

15. These papers were analyzed by John W. Lewis, "China's Secret Military Papers: 'Continuities' and 'Revelations,'" *CQ*, no. 18 (1964), and Alice L. Hsieh, "China's Secret Military Papers: Military Doctrine and Strategy," ibid. An English translation is edited by J. Chester Cheng, *The Politics of the Chinese Red Army: A Translation of the Bulletin of Activities of the People's Liberation Army* (Stanford: Hoover Institution, 1966).

16. For example, the essence of the twelve-article "Urgent Directive on the Rural Work" was summarized in an editorial in *JMJP*, 20 November 1960.

17. For an example of this kind, see editorials in *HC* and *JMJP*, "Along the Socialist or the Capitalist Road?"; *PR*, no. 34, 18 August 1967.

18. These Red Guard groups included the Chingkang-shan Corps of Tsinghua University, the Hung Ch'i Fighting Detachment of the Peking Aeronautical Engineering Institute, the Third Headquarters of the Capital Red Guards, which consisted of radical Red Guard groups in the Peking area. Most of the Red Guard materials used in this study have come from the publications of these groups.

Chapter 1

1. Mao Tse-tung, "The Question of Agricultural Cooperation," *JMJP*, 17 October 1955; *CB*, no. 364.

2. For analyses of the advances and retreats in collectivization in the 1950s, see "Agricultural cooperativization in Communist China," *CB*, no. 373, and Kenneth R. Walker, "Collectivization in Retrospect: The 'Socialist High Tide' of Autumn 1955-Spring 1956," *CQ*, no. 26 (1966).

3. For a comparative study of the Chinese and Soviet collectivization, see Thomas Bernstein, "Leadership and Mass Mobilization in the Soviet and Chinese Collectivization Campaign of 1929-1930 and 1955-1956; A Comparison," *CQ*, no. 31 (1967).

4. Teng Tzu-hui, "Speech at the National Democratic Youth League Work Conference" (15 July 1954), *CKCN*, 1 September 1954; *CB*, no. 306.

5. "State Council Directive on 1955 Spring Farming and Production" (3 March 1955), *NCNA* (Peking), 9 March 1955; *CB*, no. 318.

6. *JMST 1956* (Tientsin: Ta-kung Pao, 1956).

7. For a more detailed treatment of the dependence of China's economy on agriculture, see Choh-ming Li, *Economic Development of Communist China* (Berkeley: University of California Press, 1960), pp. 196–223.

8. Section numbers in this discussion from Mao, "Agricultural Cooperation."

9. Apparently Mao was equating himself with the "Party Center," although properly he was not.

10. This quotation and the following one from "Struggle in China's Countryside Between the Two Roads," *JMJP*, 23 November 1967; English version as released by *NCNA* is reprinted in *SCMP*, no. 4068.

11. Liu Shao-ch'i, "Confession," *MS*, 28 and 29 January 1967. Liu was reported to have made a self-criticism in a CC Work Conference on 23 October 1966; the text was made public in Red Guard wall posters and was subsequently acquired by Japanese reporters in Peking at that time. In general, the contents of Liu's confession seem to accord with events and other sources sufficiently to warrant general acceptance, especially when corroborated by other sources.

12. Teng Tzu-hui, "Speech at the National Democratic Youth League," and a speech of June 1956, "Changes in China's Rural Economy and Problems in the Agricultural Cooperative movement," in *NCAS*.

13. Li Hsien-nien, "Financial-Economic Work and Agricultural Cooperation," *TKP* (Tientsin), 8 November 1955; *SCMP*, no. 1183.

14. See two speeches he made in 1955 and 1956 in *CB*, no. 339, and *NCAS*.

15. See reports from Shantung and Hopei in *JMJP*, 23 August and 8 September 1955.

16. For a detailed study of the Central Work Conference, see Parris H. Chang, "Research Notes on the Changing Loci of Decision in the CCP," *CQ*, no. 44 (1970).

17. See "Struggle in China's Countryside Between the Two Roads," *JMJP*, 23 November 1967; *SCMP*, no. 4068.

18. Mao, "Agricultural Cooperation," section II. In a lower APC each peasant would hand over his land, draft animals, and implements to the APC but receive payment for these as well as for the labor he contributed; in a higher APC, like the Soviet Kolkhoz, he would only receive income for his labor. His land and the means of production that he contributed reverted to the collective ownership.

19. Data on Kiangsu and Shantung from *CFJP*, 21 October 1955.

20. *NFJP* (Canton), 24 September 1955.

21. *JMJP*, 19 October 1955.

22. I have treated Ch'en's career and his relations with Mao at length in *Radicals and Radical Ideology in China's Cultural Revolution* (New York: Research Institute on Communist Affairs, Columbia University, 1973), pp. 63–70.

23. "Decision on Agricultural Cooperation," *JMJP*, 18 October 1955; *SCMP*, no. 1151.

24. *MTTT*, p. 12.

25. Twenty-six provincial secretaries were promoted to the CC in the Eighth Party Congress in September 1956; most of them had been provincial first party secretaries.

26. *JMJP*, 13 November 1955; *SCMP*, no. 1177. Ch'en Yi's primary responsibility has not been in the economic field; that he had to make a self-criticism seems to suggest that the "go-slow" policy on collectivization also had the backing of officials in other sectors.

27. *SCMP*, no. 1183.

28. *MTTT*, p. 21. In addition, Mao said: "Comrade Teng Tzu-hui did a great deal of work in the past during the long-term struggle and was meritorious. However he should not allow his merits to become a burden. He needs only be a little bit more modest, not showing off his seniority, then he will be able to correct his mistakes." Mao might have had Teng in mind when he wrote these words in the Preface to a collection of essays in December 1955: "The problem today is that rightist conservativism is still causing trouble in many fields and preventing the work in these fields from keeping pace with the development of the objective situation." *SUCC*.

29. The contents of the program were reported in *NCNA* (Peking), 25 January 1956, and reproduced in *SCMP*, no. 1219.

30. If the targets were fulfilled, the grain production would increase from 183 million tons in 1956 to 450 million tons in 1967. The output for 1967, according to the estimate of an expert, was between 205 and 215 million tons.

31. "Explanations on the Draft 1956–1967 National Program for Agricultural Development," *NCNA* (Peking), 25 January 1956; *SCMP*, no. 1219.

32. This discussion is based on information from *NCNA* (Peking), 30 January 1956.

33. This discussion is based on information from Liao Lu-yen, "Explanations."

34. *NCNA* (Peking), 29 January 1956; *CB*, no. 376.

35. Liao Lu-yen, "Explanations."

36. "Democratic" personages, according to the Chinese Communists, are non-Communists who (1) supported the CCP either during the Civil War or soon after the 1949 takeover, and (2) did not occupy formal government positions after 1949.

37. The chairman of the Republic is empowered to convene and preside over the Supreme State Conference (SSC) whenever he deems necessary. The participants of this conference include the vice-chairman of the Republic, the chairman of the National People's Congress (NPC) Standing Committee, the premier, and "other persons concerned." Constitutionally, the SSC is not a decision-making body since it has no independent powers, although it can "submit" its views on important affairs of state to the NPC or its Standing Committee, the State Council, or to other bodies concerned for "their consideration and decision" (article 43).

38. For example, *KMJP* and *TKP* (Tientsin), 27 January 1956, and *CKCNP*, 28 January 1956.

39. *TKP* (Tientsin), 29 January 1956.

40. A few examples are "Struggle for a Better, Happy Life," *Szechuan Jih-pao*, 29 January 1956; "Starting a Tidal Wave Campaign for National Program for Agricultural Development," *Inner Mongolia Jih-pao*, 31 January 1956; "Diligently Study and Propagandize the National Program for Agricultural Development," *Ta-chung Jih-pao*, 2 February 1956; "Extensively Launching the Study and Discussion of the National Program for Agricultural Development," *Kiangsi Jih-pao*, 4 February 1956; "March Boldly on the Great Development of Agricultural Production," *Yunnan Jih-pao*, 6 February 1956.

41. *Shensi Jih-pao*, 24 February 1956.

42. *NFJP*, 8 April 1956.

43. *Shen-yang Jih-pao*, 17 February 1956.

44. *CKCNP*, 7 March 1956.

45. *TKP* (Tientsin), 9 March 1956.

46. Tung Ta-lin, *Agricultural Cooperation in China* (Peking: FLP, 1959), pp. 7–8.

47. *NCNA* (Peking), 19 June 1956.

48. *JMJP*, 18 December 1955; *NCNA* (Peking), 26 December 1955.

49. *JMJP*, 19 April 1957.

50. Ibid., and *JMJP*, 17 May 1956.

51. *NCNA* (Peking), 19 June 1956.

52. Speech by Teng Tzu-hui at the National Conference of Outstanding Workers, 7 May 1956, *NCNA* (Peking), 7 May 1956.

53. *TKP* (Tientsin), 2 May 1956.

54. "Changes in China's Rural Economy and Problems in the Agricultural Cooperative Movement," *NCAS*, p. 125.

55. The Seventh CC Plenum did not meet until late August; it then devoted its efforts to preparatory work for the Eighth CCP Congress and did not approve the draft program.

56. CCP Central Committee and the State Council, "Joint Directive on Running of the APC's Industriously and Economically" (4 April 1956), *NCNA* (Peking), 4 April 1956; *SCMP*, no. 1286.

57. Ibid.

58. *NCNA* (Peking), 26 June 1957; *JMJP*, 30 June 1957.

59. "Why do Double-wheel Double-share Plows Become Dull in Sale and Suspended in Production," *CHCS*, no. 9.

60. The public was not told about the meeting until five moths later. It is doubtful that the meeting merely discussed "the important questions for submission to and discussion by the Eighth Party Congress, as claimed in an *NCNA* dispatch (14 September 1956). There would have been no need to withhold the news of the conference from the public for such a long time if the April meeting of the regional secretaries had merely been to prepare for the Eighth Party Congress.

61. For an excellent analysis of the motivations behind the publication of the 5 April editorial by the Chinese leadership, see Donald S. Zagoria, *The Sino-Soviet Conflict: 1956–1961* (Princeton: Princeton University Press, 1962), pp. 42–49.

62. The 1945 version reads: "The CCP guides its entire work by the teachings which unite the theories of Marxism-Leninism with the actual practice of the Chinese revolution—the thought of Mao Tse-tung."

63. "The Reactionary Antecedents of P'eng Teh-huai," in *Down with P'eng*, pp. 12, 17.

64. It was Liu Shao-ch'i who first revealed the contents of Mao's speech in his Political Report to the Second Session of the CCP Eighth Party Congress in May 1958, *PR*, 3 June 1958. According to another party official, Wu Chih-p'u, the meeting was held on 25 April 1956 (*Hsin Chien-she*, no. 6, p. 4). If so, it must have been a different meeting from the one in early April which produced the 4 April joint directive and the 5 April *People's Daily* editorial. The full text of Mao's speech became available only during the Cultural Revolution; it is translated into English in Jerome Ch'en, ed., *Mao* (Englewood Cliffs, N.J.; Prentice-Hall, 1969), pp. 66–85.

65. It is true that the draft program was already being implemented even before the approval by the CC. However, since the CC did not approve the draft program in April 1956 as Mao envisioned, and in light of the fact that Mao resubmitted it for the CC approval in September 1957, one is led to conclude that Mao suffered a setback in 1956. After spring 1956, the draft program was rarely mentioned in the public, and press references to it were always in an unfavorable context.

66. *SUCC*, Preface. In this connection, it is interesting to note the personal charges leveled against Mao by Ch'en Ming-shu, a former KMT official, during the period of free criticism in 1957, that Mao was "very confident about the false reports and dogmatic analysis presented him by his cadres," and that Mao was "impetuous in making decisions without first making a careful study of the facts." *CB*, no. 475, p. 45.

67. See Wu Leng-hsi's "Confession" during the Cultural Revolution, translated with notes by Parris H. Chang, *CLG*, 2, no. 4, p. 72.

68. See *MTTT*, pp. 145–54, particularly pp. 151–52. In the light of this speech, Mao's "new" posture shown in his "Ten Great Relationships" was more of a tactical move under pressure than a change of heart.

69. Liu, as noted earlier, favored or at least went along with those who promoted a "go-slow" policy in collectivization, but available evidence suggests, as we shall have occasion to note later, that Liu, as an organization man, was opposed to a policy of "thaw" detrimental to the interests of the party apparatus. As far as Teng T'o, Lu Ting-yi, and Hu Chiao-mu are concerned, they, as propaganda officials, did not initiate such policy but merely articulated the leadership consensus as they perceived it.

70. NCNA (Peking), 29 January 1956; CB, no. 376. At the same meeting, Mao, too, urged the party cadres to cooperate with the non-party intellectuals, but little publicity was given to Mao's speech. It is fair to assume that at that time it was Chou, rather than Mao, who took the lead to promote the cause of the intellectuals.

71. According to a Red Guard report, which was apparently based on high-level sources, Ch'en Yun played a leading role against Mao's radical policies; see TMHC, 15 February 1967; SCMP supplement, no. 175, p. 27.

72. Mao's 2 May speech was never published, but Lu Ting-yi, director of the CC Propaganda Department, referred to it and interpreted it in a speech (JMJP, 13 June 1956). The new themes, as reflected in Lu's statement, represented a distinctly more liberal policy toward the intellectuals than was implied in Chou En-lai's speech of January.

73. Kung-jen Jih-pao (Worker's Daily), 9 May 1956.

74. Chia T'o-fu, "Problems of Light Industry in China," NCNA (Peking), 19 June 1956; CB, no. 407; JMJP, 9 July 1956.

75. Information on these economic reports from NCAS, pp. 61, 88, 97, 109–10, 112, 128–31.

76. NCNA (Peking), 18 June 1956.

77. NCNA (Peking), 25 June 1956.

78. Two examples are "Bright Future for Landlords, Rich Peasants Who Labor and Abide by Law," Editorial, KMJP, 15 May 1956 and "We Must Treat Correctly the Youth of Landlords Rich Peasant Family," Editorial, CKCNP, 26 May 1956.

79. Merely three months earlier, the Model Regulations for an APC made it clear that "during its first few years the APC shall not accept former landlords and rich peasants as members," Tung Ta-lin, Agricultural Cooperation, p. 101.

80. Information on the congress from 8NCCPC, 1:274–75; 279; 2:45–62, 157–98, 206–24.

81. In the early 1960s, as we shall see later, after the collapse of Mao's Great Leap and commune program, he encountered another setback and faced severe criticism, but the criticism again was directed ostensibly against cadres' errors in implementation.

82. "On Strengthening Production Leadership and Organizational Construction of Agricultural Producers' Cooperatives," NCNA (Peking), 12 September 1956.

83. 8NCCPC, 1:13–111.

84. For a detailed analysis of the field army factions, see William W. Whitson with Huang Chen-Hsia, The Chinese High Command (New York: Praeger, 1972). Andrew Nathan, "A Factionalism Model for CCP Politics," CQ, no. 53 (1973): 34–66, has provided a perceptive analysis of factionalism in Chinese Politics.

85. Franz Schurmann, Ideology and Organization in Communist China, 2d ed. (Berkeley: University of California Press, 1968), pp. 55–57, 196.

86. Mao Tse-tung, "On the Correct Handling of Contradictions Among the People," 27 February 1957, Supplement to People's China, 1 July 1957, Section 3 (on agricultural cooperation).

87. See JMJP, 18 June 1957.

88. In Kwangtung alone, during the winter of 1956, some 160,000 peasant households applied for withdrawal and 80,000 of them succeeded (JMJP, 22 March 1957). Numerous desertions from APC's were also reported in Honan, which will be discussed later.

89. For a detailed treatment of this subject, see Roderick MacFarquhar, The Hundred Flowers Campaign and the Chinese Intellectuals (New York: Praeger, 1960).

90. JMJP, 1 October 1957, p. 1.

91. By mid-1957, 97 percent of the total households had joined the APC's, and 93.3 percent

of these were of the advanced type (*JMJP*, 5 July 1957).

92. Teng Tzu-hui, "On the Contradictions Among People in the Countryside and the Principles and Methods of Correctly Handling these Contradictions," *CKCNP*, 1 November 1957.

93. See *JMST 1958*, p. 520.

94. See Mao's editorial remarks on an article, "The Superiority of Large Co-ops," in *SUCC*, p. 460.

95. The "three-guarantee" system refers to the production brigades' contractual arrangements with the APC's by which the brigades would fulfill certain targets and receive rewards in proportion to overfulfillment. The brigade would in turn contract with individual households which would be responsible for certain areas of work or the production of a piece of land. This kind of arrangement was called "guarantee production down to households," or individual farming within the collective framework.

96. Similar measures, as we shall see later, were readopted in the aftermath of the disastrous Great Leap Forward rural policies.

97. On 7 January 1957 the *People's Daily* published a letter from three relatively senior officials of the General Political Department of the PLA criticizing the "hundred flowers" policy. Their criticisms were not refuted until three months later by an editorial of *JMJP* (10 April 1957).

98. See speeches by K'o Ch'ing-shih, T'ao Chu, Shu Tung, and Huang Ou-tung, first party secretaries of Shanghai, Kwangtung, Shantung, and Liaoning, respectively, in *SCMP*, nos. 1694, 1682, 1700, and 1708.

99. Ch'ien Wei-ch'ang, a vice-president of Tsinghua University, was attacked by Wang Wei, another vice-president of that university, for having allegedly said "the blooming and contending was unsatisfactory because the line of Liu Shao-ch'i and P'eng Chen is against this policy" (*JMJP*, 17 July 1957). Yuan Jung-hsi, former first secretary of the Tsing-hua University Party Committee, allegedly declared: "Chairman Mao is under heavy pressure. A large number of telegrams has flowed in calling for a halt to the movement" (*JMJP*, 22 July 1957).

100. If this analysis is correct, then Mao's change of mind probably came in late May 1957, when he denounced the press in a secret speech, "Things are Undergoing a Change," which was revealed for the first time in a major article in *HC*, no. 2 (1968): 12–13.

101. Mao had been absent from Peking since June and returned to Peking from Shanghai only on 19 September for the opening of the Third Plenum the following day; see *JMJP*, 21 September 1957, on Mao's tour.

102. In this connection, it is useful to recall that it was Ch'en Po-ta, a spokesman of the "radical" collectivization policy, who in October 1955 delivered a speech on behalf of the Politburo to the CC Plenum, which subsequently passed a resolution to speed up the pace of collectivization.

103. *JMJP*, 19 October 1957. The original report of Teng may not have dealt with the draft program; it may have been rewritten for publication after the Plenum with a few passages concerning the draft program then inserted.

104. *JMST 1958*, pp. 520–24.

105. Based on his research, Michael Oksenberg suggested to me that the decision to revive the draft program was made at the Tsingtao Conference in July 1957. It is most likely that Mao made such a proposal there; the proposal, however, apparently was not accepted by his central colleagues, judging by the fact that after the conference directives underlying a moderate policy were issued, as noted before.

106. According to Teng Hsiao-p'ing, Mao called a meeting in July 1957 at Tsingtao attended by the secretaries of some of the provincial and municipal party committees (*JMJP*, 19 October 1957); Mao traveled to Honan and other provinces in August (*HJP* [Kaifeng], 4 July 1958; *CB*, no. 515, p. 11); he was in Shanghai on 17 and 18 September and returned to Peking from Shanghai the following day (*JMJP*, 21 September 1957).

107. Schurmann, *Ideology and Organization*, p. 205.

108. See *JMJP*, 25 October 1957. Teng Hsiao-p'ing, in his report to the Third CC Plenum, stated that the revised draft would be discussed by the National Party Congress toward the end

of 1957. The plan to convene a National Party Congress in 1957 did not materialize.

109. See Leo A. Orleans, "Birth Control; Reversal or Postponement?," *CQ*, no. 3 (1960), about the dispute within the party over birth control. Health officials in China began to intensify birth control propaganda at the end of 1954, and Chou En-lai had spoken in favor of it in his report on the Second Five-Year Plan in September 1956. Throughout most of 1957 birth control was official policy, but a few months after the Third Plenum, the party reversed its position.

110. Wu Chih-p'u, "From Agricultural Producers' Cooperatives to the People's Communes," *HC*, no. 8 (1958): 7.

111. *HJP*, 4 July 1958; *CB*, no. 515, p. 4.

112. The central government sent 81 million catties of grain to Honan as relief (*NCNA* [Chengchow], 30 November 1956).

113. Editorial, *HJP*, 4 July 1958; *CB*, no. 515, p. 25.

114. This discussion is based on CCP Honan Provincial Party Committee reports to the CC about the incidents in the villages, mentioned in passing in an article in *HJP*, 4 July 1958; *CB*, no. 515, p. 3.

115. Wu "Producers' Cooperatives."

116. *HJP*, 4 July 1958; *CB*, no. 515, p. 10.

117. During the Cultural Revolution, Red Guard sources charged that Li Chang-ch'uan and T'ao Chu, formerly first secretary of the Southwest Bureau and Central-South Bureau of the CCP, respectively, each maintained a Szechuanese and Cantonese restaurant in Peking to gather information on central politics. The charge, which may or may not be false, is suggestive of the "game" played by the provincial leaders to keep themselves well informed.

118. *HJP*, 4 July 1958; *CB*, no. 515, pp. 7–8.

119. "Instructions of the Jungyang Hsien Committee of the CCP to arouse Masses to Unmask and Attack Bourgeois Rightists," reprinted in *HHPYK*, no. 15 (1958).

120. CCP Honan Committee, "Instructions to Cease Struggle Against the Rightist Elements in *Hsien* Organizations and Below, 13 July 1957," ibid.; *CB*, no. 515, pp. 48–49.

121. *HJP*, 4 July 1958; *CB*, no. 515, p. 11.

122. Wu Chih-p'u, "Right Opportunism is Principal Danger in the Party Now," *HJP*, 4 July 1958; *CB*, no. 515, pp. 18–25. See also *NCNA* (Chengchow), 4 December 1957; *SCMP*, no. 1671, p. 31.

123. P'an Fu-sheng, "Survey Report on the Rural Situation in Honan," *HJP*, 20 September 1957; *SCMP*, no. 1647.

124. *HJP*, 4 July 1957; *CB*, no. 515, p. 11.

125. *NCNA* (Chengchow), 4 December 1957, *SCMP*, no. 1671, p. 31.

126. Ibid.

127. Editorial, *HJP*, 4 July 1958; *CB*, no. 515, p. 26.

128. From the fall of 1957 to the summer of 1958, P'an was again on sick leave and stayed in Peking; he may have actually been suspended, see ibid., p. 14. Since the second part of October 1957, several important conferences in Honan were presided over for the most part by Wu Chih-p'u—a fact that suggests Wu may have taken over P'an's job by that time (Roy Hofheinz, "Rural Administration in Communist China," *CQ*, no. 11 [1962]).

Chapter 2

1. Organic Regulations of the People's Government (or the Military and Administrative Committee) of the Great Administrative Areas, approved by the Government Administrative

Council (GAC) on 16 December 1949. *Compendium (1949–50)*, pp. 117–20.

2. "Decision of the 19th Meeting of the Central People's Government Council" (15 November 1952), *Compendium (1952)*, p. 38. The names of the working departments of the Administrative Committees were redesignated *Chu* [bureau] or *Ch'u* [division], instead of *Pu* [ministry] as under the Military and Administrative Committee (the same name as that of the ministry under the GAC).

3. "Decision of the 32nd Meeting of the CPGC" (19 June 1954), *Compendium (1954)*, pp. 3–4.

4. Teng Hsiao-p'ing, "Report on the Revision of the Constitution of the Communist Party of China," *8NCCPC*, 1: 204.

5. Available evidence suggests that the target of the Kao-Jao "anti-party alliance" was not Mao, but rather his top associates, Liu and Chou. According to a party resolution, the "alliance" attempted to "overthrow the long-tested nucleus of leadership of the Central Committee of the Party headed by comrade Mao Tse-tung." Moreover, Kao allegedly demanded the party's Vice-Chairmanship for himself and advocated a system of "leadership by rotation." See "Resolution on the Kao Kang-Jao Shu-shih Anti-Party Alliance" (adopted by the CCP National Conference, 31 March 1955), *JMJP*, 5 April 1955.

6. Teng, "Revision of the Constitution," pp. 204–5.

7. See "Organic Law of Local People's Congress and Local People's Councils" (adopted by the NPC, 21 September 1954), *NCNA* (Peking), 28 September 1954; *CB*, no. 302.

8. *8NCCPC*, 1: 77.

9. The supreme economic planning and coordinating agency in the government, the State Planning Commission, was swamped with the work entailed in the direct planning and coordination of all the state's economic activities; therefore, in 1956, a new planning organ, the State Economic Commission, was set up to take over the responsibility of short-term (yearly) economic planning from the State Planning Commission. See Li Fu-ch'un's speech to the Eighth National Congress of the CCP (*8NCCPC*, 2: 293–94).

10. Audrey Donnithorne, *China's Economic System* (London: George Allen and Unwin, 1967), p. 460.

11. *8NCCPC*, 1: 52.

12. Yang Ying-chieh (vice-chairman, State Planning Commission), "On Unified Planning and Decentralized Control," *CHCS*, no. 11 (1958): 3–4.

13. Jerome Ch'en, ed., *Mao* (Englewood Cliffs, N.J.: Prentice-Hall, 1969), p. 75.

14. *Ideology and Organization in Communist China*, 2d ed. (Berkeley: University of California Press, 1970), pp. 85–88.

15. The English text of Chou's speech is in *CB*, no. 398.

16. Chou En-lai, "Report on the Proposals for the Second Five-Year Plan for Development of the National Economy," *8NCCPC*, 1: 310–11.

17. Ibid.

18. For example, Ch'en Hsueh, "Further Strengthening Local Responsibility for Financial Management," *TC*, no. 1 (1956); Hu Tze-ming, "A Consideration of Certain Problems in Local Budget," *TC*, no. 8 (1957); Mao Chun-yi, "Further Discussion on Improving the Working Methods of Local Planning Organs," *CHCC*, no. 3 (1957); Yang Ching-wen, "Two Problems in the Industrial Location," *CHCC*, no. 8 (1957); Liu Jui-hua, "An Exploratory Discussion of the Problem of Decentralizing Authority for Planning the Market Supplies of Goods Subject to Unified Distribution and to Ministry Control," ibid.; Hsueh Mu-ch'iao, "A Preliminary Opinion on the Present System of Planning Control," *CHCC*, no. 9 (1957).

19. Hsueh, "Strengthening Local Responsibility."

20. Schurmann, *Ideology and Organization*, p. 198.

21. This was revealed in an editorial in *JMJP*, 18 November 1957.

22. Both Liu Shao-ch'i and Teng Hsiao-p'ing articulated this view during the Eighth Party Congress; see *8NCCPC*, 1: 76, 202–3.

23. *JMJP*, 18 November 1957. The English text of these three directives is in *SCMP*, no. 1665.

24. A State Council Staff Office constitutes, in Barnett's term, a "general system" which over-sees one broad functional field of government activities involving many ministries and agencies whose work is closely related; see A. Doak Barnett, *Cadres, Bureaucracy and Political Power in Communist China* (New York: Columbia University Press, 1967), pp. 6–9.

25. Ibid.

26. Donnithorne, *China's Economic System*, p. 152; Schurmann, *Ideology and Organization*, pp. 88–90, 188 ff.

27. The Ministry of Commerce headed by Ch'en Yun since 1956 became known as the First Ministry of Commerce in February 1958, when the Second Ministry of Commerce was established. In September 1958 the two ministries were merged into a single Ministry of Commerce and Ch'en was transferred to the post of chairman of the State Construction Commission.

28. See *Compendium (PRC)*, 7: 223–25.

29. Ibid., pp. 221, 223–25.

30. Hsu Fei-ching, "Centralized Leadership and Decentralized Administration is the Correct Policy for the National Budgetary Management," *TC*, no. 19 (1959): 13, 15.

31. *Compendium (PRC)*, 7: 266; *JMJP*, 6 June 1958. In Honan, funds collected by special districts, *hsien*, and *Hsiang* were said to have amounted to four times the sum allotted to that province by the central government—a good illustration of local initiative at work; see *CHCC*, no. 5 (1958): 10–11.

32. Jung Tzu-ho, "Several Problems in the Reform of the Financial Administrative System," *TC*, no. 1 (1958).

33. For a more detailed treatment of the sources and expenditure of the extrabudgetary funds, see Donnithorne, *China's Economic System*, pp. 389–93; also see Choh-ming Li, "China's Industrial Development," *CQ*, no. 17 (1964).

34. *Compendium (PRC)*, 8: 146.

35. Huan Wen, "Some Problems in Local Budgetary Management after the Implementation of the New Financial System," *TC*, no. 1 (1958). In the nation as a whole, according to Li Hsien-nien, whereas the investment funds outside the state plan totaled 4.65 billion *yuan* in 1957, they amounted to 5.26 billion in 1958, 5 billion in 1959, and 6 billion expected for 1960; these figures represented nearly 4 percent of budgetary capital investment in 1957, 23 percent in 1958, 19 percent in 1959, and an expected 18 percent in 1960. See Donnithorne, *China's Economic System*, pp. 390–91, and Choh-ming Li, "Industrial Development."

36. See a report by the Investigation Group of Shansi Provincial Finance Department, *TC*, no. 22 (1959).

37. Ko Chih-ta and Ling Han, "Outline Discussion of Comprehensive Financial Plan," *CCYC*, no. 2 (1960).

38. "The Central Committee-State Council Directive on the Reform of the Planning Administrative System" (24 September 1958), *Compendium (PRC)*, 8: 96–99.

39. Wang Kuei-wu, "An Important Change in the Method of Drawing up Annual Plans," *CHCC*, no. 9 (1958).

40. Liao Chi-li, "The Double Track System," *CHCC*, no. 3 (1953).

41. Wang, "Important Change," p. 13.

42. *Compendium (PRC)*, 8: 97–98.

43. "The Central Committee-State Council Directive," pp. 100–101.

44. Wu Hsia, "Enhance the Nature of Organization and Planning for Inter-Provincial Economic Cooperation," *Chi-hua yu T'ung-chi*, no. 6, (1959).

45. Liang Chih et al., "A Study in the Development of Comprehensive Financial Planning at the *Hsien* Level," *CCYC*, no. 1 (1961).

46. See "Fengling *Hsien* Resolutely Implements the Correct Policy in Developing Local Industries," *JMJP*, 9 May 1958, and a report on the development of local industries in Hsin *Hsine* of Shensi, *TKP* (Peking), 25 April 1958.

47. Liang Ying-yuan, "Which is the Correct Road for China's Industrial Leap Forward," *HH*, no. 8 (1958).

48. *8NCCPC*, 1: 311; *CB*, no. 1615.

49. Liu Shao-ch'i, "The Work Report of the CC to the 2nd Session of the 8th Party Congress," *PR*, no. 14 (1958).

50. For this point, see Schurmann, *Ideology and Organization*, pp. 209–10.

51. Donnithorne, *China's Economic System*, p. 154.

52. For example, the First and Second Ministries of Machine Building and the Ministry of Electric Machine Building were combined into the First Ministry of Machine Building; the Ministries of the Building Materials Industry, Building Construction, and Urban Construction were merged into one Ministry of Building Construction; the First and Second Ministries of Commerce were incorporated into a single ministry. For a more detailed study, see Chang Wang-shan, *The State Council in Communist China: A Structural and Functional Analysis, 1954–1965* (M.A. thesis, Columbia University, 1968).

53. Ch'en Yun, "Some Important Problems in the Current Capital Construction," *HC*, no. 5 (1959), and Wu Hsia, "Inter-Provincial Economic Cooperation."

54. Liao Chi-li, "Double Track System," p. 14. "Departmentalism" refers to the principle of putting the interests of one's own unit—province, city, ministry, or any other—above the interests of all others, the national or collective interests in particular.

55. Ibid.

56. See, for example, a report on a national conference on industry, *JMJP*, 10 April 1958.

57. For example, Liu Chieh-t'ing, "Li Ching-Ch'uan is the Khrushchev of the Great Southwest China," Radio Kweiyang, 17 June 1967, and "The Evil Deeds of the Anti-Party and Anti-Socialist Element and Counter-revolutionary Double-Dealer, Liu Chien-hsun," a pamphlet published by Revolutionary Rebel General Command of the Organs of the CCP Honan Provincial Committee, 12 March 1967, translated in *JPRS*, no. 43,357. Both provided interesting data on how these two local officials protected the interests of their own regions.

58. Liu Tsai-hsing, "On Problems in Establishing Complete Industrial Complexes in Economic Cooperation Regions," *HCS*, no. 10, (1958).

59. *Compendium (PRC)*, 8: 98.

60. In the fall of 1958 the press reported officials in the capacity of directors and deputy directors of these regions attending a conference, but nothing was ever said about their institutional setup (*JMJP*, 20 November 1958).

61. William W. Hollister, "Capital Formation in Communist China," *CQ*, no. 17 (1964).

Chapter 3

1. See reports from Chekiang, Kiangsu, Kiangsi, and Hunan in *JMJP*, 29 and 31 October 1957.

2. *JMJP*, 1 and 7 October 1957, had some fascinating reports on cadres of Shantung and Kwangtung, indicating their tendency to identify with local communities and the peasants.

3. Between 1950 and 1957, China had received Soviet credits totaling 5.194 billion yuan. A sizable share of these credits was used to finance Chinese imports of capital goods and industrial raw materials from the Soviet Union. In 1957, Soviet credits were completely exhausted. For a detailed treatment of Sino-Soviet economic relations, see Alexander Eckstein, *Communist China's Economic Growth and Foreign Trade* (New York: McGraw-Hill, 1966), ch. 4 and 5.

4. *NCNA* (Tsinan), 20 January 1958; *SCMP*, no. 1700. Mao was reportedly in Hangchow in December 1957 when a purge in Chekiang took place (Union Research Institute, *Communist China, 1958* [Hongkong, 1959], p. 1).

5. At least three regional conferences, the Hangchow Conference (January 1958), Nanning Conference (late January), and the Chengtu Conference (March 1958), were called by Mao. These meetings and their agendas were not publicized, but information about the decisions they reached was subsequently revealed by the Chinese Communists, See PR, no. 14 (1958): 14; an article by Chiang Wei-ch'ing in JMJP, 14 May 1958; LJP, 31 October 1958 (SCMP, no. 1925); and Wu Chih-pu's article in HCS, no. 6 (1960).

6. NCNA (Shanghai), 10 January 1958; SCMP, no. 1694.

7. JMJP, 25 January 1958; CB, no. 491.

8. Ibid.

9. See reports of T'ao Chu (Kwangtung), WHP (Hongkong), 8 December 1957 (SCMP, no. 1682); Shu T'ung (Shantung), NCNA (Tsinan), 20 January 1958 (SCMP, no. 1700); and Huang Ou-tung (Liao-ning), LJP, 30 November 1957 (SCMP, no. 1708).

10. JMJP, 19 October 1957.

11. JMJP, 1 and 7 October 1957.

12. JMJP, 1 October 1957.

13. For example, JMJP, 1, 5, and 7 October 1957.

14. Wu Chih-p'u, "From Agricultural Producers' Cooperatives to the People's Communes," HC, no. 8 (1958): 7.

15. JMJP, 19 November 1957. For reports of hsia-fang in other provinces, see JMJP, 10 and 29 October, 19 and 31 November, 9 December 1957, and WHP (Shanghai), 21 October 1957.

16. JMJP, 30 November 1957, and WHP (Shanghai), 21 October 1957.

17. In early 1958, the Standing Committee of the NPC passed a resolution authorizing the APC's to allocate a larger accumulation of funds; at that time, the fund constituted 8 to 12 percent of the APC collective income; JMJP, 9 January 1958.

18. Speeches by Liao Lu-yen and T'an Chen-lin, HH, no. 3 (1958), and no. 6 (1958).

19. See speeches by Teng Tzu-hui, Liao Lu-yen, and Ch'en Cheng-jen; JMJP, 10, 24, and 28 December 1957.

20. This was revealed in an article reporting the water conservancy campaign in Honan; JMJP, 13 March 1958.

21. T'an Chen-lin's speech to a water conservancy conference in Chengchow, Honan; JMJP, 31 October 1957.

22. JMJP, 15 November 1957.

23. For a typical example of this sort, see a report on Hsin Hsien of Shensi Province; TKP (Peking), 25 April 1958.

24. Editorial, TKP (Peking), 14 January 1958.

25. The model of balanced economic development—simultaneous development of agriculture and industry—and technological dualism were examined by various scholars dealing with the Great Leap period; for example, A. Doak Barnett, Communist China and Asia: A Challenge to American Policy (New York: Random House, 1960), and Eckstein, Economic Growth.

26. On 18 December 1957 the CC and the State Council issued a joint directive prohibiting rural people from moving into the city; JMJP, 19 December 1957. A JMJP editorial on the same subject appeared the same day.

27. Franz Schurmann, Ideology and Organization in Communist China (Berkeley: University of California Press, 1966), pp. 467–72. Shansi undertook a measure which turned the entire province into many huge administrative areas based on the principle of rural-urban cooperation and provided for a "reserve labor army"; JMJP, 16 May 1958.

28. See Roy Hofheinz, "Rural Administration in Communist China," CQ, no. 11 (1962): 150.

29. Discussion of the merger from Liu Kuei-hua and Huang Pi-pei, "The Amalgamation of the Three Kinds of Co-ops," JMJP, 7 July 1957.

30. Wu Chih-p'u, "Producers' Cooperatives."

31. Wu Chih-p'u, "Contradictions are the Motive Force for the Development of the Socialist Society," *HCS*, no. 6 (1960): 4.

32. In May 1958 the party issued an official directive instructing cadres to merge the APC's; this was implied by Wu Chih-p'u in "Contradictions," but it was specifically pointed out in a report from Liaoning; *JMJP*, 2 September 1958, p. 4. Schurmann's assertion that the decisions to amalgamate the APC's were made early in 1958 does not seem to be well founded; *Ideology and Organization*, pp. 142, 473, 476.

33. Chao Kuang et al., "One Red Flag—Introducing the 'Sputnik' APC of Suiping Hsien, Honan," *Cheng-chih Hsueh-hsi*, no. 44 (1958).

34. G.F. Hudson et al., *The Chinese Communes* (London: Oxford University Press, 1960).

35. These provincial secretaries were Wang Jen-chung (Hupeh), Chang Chung-liang (Kansu), T'ao Lu-chia (Shansi), Liu Chien-hsu (Kwangsi), Liu Tzu-hou (Hopei), Chou Hsiao-chou (Hunan), and Chang P'ing-hua (Hupeh). In all, twenty-five were elected alternate members of the CC in May 1958; *JMJP*, 26 May 1958.

36. T'an became the spokesman for the radical agricultural policy in the fall of 1957, apparently replacing Teng Tzu-hui as the top agricultural official of the regime. K'o's article in *People's Daily* (25 January 1958), quoted earlier, was one of the first by a top provincial leader giving all-out support to Mao's policies and, as revealed in Mao's speech at the Lushan Conference on 23 July 1959, K'o had advised Mao on many policy measures. Mao's speech, carried by a Red Guard publication, is translated in *CLG*, 1, no. 4 (1968–69): 27–43. Li, who hosted the important Chengtu Conference of March 1958 which discussed and possibly decided a number of Great Leap measures, may have also thrown his support to Mao; although Szechuan lagged in the collectivization campaign, it apparently became a pacesetter for other provinces during the Great Leap and was praised by Mao as one of the five model provinces in his Lushan speech of July 1959 (p. 37).

37. The elevation of Lin suggests that Mao may have already become dissatisfied with the performance of P'eng Teh-huai, then minister of defense and in overall charge of the regime's military affairs, and was laying the ground for P'eng's replacement. One month after the party congress in June 1958, an enlarged conference of the Military Affairs Commission was convened and severely criticized P'eng's wholesale adoption of Soviet military policies.

38. Liu Shao-ch'i, "The Report of the Work of the CC to the Second Session of the Eighth Party Congress of the Communist Party of China," *PR*, no. 14 (1958): 14–16.

39. These articles are translated into English in *CB*, no. 509 (1958).

40. Frederick C. Teiwes, "The Purge of Provincial Leaders 1957–1958," *CQ*, no. 27 (1966).

41. Roderick MacFarquhar, "Communist China's Intra-Party Dispute," *Pacific Affairs*, 31, no. 4 (1958). However, Chou appeared to have regained good standing in the fall of 1958, partly because of the Offshore Islands crisis in which his diplomatic skill was needed and partly because he was a man of great political resilience.

42. T'an Chen-lin, "Explanations on 1956–1967 National Program of Agricultural Development" (Second Revised Draft), *NCNA* (Peking), 27 May 1958; *CB*, no. 508.

43. "Thoroughly Purge the Towering Crimes of China's Khrushchev and His Gang in Undermining the Enterprises of Agricultural Mechanization," *Nung-yeh Chi-hsieh Chi-shu (Agricultural Machine Technique)*, no. 5 (1967); *URS*, 49, no. 3 (1967).

44. *NCNA* (Peking), 27 May 1958; *CB* no. 508.

45. See Robert D. Barendsen, "The Agricultural Middle School in Communist China," no. 8 (1961).

46. See Wu Chih-p'u, "Contradictions," p. 4; *JMJP*, 2 September 1958, p. 4.

47. Theodore Shabad, *China's Changing Map: A Political and Economic Geography of the Chinese People's Republic* (New York: Praeger, 1956), pp. 99, 109–13.

48. For a detailed study of the campaign, see Michael Oksenberg, *Policy Formulation in Communist China: The Case of 1957–1958 Mass Irrigation Campaign* (Ph.D. dissertation, Columbia University, 1969).

49. *NCNA* (Peking), 24 April 1958; *SCMP*, no. 1760.

50. Hofheinz, "Rural Administration," p. 154.

51. *NCNA* (Chengchow), 12 May 1958; *SCMP*, no. 1781.

52. *NCNA* (Chengchow), 20 May 1958; *SCMP*, no. 1780.

53. It is plain from the press release of the Party Congress that P'an was already dismissed from his job in Honan by May 1958 (*JMJP*, 25 May 1958); in June or July 1958 the "crimes" of P'an were denounced in a plenary meeting of the Honan Provincial Party Committee (*CB*, no. 515).

54. Schurmann, *Ideology and Organization*, pp. 467–74.

55. For example, Wu Chih-pu, "On People's Communes," *CKCNP*, 16 September 1958; *CB*, no. 524.

56. The anniversary of the Paris Commune has been commemorated by the Chinese Communists; for example, the party published a two-volume collection of the writings of Marx, Engles, Lenin, and Stalin on that subject in 1961 to celebrate the ninetieth anniversary of the Paris Commune. Many Western writings on that subject have also been translated into Chinese. During the Cultural Revolution, there was also a short-lived attempt to build a new political order in the image of the Paris Commune.

57. See "Chairman Mao's Speech at the Chengtu Conference" (22 March 1958), *Selections from Chairman Mao*, in *JPRS*, no. 49,826, p. 47.

58. According to *JMJP*, 20 July 1958, T'an attended the North China Agricultural Cooperative Conference, held from 6 to 14 July in Chengchow, and T'an announced that "the administrative methods and the remunerative system of the APC's are outmoded" and that a "commune-type" organization was being set up in various areas.

59. Li Yu-chiu, "Letter from Hsinyang, Honan," *HC*, no. 7 (1958): 22.

60. The Chinese Communists have claimed, and Western observers generally have accepted, that the first commune, "Sputnik," was established in April 1958. In fact, in July 1958, the supposed commune Sputnik was still called an APC by its party secretary and other officials; see Chao Kuang, "One Red Flag," p. 18. One *NCNA* reporter categorically stated that the commune was set up in July; *JMJP*, 2 September 1958.

61. Editorial, *LJP*, 10 September 1958, and "The Processes of Establishing People's Communes," *Haian Jih-pao*, 22 August 1958.

62. *JMJP*, 12 August 1958.

63. *JMJP*, 13 August 1958.

64. Examples from *HCS*, no. 10 (1958), no. 9 (1958).

65. Wu Chih-p'u, "Producers' Cooperatives," p. 6.

66. See Chu Teh, "People's Army, People's War," *NCNA* (Peking), 31 July 1958; *CB*, no. 514, pp. 1–2.

67. See Mao's remark in Shantung (*JMJP*, 13 August 1958) and in Ch'en Po-ta's article (*HC*, no. 4 [1958]).

68. See Fu Chiu-t'ao, "Everyone is a Soldier," *HC*, no. 10 (1958).

69. P'eng Teh-huai, Ch'en Yun, Teng Tzu-hui, Liu Shao-ch'i; Teng Hsiao-p'ing and other top party officials who were attacked during the Cultural Revolution were accused of many "crimes," but none of them was ever accused of opposing the establishment of communes in 1958.

70. Targets of major commodities, such as coal and steel, reforms of the economic planning system were also discussed; see *JMJP*, 1 September 1958, and references to the Peitaiho Conference in Mao's speech at Lushan in 1959 (*CLG*, 1, no. 4 [1968–69]: 38–39). Possibly the Offshore Islands situation was also discussed.

71. When P'eng Teh-huai and others attacked the commune and other Great Leap programs in the 1959 Lushan Conference, Mao retorted by blaming his critics for having not presented their views in the 1958 Peitaiho meeting and several subsequent party conferences. Mao castigated his critics, saying: "If they had had a set of correct views that were better than ours, they would have presented them at Peitaiho!" See Mao's remarks in "Minutes of Talks Before and After the Lushan Conference," *CLG*, 1, no. 4 (1968–69): 45–46.

72. P'eng Teh-huai, "Letter of Opinion" (14 July 1959), *Ko-ming Ch'uan-lien* (Peking: Ko-ming Ch'uan-lien Editorial Board, Peking Institute of Building Engineering), 24 August 1967; also translated in *SCMP*, no. 4032.

73. The Wuhan CC Plenum held in November-December 1958 represented the first systematic effort by the CCP to provide uniform regulations on various aspects of the commune system.

74. For example, *JMJP*, 12, 18, and 21 August, 2, 3, 4, 19, and 20 September 1958; *HC*, no. 8 (1958); and *Nung-ts'un Kung-tso Tung-hsun* (*Rural Work Bulletin*), no. 11 (1958).

75. *HC*, no. 8 (1958).

76. *TKP* (Hongkong), 31 August 1958.

77. *JMJP*, 3 September 1958.

78. *Chungking Jih-pao*, 3 September 1958, and *CJP*, 15 September 1958.

79. Based on reports in *CJP*, 15, 17, and 21 September 1958.

80. The procedures for organizing communes in Kirin, Anhwei, Szechuan, and Kwangtung provinces were briefly noted in *JMJP*, 2 and 3 September 1958; also see *TKP* (Hongkong), 4 September 1958, for a report on communization experiments of Fukien Province.

81. For a discussion of this work method, see Liu Tzu-chiu, "On Spot Experiment," *HH*, no. 10 (1953).

82. Liu Shao-ch'i, *On the Party*, quoted in Frederick T.C. Yu, *Mass Persuasion in Communist China* (New York: Praeger, 1964), p. 18.

83. Such ad hoc organizations were reported at least in Shensi, Shansi, and Heilungkiang; see *JMJP*, 4 and 14 September 1958, and *Heiho Jih-pao*, 29 August 1958.

84. *JMJP*, 2, 3, and 4 September 1958, on Kirin, Anhwei, and Hupei.

85. *Heiho Jih-pao*, 29 August 1958, and *BFPC*, p. 28.

86. *Chungking Jih-pao*, 13 September 1958.

87. *BFPC*, p. 28, and *Sian Jih-pao*, 22 August 1958.

88. *Heiho Jih-pao*, 27 August 1958.

89. Ibid.; *CJP*, 21 September 1958, on Yuhang Hsien of Chekiang; *JMJP*, 18 August 1958, on Honan.

90. See directives issued by the provincial authorities of Liaoning, Szechuan, Hopei, and Heilungkiang; *LJP*, 13 September 1958, *HC*, no. 8 (1958), and *Heiho Jih-pao*, 27 August 1958.

91. For examples, *JMJP*, 18 August 1958 and *LJP*, 16 September 1958.

92. Editorial, *Chieh-fang Jih-pao*, 22 September 1958; reprinted in *BFPC*.

93. For a systematic analysis of questions of popular political participation in China, see James R. Townsend, *Political Participation in Communist China* (Berkeley: University of California Press, 1967).

94. Mao Tse-tung, "On Methods of Leadership," in *Selected Works of Mao Tse-tung* (New York: International Publishers, 1956), 3: 113.

95. For example, "How to Establish People's Communes?—CCP Chiukiang Special District Committee's 'shih-tien' Experiences," *KJP*, 10 September 1958, reprinted in *HHPYK*, no. 19 (1958): 100–102; "How to Lead People's Commune Movement?" *JMJP*, 22 September 1958.

96. In reply to Edgar Snow's question of who launched the communes in China, a "Very High Official" (presumably Mao himself) reportedly stated "the peasants masses started them, the Party followed." Edgar Snow, *The Other Side of the River: Red China Today* (New York: Random House, 1962), p. 432.

Chapter 4

1. *JMJP*, 1 October 1958.

2. Editorial, *JMJP*, 10 September 1958.

3. For example, P'eng Teh-huai, "Letter of Opinion," *Ko-ming Ch'uan-lien (Exchange of Revolutionary Experience)* (Peking: Ko-ming Ch'uan-lien Editorial Board, Peking Institute of Building Engineering), 24 August 1967; *SCMP*, no. 4032, p. 4.

4. *JMJP*, 1 October 1958, p. 1.

5. Fukushima Masao, "Problems Confronting the Communes in Communist China," *Ajia Keizai Jum Po* (Tokyo), no. 411, 20 October 1959; translated in *JPRS*, no. 2604, p. 8. Information contained in the article was from a report made to visiting Japanese jurists by Wang Lu, director of the Bureau of Agricultural Producers' Cooperatives, Seventh Staff Office of the State Council.

6. *JMJP*, 1 October 1958.

7. Audrey Donnithorne, *China's Economic System* (London: George Allen and Unwin, 1967), p. 47; G.W. Skinner, "Marketing and Social Structure in Rural China," part 3, *Journal of Asian Studies*, May 1965.

8. "On Big Communes and Small Officials," *HC*, no. 11 (1958): 23–24.

9. "Tentative Regulations (Draft) of the Weihsing People's Commune," Articles 4 and 5, *JMJP*, 4 September 1958.

10. For example, "An Investigation and Study of the Problems of Transition from higher APC's to the People's Communes," *HCS*, no. 9 (1958); *NCNA* (Chengtu), 14 September 1958; "To Crush Mercilessly Sabotage Activities of Landlords, Rich Peasants, Counter-Revolutionaries and Wicked Elements," editorial, *Sinkiang Jih-pao*, 25 September 1958; and *JMJP*, 19 September 1958.

11. See a report from Honan, *JMJP*, 19 September 1958.

12. *TKP* (Peking), 20 February 1959; *SCMP*, no. 1980.

13. For example, *NCNA* (Tsinan), 11 October 1958; *JMJP*, 18 September 1958; Hunan Provincial Party Committee, "Plant the Red Flag," *HC*, no. 12 (1958); and *CJP*, 17 September 1958.

14. Editorial, *JMJP*, 4 September 1958.

15. See Mao Tse-tung, "Speech at the Lushan Conference" (23 July 1959), *Chairman Mao's Repudiations*, p. 7.

16. Li Hsien-nien, "What I have Seen in the People's Communes," *HC*, no. 10 (1958).

17. See reports from Honan, Anhwei, Hopei, and Shansi in *JMJP*, 19 September 1958, and *HHPYK*, no. 20 (1958): 25–26, 108–9.

18. *Anhwei Jih-pao*, 29 September 1958; reprinted in *HHPYK*, no. 20 (1958): 25–27.

19. Many peasants showed genuine enthusiasm toward the commune system, largely because they equated the system with free supply of food and other items of daily necessity. This misunderstanding partly explained the seeming smoothness with which the peasants were organized into communes in the fall of 1958. A Swedish writer who was in China at that time gives a vivid picture of the Chinese peasants' reactions to the communes; see Sven Lindqvist, *China in Crisis* (New York: Thomas Y. Crowell, 1965), pp. 89–91.

20. For example, "The Distribution Problems in the Rural Communes (Honan)," *Lun Jen-min Kung-she (On the People's Communes)* (Peking: Chung-kuo Ch'upan-she, 1958), p. 117.

21. Chang Ch'un-ch'iao, "Destroy the Ideas of Bourgeois Legal Ownership," reproduced in *JMJP*, 13 October 1958. Chang rose to great political prominence during the Cultural Revolution; for his career background, see Paris H. Chang, "Shanghai's Cultural Czar," *Far Eastern Economic Review*, no. 33 (1968): 307.

22. Wu Leng-hsi "Confession," *Hung-se Hsin-hua* (a publication of an *NCNA* "rebel" group), no. 43 (1968). An English translation of Wu's "Confession" is in *CLG*, 2, no. 4 (1969–70).

23. In essence, the "Editor's Note" stated "This problem needs discussion because it is an im-

portant issue at the present. We consider Chang's article basically correct, but somewhat one-sided, namely, it does not fully explain the historical processes. But he clearly presents the problem, and attracts people's attention." *JMJP*, 13 October 1958.

24. See *HC*, no. 12 (1958), and *CB*, no. 537, which translated a number of articles published in *JMJP*. Several radicals who achieved great political prominence during the Cultural Revolution such as Kuan Feng, Wang Li, Wu Ch'uan-chi, in addition to Chang Ch'un-ch'iao, already showed their "true colors" in 1958.

25. Wu Leng-hsi, "Confession"; Teng Hsiao-p'ing and Hu Ch'iao-mu were said to have opposed the abolition of the wage system, and Hu was said to have characterized Chang's theses as "petty bourgeois egalitarian illusions."

26. For example, reports on Kansu, Hopei, and Shansi in *HHPYK*, no. 20 (1958): 103–5, 108–11.

27. "Distribution Problems," p. 118.

28. Masao, "Problems."

29. See "Distribution Problems," p. 119.

30. For example, *Ta-chung Jih-pao*, 12 January 1959.

31. The frantic intensity with which the entire population was regimented and goaded by cadres to meet the regime's goals can be measured by a CC recommendation of December 1958 that provision should be made for the peasants to have eight hours of sleep a night. *JMJP*, 20 December 1958, p. 1.

32. *JMJP*, 11 November 1958.

33. "Communique," *Sixth Plenary Session of the Eighth Central Committee of Communist Party of China* (Peking: FLP, 1958).

34. Ibid.

35. See The Rural Work Department of the CCP Liaoning Committee, "The Structure and Organs of the People's Communes," *JMJP*, 2 December 1958.

36. It was reported that the free supply system had led to extravagant consumption on the spot, and peasants even called in their relatives to share in the free meals. See, for example, P'eng Teh-huai, "Letter of Opinion," and Cheng Ssu, "The Supply System is a Touchstone," *CKCNP*, no. 21 (1958), translated in *ECMM*, no. 155 (1959).

37. An editorial in *JMJP* on 3 September spoke of three to four or five to six years as a reasonable target for the transition from collective ownership to ownership "by the whole people."

38. For example, *JMJP*, 16 and 28 November 1958.

39. A document drafted by Mao and Liu in early 1958 clearly indicated that Mao planned to step down as Chairman of the Republic but stayed in the Chairmanship of the party and that the decision was known to the members of the CC at that time; see Article 60 of "Sixty Articles on Work Methods," *CB*, no. 892, p. 13. In January 1959 Prince Sihanouk told a Cambodian audience that Mao had revealed to him the previous August that Mao wanted to resign the Chairmanship of the Republic to work on theory and avoid ceremonial chores; I am indebted to Allen S. Whiting of the University of Michigan for this information.

40. The text of Mao's speech in October 1966 is translated in Jerome Ch'en, ed., *Mao* (Englewood Cliffs, N.J.: Prentice-Hall, 1969), p. 96.

41. In an interview with Lord Montgomery of England in 1961, Mao replied to a question regarding his succession by saying that it was clear and had been laid down—Liu Shao-ch'i was the choice; *South China Morning Post* (Hongkong), 17 October 1961.

42. Richard H. Solomon, *Mao's Revolution and the Chinese Political Culture* (Berkeley: University of California Press, 1971), pp. 374–75.

43. I am indebted to Roderick MacFarquhar, former editor of *The China Quarterly*, for this information. That Liu Shao-ch'i may not have been the unanimous choice of the CCP leaders to succeed Mao as Chairman of the Republic and that Chu Teh may have been a contender for that post was also indirectly suggested by Li Chi, director of the Propaganda Department of the Shansi Provincial Party Committee from 1960 to 1963 and Vice-Minister of Culture from 1963 to 1966,

who had read Chu Teh's 1959 written self-criticism (possibly for his support to P'eng Teh-huai's attack on the Great Leap Forward policies in July 1959) and had allegedly remarked: "After this, Liu Shao-ch'i's position is truly consolidated"; see *The Counter-revolutionary Revisionist Li Chi's Anti-Party, Anti-Socialism and Anti-Mao Tse-tung Thought Towering Crimes Exposed* (Peking: Tung-fang Hung Commune of the Peking Institute of Cinema of the Capital College Red Guard Congress, 1 April 1967), p. 8. It is interesting to note that from the fall of 1957, Chu Teh traveled to many places and attended many national conferences to campaign for Mao's Great Leap policies —political actions which he had not taken previously. Was he also "campaigning" for the Chairmanship of the Republic?

44. Anna Louise Strong, *The Rise of People's Communes in China* (New York: Marzavai and Munsell, 1960), p. 70.

45. Mao's remarks at the conference revealed that the Great Leap and commune programs had encountered criticism from within the party and resistance from the peasants; see the excerpts of Mao's two speeches in *CLG*, 1, no. 4 (1968–69): 22–24.

46. *JMJP*, 29 August 1959. The available evidence does not substantiate Franklin W. Houn's assertion that in the spring of 1959 the CCP decided, among other things, to restore the private plots of land to commune members; see his *A Short History of Chinese Communism* (Englewood Cliffs, N.J.: Prentice-Hall, 1967), p. 167.

47. "People's Communes must Establish and Consolidate the System of Production Responsibility" (editorial), *JMJP*, 17 February 1959.

48. Wu Lu, "Leave a Margin," *JMJP*, 16 May 1959; Lin I-chou, "Contracts of Production must be Practical," *HC*, no. 10 (1959).

49. The party later directed communes to take inventories of the unused materials and transfer them to factories that had the facilities to use them; editorial, *JMJP*, 26 July 1959.

50. See T'ao Chu, "The Whole Nation as a Chessboard, the Whole Provinces as a Chessboard," *NFJP*, 2 March 1959, and K'o Ch'ing-shih, "On the Whole Country as a Chessboard," *HC*, no. 4 (1959).

51. Ch'en's criticism may have been aimed at Mao for it was Mao who personally encouraged the provincial authorities to set up their own independent industrial complexes; for Mao's remarks on that subject, see *JMJP*, 16 August 1958.

52. *NCNA* (Peking), 18 April 1959; *CB*, no. 559.

53. See Mao Tse-tung, "Speech at the 8th CC Plenum" (2 August 1959), in *Chairman Mao's Repudiations*, p. 16; also in *CLG*, 1, no. 4 (1968–69): 60.

54. *Down with P'eng*.

55. P'eng Teh-huai, "Letter of Opinion."

56. This information based on Wu Leng-hsi, "Confession." Wu asserted that data collected by the *NCNA* were published in an inner-party publication "Nei-p'u Ch'an-k'ao" ("Internal References")—presumably only available to top leaders.

57. The existence of this medium was revealed by the PLA *Kung-tso T'ung-hsun* (1961); see J. Chester Cheng, ed., *The Politics of the Chinese Red Army* (Stanford, Cal.: Hoover Institution, 1966), p. 406. The date of Mao's letter, 29 April 1959, was revealed by P'eng Teh-huai's speech at the Eighth CC Plenum (*CB*, no. 851, p. 30). The text of Mao's letter is reproduced by a Red Guard publication during the Cultural Revolution and is translated in *CB*, no. 891, pp. 34–35 (erroneously dated 29 November 1959).

58. Revolutionary Rebels of CCP Southwest Bureau Offices, "From Li Ch'ing-chuan's Opposition to a Highly Important Letter of Instruction from Chairman Mao, Look at his Counter-Revolutionary Double-Dealing Features," Radio Kweiyang, 23 December 1967.

59. For example, editorials in *People's Daily*, 19 and 25 May 1959; T'ao Chu, "The Mass Line and Working Methods," *Shan Yu* (Canton, a theoretical organ of the Kwangtung Provincial Party Committee), no. 11 (1959), and Lin Tieh (first party secretary of Hopei Province), "On Increasing Production, Good Quality, and Thirft," *Tung Feng* (a theoretical organ of the Hopei Provincial Party Committee), no. 72 (1959), both reprinted in *HHPYK*, no. 13 (1959).

60. See "Resolution concerning P'eng.

61. This section draws heavily from John Gittings, *The Role of the Chinese Army* (New York: Oxford University Press, 1967); Alice L. Hsieh, *Communist China's Strategy in the Nuclear Era* (Englewood Cliffs, N.J.: Prentice-Hall, 1962); and Ellis Joffe, "The Conflict Between Old and New in the Chinese Army," *CQ*, no. 18 (1964).

62. "Hold Aloft the Banner of the Party Committee System," editorial, *CFCP*, 1 July 1958; *SCMP*, no. 1881.

63. "Opposed One-Side Emphasis on Modernization," editorial, *CFCP*, 17 August 1958.

64. PLA participation in these campaigns is to be distinguished from its own production work; the PLA has a Production and Construction Corps in Sinkiang and possibly other border provinces, and it assumes various economic tasks producing goods for the PLA's own consumption.

65. Hsiao Hua, "Participation in National Construction is a Glorious Task of the PLA," *HC*, 1 August 1959.

66. For the text, see *NCNA* (Peking), 8 February 1956; *SCMP*, no. 1234.

67. Cited in Gittings, *Chinese Army*, p. 182.

68. T'an Cheng, "Questions of Political Work at the New Stage of Army-building," *JMJP*, 24 September 1956.

69. Hsiao Hua, "Participation."

70. For the text of Mao's speech, see *CLG*, 1, no. 4 (1968–69): 15–21.

71. Summarized in Ralph L. Powell, *Politico-Military Relationships in Communist China* (Washington, D.C.: U.S. Department of State, 1965), pp. 2–3.

72. Gittings, *Chinese Army*, p. 233.

73. Ibid., pp. 225–34.

74. Ibid. The Chinese Communists claim that "in 1958 the leadership of the CPSU put forward unreasonable demands designed to bring China under military control. These unreasonable demands were rightly and firmly rejected by the Chinese government. ... On June 20, 1959, the Soviet government unilaterally tore up the agreement on new technology for national defence concluded between China and the Soviet Union on October 15, 1957, and refused to provide China with a sample of an atomic bomb and technical data concerning its manufacture." Editorial Departments of *JMJP* and *HC*, "The Origin and Development of the Differences Between the Leadership of the CPSU and Ourselves" (6 September 1963); *PR*, 13 September 1963.

75. This arrangement was revealed in P'eng Teh-huai, "Letter of Opinion," p. 1.

76. Mao, "Speech at the 8th CC Plenum" (2 August 1959), *Chairman Mao's Repudiations*, p. 16; also in *CLG*, 1, no. 4 (1968–69): 60–61.

77. Quotations from Peng appear in P'eng Teh-huai, "Letter of Opinion"; for an earlier study of the proceedings of the Lushan Conference see David A. Charles, "The Dismissal of Marshal P'eng Teh-huai," *CQ*, no. 8 (1961).

78. "Resolution concerning P'eng."

79. See "P'eng Teh-huai's Speech at the Eighth CC Plenum" (August 1959), *Down with P'eng*; *CB*, no. 851, p. 30.

80. Ibid.

81. "Chou Hsiao-chou was the Ammunition Supplier for the Attack on the Three Banners," *Repudiation against P'eng (Teh-huai)-Huang (K'e-cheng)-Chang (Wen-t'ien)-Chou (Hsiao-chou) Anti-Party Group* (The Rebelling Red Flag Regiment of the Hunan Provincial Party Committee Organs), 16 September 1967.

82. This information is revealed in *Ta P'i-p'an Tung-hsun (Mass Criticism and Repudiation Bulletin)* (Canton: Canton News Service of Shanghai T'ung-chi University Tung-fang Hung Corps), 5 October 1967. The text of Mao's speech is in *Chairman Mao's Repudiations*, pp. 6–11; also *CLG*, 1, no. 4, (1968–69): 27–43; all quotations from Mao's speech can be found here.

83. Mao figured at least 30 percent of the rural population were "activists" who actively supported the Great Leap and commune programs; another 30 percent were landlords, rich peasants, counterrevolutionaries, bad elements, bureaucrats, middle peasants, and poor peasants

who were against these programs; the remaining 40 percent were neutral but could be persuaded to follow the mainstream.

84. "Was he not without posterity who first made wooden images to bury with the dead," said Confucius as he thought that this invention gave rise to the practice of burying living persons with the dead.

85. *Down with P'eng*; *CB*, no. 851, p. 30.

86. See the Chinese text of P'eng Teh-huai's Confession to the 8th CC Plenum, *Tzu Kuo* (Hongkong), no. 50 (1968): 39. The specific remark by P'eng quoted here is not accurately translated in *CB*, no. 851, p. 30.

87. "Resolution Concerning P'eng." There were, however, several self-contradictory statements in P'eng's reported confession. At one point P'eng stated that his error "was not a mistake accidentally committed" but "a kind of action well prepared and organized," later on, he said that "no concrete plan had been mapped out" for his attack on the party. *Down with P'eng; CB*, no. 851, p. 30.

88. For example, Charles, "Dismissal of Marshal P'eng." When Khrushchev visited Peking (30 September to 5 October 1959) he allegedly produced an expensive gift for P'eng, extolled P'eng as the most promising, most courageous, most upright, and most outspoken person within the CCP, and wanted to see P'eng ("The Reactionary Antecedents of P'eng Teh-huai," in *Down with P'eng; CB*, no. 851, p. 14). At the Bucharest Conference in June 1960 Khrushchev reportedly refused to apologize for his intervention in Chinese domestic affairs and defended the right of the CPSU to communicate with members of other Communist parties.

89. This information was supplied to the author by two emigres from Communist China; one is a former cadre member who worked in the Hupei Provincial Party Committee during 1959–61 and heard intra-party briefings on the Lushan proceedings; the other is a non-Communist cadre member whose father was once a vice-chairman of the National Defense Council.

90. Charles, "Dismissal of Marshal Peng," p. 67.

91. See *Tung-fang Hung* (Peking: Capital College Red Guard Revolutionary Rebels Liaision Station), 11 February 1967; also translated in *SCMP* supplement, no. 172, p. 21. Another Red Guard publication asserted that Chu Teh made a written self-criticism in 1959, probably after the Lushan Conference, and the text was disseminated to the provincial-level cadres; see *The Counter-Revolutionary Revisionist Li Chi's Towering Crimes Anti-Party, Anti-Socialism and Anti-Mao Tse-tung Thought Towering Crimes Exposed* (Peking: Pek Tung-fang Hung Commune of the Peking Institute of Cinema of the Capital Red Guard Congress, 1 April 1967), p. 8.

92. In a letter said to have been sent by Mao to Chang Wen-t'ien on 2 August 1959, Mao chided Chang for having joined the "military club" and formed a "civilian-military alliance." Commenting on a "report" concerning the dissolution of mess halls in Anhwei, Mao wrote "There are right opportunists in the Central Committee, namely, those comrades of the Military Club, and in the provincial-level organizations. . . ." Both Mao's letter and comments are reprinted in *Chairman Mao's Repudiations*, pp. 14–15, 18; also translated in *CLG*, 1, no. 4 (1968–69): 34, 67.

93. *CLG*, 1, no. 4 (1968–69): 26; also see "P'eng Teh-huai's statements made under detention," *Down with P'eng; CB*, no. 851, p. 18.

94. In June 1957 Khrushchev, first secretary of the CPSU, was outvoted seven to four in the presidium by an "anti-party" group composed of Malenkov, Kaganovich, Molotov, Saburov, Pervukhin, Bulganin, and Voroshilov; Khrushchev and his supporters managed to convene a Central Committee Plenary session in which the presidium decision to unseat Khrushchev was reversed, and the first members of the anti-party group were expelled from the presidium (see Merle Fainsod, *How Russia is Ruled* [Cambridge: Harvard University Press, 1963], pp. 327–28).

95. The fact that an unspecified number of the CC members who did not take part in the enlarged Lushan Politburo Conference during July were later summoned to attend the CC Plenum was indicated by Mao's "Speech at the 8th CC plenum" (2 August 1959), *Chairman Mao's Repudiations*, p. 16; also translated in *CLG*, 1, no. 4 (1968–69): 61.

96. "Reactionary Antecedents of P'eng Teh-huai."

97. Mao, "Speech at the 8th CC Plenum" (2 August 1959), p. 17; trans. *CLG*, 1, no. 4 (1968–69): 63.

98. "From the Defeat of P'eng Teh-huai to the Bankruptcy of China's Khrushchev," *HC*, no. 13 (1967); *PR*, no. 34 (1967): 20.

99. Since the Cultural Revolution, the Chinese official sources have accused Liu of being P'eng Teh-huai's "behind-the-scene boss" and for using P'eng as his stalking horse in opposition to Mao at the Lushan Conference; see, for instance, editorial, *JMJP*, 16 August 1969, also *PR*, no. 34, 25 August 1967. A Red Guard publication, however, has revealed that Liu denounced P'eng Teh-huai during the Lushan showdown; see *CB*, no. 834, p. 18.

100. "Down with Ch'en Yun—An Old Hand at Opposing Chairman Mao," *Ts'ai-mao Hung Chi* (Peking), 15 February 1967; translated in *SCMP* supplement no. 175, 12 April 1967, p. 27. Ch'en's absence from the Lushan Conference was also confirmed by a more official source which reported Ch'en's inspection of the Chang Ch'un Film Studio in Manchuria on 27 July 1959; see *Ta-Chung T'ien-ying*, no. 6 (1961).

101. See Mao's speech at the Lushan Conference on 23 July 1959, in *CLG*, 1, no. 4 (1968–69): 34.

102. "P'eng Teh-huai's Speech at the 8th Plenum of the 8th CCP Central Committee," *CB*, no. 851.

103. The text of P'eng's letter is reprinted in *Down with P'eng*, translated in *CB*, no. 851, p. 16. One writer later reported that P'eng at one stage was a superintendent or deputy superintendent in a State Farm in Heilungkiang; see Charles, "Dismissal of Marshal Peng," p. 69. But a Red Guard source indicated that during 1960–62 P'eng frequently visited communes in Hunan, Kiangsu, and other provinces and that P'eng also studied in the Higher Party School; "Reactionary Antecedents of P'eng Teh-huai," pp. 14–15.

104. "Resolution concerning P'eng."

105. *Eighth Plenary Session of the Eighth Central Committee of the Communist Party of China* (Peking: FLP, 1959), p. 9.

106. For a detailed and excellent analysis of the campaign, see Charles, "Dismissal of Marshal Peng," pp. 69–73.

107. On reports of meetings in Kansu and Kiangsi, see *Kansu Jih-pao* (Lanchow), 28 November 1959; *SCMP*, no. 2184, pp. 28–32, and *Kiangsi Jih-pao* (Nanchang), 2 January 1960; *SCMP*, no. 2226, pp. 24–28.

108. Editorial, *JMJP*, 2 November 1959.

109. Editorial, *JMJP*, 6 August 1959.

110. This conclusion is also deduced from a nation-wide campaign in 1962 for the "reversal of verdicts" [*fan an*] in which victims of the "anti-rightist opportunist campaign" sought their rehabilitation.

111. A source in the early 1960s had identified Hsiao K'o, Hung Hsueh-chih, Li Ta, and Yang Cheng-wu as connected with the P'eng affair; see Charles, "Dismissal of Marshal Peng," p. 73. The information that has become available since has confirmed the dismissals of these officials (except Yang) and further revealed the identity of others who were adversely affected by the P'eng affair.

112. To the best of my knowledge, these men were never formally accused of joining the "anti-party" group in the Lushan showdown, but they were specifically charged with executing the bourgeois military line of the P'eng-Huang group and defects in their work; see *PLA Bull.*, pp. 51–53, 76–77, and 44–45, on T'an and Hung, and a Red Guard publication *Chan Pao* (Peking), no. 6 (1967) on Hsiao.

113. See *Fei-chun Fan-Mao Chi-t'uan* (The Anti-Mao Groups in the Chinese Communist Army) (Taipei: The Sixth Department of the Central Committee of the Chinese Nationalist Party, 1967), pp. 69–73, 76–80. The downfall of Hsi only came after April 1962, so his disgrace was not exclusively related to the P'eng affair and may have also been due to his support of the "three reconciliation and one reduction" policy, as claimed by a defected Chinese diplomat,

quoted on p. 72; Chang's disgrace also came only in 1961.

114. A few outstanding examples were Chia T'o-fu, a member of the CC, who was dismissed as director of the State Council Fourth Staff Office in September 1959 and lost other government posts in the early 1960s, Hsueh Mu-ch'iao, director of the State Statistical Bureau, and Yang Ying-chieh, vice-chairman of the State Planning Commission, who were dismissed in September 1959. Also see Hannspeter Hellbeck, "The 'Rightist' Movement in 1959," in *Contemporary China: 1959–1960* (Hongkong University Press, 1960), for the purges in 1959.

115. Chang Hsi-t'ing, "Defend Chairman Mao to the Death," Radio Kweiyang, 29 November 1967, and Liu Chieh-t'ing, "Li Ch'ing-chuan is the Khrushchev of the Great Southwest China," Radio Kweiyang, 17 June 1967.

116. Editorial, *JMJP*, 9 August 1960; *TKP* (Hongkong), 30 December 1960.

117. *China News Service* (Peking), 27 December 1960.

118. *TKP* (Hongkong), 30 December 1960.

119. The serious peasant uprisings in Honan in 1960–61 were not publicly reported in any known source, but they were reported in a classified PLA journal; see *PLA Bull.*, pp. 118–19, 138, 561.

Chapter 5

1. The text of the program is in *JMJP*, 12 April 1960; *CB*, no. 616, pp. 1–17.

2. *NCNA* (Peking), 6 April 1960; *CB*, no. 616, pp. 18–28.

3. Peking has not made public the figures on grain production since 1959, but Lord Montgomery was told in an interview with Mao that the grain output in 1960 was 150 million tons and that in 1959 it was probably no better; see *South China Morning Post* (Hongkong), 17 October 1961. In 1957, a year of unsatisfactory harvest, the grain output is estimated by some outside observers to have been 185 million tons.

4. Per *mou* annual rice yields in Ch'aochou and Swatou areas in Kwangtung in and before 1957 averaged over 1000 catties, and per *mou* wheat yields in Laiyang area of Shantung were over 500 catties; these areas had the longest record of using a large amount of chemical fertilizer. See *JMJP*, editorial, 16 November 1957.

5. *JMJP*, 12 April 1960; *CB*, no. 616.

6. See Senator Hubert H. Humphrey, "My Marathon Talk With Russia's Boss," *Life*, 12 January 1959, pp. 80–91, and *The New York Times*, 18 July 1959. There are indications that Mao was informed of Khrushchev's attack and that he sought to refute Khrushchev's criticism by proving the "superiority" of the people's communes; see Mao's "Remarks Concerning the Printing and Distribution of Three Articles" (29 July 1959) and "Letter to Wang Chia-hsiang" (1 August 1959), *CLG*, 1, no. 4 (1968–69): 52–53.

7. For example, Mao reportedly put forth in early 1960 "The Constitution of the Anshan Iron and Steel Company" as a substitute for the Soviet "Constitution of the Magnitorgorsk Iron and Steel Combine" as a guide for managing industry; see *JMJP*, 25 August 1967.

8. "Thoroughly Reckon with Big Renegade Liao Lu-yen's Towering Crimes in the Ministry of Agriculture," in a Red Guard pamphlet translated in *SCMP*, no. 4001, p. 11.

9. "Speech at the 10th Plenum of the 8th Central Committee," *CLG*, 1, no. 4 (1968–69): 88.

10. Not until early 1966, after a lapse of almost four years, were references again made to the program. On 27 January 1966, *People's Daily* reported that Chekiang and Hunan had organized cadres and members of communes to study the program; an accompanying editorial on the same

day, however, cautioned cadres not to set the production tasks and targets beyond "practical possibility" not to "blindly pursue high targets" or indiscriminately popularize production-increasing measures in their efforts to achieve the goals of the program.

11. See T'an Chen-lin's speech in *CB*, no. 616, p. 21. The eight points were soil improvement, increased application of fertilizer, water conservancy, seed improvement, rational close planting, plant protection, field management, and improvement of farm tools. In fact, Ma Yin-ch'u, president of Peking University and an economist, claimed in 1959 that the original idea of the "eight-point charter for agriculture" was his, adopted by Mao; see his article, "My Philosophical Thoughts and Economic Theories," *HCS*, no. 11 (1959): 22, 35, 46–47.

12. See Alexander Eckstein, *Communist China's Economic Growth and Foreign Trade* (New York: McGraw-Hill, 1966), pp. 29–37.

13. See "Nan Pa-t'ien Hsi-yu Chi" [The Story of the Southern Emperor's Western Trip], *Chih-k'an Nan-Yueh* (Canton: Editorial Department, Proletarian Revolutionary Rebels of Literary and Art Circles in the Canton Area), no. 3, 1 October 1967, as reprinted in *Hsingtao Jih-pao* (Hong-kong). This essay, while abusing and attacking Tao Chu, provided useful information on the CC Work Conference of July 1960 and the decision to set up the CC regional bureaus. Other sources that indicated the existence of the CC regional bureaus since 1960 include Li Shih-fei, "The Party's Middlemen: The Role of Regional Bureaus in the Chinese Communist Party," *Current Scene*, 3, no. 15.

14. Liao Lu-yen, "Participate in the Large-scale Development of Agriculture by the Whole Party and the Whole People," *HC*, no. 17 (1960); Editorial, *NFJP* (Canton), 16 September 1960.

15. See, for examples, Li Fu-ch'un's article in *HC*, no. 1 (1960), and T'an Chen-lin's speech to the NPC in April 1960 in *CB*, no. 616.

16. *NFJP* (Canton), 13 May 1960.

17. *NFJP*, 2 September 1960.

18. "Carry out Thoroughly the Party's Distribution Policy after the Autumn Harvest," *PJP*, 12 December 1960.

19. *NFJP* (Canton), 25 October 1960.

20. Huang Huo-ch'ing, "Factory-commune Coordination—A New Form of Strengthening the Worker-peasant Alliance," *HC*, no. 13 (1960).

21. "Industrial Enterprises must Adopt the Idea of Taking Agriculture as the Foundation," *JMJP* editorial, 17 July 1960.

22. The issuance of this directive is also mentioned in *PLA Bull.*, p. 137. The full text of this directive is not available, though a brief one-page summary of the twelve points was made available to me by Nationalist Chinese authorities.

23. In what was called "Communist styles" [*kung-ch'an feng*], cadres' excessive attempts at equalizing peasants income, in disregard of their skill, labor power, and contribution, and transferring workers and means of production from the better-off brigades or teams to the poor ones without compensation, created much conflict within the communes and adversely affected peasants' morale and incentives; *PLA Bull.*, pp. 117, 138.

24. "Communique of the 9th Plenary Session of the 8th Central Committee of the Communist Party of China," *PR*, no. 4 (1961).

25. These regional bureaus were headed by tested loyal provincial party officials or by officials sent down from Peking; for their background, see Li Shih-fei, "The Party's Middlemen."

26. For instance, under the East China Bureau, there were departments for propaganda and for finance and trade, offices for agriculture and forestry, water conservancy, finance, and policy research, and committees for planning, economic affairs, and science and technology. A. Doak Barnett, *Cadres, Bureaucracy and Political Power in Communist China* (New York: Columbia University Press, 1967), p. 112.

27. Frederick C. Teiwes, *Provincial Party Personnel in Mainland China: 1956–1966* (New York: East Asian Institute, Columbia University, 1967), pp. 42, 86.

28. A former PLA lieutenant claimed that Chang was implicated in the activities of the P'eng

Teh-huai "anti-party group"; see *Chung-kung Jen-ming-lu (Who's Who in Communist China)* (Taipei: Institute of International Relations, 1967), p. 353. If this is true, his involvement in the P'eng affair was uncovered more than one year after the 1959 Lushan meeting, as he was active throughout 1960.

29. See, for instance, Liu Shao-ch'i's "Confession" in *MS*, 28 and 29 January 1967, and Mao's speech of October 1966 as translated in Jerome Ch'en, ed., *Mao* (Englewood Cliffs, N.J.: Prentice-Hall, 1969), p. 94.

30. "Ten Crimes of Teng Hsiao-p'ing," *Pa-erh-wu Chan Pao* (Canton), 24 February 1967; *SCMM*, no. 574, p. 15; and "Uncover the Black Mask of Teng Hsiao-p'ing's 'Petofi Club,'" *Tung-fang-hung* (Peking: Capital Colleges & Universities Red Guard Revolutionary Rebel Liaison Center), 18 February 1967; *SCMP*, no. 3903, p. 2.

31. Ch'en Po-ta, "Speech to the Central Committee Work Conference, October 25, 1966" (excerpts), *Ko-ming Kung-jen Pao* (Peking: Revolutionary Rebel Headquarters of Workers from the Capital), 12 January 1967; *SCMP Supplement*, no. 167, p. 2.

32. See *PLA Bull.*, p. 405.

33. *PLA Bull.*, p. 467.

34. Ibid. "Five styles" or "Five winds" refer to cadres' "communistic" style (indiscriminately pushing egalitarian measures), commandist style (commanding by force rather than persuasion), the style of giving blind commands, the style of exaggeration (raising targets and giving false harvest reports), and the style of being special (refusal to participate in physical labor and demanding special privileges).

35. Ibid.

36. *PLA Bull.*, pp. 406, 466–67.

37. Reflecting and articulating the new mood was Foreign Minister Ch'en Yi's "Speech to the Graduates of High Institutes of Learning" (July 1961), *JMST 1961*, pp. 319–21.

38. Two notable examples are Hsueh Mu-ch'iao and P'an Fu-sheng. Hsueh was removed from the directorship of the State Statistical Bureau and other posts in September 1959, but he was reinstated as a vice-chairman of the State Planning Commission (headed by Li Fu-ch'un) in December 1960; see Cho-ming Li, *The Statistical System of Communist China* (Berkeley: University of California Press, 1962), pp. 11, 113, 114, 118. P'an Fu-sheng was purged as first party secretary of Honan in 1958 but became the acting chairman and later chairman of the All China Federation of Supply and Marketing Cooperatives in 1962.

39. "Uncover Liu Shao-ch'i's Counter-revolutionary Words and Deeds; Comments on Liu Shao-ch'i's 1961 Hunan Visit," *TFHP*, 9 March 1967.

40. "Uncover the Black Mask."

41. "Ch'en Yun is the Vanguard for the Capitalist Restoration," *TMHC*, no. 4 (1967); *SCMP*, no. 3899, p. 4.

42. P'eng visited Hunan in November 1961 and compiled several reports on the basis of his findings which he later distributed to various provincial party committees ("The Reactionary Antecedents of P'eng Teh-huai," *CB*, no. 851, p. 15). Allegedly Ch'ang Wen-t'ien obtained the approval of Liu Shao-ch'i to visit Shanghai, Chekiang, and Hunan "in the capacity of an alternate Politburo member" from April to June 1962; see "Resolutely Strike Down the Anti-Party Element Chang Wen-t'ien," *CCP* (Peking), no. 22–23 (1967); *JPRS*, no. 41,898.

43. See *PLA Bull.*, p. 405.

44. Ibid. This article has not been included in official lists of Mao's works available to the outside world.

45. Ch'en's political eclipse during the Great Leap period has generally been known to outside observers, but his reentry to the political picture since 1961 has not. Ch'en lost his influence after he was criticized by Mao at a party meeting in August 1962 and apparently ceased to participate in the deliberations of the party thereafter. Moreover, Ch'en often chose to work behind the scenes and rarely appeared in public. One of Ch'en's rare public appearances in 1961 was the Ninth CC Plenum in which he presided with other members of the Politburo Standing Committee; see the

photograph in *JMJP*, 21 January 1961, p. 1.

46. Liu was believed to have opposed the "hundred flowers" movement in 1957; see the remarks of Ch'ien Wei-ch'ang, *JMJP*, 17 July 1957.

47. Roderick MacFarquhar, "Communist China's Intra-Party Dispute," *Pacific Affairs*, December 1958. Liu's two speeches are in *JMJP*, 7 November 1957 and 25 May 1958.

48. See Mao's remarks at the 1962 Tenth CC Plenum; *CLG*, 1, no. 4 (1968–69): 92.

49. This information is deduced from a Red Guard article's references to Liu's denunciation of P'eng at Lushan; see the translation of "Down with Liu Shao-ch'i—Life of Counter-revolutionary Liu Shao-ch'i," *CB*, no. 834, p. 18.

50. "From Defeat of P'eng Teh-huai to the Bankruptcy of China's Khrushchev," editorial, *HC*, no. 13 (1967), and "P'eng Teh-huai and His Behind-the-Scenes Boss Cannot Shirk Responsibility for Their Crimes," editorial, *JMJP*, 16 August 1967; both articles are also in *PR*, no. 34 (1967).

51. See "To Take the Socialist Road or the Capitalist Road," joint editorial of *HC* and *JMJP*, 14 August 1967.

52. See the remarks of Ch'en Wei-ch'ang (vice-chancellor of Tsinghua University), *JMJP*, 17 July 1957.

53. Ma Nan-tun [Teng T'o], *Yen-shan Yeh-hua* (Peking: Peking Ch'u-pan-she, 1961); *Teng T'o Shih-wen Hsuan-chi* (Taipei: Freedom Press, 1966).

54. "The Exposé of the Plot to Usurp the Party and the State's Power Comments on the Counter-Revolutionary Incident of 'Ch'ang Kuan Lou,'" *PJP*, 7 August 1967.

55. Ibid. See also "Before and After the Counter-Revolutionary Incident of 'Ch'ang Kuan Lou,'" *Tung-fang-hung* (Peking: Peking Mining Institute Tung-fang Hung of the Capital College Red Guard Congress), 20 April 1967; *SCMP*, no. 4001.

56. Presumably the revisions were worked out in a CC Work Conference at Lushan in September 1961; see "The True Counter-revolutionary Revisionist Face of Teng Hsiao-p'ing," *CCP* (Peking), no. 12 (1967).

57. Editorial, *JMJP*, 1 January 1962; Liao Lu-yen, minister of agriculture, was quoted by a Japanese source as saying that in 1961 there were 50,000 communes (24,000 in 1959), 700,000 brigades (500,000 in 1959) and 4,600,000 teams (3,000,000 in 1959), "Observations on the Failure of the People's Communes," *Nihon Sekai Shuho* (Tokyo), 43, no. 36 (1962).

58. The excerpts of this document were made available to this writer by the Bureau of Intelligence, Ministry of National Defenses of the Nationalist Chinese government in Tapei.

59. "Down with Sung Jen-chiung—Top Capitalist-Roader in the Party in Northeast China," *Hung Ch'i T'ung-hsun* (Chiangmen Kwangtung), no. 14 (1968); *SCMP*, no. 4201, p. 11; see also "The Ten Crimes of the Counter-Revolutionary Revisionist Po I-po, *Ching-kang-shan* (Peking: Ching-kang-shan Corps, Tsinghua University), 1 January 1967.

60. Reportedly, a conference of party secretaries in charge of industry [*kung-yeh shu-chi hui-yi*] was convened in December 1961 by Teng Hsiao-p'ing to discuss and implement the new policy; see "The True Counter-revolutionary Revisionist Face of Teng Hsiao-p'ing."

61. "From the Defeat of P'eng Teh-huai."

62. See an article by the CCP CC Party School Red Flag Fighting Regiment in *JMJP*, 12 April 1967.

63. "Before and After the Counter-Revolutionary Incident of Ch'iang Kuang Lou," in *Tung-fang hung* (Peking: Peking Mining Institute Tung-fang Hung of the Capital College Red Guard Congress), 20 April 1967; *SCMP*, no. 4001.

64. "Resolutely Strike Down the Anti-Party Element Chang Wen-tien," *CCP* (Peking), nos. 22–23 (1967); *JPRS*, no. 41,890.

65. Procedures and disputes over "reversing verdicts" in Szechuan province were described by Chang Hsi-t'ing, "Defend Chairman Mao to the Death," Radio Kweiyang, 29 November 1967, and Liu Chieh-t'ing, "Li Ch'ing-chuan is the Khrushchev of the Great Southwest China," Radio Kweiyang, 17 June 1967.

66. Liu Shao-ch'i, *How to be a Good Communist*, 4th ed. (Peking: FLP, 1964), pp. 88–89. The English translation is from the Chinese text which appeared in the double issue of Red Flag, no. 15–16 (1962), in which Liu made a number of revisions, particularly in the section dealing with inner-party struggle.

67. For a sample of articles attacking Liu's book, see *JMJP*, 8 May 1967, *PJP*, 4 April 1967, and *Kwangming Jih-pao*, 8 April 1967.

68. Wu Han, *Hai Jui Pa Kuan* (Peking: Peking Ch'u-pan-she, 1961), Yao Wen-yuan, "A Criticism of the New Historical Play 'The Dismissal of Hai Jui,'" *WHP* (Shanghai), 10 November 1965, reprinted in *JMJP*, 30 November 1965.

69. "From the Defeat of P'eng Teh-huai," p. 20.

70. "Open Fire at the Black Anti-Party and Anti-Socialist Line," "Teng T'o's 'Evening Chats at Yenshan' is Anti-Party and Anti-Socialist Double-talk," *KMJP*, 8 May 1966. Key articles attacking these Maoist critics are published in *The Great Socialist Cultural Revolution in China*, 2 vols. (Peking: FLP, 1966). For a good discussion of this subject see Philip Bridgham, "Mao's 'Cultural Revolution': Origin and Development," *CQ*, no. 29 (1967); Harry Gelman, "Mao and the Permanent Purge," *Problems of Communism*, November-December 1966; Stephen Uhally, Jr., "The Cultural Revolution and the Attack on the 'Three Family Village,'" *CQ*, no. 27 (1966).

71. In 1962 when Mao's popularity declined, publication of his writing reportedly used only 0.5 percent (that is 70 tons) of the paper used for printing books in China, while books like *The Dream of the Red Chamber* and *Romance of Three Kingdoms* consumed 750 tons; see *JMJP*, 15 July 1966, p. 3. It is said that from 1962 to 1966, only 4.4 million copies of Mao's work were printed, while 17.8 million copies of Liu Shao-ch'i's *How To Be A Good Communist* were printed in the same period (see *JMJP*, 5 June 1967).

72. "From the Defeat of P'eng Teh-huai," p. 20. Allegedly, P'eng took two years to prepare the "petition," which included five "investigation reports" compiled in 1961 and 1962 when he visited communes in various provinces. "The Reactionary Antecedents of P'eng Teh-huai," *CB*, no. 851, pp. 14–15.

73. Information in this section is based on the following sources: "Thoroughly Settling Accounts with Ch'en Yun's Towering Crimes in Opposing Chairman Mao," *PKS*, 4 March 1967; "Manifold Sins of Ch'en Yun," *PKS*, 28 January 1967; Liu Shao-ch'i, "Confession," *MS*, 28 and 29 January 1967; *Ts'ai-mao Hung Ch'i* (Peking: The Finance and Trade System Rebels Liaison Committee), no. 4 (1967), also in *SCMP*, no. 3899, p. 6.

74. Joint Editorial, *People's Daily*, *Red Flag*, and *Liberation Army Daily*, 23 November 1967. English text is translated in *SCMP*, no. 4068.

75. Ibid.

76. *PLA Bull.* pp. 118–19, 138, 561.

77. Information in this paragraph and the next from "How the Evil Wind of 'Going in Alone' is stirred up in Honan," *Wei Tung* (Tientsin: Nank'ai University Wei Tung Red Guards Headquarters), 20 May 1967.

78. *The Evil Deeds of the Anti-Party and Anti-Socialist Element and Counter-Revolutionary Double-Dealer, Liu Chien-hsun* (Revolutionary Rebel General Command of Organs of the Honan CCP Provincial Committee, March 12, 1967), translated in *JPRS*, no. 43,357, p. 21.

79. Ibid., pp. 21–22.

80. Ibid. This kind of measure was also implemented in other places; in June and July 1962 T'ao Chu allegedly popularized *pao-ch'an tao-hu* in Kwangtung and other Central-South provinces; see "T'ao Chu is the Vanguard in Promoting 'Production Quotas Set at Household Level' of China's Khrushchev," *NFJP*, 26 July 1967; *SCMP*, no. 4011, pp. 14–23.

81. "Selections of Li Hsien-nien's Anti-Mao Tse-tung Thought Black Remarks," *PKS*, 27 April 1967; reprinted in *Hsing-tao Jih-pao* (Hongkong), 24 and 25 January 1968.

82. Ibid.

83. Liu Shao-ch'i, "Confession."

84. Ibid.

85. "Li Hsien-nien's Anti-Mao Tse-tung Thought Black Remarks."

86. See Mao Tse-tung, "Speech to the 10th Plenum of the 8th Central Committee" (24 September 1962), *Chairman Mao's Repudiations*, pp. 24–25; also in *CLG*, 1, no. 4 (1968–69): 85–93.

87. Li Ching-ch'uan was alleged to have said: "Only talking about class struggle is really fruitless, let us keep our energy"; "If we can settle work points every day and month, settle account every month, then we are grasping well the class struggle"; and "It is also class struggle if we check our discrepancies"; Radio Kweiyang, 29 November 1967. Ch'en Yun's reaction was reportedly similar; he allegedly said "Political and ideological work is important, but insufficient by itself"; see "Ch'en Yun is the Vanguard of the Capitalist Restoration," *TMHC*, 23 February 1967; *SCMP*, no. 3899, p. 6.

88. Communique of the Tenth Plenum, *JMJP*, 29 September 1962.

89. See "Further Consolidation of the Collective Economy and Development of Agricultural Production" (a speech by Wang Hung-shih, first party secretary of Lienchiang Hsien), *Lienchiang Documents*.

90. Some observers have reached a different conclusion, namely that "the 10th Plenum of the Central Committee brought the period of relaxation to an abrupt end"; see Charles Neuhauser, "The Chinese Communist Party in the 1960's: Prelude to the Cultural Revolution," *CQ*, no. 32 (1967): 10.

91. See *Lienchiang Documents*.

92. Ibid.

93. *Revised 60-Article Draft Regulations on Rural People's Commune* (September 1962) (Taipei: Ministry of National Defense, 1964).

94. For an excellent study of the campaign, see Richard Baum and Frederick C. Teiwes, *Ssu Ch'ing: The Socialist Education Movement of 1962–1966* (Berkeley: Center for Chinese Studies, University of California, 1968).

95. According to Mao, the important issues "solved" in these meetings were the problems of agriculture and commerce, industry and planning, the unity within the party (in that order); Mao, "Speech to the 10th Plenum of the 8th Central Committee" (24 September 1962), *CLG*, 1, no. 4 (1968–69): 85.

96. Li Tse-wen, "From the Principle of Repayment of Credits to a Discussion of the Supervisory Functions of the Banks," *HC*, no. 6 (1962).

97. Fan Yen-chun et al., "The Centralization and Unification of Financial Work," *TKP* (Peking), 25 June 1962, p. 3.

98. Ibid.; see also Ko Chih-ta and Wang Chao, "Some Inter-Relationships between Finance and Currency Work," *TKP*, 17 November 1961.

99. Franz Schurmann, *Ideology and Organization in Communist China* (Berkeley: University of California Press, 1966), p. 219, and Audrey Donnithorne, *China's Economic System* (London: George Allen and Unwin, 1967), p. 505.

100. Schurmann, *Ideology and Organization*, pp. 219, 297; also Donnithorne, *China's Economic System*, pp. 499, 505.

101. For an analysis of this important decision-making body and the shift in the locus of authority in the CCP, see Parris H. Chang, "Research Notes on the Changing Loci of Decision in the CCP," *CQ*, no. 44 (1970).

Chapter 6

1. I have dealt with the GPCR purge and its impact on China's political system in Parris H. Chang, "Mao's Great Purge: A Political Balance Sheet," *Problems of Communism*, March-April 1969.

2. All of these problems were revealed in a set of Chinese Communist materials, the *Lienchiang Documents*.

3. In the following analysis of the SEC, I have drawn heavily from Richard Baum and Frederick C. Teiwes, *Ssu-ch'ing: The Socialist Education Movement of 1962–1966* (Berkeley: Center for Chinese Studies, University of California, 1968), pp. 59–94 passim, and Charles Neuhauser, "The Chinese Communist Party in the 1960's: Prelude to the Cultural Revolution," *CQ*, no. 32 (1967).

4. This was indicated by "Draft Resolution of the Central Committee of the Chinese Communist Party on some problems in current Rural Work" (also known as the First Ten Points), Articles IV and V; an English translation of this document is in Baum and Teiwes, *Ssu-ch'ing*, Appendix II. Much of the information here is from his source.

5. Ibid., p. 73.

6. An English translation of this document is in Baum and Teiwes, *Ssu-ch'ing*, pp. 72–94.

7. Editorial Departments of *JMJP*, *HC*, and *CFCP*. "Struggle Between the Two Roads in China's Countryside," *PR*, no. 49 (1967): 17. But Liu Shao-ch'i claimed that the Second Ten Points were written by "some leading comrades at the center" on the basis of a report submitted to Mao by P'eng Chen; see Liu's reported "Confession," *MS*, 29 January 1967.

8. "Struggle Between the Two Roads in China's Countryside," *PR*, no. 49 (1967): 17.

9. Wang Kuang-mei (Madame Liu Shao-chi) allegedly claimed that Mao initially stipulated only four criteria but added two more as a result of her suggestion; she did not specify which two were her "brainchild." See "An Investigation Report of the Crimes of Liu Shao-chi and Wang Kuang-mei in the Ssu-ch'ing Movement in Pao-t'ing Special District," *Tung-fang hung* (Peking: Peking Mining Institute Tung-fang Hung of the Capital Colleges and Universities Red Guard Congress), no. 27–28 (1967).

10. Both the timing of the conference and the contents of the six criteria were disclosed in a twenty-three point directive, "Some Problems Currently Arising in the Course of the Rural Socialist Education Movement," enacted in January 1965. The English text is in Baum and Teiwes, *Ssu-ch'ing*.

11. An English translation of the document is in Baum and Teiwes, *Ssu-ch'ing*.

12. Article II of the "Organizational Rules of Poor and Lower-Middle Peasant Associations," Baum and Teiwes, *Ssu-ch'ing*, p. 96.

13. Wang Kuang-mei took part in a work team to conduct the SEC in T'aoyuan Brigade of Funin Hsien in Hopei from November 1963 to April 1964, and produced a report entitled "The Summary Experience of the Socialist Education Movement in a Brigade" in July 1964; the report, known as the "T'aoyuan Experience," was praised by Liu Shao-ch'i as having "universal significance" and became required reading for party officials and the work teams. See "The 'T'aoyuan Experience' of Wang Kuang-mei is an Anti-Mao Tse-tung Thought Poisonous Weed," *Tsao-fan Yu-li Pao* (Peking: Capital Four Clearances Revolutionary Rebel Detachment), 12 February 1967.

14. Ibid.

15. "The Line of Liu Shao-ch'i and Wang Kuang-mei in Ssu-ch'ing: Left in form but Right in Essence," *Tsao-fan Yu-li Pao* (Peking: Capital Four Clearances Revolutionary Rebel Detachment), 10 June 1967.

16. Article III of the "Revised Second Ten Points," Baum and Teiwes, *Ssu-ch'ing*, p. 108.

17. Richard Baum and Frederick C. Teiwes, "Liu Shao-ch'i and the Cadre Question," *Asian Survey*, 7, no. 4 (1969).

18. For an interesting interpretation of Liu's drastic disciplinary actions against cadres at lower

levels, see Tang Tsou, "The Cultural Revolution and the Chinese Political System," *CQ*, no. 38 (1969): 73.

19. The dispatch of "work teams" by Liu and Teng Hsiao-P'ing in June 1966 to control the Cultural Revolution in Peking's colleges and universities, we shall see later, reflected the same kind of consideration.

20. Liu Shao-ch'i, "Confession."

21. This represented a shift of emphasis away from the solution of nonantagonistic contradictions in the SEC which Liu advocated; as late as 1 October 1964 Liu's line was still affirmed by the *People's Daily* when its editorial stated that "the great historical significance of the (Socialist Education) Movement lies in the following fact—it is a movement for educating the cadres and masses in the revolutionary spirit of the general line and for correctly handling contradictions among the people."

22. For examples, compare the provisions in Article II (Section 2.3) and Article IV (Section 4.C) of the Revised Second Ten Points with those in Articles VII, and XIV, and IX (Section 5) of the Twenty-Three Points concerning squatting at points, work teams, and economic indemnities. For a more detailed comparison of the differences between the two documents, see "The Line of Liu Shao-ch'i and Wang Kuang-mei."

23. In a talk to a Central Work Conference on 25 October 1966, Mao recalled that it was during the time when the Twenty-Three Points were formulated that he became aware of the fact that those party leaders in the "first line" had assumed too much power and formed many "independent kingdoms" and that his vigilance was heightened; see Jerome Ch'en, ed., *Mao* (Englewood Cliffs, N. J.: Prentice-Hall, 1969), p. 96, for the text of Mao's talk. Chou En-lai also asserted that Mao lost confidence in Liu in the course of drafting the Twenty-Three Points; see a Tokyo dispatch of *Agence France-Presse* on 13 April 1969, quoting reports by an *NHK* reporter in Peking, *Ming Pao* (Hongkong), 14 April 1967. "A very responsible person" in China told an American writer the same thing in 1970; see Edgar Snow, "Aftermath of the Cultural Revolution," *The New Republic*, 10 April 1971, p. 19.

24. Philip Bridgham, "Mao's Cultural Revolution: Origin and Development," *CQ*, no. 29 (1967): 14–15.

25. For a more detailed treatment of this subject, see Merle Goldman, "The Unique Blooming and Contending 1961–1962," *CQ*, no. 37 (1969).

26. The full text of Mao's speech, which became available through Red Guard sources, is translated in *CLG*, 1, no. 4 (1968–69). This quotation has been repeatedly quoted by the Chinese official sources, described as part of Mao's speech to the Tenth Plenum.

27. Yao Wen-yuan, "Criticize Chou Yang, Two-faced Counter-Revolutionary Element," *HC*, no. 1 (1967).

28. For a detailed and excellent study of Chiang Ch'ing's involvement in the theatrical reform and her struggle with P'eng Chen, Lu Ting-yi, and Chou Yang, see Chung Hua-min and Arthur C. Miller, *Madame Mao: A Profile of Chiang Ch'ing* (Hongkong: Union Research Institute, 1968), chapters 8, 9, and 10.

29. See Chung and Miller, *Madame Mao*, pp. 98, 108, 127, for examples. The ill feelings she harbored against P'eng, Lu, and Chou would explain at least in part the rough treatment they got in the hands of the Red Guards at the end of 1966.

30. Yao Wen-yuan, "Criticize Chou Yang."

31. A speech by K'o at the East China Drama Festival in the end of 1963 was reproduced only in *JMJP*, 14 August 1964.

32. Quoted in Yao Wen-yun, "Criticize Chou Yang."

33. All quotations from "The Tempestuous Combat on the Literary and Art Front: A Chronicle of the Struggle Between the Two Lines on the Literary and Art Front 1949–1966," *Shou-tu Hung-wei-p'ing* (Peking: Congress of Red Guards of Universities and Colleges in Peking), nos. 34 and 35, 7 June 1967; *CB*, no. 842, 8 December 1967, pp. 17–18.

34. The speeches of Lu and P'eng were published in *JMJP*, 6 June 1964, and *HC*, no. 14, 31 July 1964, respectively.

35. It was almost three years later that Chiang Ch'ing's speech of June 1964 was finally published in *JMJP*, 10 May 1967.

36. *JMJP*, 6 June 1964.

37. "The Tempestuous Combat on the Literary and Art Front," *CB*, no. 842, p. 22.

38. Ibid.; also Yao Wen-yuan, "Criticize Chou Yang."

39. The exact date of the formation of the Five-Man Cultural Revolutionary Group is not known; judging from an article in *JMJP*, 14 May 1967, and other Red Guard sourses, the group was set up in the summer of 1964.

40. *CB*, no. 842, p. 22.

41. Chao Ts'ung, "Literature and Art in 1965 in Communist China," *Communist China 1965*, Vol. 2 (Hongkong: Union Research Institute, 1967).

42. Ibid.

43. *CB*, no. 842, p. 30.

44. Ibid., p. 26.

45. "Uncover the Black Mask of the 'Petofi Club' of Teng Hsiao-P'ing," *Tung-fang Hung* (Peking: Capital Colleges and Universities Red Guard Revolutionary Rebel Liaison Center), no. 20 (1967); *SCMP*, no. 3903, pp. 3–4.

46. Mao Tse-tung, "A Talk at the Work Conference of the Center October 25, 1966" in Ch'en, *Mao*, p. 96.

47. See the remarks of Yao Wen-yuan and Ch'i Pen-yu in *JMJP*, 24 May 1967.

48. Information in this paragraph and the next from *Counter-Revolutionary Revisionist P'eng Ch'ien's Towering Crimes of Opposing the Party, Socialism and the Thought of Mao Tse-tung* (Peking: Liaison Center for Repudiating Liu-Teng-T'ao, Tung-fang Hung Commune, China Science and Technology University, Red Guard Congress, 10 June 1967); translated in *SCMM*, no. 639, p. 2.

49. *JMJP*, 30 November 1965; the note and the article were printed on page 5, which often carried articles of "academic" nature.

50. Mao was quoted to have said "The crux of 'Hai Jui Dismissed from Office' is the question of dismissal from office. The Emperor Chia Ching (of the Ming Dynasty, 1522–1566) dismissed Hai Jui from office. In 1959 we dismissed P'eng Teh-huai from office. And P'eng Teh-huai is 'Hai Jui' too." "From the Defeat of P'eng Teh-huai to the Bankruptcy of China's Khrushchev," *PR*, no. 34 (1964): 20.

51. For example, *JMJP*, 15 and 25 December 1964, 19 January and 10 February 1966; *KMJP*, 15 December 1965, 9, 13, 19, and 29 January 1966, and *WHP* (Shanghai), 13 February 1965.

52. Also reproduced in *JMJP*, 30 December 1965. The final form of the article was allegedly examined and approved by the Secretariat of the Peking Party Committee.

53. See "Circular of the Central Committee of the Chinese Communist Party" (16 May 1966), *PR*, no. 21 (1967). The text of the "February Outline Report" is published by a Red Guard publication, *Hsin Kang-yuan* (Peking: Revolutionary Rebel Commune, Peking Iron and Steel Institute), no. 18 (1957).

54. *P'eng Chen's Towering Crimes*, in *SCMM*, no. 640, pp. 7–8.

55. *NCNA* (Peking), 28 May 1967; *SCMP*, no. 3951, p. 10.

56. Editorial, *CFCP*, 29 May 1967; *SCMP*, no. 3951, p. 21.

57. "Summary of the Forum on Literature and Art in the Armed Forces," *NCNA* (Peking), 28 May 1967; *SCMP*, no. 3951.

58. Editorial, *JMJP*, 29 May 1967; also "Two Diametrically Opposed Documents," editorial, *HC*, no. 9 (1967).

59. Uri Ra'anan, "Peking's Foreign Policy 'Debate,' 1965–1966," and Donald S. Zagoria, "The Strategic Debate in Peking," in Tang Tsou, ed., *China in Crisis*, vol. II: *China's Policies in Asia and America's Alternatives* (Chicago: The University of Chicago Press, 1968), pp. 23–71, 237–68; also

Stanley Karnow, *Mao and China: From Revolution to Revolution* (New York: Viking Press, 1972). pp. 148–51. For a somewhat different interpretation, see Harry Harding and Melvin Gurtov, *The Purge of Lo Jui-Ch'ing: The Politics of Chinese Strategic Planning* (Santa Monica, Cal.: The Rand Corporation, 1971).

60. See Karnow, *Mao and China*, pp. 150–51, and Ra'anan, "Peking's Foreign Policy 'Debate,'" p. 26 and passim.

61. *Collection of Documents concerning the Great Proletarian Cultural Revolution*, vol. I (Peking: Propagandists of Mao Tse-tung's Thought, Peking College of Chemical Engineering, May 1967); *CB*, no. 852, p. 7.

62. Ra'anan, "Peking's Foreign Policy 'Debate,'" pp. 27, 34, and passim.

63. "Reply to Red Guards' False Accusation," *Akahata* (Tokyo), 24 January 1967 (this newspaper is the daily organ of the Japanese Communist Party). Here I differ from the interpretation of Ra'anan ("Peking's Foreign Policy 'Debate,'" pp. 52, 62), who has argued that P'eng Chen consistently opposed unity of action with Moscow. The *Akahata* article indicates that several Chinese negotiators, including P'eng, consented to a communique which, among other things, called for the "broadest international united front" and only Mao was against it subsequently and scrapped the points of agreement already reached.

64. *P'eng Chen's Towering Crimes, SCMM*, p. 15.

65. Cf. Karnow, *Mao and China*, p. 152.

66. See speeches of Liu and Teng in *JMJP*, 29 April, 7 May, and 22 July 1966; also *PR*, 6 and 13 May and 29 July 1966.

67. Karnow, *Mao and China*, p. 153.

68. *P'eng Chen's Towering Crimes*, p. 9.

69. *SCMM*, no. 640, p. 10. Bowing to pressure, P'eng authorized the *Peking Daily* and *Ch'ien-hsien* to publish an "Editor's Note" on 16 April sternly criticizing the writings of T'eng T'o. This move was termed by the Maoists as "sham criticism," intended to "protect the commander through sacrificing the knights."

70. *SCMM*, no. 640, p. 12.

71. Ibid., p. 13.

72. *CFCP*, 18 April 1966; reprinted in *JMJP* in the following day.

73. The itinery of Liu, as reported in *JMJP* in March and April 1966, was rather strange and puzzling. The delegation he led arrived in Pakistan on 26 March and returned to Hotien of Sinkiang on 31 March; it arrived in Afghanistan on 4 April and returned to Urumuchi on 8 April; it arrived in East Pakistan on 15 April, left East Pakistan and arrived Burma on 18 April; it left Rangoon, Burma, on 19 April and arrived in Kunming of Yunan province on 19 April. *JMJP* on 21 April published an editorial to welcome Liu home but gave no indication on what date Liu returned to Peking; he may have gone to Hangchow directly from Kunming.

74. "Circular of the Central Committee of Chinese Communist Party" (16 May 1966), *PR*, no. 21 (1967).

75. "The Terrifying Counter-Revolutionary Incident," *Ch'uan Wu-ti* (Peking: The Yenan Commune of *Chien-k'iang Pao* and the capital Medical Revolutionary Committee), no. 9 (1967). Although policy differences and failures to carry out Mao's instructions were undoubtedly responsible for Lu's downfall, certain personal factors may be equally important. As intimated by this Red Guard source, Lu's wife, Yen Wei-ping, had over a period of time written several malicious anonymous letters to Lin Piao insulting and attacking Lin and his wife; after the identity of the author was discovered, Lu allegedly got the assistance of P'eng Chen to have medical specialists declare Yen insane in order to absolve her "counter-revolutionary" offenses.

76. The text of the poster is in *JMJP*, 2 June 1966.

77. "How Lu P'ing and Company Have Undermined the Great Cultural Revolution in Pei Ta," *Kung-jen Jih-pao*, 4 June 1966. According to the paper, the article is supplied by *CFCP*.

78. "The Great Strategic Plan," editorial, *JMJP*, 6 June 1967.

79. Liu Shao-ch'i, "Confession." The full contents of this eight-article directive remain un-

known. According to one Red Guard source, it contained provisions such as "differentiating the inside from the outside," "guarding against the leakage of secrets," and "firmly holding the fort." See "Down with Liu Shao-ch'i—Life of Counter-revolutionary Liu Shao-ch'i" in *CB*, no. 834, p. 27. It is reasonable to infer that the directive tried to limit the students' scope of activities confining them to their schools.

80. Liu Shao-ch'i, "Confession."

81. An incomplete tabulation shows that thirteen such officials in eleven universities were dismissed and publicly humiliated during June and July 1966. The more notable ones included Lu P'ing, president and party secretary of Peking University, K'uang Ya-ming, president and party secretary of Nanking University; Li ta, president of Wuhan University and a founder of the CCP in 1921; Ho Lu-ting, president of Shanghai Musical College and composer of the current national anthem "East is Red"; and K'o Lin, president and party secretary of Chungshan Medical College in Canton.

82. Liu Shao-ch'i and Teng Hsiao-ping reportedly assured members of the work teams that "Dispatching the work teams embodies the leadership of the Party. You are sent by us; to oppose you is to oppose us." "Excerpts of Teng Hsiao-Ping's Self-criticism," carried in a Canton Red Guard publication and reproduced in *Ming Pao* (Hongkong), 20 May 1968. The Sixteen-Point Decision on the GPCR also criticized those who equated opposition to work teams with opposition to the party center. See *JMJP*, 9 August 1966 (also *PR*, no. 33 [1966]).

83. Information here and in the next paragraph from "Down With Liu Shao-ch'i," p. 27.

84. Mao Tse-tung, "My First Big Character Poster" (5 August 1966), *JMJP*, 31 July 1967; also in *PR*, no. 33 (1967).

85. In several respects, the Eleventh Plenum deviated from previous practices. In addition to the presence of large number of "revolutionary teachers and students," no mention was made in the Plenum Communique of the number of the members and alternate members of the CC who attended the Plenum. A Japanese source reported that only forty-six members and thirty-three alternate members of the CC, or approximately 46 percent of the total membership, actually attended the Plenum; see *Seikai Shuho (World Weekly)* (Tokyo), no. 37 (1966).

86. The text of the Sixteen-Point Decision on the GPCR is in *JMJP*, 9 August 1966. An English text is in *PR*, no. 33 (1966).

87. Mao Tse-tung, "Big Character Poster."

88. For a detailed treatment of the tug-of-war between the Maoists and the provincial officials, see Parris H. Chang, "Provincial Party Leaders' Strategies for Survival during the Cultural Revolution," in *Elites in Communist China*, ed. Robert A. Scalapino (Seattle: University of Washington Press, 1972).

89. Ch'en, *Mao*, p. 96.

90. Richard M. Pfeffer, "The Pursuit of Purity: Mao's Cultural Revolution," *Problems of Communism*, November–December 1969, p. 19.

91. Tang Tsou, "The Cultural Revolution and The Chinese Political System," *CQ*, no. 38 (1969): 79.

92. *PR*, 17 July 1964.

93. Cf. Richard H. Solomon, *Mao's Revolution and the Chinese Political Culture* (Berkeley: University of California Press, 1971), pp. 458–60.

94. A Red Guard source quotes Chou En-lai as saying that prior to 1964 Mao had criticized Liu on several occasions; see *Wen-k'o T-ung-hsun* (Canton: Canton Municipal Organ's Red Headquarters), no. 1 (1967). Various other Red Guard sources have indicated that many policies which Liu sponsored from 1960 to 1962 had displeased Mao and that in the Peitaiho Conference in the summer of 1962 Mao openly rebuked Liu for his "rightist-leaning" stand.

95. For example, editorials, *CFCP*, 18 April, 4 May, and 20 May 1966. During April and May, the PLA paper also actively promoted Mao's GPCR and violently attacked those who obstructed it, while *JMJP* maintained silence on that matter editorially.

Chapter 7

1. See G. William Skinner and Edwin A. Winckler, "Compliance Succession in Rural Communist China: A Cyclical Theory," in Amitai Etzioni, ed., *Complex Organizations: A Sociological Reader*, 2nd ed. (New York: Holt, Rinehart and Winston, 1969), p. 426.

2. See Richard H. Solomon, *Mao's Revolution and the Chinese Political Culture* (Berkeley: University of California Press, 1971), pp. 377ff.

3. In his self-criticism, P'eng attributed the motivation of his attack on Mao to his enmity and prejudice against Mao; see *CB*, no. 851.

4. See Wu Leng-hsi, "Confession," *Hung-se Hsin-hua*, no. 43 (1968); the text of the confession is translated with notes by Parris H. Chang, *CLG*, 2, no. 4 (1969–70).

5. See "Selections of Li Hsien-nien's Anti-Mao Tse-tung Thought Black Remarks," *Peking Commune*, reprinted in *Hsing-tao Jih-pao* (Hongkong), 24 and 25 January 1968.

6. The moving force behind the regime's campaign to revolutionalize Chinese drama and theatre in 1963–64, for instance, was Chiang Ch'ing, and she played a pivotal role in it. Chang Ch'un-chiao contributed, directly or indirectly, to the experiment of the free supply system in the communes in 1958 (see ch. 4).

7. For an interesting discussion of the roles of the presidential aides in the American policy process, see Patrick Anderson, *The Presidents' Men: White House Assistants of Franklin D. Roosevelt, Harry Truman, Dwight D. Eisenhower, John F. Kennedy and Lyndon B. Johnson* (New York: Doubleday, 1968).

8. See A. Doak Barnett, *Cadres, Bureaucracy, and Political Power in Communist China* (New York: Columbia University Press, 1967).

9. Ibid., pp. 437–38.

10. See Merle Fainsod, *Smolensk Under Soviet Rule* (New York: Vintage Books, 1963), pp. 142, 180–82, 246–47.

11. For example, "How to Run the People's Communes: In Reference to the Draft Regulations of the Weihsing Commune," *JMJP*, 4 September 1958.

12. See E.E. Shattschneider, *The Semi-Sovereign People* (New York: Holt, Rinehart and Winston, 1960) for an analysis of the application of the same tactic, which he calls "socialization of conflict," in American politics.

13. Samuel P. Huntington, "Political Development and Political Decay," *World Politics*, 12, no. 3 (1956): 386–430.

14. See Parris H. Chang, "China'a Military in the Aftermath of Lin Piao's Purge," *Current History*, September 1974.

15. It is interesting to note that both Plenums, in October 1955 and September 1957, were enlarged sessions in which provincial party secretaries who were not members of the CC participated in the deliberations.

16. Written directives were often vague and ambiguous and could be subject to diverse interpretations, thus word of mouth may have helped clarify and expound the leadership's specific policy intentions and goals.

17. For instance, see reports on Mao's various trips in the provinces in *JMJP*, 21 September 1957, 14 and 27 April and 12 and 13 August 1958, *Shensi Jih-pao*, 6 and 7 April 1958, and *Kung-jen Jih-pao*, 10 April 1958.

18. "Uncover Liu Shao-ch'i's 1961 Hunan Visit," *TFHP* (Peking: Peking Institute of Geology), 9 March 1967.

19. Ibid.

20. For a "Mao in Command" model, see Michael Oksenberg, "Policy-making Under Mao, 1949–68: An Overview," in John M.H. Lindbeck, ed., *China: Management of a Revolutionary Society* (Seattle: University of Washington Press, 1971), pp. 79–115.

21. Shattschneider, *Semi-Sovereign People*, p. 68.

22. Compare the observation of Edgar Snow: "This (Central Committee) is not a faceless rubber-stamp committee packed with yes-men, but is made of strong personalities many of whom have commanded troops in battles and have at times held discretionary power over forces that could have destroyed or overthrown Mao" (*The Other Side of the River* [New York: Random House, 1961], p. 332).

23. For a discussion of "routinized charisma" see Amitai Etzioni, *A Comparative Analysis of Complex Organization* (Glencoe, Ill.: Free Press, 1961), pp. 26 ff.

24. See Articles 19 and 37 of the 1956 CCP Constitution and Teng Hsiao-P'ing's discussion of collective leadership in his "Report on the Revision of the Constitution of the Communist Party of China" (*8NCCPC*, vol. 2, pp. 192–99).

25. See A. Doak Barnett, *China After Mao* (Princeton: Princeton University Press, 1967), pp. 91–92.

26. Based on the position(s) held by these leaders, and judging from their activities, one can draw a picture of roughly who was responsible over what in the 1950s and early 1960s: political and legal affairs: Tung P'i-wu, P'eng Chen, Lo Jui-ch'ing; foreign affairs: Ch'en yi, Chang Wen-tien, Wang Chia-hsiang; intrabloc affairs: P'eng Chen, K'ang Shang; ideology and propaganda: P'eng Chen, Lu Ting-yi, Ch'en Po-ta, Hu Ch'iao-mu; military affairs: P'eng Teh-huai (until summer 1959), Ho Lung, Lo Jung-huan, Lo Jui-ch'ing; economic affairs: Li Fu-chun, Li Hsien-nien, Po I-po, T'an Chen-lin; party administration: Yang shang-k'un.

27. See Parris H. Chang, "Mao's Great Purge" A Political Balance Sheet," *Problems of Communism*, 18, no. 2 (1969): 8.

28. The text of Mao's letter was obtained by the Chinese Nationalist authorities, and reproduced in *Central Daily News* (Taipei), 18 April 1973.

Works Cited or Consulted

Non-Communist Sources in English

Articles and Books

Barnett, A. Doak. *Communist China and Asia: A Challenge to American Policy.* New York: Random House, 1960.

———. *Communist China: The Early Years 1949–1955.* New York: Praeger, 1964.

———. *China After Mao.* Princeton: Princeton University Press, 1967.

———, with a contribution by Ezra Vogel. *Cadres, Bureaucracy and Political Power in Communist China.* New York: Columbia University Press, 1967.

Bauer, Raymond A., and Gergen, Kenneth J., eds. *The Study of Policy Formulation.* New York: Free Press, 1968.

Baum, Richard, and Teiwes, Frederick C. "Liu Shao-ch'i and the Cadre Question," *Asian Survey* 8, no. 4 (1968).

———. *Ssu-Ch'ing: The Socialist Education Movement of 1962–1966.* Berkeley: Center for Chinese Studies, University of California, 1968.

Bennett, Gordon A., and Montaperto, Ronald N. *Red Guard: Political Biography of Dai Hsiao-ai.* New York: Doubleday, 1971.

Bernstein, Thomas P. "Leadership and Mass Mobilization in the Soviet and Chinese Collectivization Campaign of 1929–1930 and 1955–1956: A Comparison." *CQ*, no. 31 (1967).

Bridgham, Philip. "Mao's Cultural Revolution: Origins and Development." *CQ*, no. 29 (1967).

Brzezinski, Zbigniew. *Permanent Purge.* Cambridge, Mass.: Harvard University Press, 1956.

———, and Hungtington, Samuel P. *Political Power: USA/USSR.* New York: Viking Press, 1964.

Chang, Parris H. "Chang Ch'un-ch'iao: Shanghai's Cultural Czar." *Far Eastern Economic Review*, no. 33 (1968).

———. "The Struggle Between the Two Roads in China's Countryside." *Current Scene* 6, no. 3 (1968).

———. "Mao's Great Purge: A Political Balance Sheet." *Problems of Communism*, March–April 1969.

———. "Research Notes on the Changing Loci of Decision in the CCP." *CQ*, no. 44 (1970).

———. *Radicals and Radical Ideology in China's Cultural Revolution*. New York: Research Institute on Communist Affairs, Columbia University, 1973.

———. "China's Military." *Current History*, September 1974.

Chang, Wan-shan. *The State Council in Communist China: A Structural and Functional Analysis 1954–1965*. M.A. thesis, Columbia University, 1968.

Charles, David A. "The Dismissal of Marshal P'eng Teh-huai." *CQ*, no. 8 (1961).

Ch'en, Jerome. *Mao and the Chinese Revolution*. New York: Oxford University Press, 1965.

———, ed. *Mao*. Englewood Cliffs, N.J.: Prentice-Hall, 1969.

Ch'en, S.C., ed. *Rural People's Communes in Lien-chiang*. Stanford: Hoover Institution, 1969.

Ch'en, Theodore H.E. *Thought Reform of the Chinese Intellectuals*. Hongkong: Hongkong University Press, 1960.

Clubb, O. Edmund. *Twentieth-Century China*. New York: Columbia University Press, 1964.

Communist China 1955–1959: Policy Documents with Analysis. Cambridge, Mass.: Harvard University Press, 1965.

Dahl, Robert A. "Critique of the Ruling Elite Model." *American Political Science Review* 52, no. 2 (1958).

Donnithorne, Audrey. *China's Economic System*. London: George Allen and Unwin, 1967.

Eckstein, Alexander. *Communist China's Economic Growth and Foreign Trade*. New York: McGraw-Hill, 1966.

Etzioni, Amitai. *A Comparative Analysis of Complex Organizations*. Glencoe, Ill.: Free Press, 1961.

———, ed. *Complex Organizations: A Sociological Reader*. 2d. ed. New York: Holt, Rinehart and Winston, 1969.

Gelman, Harry. "Mao and the Permanent Purge." *Problems of Communism*, no. 6 (1966).

Gittings, John. *The Role of the Chinese Army*. New York: Oxford University Press, 1967.

Halperin, Morton H. *China and the Bomb*. New York: Praeger, 1965.

Hilsman, Roger. *To Move a Nation: The Politics of Foreign Policy in the Administration of John F. Kennedy.* New York: Doubleday, 1967.

Hofheinz, Roy. "Rural Administration in Communist China." CQ, no. 71 (1962).

Houn, Franklin W. *A Short History of Chinese Communism.* Englewood Cliffs, N.J.: Prentice-Hall, 1967.

Hsieh, Alice L. *Communist China's Strategy in the Nuclear Era.* Englewood Cliffs, N.J.: Prentice-Hall, 1962.

———. "China's Secret Military Papers: Military Doctrine and Strategy." CQ, no. 18 (1964).

Hudson, G.F., et al. *The Chinese Communes.* London: Oxford University Press, 1960.

Hughes, T.J., and Luard, D.E.T. *Economic Development of Communist China.* London: Oxford University Press, 1959.

Institute of International Relations. *Chinese Communist Who's Who.* Taipei: Institute of International Relations, 1970.

Joffe, Ellis. "The Conflict Between Old and New in the Chinese Army." CQ, no. 18 (1964).

Johnson, Chalmers A. *Peasant Nationalism and Communist Power: The Emergence of Revolutionary China.* Stanford, Cal.: Stanford University Press, 1962.

Karnow, Stanley. *Mao and China: From Revolution to Revolution.* New York: Viking Press, 1972.

Klein, Donald W. "The 'Next Generation' of Chinese Communist Leaders." CQ, no. 12 (1962).

———, and Clark, Anne B. *Biographical Dictionary of Chinese Communism 1921–1965.* Cambridge: Harvard University Press, 1971.

Lasswell, Harold. *Politics: Who Gets What, When, How.* Cleveland: World, 1958.

———. *The Decision Process: Seven Categories of Functional Analysis.* College Park: Bureau of Government Research, University of Maryland, 1956.

———, and Kaplan, A. *Power and Society: A Framework of Political Inquiry.* New Haven: Yale University Press, 1950.

Lewis, John W. *Major Doctrines of the Chinese Communist Leadership.* Ithaca, N.Y.: Cornell University Press, 1961.

———. *Leadership in Communist China.* Ithaca, N.Y.: Cornell University Press, 1963.

———. "China's Secret Military Papers: 'Continuities' and 'Revelations.'" CQ, no. 18 (1964).

Li, Choh-ming. *Economic Development of Communist China*. Berkeley: University of California Press, 1959.

————. *The Statistical System of Communist China*. Berkeley: University of California Press, 1962.

————. "China's Industrial Development." *CQ*, no. 17 (1964).

Lindbeck, John M.H., ed. *China: Management of A Revolutionary Society*. Seattle: University of Washington Press, 1971.

Lindblom, Charles E. "The Science of 'Muddling Through.'" *Public Administration Review* 19 (1959).

————, and Braybrooke, David. *A Strategy of Decisions*. New York: Free Press, 1963.

MacFarquhar, Roderick. *The Hundred Flowers Campaign and the Chinese Intellectuals*. New York: Praeger, 1960.

————. "Communist China's Intra-Party Dispute." *Pacific Affairs* 31, no. 4 (1958).

Nathan, Andrew. "A Factional Model for CCP Politics." *CQ*, no. 53 (1973).

Neuhauser, Charles. "The Chinese Communist Party in the 1960's: Prelude to the Cultural Revolution." *CQ*, no. 32 (1967).

Oksenberg, Michael. "Occupational Groups in Chinese Society and the Cultural Revolution." In *The Cultural Revolution: 1967 in Review*. Ann Arbor: Center for Chinese Studies, University of Michigan, 1968.

————. *Policy Formulation in Communist China: The Case of the 1957–1958 Mass Irrigation Campaign*. Ph.D. dissertation, Columbia University, 1969.

Orleans, Leo A. "Birth Control: Reversal or Postponement?" *CQ*, no. 3 (1960).

Ploss, Sidney. *Conflict and Decision-making in Soviet Russia: A Case Study of Agricultural Policy 1953–1963*. Princeton: Princeton University Press, 1965.

Powell, Ralph L. *Politico-Military Relationships in Communist China*. Washington, D.C.: External Research Bureau, U.S. Department of State, 1963.

Prybyla, Jan S. *The Political Economy of Communist China*. Scranton, Pa.: International, 1970.

Pye, Lucian W. *The Spirit of Chinese Politics*. Cambridge: MIT Press, 1968.

Rice, Edward. *Mao's Way*. Berkeley: University of California Press, 1972.

Robinson, James A. *Congress and Foreign Policy-making*. Homewood, Ill. Dorsey, 1962.

Robinson, Thomas, ed. *The Cultural Revolution in China*. Berkeley: University of California Press, 1971.

Scalapino, Robert A., ed. *Elites in the People's Republic of China*. Seattle: University of Washington Press, 1972.

Schram, Stuart R. *The Political Thought of Mao Tse-tung*. New York: Praeger, 1963.

———. *Mao Tse-tung*. New York: Simon and Shuster, 1967.

Schurmann, Franz. *Ideology and Organization in Communist China*. 2d ed. Berkeley: University of California Press, 1968.

Shattschneider, E.E. *The Semi-Sovereign People*. New York: Holt, Rinehart and Winston, 1961.

Skinner, G. William. "Marketing and Social Structure in Rural China," 3 parts. *Journal of Asian Studies* 24, no. 1 (1964), nos. 2, 3 (1965).

———, and Winckler, Edwin A. "Compliance Succession in Rural Communist China: A Cyclical Theory." In *Complex Organizations: A Sociological Reader*, 2d ed., Amitai Etzioni, ed. New York: Holt, Rinehart and Winston, 1969.

Snow, Edgar. *The Other Side of the River: Red China Today*. New York: Random House, 1961.

Snyder, Richard. "A Decision-making Approach to the Study of Political Phenomena." In *Approaches to the Study of Politics*, Roland Young, ed. Evanston, Ill.: Northwestern University Press, 1958.

Solomon, Richard. "One Party and 'One Hundred Schools': Leadership, Lethargy, or Luan?" *Current Scene* 7, nos. 19–20 (1969).

———. *Mao's Revolution and the Chinese Political Culture*. Berkeley: University of California Press, 1971.

Strong, Anna Louise. *The Rise of People's Communes in China*. New York: Marzavai and Munsell, 1960.

Tang, Peter S.H. *Domestic and Foreign Policies*. 2d ed. Communist China Today, vol. 4. Washington, D.C.: Research Institute on the Sino-Soviet Bloc, 1961.

Teiwes, Frederick C. "The Purge of Provincial Leaders 1957–1958." *CQ*, no. 27 (1966).

———. *Provincial Party Personnel in Mainland China: 1956–1966*. New York: East Asian Institute, Columbia University, 1967.

Townsend, James R. *Political Participation in Communist China*. Berkeley: University of California Press, 1967.

Tsou, Tang. "The Cultural Revolution and the Chinese Political System." *CQ*, no. 38 (1969).

———, ed. *China's Policies in Asia and America's Alternatives*. China in Crisis, vol. 2. Chicago: University of Chicago Press, 1968.

Uhalley, Stephen, Jr. "The Cultural Revolution and the Attack on the 'Three Family Village.'" *CQ*, no. 27 (1966).

Vogel, Ezra. *Canton Under Communism*. Cambridge: Harvard University Press, 1969.

Walker, Kenneth R. "Collectivization in Retrospect: The 'Socialist High Tide' of Autumn 1955–Spring 1956." *CQ*, no. 26 (1966).

Whiting, Allen S. "China." In *Modern Political Systems: Asia*, Robert E. Ward and Roy C. Macridis, eds. Englewood Cliffs, N.J.: Prentice-Hall, 1963, pp. 117–97.

Whitson, William W., with Huang Chen-hsia. *The Chinese High Command*. New York: Praeger, 1972.

Yu, Frederick T.C. *Mass Persuasion in Communist China*. New York: Praeger, 1964.

Zagoria, Donald S. *The Sino-Soviet Conflict 1956–1961*. Princeton: Princeton University Press, 1962.

Translations from People's Republic Sources

Current Background. Collections of articles or documents grouped according to subject, issued several times a month. (Translation: U.S. Consulate-General, Hongkong).

Daily Reports of the Foreign Broadcast Information Service. (Translation: U.S. Department of Commerce, Washington, D.C.).

Extracts (Selections) from China Mainland Magazines. Translations from periodicials, issued several times a month. (Translation: U.S. Consulate-General, Hongkong).

Joint Publication Research Service. (Translation: U.S. Department of Commerce, Washington D.C.)

Survey of the China Mainland Press. A daily collection of translations from important articles. (Translation: U.S. Consulate-General, Hongkong).

Chinese Communist Sources (in Chinese and English)

Speeches and Statements by Chinese Communists Officials;
Other Relevant Materials

Ch'en Po-ta. "Explanations of the Draft Decision on the Question of Agricultural Cooperativization." *JMJP*, 19 October 1955.

———. "New Society, New People." *HC*, no. 3, 1 July 1958.

———. "Under the Banner of Chairman Mao Tse-tung." *HC*, no. 4, 16 July 1958.

Ch'en Yi. "Comrade Mao Tse-tung's Report on the Question of Agricultural Cooperation is a Model Combination of Theory and Practice." *JMJP*, 13 November 1955; *SCMP*, no. 1177, 24–25 November 1955.

Ch'en Yun. "Speech to the 2nd Session of the 1st NPC (July 1955)." *JMST*, 1956, *CB*, no. 339, 27 July 1955.

———. "Speech to the 3rd Session of the 1st NPC" (June 1956). *NCAS*, 1956.

———. "Several Major Problems in the Current Capital Construction Work." *HC*, no. 5, 1 March 1959.

Chou En-lai. "On the Question of Intellectuals" (14 January 1956). *NCNA*, 29 January 1956: *CB*, no. 376, 7 February 1956.

———. "Report on the Work of the Government" (26 June 1957). *JMST*, 1958.

———. "Report on the Proposals for the Second Five-year Plan" (16 September 1956). *8NCCPC*, 1: 261–328.

Chou Fang. *Wo-kuo Kuo-chia Chi-kou (The State Structure of Our Country)*. Peking: Chung-kuo Ch'ing-nien Ch'u-pau-she, 1957.

Chu Teh. "People's Army, People's War." *NCNA*, 31 July 1958; *CB*, no. 514, 6 August 1958.

Hsueh Mu-ch'iao. "A Preliminary Opinion on the Present System of Planning Control." *CHCS*, no. 9, September 1957.

Kao Chu Jen-min Kung-she Ti Hung-ch'i Sheng-li Ch'ien-chin (Hold Aloft the Red Flag of the People's Communes and Victoriously March on). Peking: Fa-lu Ch'u-pan-she, 1960. 2 vols.

Li Hsien-nien. "Financial-Economic Work and Agricultural Cooperation." *TKP* (Tientsin), 8 November 1955; *SCMP*, no. 1183, 7 December 1955.

———. "What I Have Seen in the People's Communes." *HC*, no. 10, 16 October 1958.

Liao Lu-yen. "Explanations on the Draft 1956–1967 National Program for Agricultural Development," *NCNA*, 25 January 1956; *SCMP*, no. 1219, 31 January 1956.

Liu Shao-ch'i. *On Inner Party Struggle*. New York: New Century Publishers, 1952.

———. *On the Party*. Peking: FLP, 1950.

———. *How to be a Good Communist*. Peking: FLP, 1962.

———. "Political Report of the Central Committee of the Communist Party of China to the Eighth Party Congress" (15 September 1956). *8NCCPC*, 1 : 13–111.

———. "The Significance of the October Revolution" (6 November 1957). *JMJP*, 7 November 1957.

———. "Report on the Work of the Central Committee of the Communist Party of China to the Second Session of the Eighth National Congress." *JMJP*, 25 May 1958; *PR*, no. 14, 3 June 1958.

Lu Ting-yi. "Let a Hundred Flowers Blossom, a Hundred Schools of Thought Contend" (26 May 1956). *JMJP*, 13 June 1956.

Lun Jen-min Kung-she (On the People's Communes). Peking: Chung-kuo Ch'ing-nien Ch'u-pan-she, 1958.

Lun Jen-min Kung-she Yu Kung-ch'an Ch-i (On the People's Communes and Communism). Peking: People's University, 1958.

Ma Nan-tun [Teng T'o]. *Yen-shan Yeh-hua (Evening Chats at Yenshan)*. Peking: Peiching Ch'u-pan-she, 1961.

Mao Tse-tung. "The Question of Agricultural Cooperation." *JMJP*, 17 October 1955; *CB*, no. 364.

———. "On the Correct Handling of Contradictions Among the People." *People's China*, 1 July 1957. (Supplement)

———. *Selected Works*, vol. 2. Peking: FLP, 1961.

People's Communes in China. Peking: FLP, 1960.

Po I-po. "Agricultural Cooperation Should be Closely Linked Up With Technical Reform of Agriculture." *JMJP*, 17 November 1955; *SCMP*, no. 1179, 1 December 1955.

Shanghai Ti-yi-kou Jen-min Kung-she Ti T'ang-sheng (The Birth of the First People's Commune in Shanghai). Shanghai: Jen-min Ch'u-pan-she, 1958.

Socialist Upsurge in China's Countryside. Peking: FLP, 1956.

T'an Chen-lin. "Explanations on the 1956–1957 Program of Agricultural Development (Second Revised Draft)." *JMJP*, 27 May 1958.

T'ao Chu. "The Investigation Report of the Humeng Commune." *JMJP*, 25 February 1959.

———. "The Whole Nation as a Chessboard, the Whole Province as a Chessboard." *NFJP*, 2 March 1959.

Teng Tzu-hui. "Speech at the National Democratic Youth League Rural Work Conference" (15 July 1954). *CKCNP*, 1 September 1954; *CB*, no. 306, 22 November 1954.

———. "Speech at the National Conference of Outstanding Workers" (7 May 1956). *NCNA*, 7 May 1956.

————. "On the Contradictions Among the People in the Countryside and the Principles and Methods of Correctly Handling these Contradictions." *CKCNP*, no. 21, November 1957.

Tung Ta-lin. *Agricultural Cooperation in China*. Peking: FLP, 1959.

Wei Kung-ku Fa-chan Jen-min Kung-she Erh Tou-cheng (Struggle for the Consolidation and Development of the People's Commune). Honan: CCP Hsinyang Special District Party Committee, 1958.

Wu Chih-p'u. "From Agricultural Producers' Cooperatives to the People's Communes." *HC*, no. 8, 16 September 1958.

————. "Contradictions are the Motive Force for the Development of the Socialist Society." *HCS*, no. 6, June 1960.

Wu Han. *Hai Jui Pa Kuan (The Dismissal of Hai Jui)*. Peking: Peiching Ch'u-pan-she, 1961.

Yang Ying-chieh. "On Unified Planning and Decentralized Control." *CHCS*, no. 11, November 1958.

Yao Wen-yuan. "A Criticism of the New Historical Play 'The Dismissal of Hai Jui.'" *WHP* (Shanghai), 10 November 1965.

Newspapers and Periodicals

News items cited and consulted in this study but not listed individually are from the following publications:

Chekiang Jih-pao (Chekiang Daily)
Chi-hua Ching-shi (Planned Economy)
Ching-chi Yen-chin (Economic Research)
Chung-kuo Ch'ien-nien Pao (China Youth Daily)
Hsin-hua Pan-yueh-kan (New China Semi-Monthly)
Hsueh Hsi (Study)
Hung Ch'i (Red Flag)
Jen-min Jih-pao (People's Daily)
Nan-fang Jih-pao (Southern Daily)
New China News Agency
Peking Review
Ta-kung Pao (Impartial Daily)
Ts'ai Cheng (Finance)

Official Documents

The best sources for laws, regulations, directives, resolutions, and "normative enactments" are the following:

Jen-min Kung-hokuo Fa-kuer Hui-pien (The Compendium of the Laws and Regulations of the People's Republic of China) and Jen-min shou-ts'e (People's Handbook), both of which are published annually, and *Hsin-jua Pan-yueh-kan (New China Semi-Monthly)*

Documents of CCP Central Committee 1956–1969. Hongkong: Union Research Institute, 1971, vol. 1.

The following major documents are used in this study:

CCP Central Committee and the State Council. "Joint Directive on Running of the APC's Industriously and Economically" (4 April 1956). *NCNA,* 4 April 1956; *SCMP,* no. 1286, 16 April 1956.

CCP Central Committee and the State Council. "Joint Directive on Strengthening Production Leadership and Organizational Construction of Agricultural Producers' Cooperatives." *NCNA,* 12 September 1956.

"Decision on Agricultural Cooperation" (adopted at the Enlarged Sixth Plenary Session of the Seventh CC of the CCP, 11 October 1955). *JMJP,* 18 October 1955; *SCMP,* no. 1151, 15–18 October 1955.

Eighth National Congress of the Communist Party of China. Peking: FLP, 1956, 3 vols.

"1956–1967 National Program for Agricultural Development" (adopted by the NPC in April 1960). *JMJP,* 12 April 1960; *CB,* no. 616.

"Resolution of the 8th Plenary Session of the 8th Central Committee of the CCP Concerning the Anti-Party Clique Headed by P'eng Teh-huai" (excerpts), 16 August 1959. *JMJP,* 16 August 1967; *PR,* no. 34, 18 August 1967.

"Resolution on the Establishment of People's Communes in the Rural Areas" (adopted by the CCP Politburo on 29 August 1958). *JMJP,* 10 September 1958.

"Resolution on Some Questions Concerning the People's Communes" (adopted by the Sixth CC Plenum of the CCP on 10 December 1958). *Sixth Plenary Session of the Eighth Central Committee of the Communist Party of China.* Peking: FLP, 1958, pp. 12–49.

"State Council's Directive Concerning Improvement of Commercial Management Systems" (November 1957). *JMJP,* 18 November 1957. (English translation: *SCMP,* no. 1665, 5 December 1957).

"State Council's Directive Concerning Improvement of Financial Management Systems" (November 1957). *JMJP,* 18 November 1957. (English translation: *SCMP,* no. 1665, 5 December 1957.)

"State Council's Directive Concerning Improvement of Industrial Management System" (November 1957). *JMJP*, 18 November 1957. (English translation: *SCMP*, no. 1665, 5 December 1957.)

Secret Chinese Communist Documents

PLA Kung-tso T'ung-hsun (Bulletin of Activities). In J. Chester Cheng, ed., *The Politics of the Chinese Red Army: A Translation of the Bulletin of Activities of the People's Liberation Army*. Stanford: Hoover Institution, 1966.

Seventy-Article "Regulations on Industry, Mines and Enterprises" (December 1961). *Kung-fei Kung-yeh Cheng-ts'e Ch'i-shih T'iao Chu-yao Nei-yung (Main Contents of the Seventy-Article Industry Policy of the Chinese Communist)*. (Note: This is a summary, not the original text of the document.)

Sixty-Article "Draft Regulations on the Rural People's Communes" (May 1961). *Fei-wei Nung-ts'un Jen-min Kung-she T'iao-li Ts'ao-an Fu-yin-pen* (1961.5 Ting-fa). *(Reprint of the Draft Regulations on Chinese Communist Rural People's Communes)* (promulgated in May 1961).

Sixty-Article "Draft Regulations on the Rural People's Communes" (revised in September 1962). *Kung-fei Nung-ts'un Jen-min Kung-she Kung-tso T'iao-li Hsiu-cheng Ts'ao-an*, September 1962 *(Revised Draft Working Regulations on the Chinese Communist Rural People's Communes, September 1962)*. Taipei: State Security Bureau, May 1964.

The "Lienchiang Documents." *Fan-kung Yu-chi-tui T'u-chi Fukien Lienchieng Lu-huo Fei-fang Wen-chien Hui-pien (Collected Documents Captured During An Anti-Communist Raid on Lienchiang Hsien, Fukien)*. Taipei: Intelligence Bureau, Ministry of Defense, March 1964. (An English translation of the documents is in C.S. Ch'en, ed., *Rural People's Communes in Lienchiang*. Stanford: Hoover Institution, 1969.)

Twelve-Article "Urgent Directive on the Rural Work" (November 1960). *Fei-tang "Chung-yang" So Pan-pu Ti "Nung-ts'un Kung-tso Chin-chi Chih-shih"* (Kiangsi Jen-min Kwang-po T'ien-tai 1960, 11.3 Kwang-po) *(The Urgent Directive on the Rural Work" issued by the "Central Committee" of the Chinese Communist Party)*. Broadcoast by the Kiangsi People's Radio on 3 November 1960. (Note: This is only a summary of the directive.)

Red Guard Sources

Ch'iao Yi-fu. *Hung-wei-ping Husan-chi*, vol. 1 *(Selections of the Red Guard Materials)*. Hongkong, Ta-lu Ch'u-pan-she, 1967.

Down With Big Conspirator, Big Ambitionist, Big Warlord P'eng Teh-huai— Collected Materials Against P'eng Teh-huai. Peking: Ching-kang-shan Corps under the Capital Red Guard Congress, Tsinghua University, November 1967. (Translated in *CB*, no. 851, 26 April 1968.)

Liu Shao-ch'i. "Confession" (made on 23 October 1966, in a CC Working Conference, made public in Red Guard posters in Peking). *Mainichi Shimbun* (Tokyo), 28–29 January 1967. (An English translation appears in *Atlas* [New York], April 1967.)

Mao Chu-hsi Tui P'eng Huang Chang Chou Fang-Tang Chi-tuan Ti p'i-p'an (*Chairman Mao's Repudiations of the P'eng [Teh-huai], Huang [K'o-cheng], Chang [Wen-t'ien], Chou [Hsiao-chou] Anti-Party Clique*). (n.d.) Among photoduplicated material presumably published in Mainland China and released in 1968 by the U.S. Department of State's Office of External Research through the Center for Chinese Research Materials, Association of Research Libraries, Group XI, reel 2, part 9. (An English translation of the pamphlet is in *Chinese Law and Government*, vol. 1, no. 4, 1968.)

Mao Tse-tung Ssu-hsiang Wan-sui (Long Live Mao Tse-tung's Thought) (April 1967) and *Collection of Statements by Mao Tse-tung 1956–1967* (n.d.). (Some of the materials of these two collections are translated in *CB*, no. 892, 21 October 1969.)

Mao Tse-tung Ssu-hsiang Wan-sui (Long Live Mao Tse-tung's Thought) (N.P. August 1969.)

P'eng Teh-huai. "Letter of Opinion" (14 July 1959). *Ko-ming Ch'uan-lien*. Peking: Ko-ming Ch'uan-lien Editorial Board, Peking Institute of Building Engineering, 24 August 1967; *SCMP*, no. 4032, 2 October 1967.

Selections from Chairman Mao. Washington, D.C.: Joint Publications Research Service, no. 49,826, 12 February 1970.

The Evil Deeds of the Anti-Party and Anti-Socialist Element and Counter-revolutionary Double-Dealer, Liu Chien-hsun (Revolutionary Rebel General Command of the organs of the CCP Honan Provincial Committee, 12 March 1967). (Translated in *JPRS*, no. 43, 357, 16 November 1967.)

Ting Wang. *Chung-kung Wen-hua Ta Ko-ming Tzu-liao Hui-pien* (*Collected Materials of Chinese Communist Great Cultural Revolution*). Hongkong: Ming Pao Monthly, 1967–70, 5 vols.

Wu Leng-hsi. "Confession." *Hung-se Hsin-hua* (the publication of a "revolutionary" organization in New China News Agency), no. 43, May 1968; as reprinted in *Hsing-tao Jih-pao* (Hongkong), 9 July 1968. (An English translation with notes is in *Chinese Law and Government*, vol. 2, no. 4, 1969–70.)

Other Red Guard materials used in this study come mostly from the following publications (most of which are available in Ting Wang):

Chin-chun Pao. Peking: Liaison Committee for Sevagely Opening Fire on the Bourgeois Reactionary Line and the Red Guard Joint Unit of the Mao Tse-tung Thought Philosophy and Social Sciences Department, Chinese Academy of Sciences, nos. 22/23, 31 May 1967.

Chingkang-shan. Peking: Chingkang-shan corps of Tsinghua University, nos. 6/7, 1 January 1967.

Hung Ch'i. Peking: Hung Ch'i Fighting Detachment of Aeronautical Engineering Institute, no. 24, 4 April 1967.

Hung-wei-ping Pao. Peking: Red Guard Revolutionary Rebel Headquarters, Chinese Academy of Sciences, no. 6, 6 February 1967.

Pei-Ching Kung-she (Peking Commune). Peking: Central Financial and Monetary College August 8 Fighting Detachment, no. 5, 28 January; no. 12, 14 March 1967.

Shou-tu Hung-wei-ping. Peking: Congress of Red Guards of Universities and Colleges in Peking, no. 24, 21 January 1967.

Ts'ai-mao Hung Ch'i. Peking: The Rebel Liaison Committee of the Finance and Trade System, no. 3, 15 February; no. 4, 23 February 1967.

Tung-fang-hung. Peking: Peking Mining Institute Tung-fang-hung Commune of Capital Colleges Red Guard Congress, nos. 19/20, 20 April 1967.

Tung-fang-hung Pao. Peking: Peking Institute of Geology, nos. 16/17, 9 March 1967.

Index